MANAGEMENT INFORMATION SYSTEMS

Tomayess Issa
Theodora Issa
Sarita Hardin-Ramanan
Bilal Abu-Salih
Lydia Maketo
Rohini Balapumi
S Zaung Nau
Raadila Hajee Ahmud-Boodoo

MANAGEMENT INFORMATION SYSTEMS

Harnessing
Technologies for
Business & Society

§ Sage

1 Oliver's Yard
55 City Road
London EC1Y 1SP

2455 Teller Road
Thousand Oaks
California 91320

Unit No 323-333, Third Floor, F-Block
International Trade Tower
Nehru Place, New Delhi – 110 019

8 Marina View Suite 43-053
Asia Square Tower 1
Singapore 018960

Editor: Matthew Waters
Editorial Assistant: Charlotte Hanson
Production editor: Sarah Cooke
Marketing manager: Lucia Sweet
Cover design: Francis Kenney
Typeset by: C&M Digitals (P) Ltd, Chennai, India
Printed in the UK

Library of Congress Control Number: 2023938783

British Library Cataloguing in Publication data

A catalogue record for this book is available from the British Library

ISBN 978-1-5297-8119-9
ISBN 978-1-5297-8118-2 (pbk)

At Sage we take sustainability seriously. Most of our products are printed in the UK using responsibly sourced papers and boards. When we print overseas we ensure sustainable papers are used as measured by the Paper Chain Project grading system. We undertake an annual audit to monitor our sustainability.

CONTENTS

ACKNOWLEDGEMENTS

Tomayess and Theodora Issa owe special gratitude first to God, the Almighty, and their parents, V. Rev. Fr. Boutros Touma Issa, and, of course, to the Spirit of Bathqyomo Marine Khoury-Issa (2016+). Thanks are also due to their brother Dr Touma, his wife Siba, and their daughter Talitha; their sister Tamara, her husband Tony, and their children Tabitha, Antoinette, and Jacob; and finally, their bother Theodore, his wife Mary, and their children Cephas and Mary, for their continuous support and encouragement, since, without their help, this work would never have been completed. Tomayess would like to thank her co-authors for their support and commitment to this project.

Dr Tomayess Issa and Dr Theodora Issa

Thank you to Dr Tomayess Issa for giving me the opportunity to be one of the authors in this book. I would also like to thank Courtney Ramsamy and Nikhil Toolsee for their help in designing some of my chapter figures.

Dr Sarita Hardin-Ramanan

To Razan and Rashid, thank you for being a ray of sunshine in my life and teaching me more about love and patience than I ever imagined possible. I adore you both in ways that words cannot explain.

Dr Bilal Abu-Salih

I would like to acknowledge the continued support of my family: my husband John and my children Nyasha, TJ and Tino. Your support and love mean a lot to me.

Dr Lydia Maketo

I would like to express my sincere gratitude to my family for their unwavering support during the creation of this textbook. Their encouragement, understanding, and patience have been invaluable throughout the writing process, without which this achievement would not have been possible.

Dr Rohini Balapumi

Thank you, Dr Tomayess Issa and Professor Dora Marinova who have been kindly supporting my academic journey. For Meelay and Tharlay, whose endless companionship and warmth that I could never requite with a lifetime of special dog treats.

Dr S Zaung Nau

This book is the result of great cooperation between the team put together by Dr Tomayess Issa. Thank you, Dr Tomayess Issa, for your dedication and unflinching support in ensuring that your team continues to publish content that will benefit others.

Dr Raadila Hajee Ahmud-Boodoo

ABOUT THE AUTHORS

Dr Tomayess Issa, PhD, SFHEA, PREP, MACS, is a senior lecturer at the Faculty of Business and Law at Curtin University. Tomayess completed her doctoral research in web development and human factors. She is interested in establishing teaching methods to enhance students' learning experiences and resolve the problems that they face. Tomayess has published her work in several peer-reviewed journals, books, and book chapters, and participated in local and global conferences. She is a section editor for society and politics at Heliyon Elsevier Limited. Tomayess has supervised PhD, MPhil, and Masters dissertations and received Curtin Guild Awards for her teaching and supervision. She received the overall Student Guild Outstanding Achievement in Teaching Excellence 2017 Award. Tomayess also received the 2021 Green Gown Awards Australasia: Next Generation Learning and Skills, Highly Commended, for the Green Information Technology and Sustainability unit. She received the Research Supervisor Award 2022 from the Curtin Guild Excellence in Teaching Awards.

Dr Theodora Issa, PhD, SFHEA, FAIM, is a multi-award winner, an academic and author, and international volunteer. Theodora comes to academia from the financial world where she served as a high-ranking executive in an international bank for a number of years. In academia, Theodora has been a curriculum leader and a leader of a range of research groups. In addition to her academic work in Australia, Theodora was invited to design and facilitate a course under the title Sustainable Development Business and Ethical Strategies for the Master of International Business program in Europe (six runs) aimed at an international audience representing 23 countries. Theodora is the author and co-author of several journal articles, reports, edited books, textbooks, books, case studies, conference papers, conference proceedings, book chapters, and magazine articles. Theodora is a reviewer and associate editor for journals and conference papers. Her major areas of research focus on ethical mindsets, spirituality, and aesthetics.

Dr Sarita Hardin-Ramanan heads the Faculty of IT, Design and Communication at Curtin Mauritius. With over 20 years of teaching experience at both undergraduate and postgraduate levels, Sarita holds a PhD in IT Governance and Green IT from Curtin University (Australia), a Masters in Computer Science from Imperial College (UK), and a BEng in Electrical and Electronics Engineering (Mauritius). Alongside her leadership, teaching, and PhD supervision roles, her research interests include IT Governance, Green IT, and Graduate Work-Readiness.

Dr Bilal Abu-Salih is an Associate Professor at The University of Jordan and an Adjunct at Curtin University. He holds a PhD in Information Systems (with a focus on Social Big

Data Analytics) from Curtin University. He has worked on various cross-disciplinary funded research projects involving academic research, software development, and industrial implementation. Bilal's research interests include Social Big Data, Social Trust, Machine Learning/Data Mining, Knowledge Graphs, NLP, Information Retrieval, and the like.

Lydia Maketo is currently a Core Scientist at Technical University of Munich (Germany). Previously, Lydia was a lecturer at Curtin University (University). Lydia has a PhD in information systems from Curtin University. Lydia's thesis focussed on application of mobile technologies in learning in higher education. Lydia has earned an M.Sc. degree in information technology from the University of Wales and a bachelor's degree in Computer Science and Mathematics from the university of Zimbabwe. Lydia's research interests include mobile technologies, integration of technology in education and teaching and learning.

Lydia teaches Systems Analysis for undergraduate and postgraduate students. In addition, she also teaches Enterprise technologies to undergraduate students. Lydia is a Fellow of the Academy of Higher Education Academy (FHEA). Lydia has previously worked in education as a secondary school teacher and a board member. Lydia has had roles in information technology industry, working as a Helpdesk analyst and Systems administrator.

Dr Rohini Balapumi is a highly experienced lecturer in the Information Systems discipline at Curtin University. With over 20 years of experience teaching undergraduate and postgraduate courses, her expertise includes Business Information Systems, Enterprise Technologies, Business Programming, and Societal Impacts of Technological Innovations. She is a certified ICT professional with the Australian Computer Society (ACS) and a recognized Higher Education Academy (HEA) Fellow. Dr Balapumi supervises student research projects in various areas, including blockchain, security, enterprise resource planning, supply chain management technologies, social media, and online learning. Her research interests are focused on the impact of IT innovations on businesses, organizations, society, and the environment. Additionally, she is keenly interested in examining how technology influences higher education learning and teaching, as well as reflective practices in higher education.

Dr S Zaung Nau is currently a lecturer in the School of Management and Marketing, at Curtin University. For her PhD thesis, she analysed the determinants of public transport use in Western Australia and its temporal and spatial variations. Her research interests include collaborative e-learning, data mining, demand modelling and transport data analytics. She has been conducting research on travel behaviour patterns and demand planning for public transport and sustainable transportation in Perth, Western Australia. Her current research interest is the comparative analysis of private car and public transport use to identify the areas where they are competing with or complementing each other. Her other research areas are geospatial analysis on socio-economic, public health, and sustainability developments, especially in waste management, in order to reduce CO_2 emissions in this sector.

Dr Raadila Hajee Ahmud-Boodoo has a Bachelor's degree in Information Systems and Technology and a Masters in Computer Science, with a specialization in Software Engineering. She completed her doctoral research in 3.0 E-learning for developing countries. She has several publications to her credit and continues to work with renowned academics to pursue her research interests, which are currently directed towards the Semantic Web, Web 3.0 E-learning and E-learning sustainability. She has several years of experience as an academic, educator and business systems administrator, both within Australia and abroad.

INTRODUCTION

This book aims to present management information systems to undergraduate students so that they may obtain the necessary knowledge behind information systems, which have become an essential component for individuals and businesses locally and globally to enhance job performance, make the correct decisions, and most importantly, sustain the current raw materials for the next generation.

The book is divided into three parts: responsible management information systems; advances in digital information technology; and knowledge and data management technologies.

Part 1: Responsible Management Information Systems

Part 1 introduces the basic perceptions and concepts of Management Information Systems (MIS), including hardware and software technology generally and specifically, system analysis and design, project management, and team strategy. Furthermore, this part will discuss ethics, corporate social responsibility, the triple bottom line, sustainability, sustainable design, and green IT, since these concepts are of growing importance in our daily lives and help reduce the pressure on nature caused by human actions.

Chapter 1: An Introduction to Management Information Systems

Businesses, such as eBay, Amazon, Google, and Meta (Facebook) rely on information systems and technologies to conduct a variety of tasks, including liaising with clients, suppliers, and even rival businesses. This chapter will explore the value of these systems and technologies, exploring their core components (i.e., computer hardware and software), how, when, and where they are used, and how they differ from each other. Nowadays, individuals rely on information technology to carry out and manage their daily tasks, including dealing with clients, suppliers, and rival businesses. Both industrialized and developing nations use information technologies to provide their inhabitants with low-cost social, educational, retail, banking, and entertainment services. Finally, this chapter will describe several constituent parts of information systems, namely computer hardware and software, which should be recognized and understood in order to learn more about their functionality and their distinctive properties.

Chapter 2: Project Management and PMBOK

This chapter discusses the importance of project management in business and describes the five phases of the project management process. Furthermore, it discusses the 10 PMBOK knowledge areas to ensure that project deployment is successful. Project management is the process of carrying out certain project goals in accordance with predefined parameters and using specific procedures, techniques, abilities, knowledge, and experience. Project management's final deliverables are subject to time and budget constraints. In this chapter, the conflict and risks associated with project management are discussed. Since these issues are critical to successful project management, they should be addressed promptly to minimize problems related to scope, time, and cost and ensure the project's success. The relationship between project management and information systems is that information systems make up the tools and methods used to collect, combine, and distribute the results of the project management process. Information systems can contain both human and automated technologies and are used to assist every stage of the project, from planning to closure.

Chapter 3: Ethics, Ethical Mindsets, Corporate Social Responsibility, and the Triple Bottom Line

This chapter will introduce the importance of ethics, in particular in relation to the responsible management of technology use and privacy. It will also introduce corporate social responsibility (CSR) and the triple bottom line (TBL) in relation to information systems. This chapter aims to introduce these important topics and highlight their importance in an information systems context. However, it is worthwhile to note here that talking about ethics, ethical mindsets, corporate social responsibility, and the triple bottom line means we need to go back to the origin of those expressions and try to understand what they mean. Having said that, in this chapter, we shall endeavour to make this task as simple as we can, just scratching the surface of those complex expressions and trying our best to link them to the daily lives of businesspeople. Therefore, reading this chapter will not transform you into a philosopher but will equip you with basic knowledge on these important and topical subjects. It is worth stating here that reading this chapter might provide you with the tools to assist you in evaluating events and responding in a way that would be ethical and socially responsible.

Chapter 4: Sustainability, Sustainable Design and Green IT

Since organizations and individual users now rely more on computers, the Internet, and system technology than they did in the past to accomplish the same goals, these technologies are crucial tools in the 21st century. Modern technology is better able to manage situations and help people and organizations to accomplish their duties much more quickly. In addition to the widespread use of standalone computers, the Internet, World Wide Web, social networks, mobile devices, Intelligent Environments, and other technologies have greatly enhanced worldwide networking. However, as experts, researchers, and practitioners involved in the human–computer interaction domain strive to address the needs of businesses and individual users, while ensuring that new information and communication technologies are more sustainable so as to meet both current and future needs, the rise in ICT usage around the world has presented a new challenge. As a result, three concepts – sustainability, sustainable design, and green information technology – that are increasingly important to consumers and companies both locally and globally will be covered in this chapter. In order to reduce carbon emissions, global warming, energy use, and raw material waste, and conserve resources for the next generation, users, designers, HCI professionals, and businesses should take these issues into account when devising their ICT usage strategy.

Part 2: Advances in Digital Information Technology

Part 2 will discuss the latest technologies available on the market and the opportunities and challenges of using them in businesses now and in the future.

Chapter 5: Computer Networks and Information Security

The evolution of computer networks and Internet technologies has revolutionized the way businesses operate and collaborate. The emergence of network technologies such as cloud computing and mobile communication has transformed business processes and supply chain activities. Today, Internet connectivity is essential to any business organization and drives businesses' communication and collaboration with suppliers, customers, and employees. In the first part of this chapter, we will look at the various computer networks, communication media and channels, network types, and network collaboration applications that facilitate communications and collaboration within organizations. The second part of this chapter will discuss the threats to information and technology and the measures and controls that can be implemented to protect information resources in business organizations.

Chapter 6: Mobile Technologies

This chapter provides an overview of mobile technologies, discusses the history of mobile phones, and traces the evolution of mobile standards or network generations. The chapter describes several wireless networks and discusses the applications of mobile computing as well as the challenges associated with mobile technologies. Mobile technologies have come a long way, with the first handheld cellular mobile phone demonstrated in 1973 by John F.

Mitchell and Martin Cooper, with the handset weighing 2 kilograms (Anjarwalla, 2010). Over the years, mobile technologies have become ubiquitous and have gone beyond their initial function as units for verbal and text communication only. Mobile technologies have various capabilities and functionalities that are fast expanding, with applications becoming increasingly broad over time. However, although mobile technologies offer a number of benefits, there are security concerns associated with these technologies, with the portability of these technologies making them more vulnerable to security breaches.

Chapter 7: Social Computing and Social Commerce

This chapter provides an overview of social computing and social commerce. It explains the evolution of the Web with a particular emphasis on Web 2.0. It describes the conceptual model for both social computing and social commerce and discusses various relevant definitions, components, types, and tools. It critically differentiates between social commerce and traditional electronic commerce, and examines certain benefits and challenges by using social commerce tools and applications.

Chapter 8: Smart Technologies

In the 21st century, technology plays an important role in specific sectors as a means of improving job performance, providing faster and more effective communication, facilitating the development of new and innovative approaches, increasing profit, and, most importantly, decreasing waste and carbon footprints. In particular, technologies such as augmented reality (AR) and virtual reality (VR) have received much attention from individuals, industries, and scholars. These technologies involve computer programming for modelling, simulation, and augmentation that allow people to interact to achieve their goals and aspirations. These technologies are used in various sectors, including education, health, marketing, design, and gaming, among others, and the beauty of these technologies is that people can accomplish their tasks in virtual reality without creating a specific device. This chapter will explain these technologies and describe their application in specific sectors that use them to improve job performance, acquire new knowledge, and, most importantly, detect life-threatening diseases or conditions.

Part 3: Knowledge and Data Management Technologies

This part will discuss how knowledge and data management technologies are captured and processed to make decisions for businesses that will enhance job performance and accomplishment.

Chapter 9: Artificial Intelligence and Knowledge Graphs

We live in the era of big data in which data is generated at a surprising speed. These large-scale and heterogeneous datasets require advanced and sophisticated technologies that can produce hoped-for added value as well as derive knowledge from data that can benefit several industrial applications and business domains. This chapter provides an overview of two powerful technologies that are currently being incorporated in business and other operations to offer insights on obtained data, namely Artificial Intelligence (AI) and its offshoot, Machine Learning (ML). Both AI and ML are described, and their relationship and importance are explained. Then, knowledge graphs (KGs) are introduced, specifically generic and domain-specific KGs, followed by an explanation of one of the techniques used to construct a KG, and examples of real-life applications that have benefited from KGs.

Chapter 10: Data Analytics

This chapter will discuss data analytics as a method of capturing the requirements of the systems and summarizing them. Different diagramming techniques are also covered, to allow students to understand how this data will be used for decision-making in business. In the fourth industrial revolution, known as Industry 4.0, production has been decentralized so that shared facilities can achieve on-demand manufacturing and resource efficiency. Data analytics has been expediting this fourth industrial revolution by providing the means for analysing massive amounts of data. The information and patterns derived from this analysis are used to inform subsequent business decisions. The sophisticated parallel and distributed systems in big data analytics enable us to harness the volume of data currently exceeding exabytes. The emerging landscape of cloud-based environments also allows us to access any data as required, regardless of its volume, velocity, variety, veracity, and location. Additionally, significant advancements in computing memory, storage, processing power, networking infrastructure, and communication technologies have helped to increase the scope and scalability of data analytics. Evolving visualization technologies along with optimization techniques for resource utilization and parallel data processing also facilitate data analytics applications in various domains, including business and commercial applications in the fields of public health, government, environment management, etc.

Chapter 11: Emerging Technologies in the Digital Age: Big Data, IoT, Cloud Computing, and Blockchain

The ongoing development of digital technologies offers businesses many opportunities to adopt innovative solutions. Cloud computing, big data, the Internet of Things (IoT), and blockchain technologies can be collectively used for a number of business activities including data collection, storage, analytics, automation, and security, in addition to improving business performance and competitive advantage. In this chapter, we will learn about big data, cloud computing, IoT, and blockchain technologies. The concepts, components, applications, and challenges associated with each of these four technologies will be addressed in turn.

Finally, by reading this book and adopting it in your teaching, you will understand and gain the necessary knowledge of information systems (IS), as IS has become essential for individuals and businesses to enhance job performance, improve collaboration, increase productivity, and reduce risk in compliance issues. This book contains the cutting edge of knowledge that the next generation needs to learn in order to become good stewards and leaders of our global community, using smart technology, sustainability, ethics, and project management.

Reference

Anjarwalla, T. (2010, July 9). Inventor of cell phone: We knew someday everybody would have one - CNN.com. *Www.cnn.com*.

ONLINE RESOURCES

This textbook is accompanied by online resources to aid teaching and support learning. To access these resources, visit: https://study.sagepub.com/Issa-et-al. Please note that lecturers will require a SAGE account in order to access the lecturer resources. An account can be created via the above link.

For Lecturers

- **PowerPoints** that can be downloaded and adapted to suit individual teaching needs
- A **Teaching Guide** providing practical guidance and support and additional materials for lecturers using this textbook in their teaching
- A **Testbank** that can be used for both formative and summative student assessment

PART I

RESPONSIBLE MANAGEMENT INFORMATION SYSTEMS

1

AN INTRODUCTION
TO MANAGEMENT
INFORMATION SYSTEMS

1.1 Learning Outcomes

After reading this chapter, you will be able to:

- Discuss the difference between information systems and information technology
- Discuss the career opportunities offered by both
- Discuss and describe functions of computer hardware and software
- Explain the role of systems analysis in system development

1.2 Introduction

The difference between information systems and information technology is that information systems (IS) consist of several aspects, including systems, people, and processes to create, design, store, manipulate, distribute, and disseminate information. In summary, IS considers itself as the bridge between business and computer science by presenting information in a readable and feasible way to allow businesses to make decisions. On the other hand, information technology (IT) is mainly focused on the study, design, implementation, support, or management of computer-based information systems. IT typically includes hardware, software, databases, and networks. The basic goal of IT is to control how digital information (or data) created by the computer and telecommunications fields is acquired, processed, stored, and disseminated. Information technology is concerned with managing technology and maximizing its utilization to further overarching corporate objectives.

Businesses, such as eBay, Amazon, Google, and Meta (Facebook) rely on information systems and technologies to conduct a variety of tasks, including liaising with clients, suppliers, and even rival businesses. This chapter will explore the value of these systems and technologies, exploring their core components (i.e., computer hardware and software), how, when and where they are used, and how they differ from each other.

Nowadays, individuals rely on IT to carry out and manage their daily tasks, including dealing with clients, suppliers, and rival businesses. Additionally, both industrialized and developing nations use information technologies to provide their inhabitants with low-cost social, educational, retail, banking, and entertainment services. Finally, this chapter will describe several constituent parts of information systems, namely computer hardware and software, which should be recognized and understood in order to learn how, when, and where they are used, and their unique features.

1.3 Information Systems and Information Technology and Careers Opportunities

In this section, it is important to understand the key differences between the terms information systems (IS) and information technology (IT), as well as the advantages of each for both people and organizations. Information systems are more theoretical since IS experts are responsible for the planning, analysis, design, programming, testing, implementation, and maintenance of application software, such as database, Word and Excel. These applications are created and designed to be user-friendly and attractive so that users can apply them to achieve their goals and objectives efficiently. On the other hand, information technology is more practical, since it focuses on configuration systems, data centres and switches, and routers. Information technologies are responsible for implementing and maintaining these systems to ensure they meet the businesses' project aims in terms of scope, time, and budget. (Angell & Smithson, 1991; Brancheau & Wetherbe, 1987; Stolterman & Fors, 2004).

Information systems and technologies are also relevant in today's 'Internet generation', where individuals rely on digital technologies, such as smart mobiles and portable devices, to connect, communicate, and collaborate with family, friends, fellow students and colleagues while studying and working. Information and knowledge are regularly being exchanged. An understanding of information systems and technology is important to ensure they are used appropriately to achieve work and study goals. Furthermore, this generation appears to be reliant on digital technology, which is available 24 hours a day, 365 days a year, enabling them to work, listen, watch, finance, play games, and shop online.

Studying information systems and technology is crucial in today's world, as it is essential to how many businesses function. Businesses are looking to improve their performance, productivity, and customer satisfaction, as well as reducing costs, increasing competition in the market, enhancing communication, and strengthening security. Table 1.1 summarizes possible IT and IS jobs following information systems or information technology degrees. Finally, these jobs can be found in your own country or globally, since they have become essential to any organization seeking to improve its performance, productivity, and customer satisfaction, or to reduce costs, increase competition in the market, enhance communication, and strengthen security.

Table 1.1 Possible Careers after Studying Information Systems or Information Technology

Information Systems Careers	Information Technology Careers
Application Analyst	Computer and Information Research Scientists
Database Administrator	Computer Hardware Engineers
Data Analyst	Computer Programmers
Data Scientist	Desktop Administrators
Information Systems Manager	Field Service Technicians
Knowledge Management Officer	Field Tech Coordinators
Penetration Tester	Green Information Technology Officers
Software Engineer	ICT Helpdesk Technicians
Systems Analyst	ICT On-site Support Engineers
Software Developer	ICT Service Desk Officers
Web Developer	ICT Service Support Officers
	IT Support Specialists
	IT Consultants

Stop and Reflect: Information Systems

List four types of jobs related to the information systems sector.

List four types of jobs related to the information technology sector.

List the required skills that are needed to perform an information systems or information technology job.

1.4 Information Systems/Technology Strategy

To reduce costs, boost productivity, expand into new markets, boost profits, improve decision-making, and differentiate their products and services, businesses should implement an information system strategy. The use of computers at all organizational levels or through an individual as a means of modifying or developing operational goals, service outputs, and environmental connections is referred to as an information systems/technology strategy.

This strategy includes the project's goals and the steps taken to achieve them, in alignment with project constraints and requirements. Strategy is regarded as the link between organizational requirements and contemporary information technology. Therefore, the major goal is to assist an organization to apply information systems/technology to satisfy its demanding criteria for ongoing change in the corporate environment (Peppard et al., 2014; Walsham & Waema, 1994).

Definition: Information Systems/Technology Strategy

The use of computers at every level of an organization or by an individual to alter operational goals, service outputs, and environmental linkages.

Table 1.2 outlines the three different types of information systems and technology strategies, giving their aims and an example.

Table 1.2   Information Systems/Technology Strategies

Strategy Type	Strategy Aim	Example
Strategic level systems	To determine the overall trajectory of a company	**Executive Support Systems (ESS)** are used by senior managers to assist them in making decisions in the organization. ESS provide easy access to internal and external information relevant to organizational goals.
Management level systems	To obtain a competitive edge and avoid competitive disadvantage at the business level	**Decision Support System (DSS)** is a computer program that helps businesses make better decisions. The DSS analyses huge amounts of data to present the best solutions to the organization.
Operational level systems	Focus on departmental strategy to provide value to the final client	**Transaction Processing System (TPS)** is a type of information system that collects, stores, adjusts, and saves the data transactions of an enterprise.

To ensure the success of information systems/technology (IS/T) strategies in organizations, employees should have the requisite skills and knowledge to enable them to plan, analyse, design, develop, implement, and maintain such a system, with the most important aspect being the alignment of IS/T strategy with the organization's goals.

To obtain further information about information systems and information technology components, the next section of this chapter will discuss some of the components, i.e., computer hardware and computer software, which should be understood and recognized in order to learn what, when, and where they are used and the differences between them.

> **Stop and Reflect: Information Systems/Technology Strategies**
>
> List examples of information systems/technology strategies.

1.5 Hardware

Computers consist of two main parts: hardware and software. Computer hardware is the collection of the physical components that make up a computer system (Gilster, 2001). Computer hardware comprises the physical objects that are tangible and that make a computer system function. Although desktop computers and laptops differ in terms of hardware design, several core components are found in both. Some of the components are also found in smaller devices such as tablets and smartphones.

Internal Hardware Components

The hardware needed to process data and enable the CPU to interface with other devices like secondary storage, display screens, and printers is included in the internal computer hardware. The motherboard, central processing unit (CPU), and input/output controllers are the three primary internal parts of computers.

Motherboard

A motherboard is the hub through which all other hardware runs in a PC or laptop. It is the main printed circuit board of a computer (Fisher, 2021b). It can be considered as the 'backbone' of the PC. The motherboard allocates power to other components, coordinates the other components, and enables the components to communicate (Knerl, 2019). Tablets and other smaller devices like smartphones also have mother boards, generally known as logic boards (Cockerham, 2015). A motherboard contains ports that connect all internal components, a socket for the central processing unit (CPU) and a slot(s) for memory. Motherboards also have slots for a variety of cards such as video cards, sound cards, and other expansion cards. There are also ports to connect the monitor, printer, mouse, keyboard, speaker, and network cables. Motherboards also have USB ports allowing compatible devices, such as digital cameras, external drives, pen drives, etc., to be connected.

Central Processing Unit (CPU)

The central processing unit (CPU) is responsible for processing all information from programs run by the computer (Martindale, 2021). It is the electronic circuitry that executes instructions comprising a computer program. The template for modern computers is the Von Neumann architecture, the design of which comprises a digital computer with a central processing unit which has an arithmetic logic unit, processor registers, a control unit that has an instruction register and program counter, memory that stores data and instructions, and input and output mechanisms (Shipley & Jodis, 2003).

Arithmetic logic unit (ALU)

An ALU is a combinational digital circuit that performs integer mathematical calculations and bitwise operations on binary numbers (0 and 1) specified by a software program (Godse & Godse, 2007). Arithmetic operations are addition, subtraction, multiplication, and division. Logical operations include comparisons of numbers that are equal to (=), greater than (>), or less than (<) other numbers. The logic unit performs logical operations (e.g., AND, OR and NOT). The ALU performs each of these operations at the command of the control unit. Computers have multiple ALUs in the CPU and the graphic processing unit as well as the floating-point unit (Godse & Godse, 2007). The ALU uses operands and code to determine which operations to perform for input data; after processing the information this is sent to the computer's memory.

Processor register

A processor register is a location that can be quickly accessed by a computer's processor. It is a memory location within the actual processor that works at very fast speeds (Rouse, 2019). It stores instructions which await decoding or execution. Processor registers generally occupy the top-most position in the memory hierarchy. A register may contain an instruction, a storage address, or any kind of data (such as a bit sequence or individual characters). Registers are normally measured by the number of bits they can hold, for example an 8-bit register, a 32-bit register, or a 64-bit register.

Control unit

The control unit instructs the computer's memory, ALU, and input and output devices on how to respond to the instructions that have been sent to the processor (Shipley & Jodis, 2003). It brings internal instructions of the programs from the main memory to the processor instruction register, and, based on this register contents, the control unit generates a control signal that supervises the execution of these instructions.

Bus

A bus or data bus is a communication system that transfers data between components on a motherboard or between computers (Fisher, 2021a). It is a shared digital pathway linking resources with devices. This can include the transference of data to and from the memory or from the CPU to other components. The amount of data that a bus can handle is known as the bandwidth. A typical data bus is 32-bits wide. This means that up to 32 bits of data can travel through a data bus every second. Newer computers have data buses that can handle 64-bit data paths. At the same time, manufacturers are making data buses that can handle more bits, as well as devices that can handle those higher bitrates.

There are two main types of computer buses: (1) system buses, and (2) input/output buses. The system bus connects the CPU to the main memory on the motherboard. A system bus is also called a local/memory/host bus. The input/output (i/o) buses connect peripheral devices to the CPU. These i/o buses are also known as expansion/external buses.

Expansion buses

Expansion buses support add-on devices using expansion slots. There are various types of expansion buses.

Industry Standard Architecture (ISA)

An earlier hardware interface for connecting peripheral devices designed for use in the original IBM PC (Oxford University Press, 2019, Shanley and Anderson, 1995), ISA still connects legacy devices such as cash registers, Computer Numerical Control (CNC) machines and barcode scanners.

Micro Channel Architecture (MCA)

The MCA was developed by IBM as a replacement for ISA, and contains several improvements. The MCA runs at a faster speed and is supported by both 16-bit and 32-bit data, and the plug-in cards are configurable software requiring little use input during configuration. The MCA also supports bus mastering, a feature that enables devices connected to a bus to access the computer's memory independently of the CPU. This allows data transfer between the peripheral and the main system memory while the CPU is being used by other devices (Borrett, 1989).

Extended Industry Standard Architecture (EISA)

The EISA was developed as an alternative to MCA and represents an upgrade to ISA. It has 32 data channels, which is twice the number of ISA. Although EISA was not popular in desktop PCs, it was more successful in the server market as it is better suited for bandwidth-intensive tasks. EISA also offers mastering.

Video Electronics Standards Association (VESA)

This is also known as the Local bus or the VESA-Local bus. It was created to standardize the video specifications of PCs, thereby solving the problem of proprietary technology since different manufactures were attempting to develop their own buses (Computerhope, 2022). The VESA Bus was superseded by other buses due to its limited scalability, the fact that it was designed for the 80486 microprocessor, and because it was difficult to install (Giuma & Hart, 1996).

Peripheral Component Interconnect (PCI)

Intel developed the PCI bus in the early 1990s. PCI presents a hybrid of sorts between ISA and the VL-bus, PCI provides direct access to system memory for connected devices (Tyson & Grabianowski, 2001). A processor register is a location that can be quickly accessed by a computer's processor. PCI uses a bridge to connect the front side bus and CPU, which reduces CPU interference while providing higher performance. PCI became popular when Windows 95 introduced its Plug and Play (PnP) feature in 1995. Intel incorporated the PnP standard into PCI, which gave it an advantage over ISA (Casey, 2021).

Personal Computer Memory Card Industry Association (PC bus)

The Personal Computer Memory Card Industry Association was established to give laptop computers a standard bus. It is usually found in small computers.

Accelerated Graphics Port (AGP)

The Accelerated Graphics Port (AGP) was designed to accommodate computers' increased graphics needs, and is a standard type of connection for video cards (Fisher, 2023). AGP provides direct communication to the CPU and RAM, which allows graphics to be rendered more quickly (Fisher, 2023).

PCI Express (PCI-X)

This is intended for the home computer market and was designed to replace the AGP and PCI bus. The PCI-X has a 64-bit data path and incorporates full-duplex architecture which is the main performance improvement. Other internal hardware internal components are RAM, clock, and the disk drive.

Random Access Memory (RAM)

RAM is the physical hardware that temporarily stores data. It is a computer's short-term memory, which it uses to handle all active tasks and apps (Villinger, 2019). RAM is temporary storage that disappears when the power is turned off. RAM is significantly faster than running the same data off the hard disk. The more RAM a computing device has, the faster it runs. There are two types of RAM: static random-access memory (SRAM) and dynamic random-access memory (DRAM) (Knerl, 2021). SRAM data is stored in transistors, while DRAM data is stored in capacitors. SRAM uses less power, and the data can be accessed faster, while DRAM is cheaper and offers greater memory capacity.

Clock

Each CPU has clock speed, which is the speed at which the processor processes information. The clock speed is measured in hertz (Hz) (Sirois, 2018). The higher the Hz rating, the faster the processor will perform. The quality of a computer's CPU has a major effect on the overall system performance. The CPU clock synchronizes the operations of all parts of the computer and provides timing signals for the CPU.

Disk drive

A computer hard disk drive (HDD) or hard disk is a non-volatile data storage device (Hennessy, 1996). Non-volatile devices are devices that maintain stored data when powered off. HDDs were the dominant secondary storage device for general-purpose computers in the early 1960s. A HDD has an arm with several transducers that read and write data on the disk. This can be compared to the way a turntable record player works with a vinyl record (hard disk) and a needle on an arm (transducers) (Arpaci-Dusseau & Arpaci-Dusseau, 2018). The arm moves the heads across the surface of the disk to access different data. HDDs maintained this position into the modern era of servers and personal computers, although personal computing devices produced in large volumes, like cell phones and tablets, rely on flash memory storage devices.

HDDs are considered a legacy technology because they have been around longer than Solid-state Drives (SSDs). There is a decline in sales of HDDs as SSDs have higher data transfer rates, greater storage capacity and better reliability. In an SSD, data is stored in integrated circuits. This has an effect on performance. SSDs are flexible for smaller devices, can hold varying amounts of data, and require less access time (Villinger, 2019). SSDs are more expensive than HDDs per amount of storage, but the gap is closing over time. SSDs are now the rule in mainstream systems and high-end laptops like the Apple MacBook Pro. Desktops and cheaper laptops continue to offer HDDs.

Definitions: Hardware

Computer hardware is the collection of the physical components that make up a computer system, as follows

Motherboard

This is the main printed circuit board of a computer, a motherboard allocates power to other components, coordinates the other components and enables communication among the components.

(Continued)

Central Processing Unit (CPU)

This is the electronic circuitry that executes instructions within a computer program.

Bus

A bus or data bus is a communication system that transfers data between components on a motherboard or between computers.

Random Access Memory (RAM)

This is the physical hardware that stores data temporarily. It is a computer's short-term memory, which it uses to handle all active tasks and apps.

Disk drive

A computer hard disk drive (HDD) or hard disk is a non-volatile data storage device. Non-volatile devices are devices that maintain stored data when powered off.

External Components

Some external hardware components include monitor, keyboard, mouse, uninterruptible power supply (UPS), flash drive, printer, speakers, external hard drive and pen tablet (Figure 1.1).

Figure 1.1   Examples of External Hardware: Printer, Pen-tablet, External Hard Drive and a Laptop (source: https://commons.wikimedia.org/wiki/Main_Page)

Some hardware devices have changed over time. A typical example is storage devices. A floppy disk is a storage medium that was introduced into the market in the 1970s and remained popular for nearly 40 years (Deitel & Deitel, 1986). Compact disks (CDs) are digital optical data storage media that were invented in 1979 (BBC, 2019). Standard CDs hold up to 650MB of data. The USB flash drive (also called a thumb drive) first appeared on the market in the early 2000s (Fisher, 2021a). The flash drive includes flash memory with an integrated USB interface. Compared with floppy disks or CDs, they are smaller, faster, have significantly more capacity, and are more durable due to the absence of moving parts (Figure 1.2).

Additionally, USBs are less vulnerable than floppy disks to electromagnetic interference and are unharmed by surface scratches (unlike CDs). However, storage has shifted from hardware devices to cloud storage. It is believed that cloud storage dates back to the 1960s, invented by Dr Joseph Carl Robnett Licklider (Mohamed, 2018). There are several file-hosting services which are currently active that include Amazon Drive, Backblaze, Baidu cloud, Dropbox, Google Drive, iCloud, and Microsoft oneDrive. Such services are designed for online storage with both different and common features.

Figure 1.2 Earlier storage media: floppy disk, compact disk and USB (source: https://commons.wikimedia.org/wiki/Main_Page)

Hardware Procurement

Users continue to purchase computer hardware for personal or organizational use. When procuring hardware, larger businesses can choose from a variety of options. Some organizations still prefer to buy their own hardware, others prefer the traditional hardware leasing approach, and some companies opt for the more contemporary hardware-as-a-service (HaaS) (Parashar, 2022). Hardware leasing remains popular, with printers being the most popular devices to be leased. Other devices that are leased are servers, networking equipment, desktops, laptops and mobile devices. Most leased devices are managed/supported in-house.

HaaS is similar to leasing, in that the hardware that belongs to a provider is installed at the customer's site and a service level agreement (SLA) defines the responsibilities of both parties. Unlike the type of leasing where the customer benefits from using the equipment and is usually responsible for maintenance, management, and eventual replacement of the specific hardware, HaaS requires the customer to pay for using the hardware without the burden of the maintenance and replacement of the specific hardware. Essentially, HaaS is similar to paying for a utility.

Stop and Reflect: Computer Hardware

Some computer hardware has changed over time. Using examples, discuss how computer hardware has evolved to suit the changing needs of individuals and organizations.

1.6 Software

Software is a set of instructions, data or programs used to operate computers and execute specific tasks (Bidgoli & Prestage, 2003). It is the opposite of hardware, which comprises the physical aspects of a computer. Software is a generic term used to refer to applications, scripts, and programs that run on a device. Software is used to control a computer. There are different types of software that can run on a computer. There are four main classifications of software namely system software, application software, utility and computer programming tools (Table 1.3) (Wilcox, 2021).

Table 1.3 Software Classifications

Software Classifications	Example
System Software	Operating Systems, Firmware, Device Drivers, Networking Software, Assemblers, Compliers, and Translators
Application Software	Word Processing Software, Spreadsheets, Web Browsers, Database Software, Multimedia Software, Simulation Software, Business Application Software (i.e. enterprise resource planning (ERP) application software, and customer relationship management (CRM))
Utility	Antivirus, File Management System, Backup Software, Disk Clean-Up Tool, and Data Synchronisation Tools
Computer Programming Tools	Javascript, Python, Java, PHP, C and C++, HTML and SQL

System Software

System software is intended to manage the system resources. It is designed to manage and coordinate computer hardware behaviour and develop and run applications. System software provides a platform for running application software and forms the interface between the hardware and user applications (Business Insider, 2020). Examples of system software are available in Table 1.3.

Application software

Application programs (applications or apps) are specific in their functionality as they are designed for specific tasks (Encyclopaedia Britannica, 2022). Users directly interact with the application software. Application software is developed to assist with a specific process that may be related to creativity, productivity, or improved communication for an end-user.

Mobile applications are the apps used on mobile devices, such as WhatsApp, weather apps, and Candy Crush. Application software also includes software that is developed to meet the needs of an organization. Application software can be classified according to its chargeability and accessibility.

Freeware

Freeware software is software that is available for use at no monetary cost or for an optional fee for unlimited time (Stouffer, 2022). There is no paid licence required to use the application and no restrictions on how often the application can be downloaded or opened. Copyright owners have the exclusive right to distribute copies of their work (Mueller, n.d.). Freeware applications may or may not have their source code available. Freeware applications may be restrictive, limiting users to using the application for personal, not commercial, use. Freeware is often used as an advertising tool to promote a developer's commercial software. In some cases, freeware will be a version with limited features, while the commercial version has all the features. Some freeware applications for educational purposes are not profit-seeking and provide all the features at no cost to the user e.g., GeoGebra. Other examples of freeware applications include Skype software, Adobe PDF, Mozilla Firefox, and Google Chrome.

Shareware

Shareware is commercial/proprietary software that is distributed free to users by the owner for trial use at little or no cost, with the understanding that users will pay for it if they continue to use the software (Stouffer, 2022). Shareware usually has limited functionality or incomplete documentation but can be upgraded upon payment. Shareware allows users to trial an application before committing to buy it. An example of shareware includes WinZip, Anti-virus, and Adobe Reader. Various types of shareware are listed and described in Table 1.4.

Table 1.4 Types of Shareware

Type of Shareware	Description
Adware	Displays advertisements within a browser or program to monetise content. Adware often gathers personal information from user's device and shares it with advertisers so that advertisements are tailored to meet the needs of the user (Gorrie, 2023). Adware can spam a user with unwanted pop-up advertisements. Sometimes it uses Trojan viruses. Adware is usually loaded onto a computer undetected.
Demoware	This is also known as trial ware. Usually it has limited features and users can use it for a limited time. Crippleware is a version of demoware that stops performing vital functions unless the full version is purchased (Computerhope, 2020).
Donationware	A fully functional and operational application that requires a donation to support future development or other causes such as charity work or non-profit organizations (Milian, 2011).
Nagware	Shareware that repeatedly requests the user to pay for a licence, reminders are continuous until payment has been made (Cambridge Dictionary, 2023).
Freemium	Offers basic features for no payment and offers 'premium' upgrades for a fee. The fee 'buys' an enhanced experience. Freemium has been driven by the rise of online and mobile gaming.

Security concerns

There are security concerns with shareware. Although shareware is generally safe, it is more vulnerable to security threats because the programs are not fully licensed, and patches and upgrades are not available. Some known cybersecurity risks associated with shareware are:

- Malware – This is malicious software hidden within the shareware or with links to outside sources that can lead to viruses being downloaded on your device (Cisco, 2023). Deceptive URL links can be used by cybercriminals, taking users to webpages where they download malware instead of a safe shareware application.
- Spyware – A type of malware that spies on a user's activity in order to gather sensitive information (Stouffer, 2021). The use of shareware in business and government networks can exacerbate spyware risks if sensitive data is leaked.
- Zero-day exploits – Software security flaws that hackers exploit without the developer's knowledge (Bogna, 2022).
- Affiliated software – The shareware developer may earn a commission by linking to other programs for download, although there is no guarantee that these secondary programs are protecting user data and privacy.

Open-source

Open-source software is software that is released under a licence where the copyright holder grants users the rights to inspect, use, study, modify, improve and distribute the software and its source code to anyone for any purpose (Laurent, 2004). Users can fix bugs, augment the software functionality and redistribute the software or its derivative (for free, or at a charge) (Sen, 2007). Open-source application software includes GIMP, Sendmail, WordPress, and Mozilla Firefox. Open-source software has several advantages (Bromhead, 2017) as listed below.

- Better security: since many developers work on the source code, it is easier to spot security flaws.
- Better quality: since many developers work on the source code, this reduces the number of flaws and improve the quality.
- More control: users have more control over the code and how they can use the code.
- No vendor dependence: users are not locked into a relationship with software suppliers.
- Easier licence management: generally, users can use software however they wish and as frequently as they wish. There are specific licences for open-source software, and users must comply with the specific licence conditions.

However, open-source software can have several disadvantages (Verma, 2020) as listed below.

- Difficult to use: some software may have interfaces that are not user-friendly, which can decrease productivity.
- Compatibility issues: Many proprietary hardware needs specialized drivers to run open-source programs. This can lead to incompatibility issues or additional costs in purchasing compatible elements.
- Liabilities and warranties: Open-source software licences typically contain only limited warranty and no liability or infringement indemnity protection.
- Hidden costs: Although open source is free, there may be costs required later e.g., setting-up costs, training costs if users are not familiar with the software, maintenance costs.

Proprietary software

This is sometimes referred to as 'closed source software', which is software that legally remains the property of the organization or individual who created it (Gartner, n.d.). The software's publisher reserves some licensing rights to use, modify, share modifications, or share the software, thus reducing user freedom with respect to the software they lease. Examples of proprietary software are Microsoft Windows, Adobe Flash Player, iTunes, and Google Earth.

Utility Software

The utility software is system software that is designed to help analyse, configure, optimize or maintain the proper and smooth functioning of a computer system. It assists the operating system to manage, organize, maintain, and optimize the functioning of the computer system. Utility software provides key functions such as data compression, data recovery, disk fragmentation, system diagnosis and file management (Oja & Parsons, 2014). Examples of utility software include antivirus software, file management systems, backup software, disk clean-up tools, and data synchronization tools.

Computer Programming Tools

A computer programming tool is a software application that helps software developers or programmers create, modify, debug, maintain, or carry out any task relevant to programming or development (Lobb & Harlow, 2016). Examples of computer programming tools are Javascript, Python, Java, PHP, C and C++, HTML and SQL.

Accessing Software Applications

In the past, in order to use most software applications, one had to install and run the software application, requiring an IT specialist to download the software onto several computers and then install the software. Software as an application (SaaS) allows users to access software from any device at any time as long as there is an Internet connection. SaaS uses cloud-based applications, with the cloud provider developing and maintaining the cloud application software (Oracle, 2014). All the underlying infrastructure, application software and application data are located in the service provider's data centre. Examples of SaaS include web-based email services like Outlook, Hotmail, Yahoo email, and Gmail. Several SaaS providers use a subscription model, with subscriptions including maintenance, compliance and security services.

Definitions: Software

Software is a set of instructions, data or programs used to operate computers and execute specific tasks.

Application software

Application programs (applications or apps) have specific functions and are designed to complete a certain task.

Freeware

Freeware software is software that is available for use at no monetary cost or for an optional fee for unlimited time.

Shareware

Shareware is commercial/proprietary software that is distributed free to users by the owner for trial use at little or no cost, with the understanding that users will pay for it if they continue to use the software.

Malware

This is malicious software hidden within the shareware or with links to outside sources that can lead to viruses being downloaded on your device.

Open-source

Open-source software is software that is released under a licence in which the copyright holders grant users rights to inspect, use, study, modify, enhance, and distribute the software and its source code to anyone for any purpose.

Proprietary software

This is sometimes referred to as closed source software, this is software that legally remains the property of the organization or individual who created it.

Utility software

Utility software is system software that is designed to help analyse, configure, optimize, or maintain the proper and smooth functioning of a computer system.

Stop and Reflect: Computer Software

Discuss challenges that may be faced when sourcing software. Consider the use of propriety and open-source software.

1.7 Systems Analysis

Information technology is the combination of hardware, software and services that people use to manage, communicate and disseminate information. Systems analysis and design (SAD) is a broad term used to describe the methodologies employed to develop high-quality information systems which combine IT, stakeholders' requirements, and data to support business operations. The development of quality information systems requires an understanding of the problem that needs to be fixed. This also involves understanding how the current system works. Information systems are developed to meet specific business needs. System analysis involves comprehensively defining what the information system needs to accomplish so as to provide an organization with the desired benefits (Satzinger et al., 2015). Some major activities of system analysts include investigating system requirements, modelling system requirements, and determining development strategies.

Investigating System Requirements

The investigation of system requirements requires one to fully understand the business area that the system will support. When developing a system, system analysts work with various stakeholders to gather information about the system requirements. This information can be gathered in various ways, including brainstorming, interviewing the end-users (individual interviews or focus groups), observing the end-users at work, and distributing questionnaires to the end-users. Information about system requirements can also be obtained from an analysis of documents pertaining to the existing system, for example contracts, invoices, memos, etc. (Satzinger et al., 2015; Tilley, 2019). Other approaches include researching vendor solutions, prototyping, and conducting requirements workshops.

System requirements can be classified as functional or non-functional. A functional requirement is what the system should do. Examples of functional requirements are:

- The system should allow users to add reviews.
- The system should show how many items are in stock.
- Each input must have a date of birth and a place of birth.

A non-functional requirement is an operational system constraint, also known as a quality attribute. Examples of non-functional requirements are:

- The operating system that the system should work on.
- The number of people supported by the system simultaneously.
- The length of response time.

Modelling System Requirements

The information gathered when determining the system requirements is used to develop models that show what the system should do (Satzinger et al., 2015). A variety of models can be developed, such as data flow diagrams (DFDs) that show how the system transforms input data into useful information. An object/entity represents a place, person, event, or transaction that is important to the information system. Objects/entities can be modelled using an entity relationship diagram or a domain model class diagram. Other models include use case diagrams. A use case provides a description of how a user interacts with a system. Other models used for systems analysis are activity diagrams, decision trees, system sequence diagrams, and state machine diagrams.

Determining Development Strategies

The approach to system development can be either traditional (predictive approach) or more contemporary (adaptive approach). The predictive approach to system development strives to foresee the complete project's scope and carry it out in one lengthy procedure, involving low risk, while the adaptive approach is applied for high-risk projects and the project is not well understood (Satzinger et al., 2015). Adaptive approaches involve the incremental addition of features so that the development is iterative.

1.8 Chapter Summary

Information systems and information technology are necessary for companies' and people's operations, management, and decision-making. Information systems relate to the information and communication technology (ICT) that a business uses, as well as the manner in which personnel use this technology to support business operations. The present age, which includes you, is referred to as the 'Internet generation' because people commonly utilize smart phones and other portable electronics to stay in touch with their loved ones and co-workers while they study or work. People increasingly rely on digital technology more frequently as a result. Users must be aware of the functionalities of the hardware and software components and understand how to utilize them effectively in order to successfully employ digital technology and supply management with the accurate data they need to make decisions that will improve an organization's performance and productivity.

Discussion Questions

1   How can organizations benefit from adopting the SaaS and HaaS models?
2   Why is system analysis essential for the development of information systems?
3   Discuss the difference between information systems and information technology.
4   Discuss the difference between hardware and software.

Case Study: Information Systems – What and Why?

By Sumaiya Pervaiz, a Business Analyst at MicroMerger Pakistan (Pty Ltd)

Information systems (IS) are comprised of many components (e.g., software, hardware, computer connections, system users, the system housing, and information about the computer) that help gather, process, store, and disseminate information. The purpose of an information system is to store operational data, communication records, documents, and revision histories. It is inconvenient to store data manually, especially if one is trying to search for something specific. The information systems of an organization keep track of its environment and its operations. Organizations use information systems for disseminating information to employees by storing data in folders and documents that can be seamlessly shared. Organizations have three main types of information systems: operational, management, and strategic. A common operational-level system is one that tracks the number of hours employees work each day in a factory, for example. Management-level systems support middle managers' monitoring, controlling, and administrative activities, as well as decision-making. The use of strategic-level systems enables senior management to address strategic issues and long-term trends, both internally and externally.

(Continued)

In today's constantly changing and fast-paced environment, customers' requirements and preferences are always evolving. Innovation is the only way for businesses to remain competitive and continue to meet their customers' needs and expectations. Success in business depends on the ability to use information correctly. Information systems have become increasingly significant for businesses, and many have been driven to implement them in order to maintain a competitive edge. There is no business today that can function without an effective digital information system. Information systems are beneficial in many ways, but their greatest advantage is that they provide users with the information they need for their various activities.

The following are some business activities that require the intervention of an information system. An enterprise resource planning system (ERP) can be applied to automate business administration and planning. Supply chain management (SCM) provides a forum for interacting with different parties in the supply chain. As a result, communication between parties is made easier and more resourceful. Various information systems, including customer relationship management (CRM), facilitate the realization of customer needs. Furthermore, other information applications allow companies to communicate with their clients easily and affordably. Also, business data creation and utilization have been greatly facilitated by information systems.

Some examples of information systems include transaction processing systems, management information systems, customer relationship systems, decision support systems, office automation systems, business intelligence systems, knowledge management systems, etc. Information systems contribute to efficiency in operations, cost reduction, better customer service, constant system availability, and the development of communication methods and capabilities. Apart from improving business operations, information systems play an important role in the fight against violence, terrorism, cyber-crimes, and other threats to cyber security (Chen, Chiang, & Storey, 2012).

Questions

- What is an information system?
- Why do organizations need information systems?
- What are the benefits of having an information system?

1.9 References

Angell, I. O., & Smithson, S. (1991). Information technology and information systems. In *Information Systems Management* (pp. 77–93). Springer.

Arpaci-Dusseau, R. H., & Arpaci-Dusseau, A. C. (2018). Hard disk drives. In *Operating Systems: Three Easy Pieces*. Arpaci-Dusseau Books, LLC.

BBC. (2019, March 12). History of the CD: 40 years of the compact disc. *CBBC Newsround*. https://www.bbc.co.uk/newsround/47441962

Bidgoli, H., & Prestage, A. (2003). Operating systems. In *Encyclopedia of Information Systems*. Academic Press.

Bogna, J. (2022, March 24). What are zero-day exploits and attacks? *PCMag Australia*. https://au.pcmag.com/security/93117/what-are-zero-day-exploits-and-attacks

Borrett, L. (1989). IBM's micro channel architecture. http://www.borrett.id.au/computing/art-1989-03-01.htm

Brancheau, J. C., & Wetherbe, J. C. (1987). Key issues in information systems management. *MIS Quarterly*, 23–45.

Bromhead, B. (2017). 10 advantages of open source for the enterprise. https://opensource.com/article/17/8/enterprise-open-source-advantages

Business Insider. (2020, December 28). *Difference between Application Software and System Software*. https://www.businessinsider.in/difference-between-application-software-and-system-software/

Cambridge Dictionary. (2023, March 22). Nagware. *@CambridgeWords*. https://dictionary.cambridge.org/dictionary/english/nagware

Casey, M. (2021, October 17). What is peripheral component interconnect (PCI)? *Lifewire*. https://www.lifewire.com/what-is-pci-2640242

Chen, H., Chiang, R. H., & Storey, V. C. (2012). Business intelligence and analytics: From big data to big impact. *MIS Quarterly*, 1165–1188.

Cisco. (2023). What is malware? *Cisco*. https://www.cisco.com/site/us/en/products/security/what-is-malware.html

Cockerham, R. (2015, April). What is a logic board? *Techwalla*. https://www.techwalla.com/articles/what-is-a-logic-board

Computerhope. (2020, April 30). What is crippleware? https://www.computerhope.com/jargon/c/cripware.htm

Computerhope. (2022). What is a bus? https://www.computerhope.com/jargon/b/bus.htm

Croasdell, D., McLeod, A., & Simkin, M. G. (2011). Why don't more women major in information systems? *Information Technology & People*.

Deitel, H. M., & Deitel, B. (1986). *An Introduction to Information Processing*. Academic Press.

Encyclopaedia Britannica (2022, May 19). Application software. *Encyclopedia Britannica*. https://www.britannica.com/technology/application-software

Fisher, T. (2021a, September 20). What is a flash drive? *Lifewire*. https://www.lifewire.com

Fisher, T. (2021b, November 5). Everything you need to know about computer hardware. *Lifewire*. https://www.lifewire.com/computer-hardware-2625895

Fisher, T. (2023, February 28). What is accelerated graphics port (AGP)? *Lifewire*. https://www.lifewire.com/

Gartner. (n.d.). Definition of proprietary software. *Gartner Information Technology Glossary*. https://www.gartner.com/en/information-technology/glossary/proprietary-software

Gilster, R. (2001). *PC Hardware: A Beginner's Guide*. McGraw Hill Professional.

Giuma, T. A., & Hart, K. W. (1996). *Microcomputer Bus Architectures*. Paper presented at the Southcon/96 Conference Record.

Godse, A. P., & Godse, D. A. (2007). *Digital Logic Circuits*. Technical Publications Pune.

Gorrie, M. (2023). What is adware? https://us.norton.com/blog/emerging-threats/what-is-grayware-adware-and-madware

He, J., & Freeman, L. A. (2010). Are men more technology-oriented than women? The role of gender on the development of general computer self-efficacy of college students. *Journal of Information Systems Education, 21*(2), 203–212.

Hennessy, J. L. (1996). *Computer Organization and Design: The Hardware/Software Interface*. Morgan Kaufmann.

Kohlberg, L. (1958) The development of modes of moral thinking and choice in the years 10 to 16 (Doctoral dissertation, The University of Chicago).

Kohlberg, L. (1971) Stages of moral development. *Moral Education, 1*(51), 23-92.

Knerl, L. (2019, October 17). What does a motherboard do? *HP®Tech Takes*. https://www.hp.com/us-en/shop/tech-takes/what-does-a-motherboard-do#:~:text=The%20motherboard%20is%20the%20backbone

Knerl, L. (2021, April 2). What is DRAM (Dynamic Random Access Memory)? https://www.hp.com/us-en/shop/tech-takes/what-is-dram-dynamic-random-access-memory

Laurent, A. M. S. (2004). *Understanding Open Source and Free Software Licensing: Guide to Navigating Licensing Issues in Existing & New Software*. O'Reilly Media, Inc.

Lindsay, S., Taylor, A., Woodward, B., & Milligan, M. (2016). A male thing: why college women are not choosing STEM majors. *Issues in Information Systems, 17*(3).

Lobb, R., & Harlow, J. (2016). Coderunner: A tool for assessing computer programming skills. *ACM Inroads, 7*(1), 47–51.

Martindale, J. (2021, October 18). What is a CPU? *Digital Trends*. https://www.digitaltrends.com/computing/what-is-a-cpu/

Milian, M. (2011, June 13). Reading apps sell subscriptions to fuzzy feelings. http://edition.cnn.com/2011/TECH/web/06/13/subscription.donations/

Mohamed, A. (2018, April 9). A history of cloud computing. *ComputerWeekly.com*. https://www.computerweekly.com/feature/A-history-of-cloud-computing

Mueller, J. (n.d.). *Copyright Laws for Freeware and Shareware* https://legalbeagle.com/12719843-copyright-laws-for-freeware-and-shareware.html

Oja, D., & Parsons, J. J. (2014). *Computer Concepts 2014: Comprehensive*. Course Technology, Cengage Learning.

Oracle. (2014). Learn about SaaS. Oracle.*com*. https://www.oracle.com/au/applications/what-is-saas/

Oxford University Press. (2019). *Industry Standard Architecture (ISA)* Oxford University Press. https://www.oxfordreference.com/display/10.1093/acref/9780199688975.001.0001/acref-9780199688975-e-1660?rskey=MhyH4N&result=7

Parashar, N. (2022, March 17). Hardware as a Service (HaaS): A five-point guide. *Medium*. https://medium.com/@niitwork0921/hardware-as-a-service-haas-a-five-point-guide-5026610a0d84

Peppard, J., Galliers, R. D. & Thorogood, A. (2014). Information systems strategy as practice. *The Journal of Strategic Information Systems, 23*(1), 1–10.

Rouse, M. (2019, February 5). *Processor Register*. https://www.techopedia.com/definition/27596/processor-register

Satzinger, J. W., Jackson, R. B., & Burd, S. D. (2015). *Systems Analysis and Design in a Changing World*. Cengage Learning.

Sen, R. (2007). A strategic analysis of competition between open source and proprietary software. *Journal of Management Information Systems, 24*(1), 233–257.

Shanley, T. and Anderson, D., 1995. *ISA System Architecture*. Addison-Wesley Professional.

Shipley, C., & Jodis, S. (2003). Programming languages classification. https://www.sciencedirect.com/topics/computer-science/computer-language

Sirois, S. (2018, December 18). What is processor speed and why does it matter? https://www.hp.com/us-en/shop/tech-takes/what-is-processor-speed

Snyder, J., & Slauson, G. (2014). Majoring in information systems: reasons why students select (or not) information systems as a major. *Information Systems Education Journal, 12*(3), 59.

Stolterman, E. & Fors, A. C. (2004). Information technology and the good life *Information Systems Research* (pp. 687–692). Springer.

Stouffer, C. (2021, December 13). Types of ransomware to recognize + ransomware protection tips. https://us.norton.com/blog/malware/spyware

Stouffer, C. (2022, February 8). Shareware: An overview + the cost of 'free' software. https://us.norton.com/blog/emerging-threats/shareware

Teubner, R. A. & Stockhinger, J. (2020). Literature review: understanding information systems strategy in the digital age. *The Journal of Strategic Information Systems, 29*(4), 101642.

Tilley, S. (2019). *Systems Analysis and Design*. Cengage Learning.

Tyson, J., & Grabianowski, E. (2001, May 2). How PCI works. *HowStuffWorks*. https://computer.howstuffworks.com/pci.htm

Verma, M. (2020, December 7). Advantages & disadvantages of open source software, explained! *Medium*. https://medium.com/quick-code/advantages-disadvantages-of-open-source-software-explained-2fd35acd413

Villinger, S. (2019, November 7). What is RAM and why is it important? *Avast*. https://www.avast.com/c-what-is-ram-memory

Walsham, G. & Waema, T. (1994). Information systems strategy and implementation: a case study of a building society. *ACM Transactions on Information Systems (TOIS), 12*(2), 150–173.

Wilcox, L. (2021, March 30). The 4 main types of software. https://www.leadwithprimitive.com

2
PROJECT MANAGEMENT AND PROJECT MANAGEMENT BODY OF KNOWLEDGE (PMBOK)

2.1 Learning Outcomes

After reading this chapter, you will be able to:

- Discuss what project management is
- Explain what information technology projects are
- Discuss what project management processes are
- Explain what project management knowledge areas are
- Explain how mapping is used to process groups and knowledge areas
- Discuss what is meant by conflict in project management
- Discuss what is meant by risk in project management

2.2 Introduction

This chapter discusses the importance of project management in business and describes the five phases of the project management process. Furthermore, it discusses the 10 project management body of knowledge (PMBOK) areas to ensure that project deployment is successful. Project management is the process of carrying out certain project goals in accordance with predefined parameters and using specific procedures, techniques, abilities, knowledge, and experience. Project management's final deliverables are subject to time and budget constraints. In this chapter, the conflict and risks associated with project management are discussed. Since these issues are critical to successful project management, they should be addressed promptly to minimize problems related to scope, time, and cost in order to ensure project success.

The relationship between project management and information systems is that information systems are made up of the tools and methods used to collect, combine, and distribute project management process results. Information systems can contain both human and automated technologies and are used to assist at every stage of the project, from planning to closure. Through one or more software applications, project management information systems (PMIS) collect, arrange, and use project data. These tools help project managers plan, carry out, and wrap up their projects, as well as organise information flow. Information gathering, scheduling, delivery, and, most crucially, the gathering and reporting of automated key performance indicators (KPIs) are all elements shared by several PIMS software types.

2.3 What is Project Management?

'A project is a temporary endeavor undertaken to create a unique product, service, or result' (Project Management Institute, 2017a, p. 4). The temporary nature of projects implies that they have a definite start and end, irrespective of their duration. As opposed to operations, which are ongoing and do not produce distinctive outcomes, projects generate unique output(s) also known as deliverables. Projects can emerge from: (1) the need to resolve a problem, such as one linked to an environmental issue; (2) an opportunity, such as a technological breakthrough; or (3) a directive such as a legal requirement.

The world is constantly faced with disruptions. As industries become more competitive, and delivery speeds along with quality exigencies escalate, companies are increasingly expected to be more effective and efficient. The need to adapt and operate efficiently in rapidly changing environments was further accentuated by the COVID-19 pandemic and its resulting economic challenges. Companies which successfully navigated their way through the impacts of the virus adopted innovative practices, people-centric strategies, and an agile mindset, while embracing the change to lead, plan and execute tasks differently. The level of competence in organizations determines the success or otherwise of company operations. Hence, successful companies meticulously plan their projects, manage risks, and control their project scope to deliver timely and budget-contained project outcomes. Such project management key practices are essential for successful project outcomes, organizational resilience, and creating a competitive edge. Project management, therefore, refers to 'the application of knowledge, skills, tools and techniques to project activities to meet the project requirements' (Project Management Institute, 2017a).

2.4 Information Technology (IT) Projects

An IT project could range from the acquisition of an entirely new item (e.g., a new piece of hardware or new software) to the establishment of a service (e.g., setting up a help desk) or a result (e.g., a product manual). A project could also involve a unique combination of product, service, and result (e.g., tailored software, its customer service, and help guide) or even one or more amendments to each (e.g., a software upgrade).

Once the objectives have been achieved, successful projects help drive positive organizational change and create business value. Unfortunately, more than 50% of projects are unsuccessful, while 17% of IT projects fail so badly that they generally bankrupt the company (Djurovic, 2021). Following their 9th global project management survey, the Project Management Institute (2017b) reported that 37% of projects do not succeed due to a lack of clearly-defined objectives and milestones. This appears to be the biggest cause of project failure, followed by poor communication. In fact, all project journeys are fraught with pitfalls. Lack of stakeholder engagement, poor planning, insufficient management of risks, and the inability to adapt to change could easily lead a project astray. Projects could run late, exceed their budget, and/or produce poor quality deliverables resulting in unhappy stakeholders and damage to the company reputation. Conversely, agile, people-focused organizations with strong leadership, effective communication and risk management, and well-defined project scopes tend to experience greater project success. These companies value their people, help them work smartly, and demonstrate constant empathy while nurturing trusting relationships, innovative, flexible mindsets, and a collaborative culture.

In successful companies, project roles and responsibilities are carefully delineated and there is clear visibility in terms of how they all fit together to achieve business objectives (Project Management Institute, 2021). Such organizations demonstrate superior project management maturity which, as stated by Mir and Pinnington (2014), is likely to translate into higher project success rates.

2.5 Project Management Constraints

As indicated in Figure 2.1, project management requires careful juggling and prioritization of competing project constraints including scope (or the set of deliverables defining the project boundaries), time, cost, quality, risks, resources, and stakeholder expectations. A change in one project constraint can affect one or more of the others and therefore needs to be carefully evaluated, planned, and managed. For example, following the discovery of a security issue breaching the data privacy of more than 500,000 users, Google's Google+ social media platform was shelved in 2018 after the amount of work required to correct the problem was found to require too much time and money (Nelson, 2021). IT projects also often suffer from gold-plating or the tendency for developers to get carried away by new technology, thereby introducing features which might not be a client requirement, but which result in an avalanche of new tasks such as additional testing, increased risk management, and quality assurance. This is a classic example of uncontrolled project scope change (or scope creep), which has a direct impact on the project's time frame and cost, while potentially giving rise to additional project risks, quality issues, and stakeholder impacts.

Resource requirements are also heavily dependent on the project tasks, their duration, costs, quality expectations, and risks, which, if managed correctly, should result in stakeholder satisfaction. Additionally, risk oversight is critical to prevent the project from falling apart. Therefore, risks are situated at the base of the pyramid in Figure 2.1, as their management is critical for the project to remain stable and on track. Typical risks in IT projects include scope creep, poorly defined user requirements or even contractor failure (especially in cases where tasks have been outsourced).

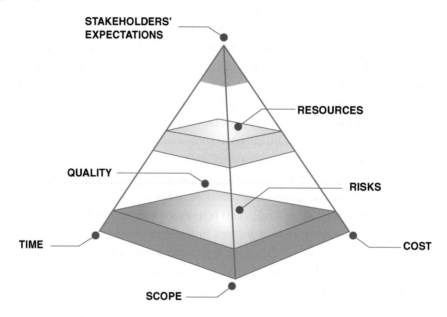

Figure 2.1 The Six Competing Project Constraints (adapted from Project Management Institute (2017a) by the authors and designed by Courtney Ramsamy – Curtin University Mauritius)

Stakeholder management is also critical as stakeholders can either make or break a project. Stakeholders refer to individuals, groups of people or organizations which are influenced by the project execution or its outcomes. They can be either internal or external to the organization, and can comprise:

• those involved in defining the requirements, scope and expected outcomes of the project (e.g., the project sponsor or customer);
• those responsible for the management and/or execution of the project (e.g., project manager and team members);
• those directly or indirectly affecting or being affected by the project and/or its outcomes (e.g., project enablers/blockers or regulatory bodies).

The project manager has the crucial responsibility of eliciting, understanding, and addressing stakeholder requirements in order to achieve project success. To ensure stakeholder satisfaction, it is essential that all the other project constraints be managed efficiently. For this reason, stakeholder expectations are located at the apex of the pyramid in Figure 2.1.

2.6 Project Management Processes

The key to a successful project lies in the correct application of project management processes for efficient and effective project execution. As indicated in Figure 2.2, project management processes can be categorized under five process groups (Project Management Institute, 2017a).

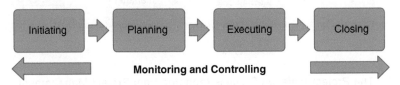

Figure 2.2   Project Management Process Groups (adapted from Project Management Institute (2017a) by the authors)

Stop and Reflect: Project Management Processes

List and reflect on the five project management processes.

Project Initiation

Project initiation groups together all tasks related to the kick-starting of the project. Pre-initiation could involve the approval of a business case to justify the project rationale, and the documentation of a business brief that clearly specifies the project customer/sponsor expectations. The project's operational environment also needs to be understood so that environmental influences can be better managed. These include enterprise environmental factors (EFFs) and organizational process assets (OPAs).

EFFs are factors present outside the project or even the enterprise and, although they may influence the project, they cannot be controlled by the project team. An example is the organizational culture which includes but is not limited to the organizational structure, strategy, and values.

OPAs, on the other hand, are internal to the organization and could comprise project templates, as well as historical data and lessons learnt documented from past similar projects. Once the project environment and its influences are understood, project initiation includes the identification of project stakeholders, constraints, assumptions, and objectives. These are documented in the project charter, which is typically signed off by the project sponsor, manager, and team members to formalize their buy-in. The charter provides the high-level requirements of the project and serves to formalize its existence, while also authorizing the project manager to commit resources. The project initiation process is summarized in Figure 2.3.

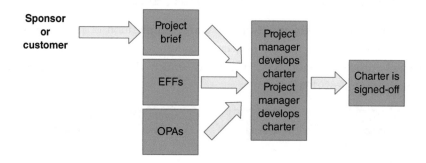

Figure 2.3   The Project Initiation Process (adapted from Project Management Institute (2017a) by the authors)

Project Planning

During the planning process, project objectives are refined to clearly define the scope and tasks associated with the project. This forms the basis of the project time plan where activities are carefully sequenced, and their duration, start, and completion times are identified to develop the project schedule before the project budget is determined. Planning also includes quality, resource, communications, procurement, and stakeholder management. Risks are also identified and prioritized, before establishing response strategies.

Project Execution

At execution, the project plan is put into action. Resources are allocated, the project team is managed, and project communication is undertaken according to the communication management plan. Stakeholders are managed, procurements conducted, and quality overseen. Risk response strategies are also implemented, with the execution of contingency plans when required. It is also important to collect actual data during the execution of the project. This will be part of the OPAs used as input to the development of the project charter at the initiation phase of future, similar projects.

Monitoring and Controlling

As indicated in Figure 2.2, monitoring and control occur throughout the lifetime of a project, although they normally peak during project execution. Monitoring requires the comparison of actual data (regarding project scope, schedule, cost, resources, quality, procurement, etc.) with the project plan. Discrepancies between actual and planned data might require changes in the project plan, and actions to bring the project back on track. This is known as project control.

Project Closing

Project closure involves client sign-off and/or contract closure, which may also be required if the project is cancelled or aborted. Post-implementation reviews are also conducted to document lessons learnt such as good practices on the project and suggestions for improvement. The review document is then added to OPAs along with other project documents/data to constitute historical data.

Figure 2.4 depicts the project management life cycle phases and tasks, which should be followed by the project manager and his/her team to ensure that the project aims will be achieved and the project time, cost, and scope are conducive to achieving a successful project at the end which meets the needs of the organization and the client.

Figure 2.4   Project Life Cycle

> ### Stop and Reflect: Project Management Processes
>
> Create a project life cycle in project management.

2.7 Project Management Knowledge Areas

Project processes can also be classified under knowledge areas which relate to specific project dimensions. The different knowledge areas are summarized in Table 2.1.

Table 2.1   Project Management Knowledge Areas (adapted from Project Management Institute (2017a) by the authors)

Project Knowledge Area	Description	Examples of Key Deliverables
Project Integration Management	This knowledge area is the glue that binds all other knowledge areas together. It includes processes for the identification and/or coordination of project management tasks.	The project charter specifies project objectives, expectations, and outcomes for stakeholder alignment and buy-in. An effective project management plan maps out how each project knowledge area will be coordinated.
Project Scope Management	Groups activities for the correct identification and control of the work to be done on the project.	The Work Breakdown Structure (WBS) assists in identifying all work to be carried out on the project. Only work in the WBS needs to be completed for project success.
Project Schedule Management	Includes activities required to successfully manage the time taken to complete project activities and meet the project deadline.	The project schedule provides an overview of project tasks, duration, sequence and resource allocation.
Project Cost Management	Covers all tasks related to budget setting, managing and control to prevent the project from going over-budget.	The project budget provides an estimation of the total cost of the project including the cost of labour, and other project resources such as hardware/software.
Project Quality Management	Includes quality planning, assurance, and control tasks for the project to operate within quality requirements.	Software test outcomes constitute a key quality control deliverable on IT projects.
Project Resource Management	Encompasses activities related to the identification of resources and the allocation of roles and responsibilities, as well as their management.	The resource plan identifies the project resources required to complete the project, when they are needed during the project and how they are used for efficient resource allocation.
Project Communications Management	Activities under this knowledge area relate to the identification of what needs to be communicated and why, as well as how the information will be collected, stored, and distributed, by whom and at what frequency to ensure timely and appropriate dissemination of the project information.	Minuted project team meetings constitute a key communication requirement to update all team members of project progress. In the communication management plan, these could be run face-to-face, on a monthly basis, organized by the project manager and including all team members.

Project Knowledge Area	Description	Examples of Key Deliverables
Project Risk Management	Includes risk planning, identification, prioritization, and response activities.	A risk register is a live document which enables risk tracking. It includes information such as the project risk description, its probability of occurrence and impact, the risk owner, mitigation strategies, etc.
Project Procurement Management	Covers all tasks related to procurement management, acquisitions, and control.	Procurement contracts are typically used to legally define the buyer–vendor relationship for products/services required to complete the project.
Project Stakeholder Management	Activities include project stakeholder identification, understanding their expectations and the management of stakeholder engagement strategies.	A stakeholder management plan documents key characteristics of project stakeholders, as well as strategies on how to most effectively manage them, e.g., a project sponsor who likes to be aware of every project detail might need more regular meetings with the project manager.

Stop and Reflect: Project Management Processes

What are the challenges that could be faced in the project management knowledge area?

2.8 What is Conflict in Project Management?

In this section, the issue of conflict in project management will be discussed to learn how it may occur in projects and how it can be tracked and managed. In this context, conflict 'is the process which begins when one party observes that the other has frustrated or is about to frustrate, some concern of his or hers' (Thomas, 1992, p. 265).

Conflict can occur in project management due to lack of communication, which is considered the main source of conflict during project development. Furthermore, lack of honesty, trust, or commitment, cross-cultural factors, inattentive listening, and perceptual disagreements can lead to severe communication problems. Failure to address these issues appropriately will lead to conflict in the project and among the teams. Therefore, the project manager should take responsibility for resolving issues associated with complex project organizational structures, conflict, and risks by using effective communication, which is an essential skill for project managers, particularly in terms of listening. The project's goal, group disagreements, a lack of communication, subpar leadership, and personal conflict are examples of sources of conflict in project management.

There are three traditional types of conflict: goal-oriented, authority-based, and inter-personal (Table 2.2) (Meredith & Shafer, 2022).

Table 2.2 Types of Conflict

Conflict Types	Examples
Goal-oriented conflicts	Associated with end results, performance specifications and criteria, priorities, and objectives
Authority-based conflicts	Related to management structure and philosophy are mainly based on the definition of roles and reporting relationships, and on responsibilities and authority regarding tasks, functions, and decisions
Interpersonal conflicts	Result from differences in the work ethics, styles, egos, and personalities of the participants

Stop and Reflect: Project Management Processes

List and give examples of the three types of conflict.

There are other sources of conflict in addition to those given above. Table 2.3 presents other types of conflict in project management and provides a suggested solution to pre-vent the reoccurrence of the conflict and to ensure the success of the current and future projects. This table will assist the project manager and his/her team to understand the sources of conflict and adopt solutions to ensure the project proceeds smoothly and is completed on time and within scope and budget constraints (Butler Jr, 1973; El Khatib et al., 2022; McCarthy, 2010; Meredith & Shafer, 2022).

There are several approaches available for resolving interpersonal conflict in project management: withdrawing; smoothing; compromising; forcing; collaborating, and prob-lem solving. Although any of these approaches can be taken to resolve conflict, it is important to consider the one that will be most appropriate and effective. Table 2.4 is divided into three columns, namely: style, description, and effect. As shown in the table, withdrawing is less time-consuming than problem solving. However, it does not resolve the conflict and results in personnel withdrawing from (in other words, leaving) the project. On the other hand, problem solving is time-consuming since is requires effort from the project manager and his/her team, to identify the conflict, discuss it with those involved in order to understand the problem, and create a solution to the conflict. The proposed solution must be approved by the project manager and his/her team prior to implementation. Most importantly, once implemented, the solution must be tracked and monitored to determine whether it is effective and whether subsequent changes need to be made to the project scope, cost, and time. Team members, clients, sponsors, and other stakeholders must be informed of any changes.

Table 2.3 Sources of Conflict and Suggested Solutions

Sources of Conflict	Definitions	Suggested Solutions
Conflict over project priorities	Project participants differ in regard to **sequence of activities and tasks**. Includes goals incompatibility and differences in long-term vs. short-term perspectives	Develop a **master plan** compatible with long-term strategies
Conflict over administration procedures	Conflicts over **managerial and administrative issues**; i.e., how the project will be organized and managed	Clarify **roles, responsibilities**, and reporting relationships at the beginning of the project
Conflict over technical opinions and performance trade-offs	Disagreements over **technical issues**, performance specifications, and technical trade-offs	Use **peer review and steering committees** to review specifications and design
Conflict over human resources	Conflicts concerning **staffing and allocation of project personnel**, and recruitment	Develop a **work breakdown structure** and a corresponding responsibility matrix
Conflict over costs and budget	Conflict over **cost estimates** from support areas regarding work breakdown structures and estimation techniques	Develop **overall budgets** supported by detailed budget and cost estimates of sub-project tasks and activities
Conflict over schedules	Disagreements about the **timing**, sequencing, and scheduling of project-related tasks and information systems to prepare and monitor project schedules	Develop an **overall schedule** that integrates schedules for sub-projects with staffing and other life constraints
Personality conflict	Disagreements on **interpersonal issues**	Emphasize **team building** and create an environment that emphasizes respect, mixture and fairness

Table 2.4 Interpersonal Conflict

Style	Description	Effect
Withdrawing	**Withdrawal** from an actual or possible conflict situation – this process is less time consuming than problem solving.	Does not resolve the conflict
Smoothing	Emphasizes area of **agreement** rather than area of **differences**	Provides only a short-term solution
Compromising	Searches for and agrees on **solutions** that bring some degree of **satisfaction** to all parties	Provides definitive resolution
Forcing	Promotes **one's own viewpoint** at the expense of others; offers only win–lose situations	Hard feelings may be expressed later in other ways
Collaborating	Incorporates **multiple** viewpoints and insights from different perspectives; leads to agreement and commitment	Provides long-term resolution
Problem Solving	Treats **conflict as a problem** to be resolved by examining alternatives; requires **give-and-take attitude and open dialogue**	Provides final resolution

Conflict can occur in any phase of the project life cycle, i.e.: project formation; build-up: main programme and phase-out (McCarthy, 2010; Meredith & Shafer, 2022; Project Management Institute, 2022; Sage et al., 2014).

During the project formation phase, conflict can arise from the confusion generated by the starting of a new project, since many of the policies and procedures have not yet been established and the objectives of the project are yet to be finalized. Therefore, conflict during this phase cannot be avoided. However, this type of conflict is considered good conflict, since it makes the project manager and his/her team aware of potential new conflicts and the need to address them promptly in order to begin working on the project as soon as possible.

In the build-up phase, the conflict may arise due to project priorities, schedules, and administrative procedures. The project manager will seek commitment from the functional department in order to ensure that the project stays on track in terms of its scope, cost, and time requirements. In each case, the project manager seeks commitment from the functional managers who are under pressure to deliver support to other projects.

During the main phase of project development, a major cause of conflict is the scheduling of tasks. To address this conflict, the project manager and his/her team should adjust the project tasks schedule by requesting extra resources from the functional departments or outsourcing in order to complete the tasks on time, and within budget and project scope. Technical conflicts may arise during this phase and their resolution is the first priority of the project manager. Any proposed solution must be tracked and monitored following its implementation to determine whether new changes affect the project scope and the achievement of project goals.

In order to manage conflicts that arise in projects, a project manager needs to be a skilful negotiator with effective communication skills. The term 'negotiation' refers to a planned conversation that finds a mutually agreeable solution to a problem. All parties concerned attempt to prevent conflict through negotiation while agreeing on a compromise. Significant communication abilities are required to assist in the resolution of conflict in projects (Meredith & Shafer, 2022; Smith, 2014).

Finally, conflict resolution requires the project manager to have a combination of analytical and interpersonal skills. To permanently resolve an issue, the project manager, his or her team, and stakeholders must seek the root cause of the conflict by listening to others and discussing the issue in depth. They must create a win–win situation to avoid losses when necessary, and use an effective strategy to be implemented immediately after first obtaining approval from all stakeholders, making the necessary changes to the project scope, time, and cost, and tracking the new changes to ensure that the work on the project can continue.

2.9 What is Risk in Project Management?

Risk is the result of uncertainty or chance events (e.g., the COVID-19 pandemic) that pre-planning cannot prevent or control, and this will affect the scope, cost, and time of projects. Risk exists throughout the whole project life cycle; therefore, project managers must be vigilant in spotting new risks and managing and monitoring them effectively to minimize their negative effects or seize any opportunities that unexpected events may offer (Barber, 2005; Le et al., 2022).

To minimize the risks that may pose a threat to a project, a risk management approach should be implemented, which is a practical attempt to recognize and manage internal events and external threats that are likely to affect the success of the project. Several questions should be asked at the beginning of risk assessment: what can go wrong (risk event)? How can the impact of a risk event (penalties/costs) be minimized? What can be done before an event occurs (expectation) and what to do when an event occurs (contingency plans)? For project managers to avoid losses and maximize opportunities, their primary risk-management goal is to identify and establish the context, and assess, evaluate, treat, monitor, and communicate the risks connected with any activity or process (Edwards & Bowen, 2013; Loosemore et al., 2012; Wideman, 2022).

Risk management has several advantages. For example, it mitigates the impact of unpleasant surprises and their consequences, prepares the project manager to take advantage of the circumstances created by a risk event, gives project managers better control over the future, and increases the likelihood of achieving project performance goals on time and within budget. On the other hand, risk-management measures may be difficult to implement and difficult to calculate. This is because risk management requires a lot of time to gather data regarding the current risk and prepare the best course of action to address it. Furthermore, uncontrolled losses occur because the organization incurs costs resulting from poor risk-management planning (Qazi et al., 2016; Willumsen et al., 2019).

Several studies (Meredith & Shafer, 2022; Pekkinen & Aaltonen, 2015; Wideman, 2022) indicate that the following steps should be taken to manage project risks:

- Step 1: Risk Identification
- Step 2: Risk Assessment
- Step 3: Risk Response Development
- Step 4: Risk Response Control

Step 1: Risk Identification

In this step, the project manager and his or her stakeholders brainstorm a list of potential risks by paying attention to and discussing the sources of those risks, and then they develop an action plan to minimize the risks and maximize the project's opportunities (Meredith & Shafer, 2022; Smith, 2014).

Step 2: Risk Assessment

The second step involves identifying the project's risks using a range of methodologies and examining how they may affect the project's scope, cost, and time. A risk assessment matrix tool is used to assist project managers and stakeholders to identify specific types of risks, their likelihood and severity, and obtain a real-time view of the evolving risk environment. Net present value (NPV), for example, is a financial metric used to determine whether an investment in a new project will be profitable now and in the future (Masár & Hudáková, 2019; Meredith et al., 2022).

Step 3: Risk Response Development

Based on the outcomes from Steps 1 and 2, the project manager should share with his/her stakeholders including the project client, the new solution proposed to minimize the risk. Generally, several solutions are proposed in this phase, and one of them should be adopted and monitored in terms of scope, cost, and time so that the project can be finalized. The solutions are: justifying risk (reducing the likelihood that an adverse event will occur); avoiding risk (changing the project plan to eliminate the risk); transferring risk (recruiting sub-contractors to complete the tasks that involve risk); and finally, retaining risk (accepting the risk, i.e., earthquake, flood, bushfire, or pandemic, i.e., COVID-19) (Liew et al., 2019; Wideman, 2022).

Step 4: Risk Response Control

The final step in managing risk is risk response control. In this step, the project manager should consider both risk control and establishing a change management system. This requires the project manager to execute and monitor the risk response strategy, establish contingency plans, and watch for new risks that could arise in the project. As for the change management system, the project manager should monitor, track, and report risks to the project stakeholders, including the project client. Finally, the project manager should document all the risks that arose during the project, as well as the solutions and lessons learned (Ahmadi-Javid et al., 2020; Wideman, 2022).

***

Project risk is the possibility that a circumstance could arise that would alter the path of a project, either favourably or unfavourably. Scope, cost, and time are all impacted by project risks, and have the potential to cause project failure if not addressed properly. Social, economic, technological, environmental, political, and pandemic issues can all contribute to project risks. Risk management and contingency plans should be established at the beginning of the project to prevent or minimize threats due to poor project management practices, supply chain delays, unexpected staff illnesses, a pandemic, etc. To manage and resolve these risks in projects without wasting time or money and to produce high-quality projects that match the project's scope, schedule, and cost, the project manager and his or her stakeholders should be well versed in the use of risk management tools.

> **Stop and Reflect: Project Management Processes**
>
> List and discuss the four steps taken to manage risk in project management.

2.10 Chapter Summary

The significance of project management in business is covered in this chapter, which also outlines how the project manager and his or her team should collaborate to determine the project's scope. Based on this, an action plan will be created to specify the teams and their tasks. Subsequently, a plan based on the tasks, time, and cost will be created. All project stakeholders, including the client and top management, will need to review and approve this plan. This chapter also covered the 10 PMBOK knowledge domains and the five project management methods used to ensure the success of a project. Additionally, two key project-related concepts are covered: project conflict and project risk, both of which need to be dealt with promptly to reduce losses and maximize opportunities. Finally, information systems played a key role in project management, as information systems are made up of the tools and methods used to collect, combine, and distribute project management process results. They can include both human and automated technologies and are used to assist at every stage of the project, from planning to closure.

> **Discussion Questions**
>
> 1 What is project management?
> 2 What is a conflict?
> 3 What is a risk?
> 4 What is the project life cycle?

> **Case Study: The Interpersonal Conflict during COVID in Western Australia**
>
> **By Sumaiya Pervaiz, a Business Analyst at MicroMerger Pakistan (Pty Ltd)**
>
> This case study is about the XYZ building that was constructed in Perth, Western Australia in January 2020. For this project, one of the world's best project managers,
>
> *(Continued)*

David, was hired. To stay focused and on track throughout any task of such a project, it is essential to set clear goals and objectives at the start. A lack of goals complicates the situation, resulting in poor results. Therefore, this project's aims and goals were set to run smoothly. Moreover, the roles and responsibilities of the manager and each of the team members were well-defined and aligned with the project objectives and aims. Therefore, the project manager and stakeholders were able to make relevant, reliable, and timely decisions and receive support from the project team.

To manage a project successfully, it is crucial to hire the right people at the right time. For this purpose, the building company hired a team of talented people to streamline the workflow. After hiring, training to manage a team became a real challenge. As a project manager, it was David's responsibility to train his team. Training included everything from briefings to instructions to post-project work. Along with hiring and training the workers, social skills were one of the project manager's strengths. David's leadership kept the team on track and the project progressed effortlessly. Due to David's good public relations, he overcame numerous challenges faced by builders and contractors. To develop a healthy working relationship with his team, David believes in good, open, and transparent communication.

As a result of the team's hard work and efforts being appreciated, the whole team was motivated. It was evident that they were extremely passionate about their work, which led to excellent results, and the workflow of the project stayed within budget and time constraints. Overall, the team members worked in a very stress-free environment and weren't pressed or forced to do anything. Moreover, the project manager prepared them mentally for the contingency plan so that they could handle it effectively and efficiently. A good risk assessment made them feel confident and kept their morale high.

A sudden outbreak of COVID-19 occurred in Western Australia in 2020, creating an unexpected situation. The entire world was shocked and frightened at that time. As a result, the project had to be stopped for eight months. The project was delayed, and every task was behind schedule. Due to this situation, the administration decided, without consulting project team members, that vaccination would be mandatory for everyone. No vaccine, no job!

This decision resulted in an interpersonal conflict. Project managers faced the challenge of having to deal with interpersonal conflict in their teams. Conflicts between individuals can derail a project's success, harming a team's collaboration and cohesion as well as threatening the project's survival. In most cases, this conflict results from differences in work ethics, styles, egos, and personalities. Despite their unwillingness, the workers felt pressured to comply with the vaccination mandate. This issue halted the project for another month. Time management was a serious problem at that point. This occurred because the team members' strike disrupted roles and responsibilities, authority over tasks, functions, and decisions. To resolve this deadlock, the administration and project manager emphasized team building and creating an environment that values respect, trust, and care. Therefore, they began negotiating with their workers to resolve the interpersonal conflicts. During negotiations, they decided not to impose vaccinations on them, instead allowing them to make their own choices. It gave the team members a sense of freedom and relaxation. As a result, the interpersonal conflict was resolved. The project manager should view conflicts as opportunities to grow and to move the project forward. It is through conflicts that project managers, stakeholders, or any other member of the team can identify and address unforeseen problems. Consequently, it helps people become more real, recognize their differences, and maximize their potential.

Questions

1   What was the conflict in this case?
2   Why did the conflict occur?
3   How could it be resolved?
4   What are the challenges and opportunities created by conflict in modern projects?

Bibliography

Hope, K. L., & Amdahl, E. (2011). Configuring designers? Using one agile project management methodology to achieve user participation. *New Technology, Work and Employment, 26*(1), 54–67.

Meredith, J. R., & Shafer, S. M. (2022). *Project Management: A Strategic Managerial Approach* (11th edition). John Wiley & Sons.

Smith, P. (2014). Project management. *Journal of Project Management, 23*(4), 1–20.

2.11 References

Ahmadi-Javid, A., Fateminia, S. H., & Gemünden, H. G. (2020). A method for risk response planning in project portfolio management. *Project Management Journal, 51*(1), 77–95.

Barber, R. B. (2005). Understanding internally generated risks in projects. *International Journal of Project Management, 23*(8), 584–590.

Butler Jr, A. G. (1973). Project management: A study in organizational conflict. *Academy of Management Journal, 16*(1), 84–101.

Djurovic, A. (2021). 25 astounding project management statistics [2020 Update]. https://goremotely.net/blog/project-management-statistics/#:~:text=More%20than%2050%25%20of%20projects%20fail.&text=More%20than%20half%20of%20all%20projects%20fail.,could%20bankrupt%20the%20whole%20company

Edwards, P., & Bowen, P. (2013). *Risk Management in Project Organisations.* Routledge.

El Khatib, M., Kherbash, A., Al Qassimi, A., & Al Mheiri, K. (2022). How can collaborative work and collaborative systems drive operational excellence in project management? *Journal of Service Science and Management, 15*(3), 297–307.

Le, P. T., Kirytopoulos, K., Chileshe, N., & Rameezdeen, R. (2022). Taxonomy of risks in PPP transportation projects: A systematic literature review. *International Journal of Construction Management, 22*(2), 166–181.

Liew, K., Low, W., Wong, K., & Wong, S. (2019). *Risk Assessment of Infrastructure Projects on Project Cost*. Paper presented at the IOP Conference Series: Materials Science and Engineering.

Loosemore, M., Raftery, J., Reilly, C., & Higgon, D. (2012). *Risk Management in Projects*. Routledge.

Masár, M., & Hudáková, M. (2019). *The Current State of Project Risk Assessment and Education Needs in Project Risk Management*. Paper presented at the CBU International Conference Proceedings.

McCarthy, J. F. (2010). *Construction Project Management: A Managerial Approach*. Pareto.

Meredith, J. R., & Shafer, S. M. (2022). *Project Management: A Strategic Managerial Approach* (11th edition). John Wiley & Sons.

Mir, F. A., & Pinnington, A. H. (2014). Exploring the value of project management: Linking project management performance and project success. *International Journal of Project Management, 32*(2), 202–217. https://doi.org/10.1016/j.ijproman.2013.05.012

Nelson, R. R. (2021). *IT Project Management: Lessons Learned from Project Retrospectives 1999–2020*. Now Publishers.

Pekkinen, L., & Aaltonen, K. (2015). Risk management in project networks: An information processing view. *Technology and Investment, 6*(01), 52.

Project Management Institute. (2017a). *A Guide to the Project Management Body of Knowledge (PMBOK Guide)* (6th edition). Project Management Institute, Inc.

Project Management Institute. (2017b). *Success Rates Rise. Transforming the High Cost of Low Performance*. Pulse of the Profession®. https://www.pmi.org/-/media/pmi/documents/public/pdf/learning/thought-leadership/pulse/pulse-of-the-profession-2017.pdf

Project Management Institute. (2021). *Beyong Agility: Flex to the Future*. Pulse of the Profession®. https://www.pmi.org/-/media/pmi/documents/public/pdf/learning/thought-leadership/pulse/pulse-of-the-profession-2017.pdf

Project Management Institute. (2022). *What is Project Management?* Retrieved 16 Jan 2023, from https://www.pmi.org/about/learn-about-pmi/what-is-project-management

Qazi, A., Quigley, J., Dickson, A., & Kirytopoulos, K. (2016). Project Complexity and Risk Management (ProCRiM): Towards modelling project complexity driven risk paths in construction projects. *International Journal of Project Management, 34*(7), 1183–1198.

Sage, D., Dainty, A., & Brookes, N. (2014). A critical argument in favor of theoretical pluralism: Project failure and the many and varied limitations of project management. *International Journal of Project Management, 32*(4), 544–555. doi:http://dx.doi.org/10.1016/j.ijproman.2013.08.005

Smith, P. (2014). Project management. *Journal of Project Management, 23*(4), 1–20.

Thomas, K. W. (1992). Conflict and conflict management: Reflections and update. *Journal of Organizational Behavior, 13*(3), 265–274.

Wideman, R. M. (2022). *Project and Program Risk Management: A Guide to Managing Project Risks and Opportunities*: Project Management Institute, Inc.

Willumsen, P., Oehmen, J., Stingl, V., & Geraldi, J. (2019). Value creation through project risk management. *International Journal of Project Management, 37*(5), 731–749.

3

ETHICS, ETHICAL MINDSETS, CORPORATE SOCIAL RESPONSIBILITY, AND THE TRIPLE BOTTOM LINE

3.1 Learning Outcomes

After reading this chapter, you will be able to:

- Identify the prerequisites for understanding ethics

    o Schön's reflective practice
    o Kohlberg's moral stages

- Define and explain

    o ethics
    o ethical mindsets
    o ethical principles
    o values
    o models, including the responsible management of technology use and privacy
    o the most popular ethical theories

- Define and understand the components of ethical mindsets
- Define corporate social responsibility
- Differentiate between corporate social responsibility, government responsibility and individual responsibility

- Define the triple bottom line
- Critically distinguish between ethical/moral and legal

3.2 Introduction

This chapter will introduce the importance of ethics, related to responsible management of technology use and privacy. This chapter will help you to understand the importance of being honest, considerate, and reflective whenever you deal with clients, by way of technology. You need to always consider the consequences of your actions prior to acting, considering the benefits and the shortcomings of your product for the purpose it is designed for. Simply put, you need to be honest in your dealings with systems, people, and the planet. This chapter will also introduce corporate social responsibility (CSR) and the triple bottom line (TBL) in relation to information systems.

   This chapter aims to introduce these important topics and highlight their importance in an information systems context. However, it is worth noting here that talking about ethics, ethical mindsets, corporate social responsibility, and the triple bottom line means we need to go back to the origin of those expressions and try to understand what they mean. Having said that, in this chapter, we shall endeavour to make this as simple as we can, just scratching the surface of those complex expressions and trying our best to link them to the daily lives of businesspeople. Therefore, reading this chapter will not transform you into a philosopher but will equip you with minimal knowledge on these important yet topical subjects.

   It is worth stating here that reading this chapter might provide you with the tools to assist you in evaluating events and responding in ways that would be ethical and socially responsible.

3.3 Reflective Practice and Moral Stages

At work people are guided by law, regulations, and internal guidelines, and thus, after a while, individual workers can become like robots, and this is the danger in applying the law. Here, there is a need for reflection, as whatever the individual does at work will not only impact that individual, or the work they do, but also the community and society. Currently, as we are living in what is referred to as a 'global village', what I might do in my work in one corner of the world could impact on others around the world. Thus, we as individuals, need to consider our impact on others. To allow us to do that we need to think beyond the law and consider whether our actions are the result of an ethical decision. The best way to be able to think along these lines would be to become a reflective practitioner and understand the Kohlberg moral stages of humankind. An understanding of these two approaches, which is considered a prerequisite of understanding ethics, would help the individual to take not only legal, but also ethical decisions that would benefit if not all, then most of humanity. This is crucial, especially in the field of information systems and technology and with the introduction of Artificial Intelligence (AI). Although AI is not considered a part of information technology, the link is significant, and any development in this area that is done without considering the ethical side of such work would be disastrous for humankind. Therefore, as specialized individuals in information systems and technology, we need to be careful to stop, reflect, and think about our own actions, as well as the short- and long-term impacts of such actions on everyone else, before we consider implementing such ideas.

In this regard, Porter (1990) and Porter and Kramer (2006) indicate that we are facing a range of problems, such as: access to water; climate change; deforestation, pollution; lack of healthcare; inequality. Here, we can add several other problems that are on the increase: computer hacking and cybercrime; ongoing wars; the danger of nuclear war; famine; pandemics; and more and more. Unfortunately, business is not the solution, and it seems that the build-up of wrong and selfish decisions has created or contributed to some of the problems that humankind and the environment are facing, all in the name of increasing profits, and maximizing the money generated from those businesses in the market.

In this respect, Sandel (2009; 2010) opines that there is a need for all of us to rethink the role of money in the market, stating that, in this corrupt age, it seems there is nothing money cannot buy. We need to rethink this role because we need to consider how giving freedom to the markets and money might increase inequality.

This section introduces the concept of reflective practice. I was introduced to this way of thinking by my Doctor of Philosophy Supervisor, who always insisted on students having the ability to maintain good reflective practice and to think critically.

To assist you with these two issues, this chapter offers a very brief overview of Kohlberg's Moral Stages, Schön's Reflective Practice (e.g., Kohlberg, 1963; Kohlberg & Symptom Media, 2012; Schön, 1967; 1971a; 1971b; 1983; 1987a; 1987b; 1991; 2001; 2017; Schön & Rein, 1994; Schön et al, 1999; Schonemann, 1990) and the principles of Critical Thinking (e.g., Biesta & Stams, 2001; Mahin, 1998).

3.4 Kohlberg's Moral Stages

Kohlberg (1958) considers that humans have four issues that will impact their development stages: self, family, community, and humanity. Kohlberg identifies three levels and each level has two stages, thus outlining a total of six stages in the moral development of the individual (see Figure 3.1)

- Pre-Conventional Level

    o   Stage 1: The punishment and obedience orientation
    o   Stage 2: The instrumental relativist orientation.

- Conventional Level

  o Stage 3: The interpersonal concordance or 'good boy–nice girl' orientation
  o Stage 4: The 'law and order' orientation.

- Post-Conventional, Autonomous, or Principled Level

  o Stage 5: The social-contract legalistic orientation (generally with utilitarian overtones)
  o Stage 6: The universal ethical-principle orientation.

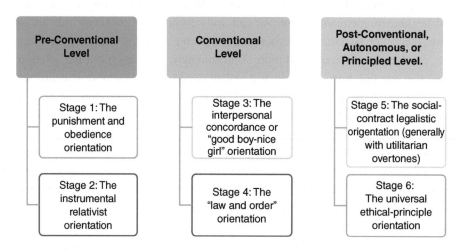

Figure 3.1 Stages of Moral Development (derived from Kohlberg (1971) and designed by the author)

While Kohlberg,[1] had identified age groups for each of these stages, however, in business, we might be able to spot all these different stages, as in my opinion they are not only linked to the age of the individual, but can be linked to their emotional intelligence, as well as their conscience and ability to cope with the pressures of family, community, and humanity, and to deal with each of the stages.

Kohlberg[2] provides simple examples to illustrate these stages. Firstly, people might only be moved to act in order to obey a higher authority or because they are scared of punishment, or only act out of self-interest, their sense of right and wrong being derived from the prospect of punishment or reward, that they will suffer or enjoy, and this corresponds to the 'pre-conventional' stage. Secondly,

---

[1]References mentioned in the paragraph above, under 3.1.

[2]For other sources that can be consulted in relation to Kohlberg, see Brady & Hart (2007), Hayes (1994), Heilbrun (1990), Kay (1982), Kjonstad & Willmott (1995), Weber (1991).

when someone considers that being good is pleasing others and society, and thus acts to receive compliments and be described as a good boy/girl, being seen as someone who always abides by the norms of law and order, this would be referred to as the conventional stage. Finally, the last stage is when the individual's sense of right and wrong is only determined by referring to their personal values and by looking at the deeply held principles that they consider as more important than the law of the land. Thus, these individuals would act out of their commitment to the social contract and specifically out of their principled conscience, and this would be referred to as post-conventional behaviour.

Stage of moral development

Pre-Conventional Level

- Stage 1: The punishment and obedience orientation
- Stage 2: The instrumental relativist orientation

Conventional Level

- Stage 3: The interpersonal concordance or 'good boy–nice girl' orientation
- Stage 4: The 'law and order' orientation

Post-Conventional, Autonomous, or Principled Level

- Stage 5: The social-contract legalistic orientation (generally with utilitarian overtones)
- Stage 6: The universal ethical-principle orientation

3.5 Schön's Reflective Practice

Being active, and working with other individuals in an organization that is part of society, thus part of the world, you need to always be mindful of what you are doing as an individual, and consider the long-term effects of your actions. This applies to all industries, and as the field of information systems and technology is taking over the world, it applies here too. Therefore, as an individual working in this field, there is a need to not only comply with the requirements of organizations' leaders, and bring in quick solutions, but also to stop, think and reflect on what the consequences might be prior to coming up with the final product.

Thus, there is a need for anyone in business to reflect, and Schön's[3] idea was that you might need to both reflect-in-action and reflect-on-action. The reflection in action

---

[3]References mentioned in the first paragraph under 3.1.

can be conducted while you are undertaking the work, thus, with your reflection you will be able to evaluate whether what you are doing is right or wrong. In business the choice might usually be between being legal or illegal, but when you consider ethics, you need to always think beyond the legal and enter the realms of the moral and ethical. Thus, comes 'reflection-on-action', which would take place at the review stage, when you would assess the actions you have taken and learn the appropriate lessons.

In Figure 3.2 Schön's (1983) model of reflection-in-action and reflection-on-action is detailed.

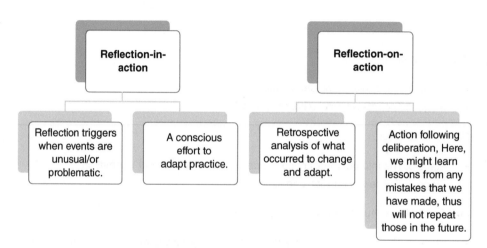

Figure 3.2   Reflection-in-Action and Reflection-on-Action Model (derived from Schön (1983) and designed by the authors)

Now, let us conclude this section by reiterating, using the words of Schön (1983), what reflective practice means:

Definition: Reflective Practice

Reflection-in-action: reflection is triggered when events are unusual/or problematic; a conscious effort is then made to adapt practice.

Reflection-on-action: involves a retrospective analysis of what has occurred in order to change and adapt. Action follows deliberation. Here, we have the opportunity to learn lessons from any mistakes that we have made, and thus not repeat them in the future.

Pick (2010) has identified a number of questions that you might need to ask yourself when you practice reflection:

- On what ethical basis did I make my decision?
- How well did I recognize various stakeholders?
- On what basis did I prioritize various interests/values?
- How well did I communicate with others about my decisions, before, during and after I acted?
- How well did I reason things through?
- Were there any biases in my decision-making?
- How can I improve and what effects will this have?
- How can I do it better next time?!

Thus, as individuals we need to always be thinking about what we are doing, and what the impact of our actions would be on ourselves, our family, society, and humanity, including thinking about the impact of our actions on the environment.

3.6 Critical Thinking

We need to always remember when acting that although we are one person, we may have an impact, either directly or indirectly, on other individuals, society, and the environment; thus, it is a great idea to always think critically about the tasks given to us by our leaders, especially in the business environment. However, if we have trained ourselves throughout our lives to be critical thinkers, we will find it easy not to jump on the first opportunity presented to us without posing the necessary questions that will allow us to identify the task and its potential impact.

Hilsdon (2010) provides a model to generate critical thinking. At the heart of this model lies the topic/issue/title. Hilsdon (2010) identifies three areas that need attention:

- Description
- Analysis
- Evaluation

You need to ask the questions: What? When? Who? Where? Why? How? What if? So What? and What next? By doing so you can reach an understanding of the nature of the topic/issue/title, analyse it further, and then evaluate the action taken, which might lead you to the beginning of the model, at which point you can repeat the process again and again until you reach a full understanding of the action, its impact and consequences on all areas of interest, not only in terms of the individual but at the corporate, family, social and environmental levels.

This model, together with some knowledge of the nature of ethics, ethical mindsets, corporate social responsibility, and the triple bottom line, might assist you to take a moral position about everything around you, from the nature of capitalism to international business and environmental ethics, for example.

3.7 Ethics and Ethical Theories

To answer the question 'What is ethics?' we need to consider some of the scholars whose work takes in ethics and professions.

De George (1986) is a very well-known scholar in relation to ethics. In 1999 De George outlined a contemporary discussion on and definition of ethics, stating: 'Ethics is the study of morality, and morality is a term used to cover those practices and activities that are considered importantly right or wrong; the rules that govern those activities; and the values that are embedded, or pursued by those activities and practices' (De George, 1999 p. 19).

Indeed, understanding ethics would enable the individual to understand the morality behind any practice or action, and that these need to be governed by the values that this individual holds high.

Lawrence (1999) posed the question, 'Why is it especially important for professions and professionals to be able to justify morally their actions?' Lawrence responded with a brief answer stating that professionals hold skills and power that place them in the higher ranks of trust and power in any society. Having said that, Lawrence qualifies this response by stating that giving professionals this power comes with the assumption that they will be using it for morally justified purposes. Lawrence (1999) further opines that a crucial feature of a profession is hence its so-called 'ethics', which supposedly guarantees that a profession serves rather than exploits the society in which it operates. Moral or ethical reasoning provides the grounding argument for appropriate action.

Shaw et al. (2013; 2016; 2021) have identified several normative theories, as well as other issues relating to corporate social responsibility. Fisher and Lovell (2006; 2009) and Fisher and Malde (2011) have produced major works in relation to ethics and morality. For example, Fisher and Lovell define business ethics as the study of what constitutes right and wrong, or good and bad human conduct in a business context (Fisher & Lovell, 2006), while, in their opinion, morality refers to how choices are made from among alternative courses of action.

It is worthwhile noting here that professional ethics has become the focus of a great deal of recent writing within individual occupations and, to some extent, more generally (see Table 3.1)

Table 3.1 The Marriott School Ethics Toolkit (adapted by Theodora Issa from the Marriott School Ethics Toolkit – developed by Brad Agle, Jeff Thompson, and Dave Hart)

Theoretical Roots	An Action is Ethical When	Questions I Should Ask Myself	Relevant Scholars	Limitations	Discussion Starters (in 'business speak')
Deontology	I would be willing for it to become a universal law. (*Universal Principles*) It treats other people as ends in themselves and not just as means. (*Rights*) It is reversible (as per the Golden Rule). (*Reversibility*) Benefits and costs are equitably distributed. (*Justice*)	What are the core principles at stake? Am I protecting others' rights? Does my decision preserve others' dignity and ability to choose? Would I be willing to be the other party to the transaction? Will this decision be fair to all involved?	Emanuel Kant W. D. Ross	Difficult to manage competing principles. Difficult to bound the conditions. Difficult to balance conflicting rights. Lack of agreement on fair shares. Multiple parties to satisfy. Difficult to anticipate how others really feel. Difficult to measure costs and benefits. Lack of agreement on fair share.	Would we be content if others (competitors, employees, partners) did what we plan to do? Will our decision make some people feel that they are just being used? Are we treating our stakeholders as we would like to be treated? Will any of our stakeholders feel this decision is unfair to them?
Utilitarianism	It provides the greatest benefit to most people (i.e., the greatest good for the greatest number of people).	Who will be affected by my decision? Who will benefit? Who will be harmed?	Jeremy Bentham John Stewart Mill	Difficult to measure costs and benefits. Majority may disregard the rights of the minority.	Let us talk about whom our decision will impact the most. Who are the key stakeholders here? What decision would add the most value to us and our stakeholders?
Virtue Ethics	It helps me become a better person (an excellent person – the character of a person). I would be willing to have it broadcast to the public.	Who am I? What kind of person would this action make me? How would I feel if my reasoning and approach appeared on the news?	Aristotle Plato Thomas Aquinas Bernard Williams Alasdair McIntyre	Relies on individual feelings. Everyone has implicit self-serving biases. The public is not always right. Historical/cultural biases.	Let us consider what kind of organizational identity we want to convey to the public. How will this action affect our image or reputation if it becomes public?
Ethics of Care	It benefits those with whom I have a special trust and obligation or the most vulnerable.	Am I taking care of the people who are most important to me, or those who are most vulnerable?	Carol Gilligan Nel Noddings	Danger of favouritism or nepotism. Difficult to balance competing relationship demands.	How does this decision affect the people or groups who trust us the most? (e.g., employees/customers, etc.)

3.8 Ethical Mindsets and Ethical Theories

Ethical mindsets was coined by Issa (2009), who concluded that there are eight major components of these mindsets (i.e. aesthetic spirituality, religious spirituality, optimism, harmony and balance, personal truth, contentment, making a difference, and interconnectedness).

Therefore, to fully comprehend the situation you need to develop your thinking towards moral and ethical decision-making, thus attaining the ability to see the moral dimension in business through an understanding of normative theories of ethics. Shaw et al. (2013; 2016; 2021) highlight the normative theories as:

- **Virtue Ethics:** Those ethics are based on character – there are two branches of these types of theories:
    - ○ Aristotle's virtue: The development of virtues to become an 'excellent' person
    - ○ Ethics of care: Caring for others

- **Teleology:** These theories are based on consequences – there are two branches of these types of ethics theories:
    - ○ Egoism: Achieving the moral agent's best long-term interest
    - ○ Utilitarianism: Achieving the greatest good for the greatest number

- **Deontology:** These theories are based on duty – there are two branches of these types of ethics theories:
    - ○ Kant: Universal law, good will, treating others as an end, never as a means to an end
    - ○ W.D. Ross: Where principles conflict, prioritize the most important.

On the other hand Fisher and Lovell (2006; 2009), Fisher and Malde (2011) provide a framework for ethical theories, dividing them into four categories: (a) individual processes, such as adaptability and responses; (b) institutional structure, such as fixity and consistency; (c) policy ('doing good'); and (d) principle ('doing right').

Within this framework, Fisher and Lovell (2006, p. 100) have come up with the four ethical theories:

1   Virtue Ethics, including virtue ethics and ethical care. In the framework of Fisher and Lovell (2006; 2009), Fisher and Malde (2011) this virtue ethics sits between individual processes and the principle (doing right).
2   Ethical learning and growth, including individual growth, communitarianism, and ethical egoism. In the framework of Fisher and Lovell (2006; 2009), Fisher and Malde (2011) this ethical learning and growth sits between individual processes and policy (doing good).
3   Deontological ethics, including Kantian imperatives, rights, and justice as fairness. In the framework of Fisher and Lovell (2006; 2009), Fisher and Malde (2011) this

deontological ethics sits between the principle (doing right), and institutional structure, such as fixity and consistency.

4   Teleological ethics, including discourse ethics and utilitarianism. In the framework of Fisher and Lovell (2006; 2009), Fisher and Malde (2011) this teleological ethics sits between policy (doing good) and institutional structure, such as fixity and consistency.

The knowledge of ethical theories might help you with taking a moral position in relation to your own work, while other trends in the market might affect this work negatively or positively, trends such as capitalism, corporate social responsibility and corporate governance, morality and ethics of consumption, international business, globalization and environmental ethics in business, ethics and human talent, and ethics at work, managing business ethics, leadership, and culture. Thus, if you incorporate ethical theories into whatever you do, you will be satisfying yourself, your organization, your consumers, the environment, and society.

3.9 Corporate Social Responsibility

In this section we shall provide a brief overview of 'corporate social responsibility', trying to highlight some of the ethical responsibilities of technology. This is important these days as technology is present in every aspect of our lives.

One very famous tool for understanding CSR is Carroll's (1999) pyramid (see Figure 3.3).

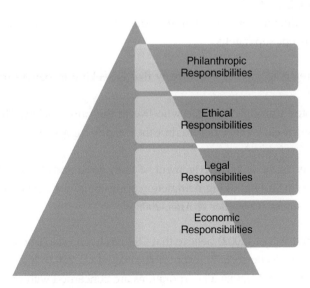

Figure 3.3 Corporate Social Responsibility Pyramid (derived from Carroll (1991) and designed by the authors)

> ## Definition: Corporate Social Responsibility
>
> Over the years, a number of scholars have discussed and evaluated CSR from different perspectives, for example: Bravo et al. (2012), Fransen (2013), Girard and Sobczak (2012), Harjoto and Jo (2015), Holder-Webb et al. (2009); Jo and Harjoto (2012), Kolstad (2007), Lii and Lee (2012), Mitra (2012), Norman (2011), Ofori (2010), Perrini et al. (2011), Vanhammen et al. (2012), Yakovleva and Vazquez-Brust (2012).
>
> Corporate social responsibility (CSR) is the continuing commitment by business to behave ethically and contribute to economic development while improving the quality of life of the workforce and their families as well as of the local community and society at large (Van Marrewijk, 2003).

Corporate Social Responsibility, Government Responsibility, and Individual Responsibility

When CSR is mentioned, Government Responsibility (GR) and Individual Responsibility (IR) immediately come to the fore. CSR can be simply defined as the continuing commitment by business to behave ethically and contribute to economic development while improving the quality of life of the workforce and their families, as well as of the local community and society at large. CSR can also be described as the commitment of business to contribute to sustainable economic development, working with employees, their families, the local community, and society at large to improve their quality of life.

Therefore, and drawing on Crowther and Aras (2008), let us take the three words that make up this concept separately:

* 'Corporate' refers to any large company that is seeking to benefit from several activities.
* 'Social' denotes a group of people who live in the same society. They may or may not have known each other before, but they can forge a relationship and help each other.
* 'Responsibility' is the acknowledgement of both good and bad results from all actions taken, including taking complete responsibility for developing and sustaining business (Crowther & Aras, 2008).

Post, Lawrence, and Weber (2002) believe that CSR has been established as a guideline that expects organizations to be socially responsible (Post et al., 2002). It is worth noting here, along with Attig et al. (2013), that all corporations are concerned with profit, but they must be more concerned with short-term and long-term social impacts (Attig et al., 2013).

In their research Baird et al. (2012) shed new light on the empirical link between corporate social performance (CSP) and corporate financial performance (CFP), showing both a significant overall CSP effect as well as significant industry effects between CSP and CFP. Their results confirm the existence of disparate CSP dimension–industry effects on CFP, thus the results of our actions provide important and actionable information to decision-makers considering whether and how to commit corporate resources to social performance.

According to Rangan et al. (2012), the responsibilities towards shareholders or investors can be briefly described as respect for stakeholders, directors and managers, employees, consumers, business partners, the community and environment, and business competitors. In business of all sorts, including companies dealing with technology, and with regard to the responsibilities towards shareholders, according to Rangan et al. (2012), there is a need to reveal all necessary information to shareholders and investors and maintain the confidentiality of internal information. At the same time, the responsibilities towards the directors and managers may be apparent in the provision of support for them in the pursuit of good governance, the development of managing systems, the provision of accurate financial reporting, and the disclosure of all financial reports. As for the responsibilities towards employees, these can be briefly stated as the payment of fair wages, offering welfare according to labour protection law, looking after employees' health and security in the workplace, developing employees' skills, and the provision of staff training. As for the responsibilities towards consumers, these can be briefly described as the provision of products and services, making available to customers/consumers information about the company and its products, concern for the customers' health, and responding appropriately to all complaints.

Further, and according to Rangan et al. (2012), the responsibilities to business partners consist in offering a fair contract and rejecting all forms of corruption and bribery. As for the responsibilities towards community and environment, these can be briefly outlined as supporting the local workers, establishing a policy of environmental protection, and learning about the local culture. The responsibilities towards business competitors would be the promotion and maintenance of fair competition.

From the above, it might be considered that CSR could be difficult for some businesses to cope with, especially those who came late to the market, when CSR was considered as an add-on rather than a basic requirement of any business. Having said that, there are several benefits to CSR, and, according to Forte (2013), these are:

- CSR can improve profitability, promote long-term profits, increase financial performance, increase the return on investments, and raise sales volumes.
- CSR enhances community relations because it is proactively attempting to benefit society, thereby establishing positive relationships between individuals, companies, and government.

- CSR improves the business ethics within the company, and among business partners and competitors.
- CSR can maintain a favourable public image and enhance the company's reputation.
- CSR helps to create a better environment and improve the welfare of the community.

Moreover, it is worth mentioning here that, according to Steckstor (2012), there are several types of CSR, as follows:

Cause Promotions: includes capital, materials, or other resources for expanding awareness and concern about social issues.

Cause-Related Marketing: related to marketing activities and supporting community projects or charities.

Corporate Social Marketing: aims to change people's behaviour and show how organizations can affect customer behaviours.

Community Volunteering: organizations promote and encourage all employees and business partners to devote time and effort to helping the local community.

Socially Responsible Business Practices: all business activities are carefully managed in order to prevent and avoid causing social and/or environmental problems.

Developing and Delivering Affordable Products and Services: concerns the production and selling of low-priced goods and services which enable people with a low income to purchase them.

Furthermore, while CSR used to be an add-on, currently, in the context of everything that is happening in terms of the misuse of technology and the awareness of customers, it is a must; and those working in technology need to be aware that this industry and the services it renders have to fully adopt CSR and act for the benefit of their business, people, and the planet.

This leads us nicely to the next and final section of this chapter where we will provide a brief overview of the triple bottom line. While some large corporations have moved towards five bottom lines, we shall only concentrate here on the triple bottom line.

3.10 The Triple Bottom Line (TBL)

Breton and Largent (2008), posing the questions 'Is greed good?' discuss the issue of the triple bottom line (TBL), highlighting that monopoly driven by greed has led to a disastrous situation in the world. Breton and Largent go on to state that dealing with greed goes beyond the economic system, or technology, and moves directly towards morality and ethics. Thus, no matter what type of business we are in, we need to consider dealing with the issues around us, including greed, and thinking about the ethical and moral dimension of every action with respect to the people, planet, and profit (see Figure 3.4).

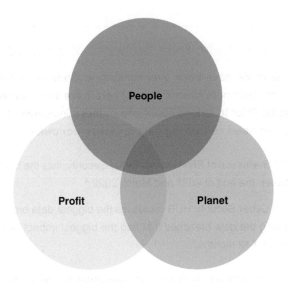

People

Profit   Planet

Figure 3.4   The Triple Bottom Line

According to Fry and Slocum (2008) One of the greatest challenges facing leaders today is the need to develop new business models that accentuate ethical leadership, employee well-being, sustainability, and social responsibility without sacrificing profita-bility, revenue growth, and other indicators of healthy financial performance. Fry and Slocum address top managers' need to simultaneously maximize the so-called triple bottom line, or 'People, Planet, Profit'.

On the other hand, Johnson (2008) posits that it is possible to do well and do good at the same time in corporate America. Soul care and the bottom line are not the 'odd couple' in corporate America. Johnson (2008) is of the opinion that business thrives because of the ethical principles of goodness and compassion.

3.11 Chapter Summary

In this chapter we have attempted to provide a very simple and brief outline of Kohlberg's six moral stages of human development and Schön's idea of reflective practice, including reflection-in-action and reflection-on-action. Also, we have provided a brief look at Issa's ethical mindsets, and its components, which led to the introduction of normative ethical theories, as identified by Shaw et al. and Fisher and Lovell.

Following on from this, we discussed the idea of corporate social responsibility high-lighting its importance for individuals, businesses, governments, and society. Finally, we briefly discussed the idea of the triple bottom line, urging those studying to spread their consideration beyond monetary profit, and think of the consequences of their action on people and planet.

Case Study: Data Breaches Worldwide

Recently in the news we have been over-consuming stories about hacking and the illegal accessing of customers'/clients' data. There have been several examples of hacking in Australia. Prior to talking about one of these incidents, it is worth sharing with you some of the news concerning data breaches worldwide:

> Dr Rey LeClerc Sveinsson of ERM Protect Cyber Security, lists the top 10 data breaches recorded between the end of 2021 and March 2022.[4]

> Olivia Powell of Cyber Security HUB discusses the biggest data breaches and leaks of 2022, highlighting the data breaches that had the biggest impact in the cyber security world over the past 12 months.[5]

As we can see, these represent very serious data breaches and leaks, indicating that there is something wrong here, either within those organizations or in the way those with immense knowledge deal with computers and data.

---

[4]These are given as: 1. Crypto.com Crypto Theft; 2. Microsoft Data Breach; 3. News Corp Server Breach; 4. Red Cross Data Breach; 5. Ronin Crypto Theft; 6. FlexBooker Data Breach; 7.GiveSendGo Political Data Breach; 8. Cash App Data Breach; 9. Marquard & Bahls Supply Chain Breach; 10. PressReader Data Breach (https://ermprotect.com/blog/top-10-data-breaches-so-far-in-2022/).

[5]These are listed as: 10. Revolut data breach exposes information for more than 50,000 customers; 9. SHEIN fined US$1.9mn over data breach affecting 39 million customers; 8. Student loan data breach leaks 2.5 million social security numbers; 7. Twitter confirms data from 5.4 million accounts was stolen; 6. Hacker allegedly hits both Uber and Rockstar; 5. 9.7 million people's information stolen in Medibank data leak (Australia); 4. Hacker attempts to sell data of 500 million WhatsApp users on dark web; 3. Personal and medical data for 11 million people accessed in Optus data breach. (Australia); 2. More than 1.2 million credit card numbers leaked on hacking forum; 1. Twitter accused of covering up data breach that affects millions (https://www.cshub.com/attacks/articles/the-biggest-data-breaches-and-leaks-of-2022).

Questions

1   Can you evaluate which of the ethical theories discussed you would think that these hackers have been adhering to, if any?
2   How would you have benefited from Schön's reflection-in- and on-action.

Case Study: The Case of Optus

Please review the following articles:

Financial Review: 'Inside the Optus hack that woke up Australia: A huge cyberattack on the telco in September caused a political storm and made Australians aware of the power of their personal data. Behind the scenes, it was a time of high drama'[6]

7news.com.au: 'The "Optus hacker" claims they've deleted the data. Here's what experts want you to know. You may think the turmoil is over. It's not'[7]

The Sydney Morning Herald: 'Optus hack to cost at least $140 million'[8]

The Guardian: 'The biggest hack in history: Australians scramble to change passports and driver licences after Optus telco data debacle'[9]

Then, taking the approach of Pick (2010), imagine yourself to be the CEO of Optus and ask yourself the following questions, deriving your answers from the material in this chapter:

1   On what ethical basis did I make my decision?
2   How well did I recognize various stakeholders?

(Continued)

---

[6]https://www.afr.com/technology/inside-the-optus-hack-that-woke-up-australia-20221123-p5c0lm

[7]https://7news.com.au/technology/optus/the-optus-hacker-claims-theyve-deleted-the-data-heres-what-experts-want-you-to-know-c-8400749

[8]https://www.smh.com.au/business/companies/optus-puts-aside-140m-to-replace-customers-hacked-identity-documents-20221110-p5bx4g.html

[9]https://www.theguardian.com/business/2022/oct/01/optus-data-hack-australians-scramble-to-change-passports-and-driver-licences-after-telco-data-debacle

3   On what basis did I prioritize various interests/values?

4   How well did I communicate with others about my decisions, before, during and after I acted?

5   How well did I reason things through?

6   Were there any biases in my decision-making?

7   How can I improve and what effects will such an improvement have? How can I do better next time?

In addition to the above questions, please respond to the following questions:

1   How would you have benefited from Schön's reflection-in- and on-action.

2   Analyse your personality and see where you (as the CEO of Optus) are situated within Kohlberg's six moral stages.

Please note there are no right or wrong answers, but in every attempt to answer any of these questions you need to support your answer with the necessary theory.

3.12 References

Ardichvili, A., Jondle, D., Kowske, B., Cornachione, E., Li, J., & Thakadipuram, T. (2012). Ethical cultures in large business organizations in Brazil, Russia, India and China. *Journal of Business Ethics, 105*(4), 415–428.

Arel, B., Beaudoin, C. A., & Cianci, A. M. (2012). The impact of ethical leadership, the internal audit function, and moral intensity on a financial reporting decision. *Journal of Business Ethics, 109*(3), 351–366.

Attig, N., El Ghoul, S., Guedhami, O., & Suh, J. (2013). Corporate social responsibility and credit ratings. *Journal of Business Ethics, 117*(4), 679–694.

Baird, P. L., Geylani, P. C., & Roberts, J. A. (2012). Corporate social and financial performance re-examined: industry effects in a linear mixed model analysis. *Journal of Business Ethics, 109*(3), 367–388.

Baron, R. A., Zhao, H., & Miao, Q. (2015). Personal motives, moral disengagement, and unethical decisions by entrepreneurs: cognitive mechanisms on the 'slippery slope'. *Journal of Business Ethics, 128*(1), 107–118.

Biesta, G. J. J., & Stams, G. J. J. M. (2001). Critical thinking and the question of critique: Some lessons from deconstruction. *Studies in Philosophy and Education, 20*, 57–74.

Bishop, J. D. (2000). A framework for discussing normative theories of business ethics. *Business Ethics Quarterly, 10*(3), 563–591.

Brady, N., & Hart, D. (2007). An exploration into the developmental psychology of ethical theory with implications for business practice and pedagogy. *Journal of Business Ethics, 76*, 397–412.

Bravo, R., Matute, J., & Pina, J. M. (2012). Corporate social responsibility as a vehicle to reveal the corporate identity: A study focused on the websites of Spanish financial entities. *Journal of Business Ethics, 107*(2), 129–146.

Breton, D., & Largent, C. (2008). The soul of economies: The power of philosophies to transform economic life – 4 parts. *Business Spirit Journal Online, 34.*

Carroll, A.B. (1991) The pyramid of corporate social responsibility: Toward the moral management of organizational stakeholders. *Business Horizons, 34*(4), 39-48.

Carroll, A. B. (1999). Models of management morality for the new millennium. *Vital Speeches of the Day, 66*(2), 48–50.

Crowther, D., & Aras, G. (2008). *Corporate Social Responsability.* Aras Güler & Ventus Publishing ApS.

De George, R. (1986). Theological ethics and business ethics. *Journal of Business Ethics, 5*, 421–432.

De George, R. T. (1999). *Business Ethics* (5th edition). Prentice Hall.

Dreier, J. (1993). Structures of normative theories. *The Monist, 76*(1), 22–40.

Fisher, C., & Lovell, A. (2006). *Business Ethics Values. Individual, Corporate and International Perspectives* (2nd edition). Pearson Education Limited.

Fisher, C., & Lovell, A. (2009). *Business Ethics and Values: Individual, Corporate and International Perspectives* (3rd edition). Pearson Education Limited.

Fisher, C., & Malde, S. (2011). Moral imagination or heuristic toolbox? Events and the risk assessment of structured financial products in the financial bubble. *Business Ethics: A European Review, 20*(2), 148–158.

Forte, A. (2013). Corporate social responsibility in the United States and Europe: How important is it? The future of corporate social responsibility. *The International Business & Economics Research Journal (Online), 12*(7), 815–824.

Fransen, L. (2013). The embeddedness of responsible business practice: Exploring the international between national-institutional environments and corporate social responsibility. *Journal of Business Ethics, 115*(2), 213–227.

Fry, L. W., & Slocum, J. W. J. (2008). Maximizing the triple bottom line through spiritual leadership. *Organizational Dynamics, 37*(1), 86–96.

Girard, C., & Sobczak, A. (2012). Towards a model of corporate and social stakeholder engagement: Analyzing the relations between a French mutual bank and its members. *Journal of Business Ethics, 107*(2), 215–225.

Harjoto, M. A., & Jo, H. (2015). Legal vs. normative CSR: Differential impact on analyst dispersion, stock return volatility, cost of capital, and firm value. *Journal of Business Ethics, 128*(1), 1–20.

Hayes, R. L. (1994). The legacy of Lawrence Kohlberg: Implications for counseling and human development. *Journal of Counselling and Development, 7*, 261–267.

Heilbrun, A. B. J. (1990). The measurement of principled morality by the Kohlberg Moral Dilemma Questionnaire. *Journal of Personality Assessment, 55*, 183–194.

Hilsdon, J. (2010). Reflection. In: Plymouth, U. o. (ed.). Plymouth: University of Plymouth.

Holder-Webb, L., Cohen, J. R., Nath, L., & Wood, D. (2009). The supply of corporate social responsibility disclosures among U.S. firms. *Journal of Business Ethics, 84*, 497–527.

Issa, T. (2009). Ethical mindsets, aesthetics and spirituality: A mixed-methods approach analysis of the Australian services sector. Curtin University of Technology. http://espace.library.curtin.edu.au/R/?func=dbin-jump-full&object_id=131986&local_base=GEN01-ERA02

Jo, H., & Harjoto, M. A. (2012). The causal effect of corporate governance on corporate social responsibility. *Journal of Business Ethics*, *106*(1), 53–72.

Johnson, C. (2008) How to do well and do good in business: Taking care of the soul and the bottom line, 2008. bizspirit.com/bsj/archive/articles/cedric1.html

Kay, S. R. (1982). Kohlberg's theory of moral development: Critical analysis of validation studies with the defining issues test. *International Journal of Psychology*, *17*, 27–42.

Kjonstad, B., & Willmott, H. (1995). Business ethics: Restrictive or empowering? *Journal of Business Ethics*, *14*, 445–464.

Kohlberg, L. (1958) The development of modes of moral thinking and choice in the years 10 to 16 (Doctoral dissertation, The University of Chicago).

Kohlberg, L. (1963, reprinted in 2008). The development of children's orientations toward a moral order i. sequence in the development of moral thought. *Human Development* (Reprint of Vita Humana 1963 6, 11–33), *51*, 8–20.

Kohlberg, L. (1971) Stages of moral development. *Moral Education*, *1*(51), 23–92.

Kohlberg, L. & Symptom Media. (2012). *Kohlberg Moral Developmental Stages Index*. Level 3. Episode 11, Conventional universal ethical principles 2. Symptom Media.

Kolstad, I. (2007). Why firms should not always maximize profits. *Journal of Business Ethics*, *76*, 137–145.

Lawrence, T.B. (1999). Institutional strategy. *Journal of Management*, *25*(2), 161-187.

Lii, Y.-S., & Lee, M. (2012). Doing right leads to doing well: When the type of CSR and reputation interact to affect consumer evaluations of the firm. *Journal of Business Ethics*, *105*(5), 69–81.

Mahin, L. (1998). Critical thinking and business ethics. *Business Communication Quarterly*, *61*(3), 74–78.

Mitra, R. (2012). 'My country's future': A culture-centered interrogation of corporate social responsibility in India. *Journal of Business Ethics*, *106*(2), 131–147.

Norman, W. (2011). Business ethics as self-regulation: Why principles that ground regulations should be used to ground beyond-compliance norms as well. *Journal of Business Ethics*, *102*(1), 43–57.

Ofori, D. (2010). Executive and management attitudes on social responsibility and ethics in Ghana: Some initial exploratory insights. *Global Partnership Management Journal*, *1*(1–2), 14–24.

Perrini, F., Russo, A., Tencati, A., & Vurro, C. (2011). Deconstructing the relationship between corporate social and financial performance. *Journal of Business Ethics*, *102*(1), 59–76.

Pick, D. (2010). Being a Reflective Practitioner – Based on Schön's (1967) *Educating the Reflective Practitioner* – Chapter 2, [Lecture]. Curtin University unpublished.

Porter, M. E. (1990). The competitive advantage of nations. *Harvard Business Review*, https://hbr.org/1990/03/the-competitive-advantage-of-nations

Porter, M. E., & Kramer, M. R. (2006). Strategy and society: The link between competitive advantage and corporate social responsibility. *Harvard Business Review*, December, 78–92.

Post, J. E., Lawrence, A. T., & Weber, J. (2002). *Business and Society: Corporate Strategy, Public Policy, Ethics*. McGraw-Hill Companies.

Rangan, K., Chase, L. A., & Karim, S. (2012). Why every company needs a CSR strategy and how to build it. http://www.hbs.edu/faculty/Publication%20Files/12-088.pdf

Sandel, M. J. (2009). *Justice: What's The Right Thing To Do?* Farrar, Straus and Giroux.

Sandel, M. (2010). We need a public life with purpose. *The Guardian*.

Schön, D. A. (1967). *Technology and Change: The New Heraclitus*. Pergamon Press.

Schön, D. (1971a). *Beyond the Stable State: Public and Private Learning in a Changing Society*. Maurice Temple Smith Ltd.

Schon, D. A. (1971b) *Beyond the Stable State*. New York: The Norton Library.

Schön, D. A. (1983). *Reflective Practitioner: How Professionals Think in Action*. Basic Books Inc.

Schon, D. (1987a) *Educating the Reflective Practitioner*. Available online: http://educ.queensu.ca/~ar/schon87.htm

Schon, D. (1987b) *Educating the Reflective Practitioner: Toward a New Design for Teaching and Learning in the Professions*, Jossey-Bass Inc.

Schön, D. (1991). *The Reflective Practitioner: How Professionals Think in Action* (2nd edition). Ashgate Publishing Limited.

Schön, D. (2001). The crisis of professional knowledge and the pursuit of an epistemology of practice. In J Raven & J Stephenson (eds), *Competence in the Learning Society*. Peter Lang, pp. 183–207.

Schön, D. A. (2017). *The Reflective Practitioner: How Professionals Think in Action*. London: Routledge.

Schön, D. A., & Rein, M. (1994) *Frame Reflection: Toward the Resolution of Intractable Policy Controversies*. Basic Books.

Schön, D. A., Sanyal, B., & Mitchell, W. J. (eds) (1999). *High Technology and Low-Income Communities: Prospects for the Positive Use of Advanced Information*. Massachusetts Institute of Technology.

Schonemann, P. H. (1990). Facts, fictions, and common-sense about factors and components. *Multivariate Behavioral Research*, *25*(1), 148–154.

Shaw, W. H., Barry, V., Issa, T., & Catley, B. (2013). *Moral Issues in Business* (2nd Asia Pacific edition). Cengage Learning.

Shaw, W. H., Barry, V., Issa, T., Catley, B., & Muntean, D. (2016). *Moral Issues in Business* (3rd Asia-Pacific edition). Cengage Learning.

Shaw, W. H., Barry, V., Muntean, D., Issa, T., Ilott, G., & Catley, B. (2021). *Moral Issues in Business* (4th Asia Pacific edition). Cengage Learning.

Steckstor, D. (2012). *The Effects of Cause-related Marketing on Customers' Attitudes and Buying Behavior*. Springer.

Vanhammen, J., Lindgreen, A., Reast, J., & van Popering, N. (2012). To do well by doing good: Improving corporate image through cause-related marketing. *Journal of Business Ethics*, *109*(3), 259–274.

Van den Hoven, J. (2010). The use of normative theories in computer ethics. In L. Floridi (Ed.), *The Cambridge Handbook of Information and Computer Ethics*. Cambridge University Press, pp. 59–76.

Van Marrewijk, M. (2003). Concepts and definitions of CSR and corporate sustainability: Between agency and communion. *Journal of Business Ethics, 44*(2–3), 95–105.

Weber, J. (1991). Adapting Kohlberg to enhance the assessment of managers' moral reasoning. *Business Ethics Quarterly, 1*, 0293–0318.

Yakovleva, N., & Vazquez-Brust, D. (2012). Stakeholder perspectives on CSR of mining MNCs in Argentina. *Journal of Business Ethics, 106*(2), 191–211.

4

SUSTAINABILITY, SUSTAINABLE DESIGN, AND GREEN IT

4.1 Learning Outcomes

After reading this chapter, you will be able to:

- Define and explain what sustainability is and its importance to users and businesses
- Identify and discuss the 17 United Nations Sustainable Development Goals
- Define and discuss sustainable design
- Define and discuss human-computer interaction (HCI)
- Understand what is meant by usability
- Define and discuss green information technology

4.2 Introduction

Since organizations and individual users now rely more on computers, the Internet, and systems technology than they did in the past to accomplish the same goals, these technologies are crucial tools in the 21st century. Modern technology is better able to manage and help people and organizations to fulfil their duties much more quickly. In addition to the widespread use of standalone computers, the Internet, the World Wide Web, social networks, mobile devices, Intelligent Environments, and other technologies have greatly enhanced worldwide networking. However, as experts, researchers, and practitioners involved in the human–computer interaction (HCI) domain strive to address the needs of businesses and individual users, while ensuring that new ICT technologies are more sustainable so as to meet both current and future needs, the rise in ICT usage around the world has presented a new challenge. As a result, three concepts that are increasingly important to consumers and companies both locally and globally – sustainability, sustainable design, and green information technology – will be covered in this chapter. In order to reduce carbon emissions, global warming, energy use, and raw material waste, and conserve resources for the next generation, users, designers, HCI professionals, and businesses should take these issues into account when devising their ICT usage strategy.

4.3 What is Sustainability?

In her book, *Silent Spring*, published in 1962, Rachel Carson warned the world about the dangers that chemicals present to the ecosystem (Mozlin, 2007). In 1968, Garret Hardin's 'Tragedy of the Commons' highlighted the dangers of over-exploiting the world's limited resources (Hawkshaw et al., 2012). Later, in 1972, leaders of nations worldwide met in Stockholm to voice their strong concerns about environmental issues and international human well-being (Rowland, 1992). Yet, it was only in 1987 that the concept of sustainable development (SD) was propelled to the limelight by the Brundtland Report. Titled *Our Common Future*, the report presented a global agenda aimed at uniting countries in the fight against poverty, environmental degradation, and inequality. It defined sustainable development as 'development that meets the needs of the present without compromising the ability of future generations to meet their own needs' (Brundtland Commission, 1987, p. 41).

The Brundtland definition of sustainability is one of the most frequently cited, particularly due to its long-term focus and ethical premise of equality between both current and future generations (Mensah, 2019). Several other definitions followed, centred on economic, social, and environmental considerations. For example, Diesendorf (2000) categorized any social or economic development supporting the environment and social equity as sustainable. He defined sustainable development as comprising 'types of economic and social development which protect and enhance the natural environment and social equity' (Diesendorf, 2000, p. 3). Mensah (2019) added that the end goal of sustainable development is to reach a balanced state of the three pillars of SD: economic, environmental, and social sustainability. With sustainability being the result of the sustainable development process, a deeper understanding of sustainability requires a more substantial explanation of each SD pillar.

Economic sustainability is 'often seen as a matter of intergenerational equity' (Anand & Sen, 2000, p. 2029). Natural resources are neither unlimited nor always replaceable, thus emphasizing the need for controlled growth and sustainable consumption. Hence, economic sustainability requires sound production, distribution, and consumption practices in order to avoid compromising future needs (Mensah, 2019). Social sustainability includes multiple dimensions such as social equity, poverty alleviation, literacy, justice, and decent housing, as well as a safe and healthy community (Dempsey et al., 2011; Eizenberg & Jabareen, 2017). Environmental sustainability seeks to maintain systems that support human life, namely food, water, air, energy, and the capacity to absorb waste (Goodland, 1995).

> More specifically, environmental sustainability could be defined as a condition of balance, resilience, and interconnectedness that allows human society to satisfy its needs while neither exceeding the capacity of its supporting ecosystems to continue to regenerate the services necessary to meet those needs nor by our actions diminishing biological diversity (Morelli, 2011, p. 5)

Hence, sustainability requires concerted efforts to integrate social, economic, and environmental considerations within development (Mensah, 2019). Figure 4.1 depicts the three pillars of sustainability.

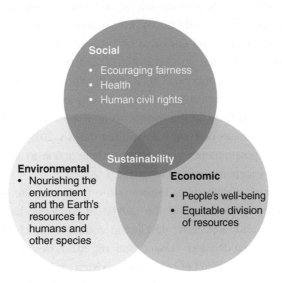

Figure 4.1 The Three Pillars of Sustainability

Definition: Sustainability

Sustainability is defined as 'development that meets the needs of the present without compromising the ability of future generations to meet their own needs' (Brundtland Commission, 1987, p. 41).

4.4 Why Sustainability?

In April 2021, A68, the largest iceberg in the world, melted into smaller fragments deemed unworthy of tracking. While the demise of A68 alone cannot be directly attributed to global warming, the fivefold increase in the loss of ice in the Antarctic Region since the 1990s is a result of the increase of ocean temperatures (Goddard, 2021). According to United States National Oceanic and Atmospheric Administration (NOAA) data, the top 10 warmest years have been recorded since 2005, with 2020 registered as the second hottest year following a surface temperature 0.98 °C warmer than the 20th-century average of 13.9 °C (Lindsey & Dahlman, 2021). In 2005, 154 states committed to the United Nations Framework Convention on Climate Change (UNFCCC) Kyoto Protocol to collaboratively fight against excessive atmospheric greenhouse gas (GHG) emissions and the resulting global warming and climate change (UNFCCC, 2008).

Later, the 2015 Paris Climate Conference (COP21) resulted in 195 nations pledging to contain the global average temperature increase within 2 °C – a threshold beyond which the world was predicted to face catastrophic environmental, economic, and social impacts. This ceiling was lowered to 1.5 °C following the release of the Intergovernmental Panel on Climate Change (IPCC) 2018 special report (IPCC, 2018). To remain within the 1.5 °C limit, the report recommended that net global GHG emissions be brought down by 45% compared to 2010 levels by 2030, and reduced to net zero by 2050 (IPCC, 2018). Despite some countries' open scepticism about the report (Ogunbode et al., 2020), the impacts of climate change are undeniable. These include extreme weather conditions (such as storms, floods, and droughts), reduced agricultural productivity, health threats, rising sea levels, and damaged ecosystems with destroyed natural habitats both on land and sea (NOAA, 2019). Therefore, it is imperative that communities, governments, and industries take action to limit climate change to 1.5 °C and ensure environmental sustainability (Steg, 2018).

While environmental sustainability improves the quality of life, several other issues must also be addressed. For example, the COVID-19 pandemic has had unprecedented impacts on developed and, especially, developing countries, which have battled to meet health, economic and social demands (United Nations, 2021). Despite a global success story of poverty reduction, with the number of people surviving under extreme poverty (living on less than $1.90 per day) falling from 1.9 billion in 1993 to 689 million in 2017, the battle to achieve zero poverty continues to be fought (The World Bank, 2020). In fact, since the emergence of COVID-19 in 2019:

- It has been predicted that over 71 million people would be living in intense poverty in 2020.
- Slum dwellers, older people, people with disabilities, migrants and refugees have become even more susceptible to health and socio-economic problems.
- Women and children have borne the brunt of virus-related lockdowns, with a global increase in domestic violence, as well as limited healthcare and food supplies in poorer nations.
- Children and youth are dropping out of the education system as more and more schools and universities close, resulting in a rise in social problems, and increased child labour to combat poverty.

- Poorer nations are increasingly faced with food insecurities, clean water shortages, job losses, inadequate health facilities, and declining social protection.
- World trade is forecast to decrease by 13–32% and foreign direct investment predicted to fall by up to 40%.
- It is imperative that the world use its resources more sustainably through efficient production, consumption, and waste management.
- The chasm of inequality between high-, middle-, and low-income nations continues to widen, as poorer nations struggle to keep their economies afloat (United Nations, 2021).

More than ever, sustainable development is required in order to address global concerns. Nonetheless, one of the biggest issues with sustainability is the constant battle between development and environment (Rowland, 1992). This could explain why the IPCC special report stating the urgency of taking action to reduce climate change generated a negative political response from several countries including the United States (Ogunbode et al., 2020). The high investment and operational costs of SD (Dulebenets, 2016; Zhang & Song, 2020) do not help. Despite several advantages of SD, including enhanced business reputation, stronger competitiveness, and customer loyalty, businesses are also concerned about the costs associated with sustainability reporting (James, 2015).

While carbon tax is an incentive that encourages the adoption of alternative methods that will reduce GHG emissions, poorer households need to be compensated for spending a greater proportion of their income on carbon-intensive goods and services (such as energy), and businesses (particularly energy-manufacturing companies) are driven to zero-carbon tax havens (Ionescu, 2019), leaving significant economic voids. A similar issue is seen with carbon emissions trading systems such as 'cap-and-trade'. With pollution limits capped at an upper limit, a corresponding number of emission permits issued, and excess permits traded to companies unable to conform to required standards, emissions trading is an excellent means of reducing GHG. Nevertheless, this scheme results in a lack of competitiveness between energy production companies, thereby encouraging them to relocate, and resulting in substantial macroeconomic impacts (Kuik & Mulder, 2004).

Industry 4.0 is often perceived by businesses and researchers alike as the holy grail of sustainable development. Based on advanced technologies, Industry 4.0 can boost operational efficiency, while promoting smarter, cleaner, and more sustainable production (Nascimento et al., 2019). One example is the Internet of Things (IoT), which comprises devices such as sensors that record and transfer real-time data, as well as cloud-based software that processes the data and triggers automated actions and/or displays the outcome. Another example of Industry 4.0 technology is blockchain, which stores encrypted records of transactions in the form of blocks, each linked to the previous one. Data in a blockchain cannot be amended or deleted without affecting the entire chain, and, consequently, the blockchain data is immutable, secure, and transparent. IoT, cloud services and blockchain technologies often work together, especially across supply chains, enabling real-time data to be collected, efficiently processed, and securely shared.

Therefore, the adoption of Industry 4.0 can help to reduce carbon emissions through efficient carbon monitoring, resource efficiency that minimizes waste and energy demands, smarter logistics management, and an improved work–life balance, with robots taking care of the more monotonous and physically demanding tasks. Conversely, Industry 4.0 comes with high initial costs, and several social issues, including digital exclusion, widening inequalities in job incomes, upskilling/deskilling, resistance to change, cyber security and data privacy (Sony, 2020). In addition, the environmental impacts of electronic waste cannot be ignored (Tjoa & Tjoa, 2016).

Although sustainable development presents several problems that need to be addressed collaboratively by governments, businesses, and communities, this should not deter the world from fighting against the environmental, economic, and social issues that have negative impacts. Despite its disadvantages, the quest for sustainability must continue.

4.5 Sustainable Development Goals – 17 United Nations Goals

The 1987 Brundtland Report provided a wake-up call for populations around the world, with sustainable development occupying a prominent position among governments, businesses, and academics. In 1992, sustainability raised further international alarm when it featured at the centre of the United Nations Conference on Environment and Development (UNCED), commonly known as the Rio de Janeiro 'Earth Summit'. The conference underlined the pressing need to balance social, economic, and environmental considerations – the triple bottom line. Along with the Rio Declaration on Environment and Development, where a global partnership for sustainable development was sealed, the Conference culminated in Agenda 21 – a series of actions and goals addressing environmental issues and catalysing sustainable development.

Agenda 21 recommendations were revolutionary and ranged from combating poverty to sustainable production and consumption, education, health, sustainable management of ecosystems, sustainable agriculture, waste management, and the welfare of women and children (United Nations, n.d.-b).

Eight years later, after several other conferences and summits, the United Nations Millennium Summit resulted in eight people-centric Millennium Development Goals (MDGs). These ranged from the eradication of poverty and hunger to universal primary education, gender equality and empowerment for women, the reduction of child mortality, improved maternal health, the fight against AIDs and other diseases, environmental sustainability, and a global partnership for development (United Nations Development Programme, 2021).

Managed by the United Nations Development Programme (UNDP), the MDGs had a deadline of 2015, and by the end of this year UNDP reported an unprecedented success in their battle against poverty through the combined efforts of governments, the international community, civil society, and the private sector (UNDP, 2021). Nonetheless, the goal for sustainable development remained to be achieved, and on 25 of September 2015, 150 world leaders pledged their allegiance to the 2030 Agenda for Sustainable Development and the 17 Sustainable Development Goals (SDGs) (see Figure 14.2) (UNDP, 2015).

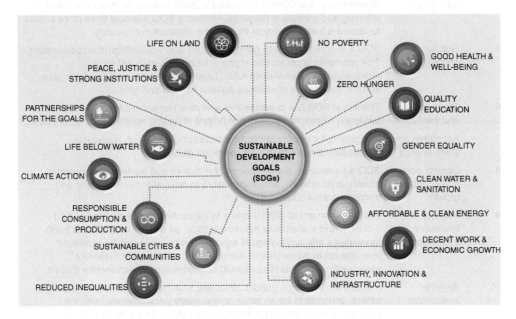

Figure 4.2 The 17 Sustainable Development Goals

As can be seen from Figure 4.2, SDGs build on the MDGs to focus on the eradication/ reduction of the world's most prominent economic, social, and environmental problems, including poverty, hunger, disease, inequality, lack of access to quality education, unsustainable energy production, poor infrastructure, shortage of safe housing, uncontrolled production and consumption, climate change, damage to the oceans and ecosystems, war, and injustice (United Nations, 2015). Table 4.1 provides a brief description of each SDG.

Table 4.1 A Summary of Each Sustainable Development Goal (United Nations, n.d.-a)

SDG#	SDG	Summary
1	No poverty	The goal is to end poverty in all its forms everywhere and ensure that everyone can satisfy their basic needs: health, education, and access to water.
2	Zero hunger	Exacerbated by climate change, global conflicts, economic turbulences, and the COVID-19 pandemic, millions of people suffer from hunger or starvation globally. SDG 2 therefore focuses on solutions to ensure the eradication of this problem.

(Continued)

Table 4.1 (Continued)

SDG#	SDG	Summary
3	Good health and well-being	SDG 3 aims to eliminate existing and emerging diseases and to promote good health through improved hygiene and health services.
4	Quality education	More than 91% of students worldwide were affected as schools temporarily closed due to the COVID-19 spread in 2020, leading to major disruption in learning and education progress. Achieving SDG 4 is now even more critical to ensure a better quality of life and the elimination of poverty.
5	Gender equality	SDG 5 is concerned with gender equality and women's/girls' empowerment. The emphasis is on women's/girls' education, significant female representation in leadership roles, legal reforms favouring gender equity, and the elimination of violence against women and girls.
6	Clean water and sanitation	The aim of SDG 6 is to ensure that everyone has access to clean water and sanitation – basic necessities that billions of people worldwide still do not have.
7	Affordable and clean energy	The goal is for energy to become increasingly efficient, renewable accessible, and affordable for everyone globally.
8	Decent work and economic growth	SDG 8 focuses on the promotion of inclusive and sustainable economic growth, employment, and decent work to raise standards of living and people's overall quality of life.
9	Industry innovation, and infrastructure	The achievement of SDG 9 is key to supporting new technologies and inclusive and sustainable industrialization, as well as international trade. Innovations and technological advancements, promoted by increased investments in research and development, are a critical means of safeguarding communities against economic and environmental threats.
10	Reduced inequalities	Inequalities based on gender, disability, income, and economies among others, continue to be an issue across many parts of world, with the COVID-19 pandemic exacerbating the situation for many. SDG 10 is therefore essential to bridge equality gaps both within and across countries.
11	Sustainable cities and communities	SDG 11 aspires to create safe, inclusive, and sustainable cities for one and all, as opposed to chaotic, congested, and polluted urban areas.
12	Responsible consumption and production	The aim of this goal is to ensure sustainable consumption and production patterns characterized by resource efficiency paired with environmental and social responsibility.
13	Climate action	SDG 13 is intended to combat climate change and its effects, as world temperatures continue to escalate and GHG emission levels remain high.
14	Life below water	Pollution and acidification are destroying our oceans and marine life. The conservation and sustainable harvesting of oceans is essential for their protection and for a healthy planet.
15	Life on land	SDG 15 concerns the protection of forests and biodiversity, as well as the prevention of desertification and land degradation resulting from uncontrolled human activity and climate change.
16	Peace, justice, and strong institutions	SGD 16 promotes access to justice, as well as the elimination of wars, conflicts, and insecurities to build peaceful and inclusive societies.
17	Partnerships for the goals	This goal emphasizes the importance of global collaborations and a shared vision, whereby countries work together to achieve economic, environmental, and social sustainability.

Unfortunately, the battle is far from being won and the 2020 SDG report paints a gloomy picture of the progress achieved so far, in particular with regard to the social and environmental pillars (United Nations, 2021). The COVID-19 pandemic has caused new health, economic, and social challenges in its wake, further curtailing countries' ability to implement sustainability actions (Halkos & Gkampoura, 2021). The need to consolidate the global partnership, as stated in SDG 17, is greater than ever for nations around the world – all of which must join forces if they are to achieve sustainability.

Stop and Reflect: Sustainability

Discuss examples of sustainability practices applied by individuals and businesses that you are aware of and answer the following questions:

- Why is sustainability important?
- List six Sustainable Development Goals and discuss how we can contribute to achieving them, giving examples for each.

4.6 What is Human–Computer Interaction (HCI)?

Before discussing sustainable design, it is necessary to understand two important design-related terms: human–computer interaction (HCI) and usability. Let us discuss them and learn about how they are used in design in general, and in sustainable design in particular.

The term human–computer interaction (HCI) was used to describe this emerging area of research in the mid-1980s. 'This term acknowledged that the focus of interest was broader than just the design of the interface and was concerned with all those aspects that relate to the interaction between users and computers' (Preece et al., 1994, p. 7).

HCI 'is a discipline concerned with the design, evaluation, and implementation of interactive computing systems for human use and with the study of major phenomena surrounding them' (Preece et al., 1994, p. 7). Therefore, in order to produce interactive computer systems that are both practical and usable, it is necessary to consider HCI during the development process (Head, 1999).

The design, implementation, and assessment of interactive systems 'in the context of the user's task and work' are some of the steps in the development process that are covered by the 'human–computer interaction' (Dix et al., 2004, p. 4). Because this development necessitates a wide range of competencies, including an understanding of the user and his/her needs, an appreciation of software engineering capabilities, and the application of appropriate graphical interfaces, the implementation of HCI can be seen as both an art and a science. If we want to be seen as experts, as informed practitioners, and as developers, we must understand what makes an application dynamic, instructional, and productive (Rahm-Skågeby & Rahm, 2021).

Finally, HCI is a crucial aspect of system development (Issa, 2008; Issa & Issasias, 2022). HCI requires users, analysts, and (internal and external) designers to determine whether a website's design, or a portable device is workable. When building Internet pages or developing a portable device, several specific factors must be taken into account, including text style, fonts, layout, images, and colour (see Figure 4.3).

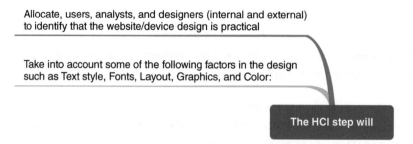

Allocate, users, analysts, and designers (internal and external) to identify that the website/device design is practical

Take into account some of the following factors in the design such as Text style, Fonts, Layout, Graphics, and Color:

The HCI step will

Figure 4.3 HCI Step in the New Participative Methodology for Marketing Websites (NPMMW) (Issa, 2008; Issa & Issaias 2022), prepared by Tomayess Issa

4.7 What is Usability?

Usability is the level of a user's interaction with a product or system in terms of factors including how long it takes to perform tasks, how many mistakes are made, and how long it takes for a user to master the product or system (Benyon et al., 2005). Moreover, usability is related to the ease and simplicity with which an interface can be used. Throughout the design process, several techniques are applied that will improve usability (Nielsen, 2003). A software development team can identify the good and bad features of its prototype releases during the usability evaluation stage and make the necessary adjustments before the system is made available to the intended consumers. Usability evaluation involves observing consumers in order to identify what can be improved or the new products that can be or need to be developed (McGovern, 2003). HCI experts observe and converse with users who are undertaking and testing a genuine task on a site (or system), and this enables them to build a thorough image of the site as it is being navigated by the user. According to Rhodes (2000), this approach is based on human psychology and user research.

Several studies (Gauthier, 2015; Issa & Issaias, 2014; 2022; Sulaksono et al., 2020; Wakefield et al., 2015) indicate that usability is a crucial element of system development, whether it's for software, hardware, or websites. To prevent the user from becoming frustrated or impatient, and to ensure that the system provides an enjoyable experience, usability should comprise functionality, efficiency, effectiveness, satisfaction, special user requirements, particular aims, and the specific context of use. In the business sector, the incorporation of these principles into the design process will strengthen consumer loyalty, reduce expenses, and increase competitiveness.

To summarize: usability is a crucial step in the development of systems (Issa, 2008; Issa & Issaias, 2022). This is because usability enables users, analysts, and designers (internal and external) to confirm that the website design is effective, safe, practical, visible, easy to learn, easy to remember, and easy to use and evaluate (see Figure 4.4).

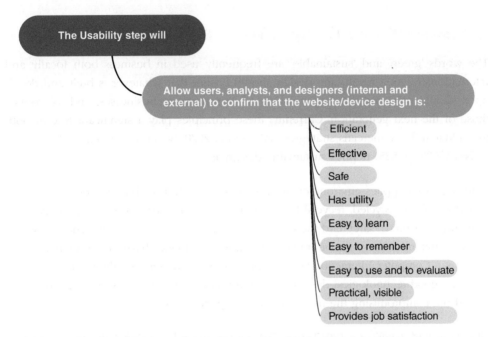

The Usability step will

Allow users, analysts, and designers (internal and external) to confirm that the website/device design is:

Efficient

Effective

Safe

Has utility

Easy to learn

Easy to remenber

Easy to use and to evaluate

Practical, visible

Provides job satisfaction

Figure 4.4 Usability Step in the New Participative Methodology for Marketing Websites (NPMMW) (Issa, 2008; Issa & Issaias, 2022), prepared by Tomayess Issa

Finally, Issa & Issaias (2022) indicate that in light of the environmental issues the world is currently facing, it is crucial for businesses, users, and designers to reorient their techniques and strategies towards sustainable design and sustainability. Furthermore, it is critical that users, businesses, HCI professionals, and designers comprehend how their actions affect the environment, especially when using technology. Therefore, it is imperative that these issues be considered and addressed through innovative and creative sustainable solutions. This can be done by educating users, organizations, HCI experts, designers, and top management about the significance of sustainable design and sustainability methodologies and strategies, which will improve technology performance and efficiency and reduce carbon emissions.

Finally, HCI designers and users of systems and devices should consider the sustainability step, which is part of the design stage from the New Participative Methodology for Sustainable Design (NPMSD) (Issa & Issaias, 2022), as this step addresses the issues of design, manufacturing and energy, recycling, safety efficiency, and social impact. The resources for the next generation will be conserved, and our planet will be protected from harmful pollutants and diseases if the aforementioned issues are taken into account in the design of new smart technology and portable devices. These elements are taken into account during the design stage's sustainability step, which includes goals for usability, HCI, navigation and prototyping.

4.8 Sustainable Design: What and Why?

The words 'green' and 'sustainable' are frequently used in business both locally and internationally. As a result, any design should ensure that whatever is built and developed should first meet the requirements of current users, businesses, and, of course, those of the next generation. Currently, these principles play a significant role in both individual and commercials strategies (Jaffe et al., 2020; Şeker and Aydinli, 2022).

Issa (2023, p. 525) defines sustainable design as:

[design] that applies environmental principles to create portable devices and services from recycled, recyclable, and renewable materials in order to conserve natural resources, safeguard the environment, and ensure energy efficiency. If we are to minimise the negative impacts that human activities have on the planet, Human Computer Interaction (HCI) experts and researchers should continue to create good technological design to meet the needs of businesses and individuals without compromising the needs of the next generation.

Silberman and Tomlinson (2010, p. 3470) discuss the relationship between sustainable design and HCI, confirming that, previously, HCI researchers were concerned with 'what do users do? when? how often? why? how do they feel about it? what do they know about what they are doing? how do they know?' However, in the modern era, HCI researchers should be aware of the interaction between users and technologies and how this might help designers to streamline designs so as to foster greener user habits. Furthermore, DiSalvo et al. (2010) affirm that top management and HCI researchers should be encouraged to work together on the design and development of applications, interfaces, tools, and services with more sustainable outcomes; these designs should also adhere to the principles of economic, social, and ecological sustainability.

In order for practitioners to be aware of the environmental impact of the technologies they use, Smith and Sharicz (2011) contend that HCI and information technology researchers and professionals must address the environmental impact of the design of present and future technologies. Above all, sustainable design must satisfy user needs. Only with the awareness and creativity of designers and users can sustainable design be accomplished. Awareness can create the opportunity to be outstanding in terms of distinctive design, which can inspire creativity and lead to research advances.

The expansion of the global community, social equality, and economic prosperity can all benefit from a greater understanding of the need for change. This awareness will inspire designers to act, study, and be excited about new design prospects, and to develop a greater degree of caring based on their newly acquired knowledge and dedication. Participation in sustainable design is crucial to achieving this goal, and as designers should not act autonomously, they must consider the viewpoints and opinions of potential users and invite them to collaborate in the design.

The world is currently under environmental stress resulting from human activities that endanger sustainability. Approximately 53.9 million tonnes of e-waste were produced globally in 2020, according to Reuters (2020). It is expected that this figure will increase to 74.7 million tonnes by 2030 (Tiseo, 2021), reflecting an increase in growth rate of 4–5%, assuming developers continue to design systems using their current methods without taking sustainability into account. Figure 4.5 shows the amount of electronic garbage produced by the five continents; Asia produced 24.9 MT in 2019 whereas Oceania produced only 0.7 MT (Forti et al., 2020).

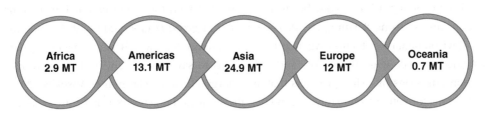

Figure 4.5 E-Waste Generation per Continent in 2019 (adopted by Forti et al. (2020), prepared by the authors) (MT = million tonnes)

According to the data shown in Figure 4.5, unsustainable human activity is having a significant effect on the environment, mandating a plan of action to alter how we live. Therefore, designing products and electronic devices that adhere to the concepts of social, economic, and ecological sustainability should be a priority for designers, users, and organizations) (Rahm-Skågeby & Rahm, 2021; Soden et al., 2021).

Definition: Sustainable Design

Sustainable design 'applies environmental principles to create portable devices and services from recycled, recyclable, and renewable materials in order to conserve natural resources, safeguard the environment, and ensure energy efficiency. If we are to minimise the negative impacts that human activities have on the planet, Human Computer Interaction (HCI) experts and researchers should continue to create good technological design to meet the needs of businesses and individuals without compromising the needs of the next generation' (Issa, 2023, p. 525).

> **Stop and Reflect: Sustainable Design, HCI, and Usability**
>
> - What is meant by 'sustainable design'?
> - Why is sustainable design important?
> - What is HCI?
> - What is usability?
> - Why are HCI and usability important for sustainable design?

4.9 What is the Meaning of 'Green' and 'Green Information Technology' (Green IT)?

Green is a term that emerged in the marketing domain in the late 1980s to early 1990s, quickly becoming a buzz word because it coincided with the environmental awakening of consumers (Tseng & Hung, 2013). The concept of *green IT* emerged in 1992, when the US Environmental Protection Agency launched Energy Star which is a labelling system intended to encourage businesses and individuals to save energy and water and reduce carbon emissions by using products that are energy efficient (Harmon & Auseklis, 2009).

Green information technology (green IT) is the study and practice of using computers and IT resources in a more efficient and environmentally responsible way, made possible by the design, use, and disposal of technology products. Computers and computing consume massive amounts of natural resources, from the raw materials needed to manufacture them, the power used to run them, and the problems of disposing of them at the end of their life (McCabe, 2010). Green IT is used by businesses and individuals to minimize the negative environmental impacts resulting from the use of technologies, in order to achieve environmental sustainability and to increase green awareness locally and globally (Ali et al., 2022).

Green IT should not be viewed simply as a means of cutting costs, although green IT reduces electricity consumption by about 90 percent, and reduces cooling costs by about 87 percent, which are the most important reasons that businesses locally and globally use green IT for production and manufacturing (Bernstein, 2009).

In order to give both specific and general definitions of green IT, Dastbaz et al. (2015) divided green IT into two categories. These categories are known as 'Greening for IT' and 'Greening by IT'. 'Greening for IT' is frequently used in the IT industry to refer to energy conservation, the minimizing of the negative environmental effects, and achieving energy efficiency throughout the whole life cycle of an IT service or product, from the design stage through to production, use, and disposal. On the other hand, 'Greening by IT' is mainly concerned with eco-friendly activities and is used to mitigate the environmental impact of various industries, including power, transportation, manufacturing, agriculture, construction, and the consumer and service sectors (Pichlak & Szromek, 2021; Yoon, 2018).

Definition: Green IT

Green information technology (IT) is the study and practice of using computers and IT resources in a more efficient and environmentally responsible way, beginning with the design, and including the use and disposal of technology products. Computers and computing consume enormous amounts of natural resources, ranging from the raw materials needed to manufacture them, the power used to run them, and their disposal at the end of their life cycle (McCabe, 2010).

Currently, organizations have started to use green IT to tackle the challenges of climate change by: (1) providing opportunities to think differently and find new ways by which to create the capacity for innovation; (2) creating low-cost platforms for growth and to minimize compliance costs and risks; and (3) involving the entire eco-system of an organization and offering both technology and business innovations that reduce carbon emissions by working more intelligently (Smith, 2014; Thabit et al., 2021).

Here is a list of green information technologies:

- **The Internet of Things (IoT)** is the network that connects many individually identifiable 'objects' that have sensing and acting capacities. Hence, 'things' can have their status remotely adjusted so as to gather information at any time and from any location. Put simply, IoT is a system of coordinated computing devices, automated and digital equipment, objects, animals, or people with the capacity to transfer data over a network without the need for human-to-human or human-to-computer contact (Mouha, 2021).
- **Augmented Reality (AR)** technology enables any data from the real environment to be presented virtually (Chen et al., 2019). AR can significantly reduce the production-related waste of materials and energy consumption (Chen et al. 2019). AR is used in apps for smartphones and tablets. Apps can use AR for recreational purposes, an example of which is the game Pokémon GO (Chen et al., 2019).
- **Virtual Reality (VR)** users can experience a virtual environment that is identical to or completely different from the real world by means of specialized software or electronic equipment. The distinction between VR and AR is that whereas AR combines virtual things exhibited in the real world, VR displays an entirely virtual space. You can view virtual reality through a special VR viewer, such as the Oculus Rift. Other virtual reality viewers use their phone and VR apps such as Google Cardboard or Daydream View (Chandrasiri et al., 2020; Xiong et al., 2021).
- **Artificial Intelligence (AI)** is a branch of computer science that focuses on building intelligent machines which function and behave like people. AI refers to machines that have been created and programmed to function similarly to humans.

Speech recognition, lesson planning, and problem solving are some of the tasks that are performed by AI-powered computers (Zhang and Lu, 2021).

- **Big data** is a field that explores methods for analysing datasets that are too huge or complicated to be handled by conventional data-processing application software, extracting information from them logically and methodically, or handling them in other ways (Naeem et al., 2022).
- **Blockchain** is a peer-to-peer technology which records information shared between parties in a legitimate/real and immutable/complete way. Once a record has been added to the blockchain network, it is protected using encryption methods, which secures the data because no one, not even the block's owner, is able to alter the data that has been put there. People now trust blockchain because of its secure encryption method (Verma & Garg, 2017).

To minimize the amount of hardware, monitors, and unwanted computers that end up in landfill, individual users and businesses should reuse, refurbish, and recycle. If devices are still suitable for work tasks, they should be used for at least 3–5 years, or they can be moved to other departments in the organizations or given to others who can use them for work tasks. This will reduce the total environmental footprint caused by computer manufacturing and disposal. Furthermore, users and businesses can refurbish and upgrade old computers, servers, and devices to meet their needs by adding and replacing some parts rather than buying new computers. The adoption of this approach will reduce raw material consumption and conserve it for the seventh generation in the future. Finally, the recycling of computers and other devices should be on the agendas of businesses and users, so they can be recycled appropriately without causing further damage to the planet. By following these three techniques, users and businesses will be part of the solution, moving forward to become more sustainable in their actions, acting as good stewards, and conserving resources for future generations (Issa et al., 2017; 2020; Murugesan, 2008; Murugesan & Gangadharan, 2012; Newton, 2000; 2003).

Lastly, everyone can cooperate to reduce energy consumption and carbon emissions by using thin-client PCs, using a blank screensaver, turning the system off when not in use, and activating power management tools (Issa & Issa, 2019; Molla & Cooper, 2010; Smith, 2014).

Stop and Reflect: Green Information Technology

- Why is green IT important for users and businesses now?
- List and discuss three types of green IT.
- How can users and businesses minimise technology use and reduce its impact on the natural environment.

4.10 Data-Driven Sustainability

The world is far from being close to achieving its SDGs by 2030, especially with the COVID-19 pandemic considerably slowing down progress. To get back on track in achieving their sustainability targets, the gathering of timely and reliable data is crucial if nations are to accurately evaluate economic, social, and environmental impacts before shaping effective strategies. However, there are significant gaps in the available data and several countries struggle to gather and organize data and derive useful information from it. Digital innovations in data gathering and analysis are urgently sought to speed up SDG actions (United Nations, 2021), and support data-driven governance for both governments and businesses to monitor progress and achieve their sustainable development goals (ElMassah & Mohieldin, 2020).

In addition, in order to sustain a circular economy (CE) where resources are recycled and waste is minimized, data-driven manufacturing backed by Industry 4.0 technology is critical for high volumes of data (such as energy data) to be mined prior to implementing environmentally, socially, and economically responsible operations (Ma et al., 2020). Big-data-driven technologies are key to smart manufacturing and sustainable supply chain operations (Tsai et al., 2021). For example, data-driven, digital agricultural supply chains are at the centre of sustainable food production and consumption. The Internet of Things enables data to be collected and shared in real time, thereby improving communication and cooperation among various supply chain members such as farmers, customers, logistics and distribution networks, and retailers.

Thus, the demand–supply gap is bridged as customer needs are better satisfied, products better tracked, and inventories more efficiently managed, while the large amount of data collected can be mined to identify and address any weaknesses in the system. Blockchain, cloud services and other emerging technologies also help improve the visibility of information across all nodes of the supply chain to support timely decision-making and strategies for waste minimization, improved food quality, and better security (Kamble et al., 2020).

Similarly, smart cities rely on the IoT, with real-time data capturing sensors and big data analytics helping to foster sustainable behaviours and lifestyles. On a social level, public safety is improved as the IoT can reduce response times during emergencies. Also, the IoT enables residents to feel more connected to the community and improves the health of community members by reducing the burden of disease. Environmentally, GHG emissions, energy consumption, waste recycling, and water usage can be better controlled via the IoT. At an economic level, cost savings through efficient resource usage and the creation of jobs bring additional benefits (Hodgkins, 2020).

4.11 Chapter Summary

This chapter discussed three concepts: sustainability, sustainable design, and green information technology, which are increasingly relevant for individuals and businesses locally and globally. These concepts should be considered and addressed by users, designers,

HCI experts, and businesses in their strategies, especially in developing or maintaining new smart technology and portable devices to minimize carbon emissions and global warming, reduce energy, and save raw materials for the next generation. Finally, we need to solve this problem before it is too late to preserve the globe since there is 'No Plan B for the Earth'. Our planet is suffering as a result of our activities (Issa & Issaias, 2022).

Discussion Questions

1   What is sustainable design?
2   What are HCI and usability?
3   List three types of green IT.
4   List five Sustainable Development Goals (SDGs).

Case Study: Small Island Developing States and the Mauritian Commitment to Sustainable Development

Small Island Developing States (SIDS) comprise 52 small, remote islands listed by the United Nations. Despite differing demographics, locations, political situations and economies, SIDS are characterized by limited natural resources and are particularly vulnerable to the impacts of climate change and global economic fluctuations. Constrained by their size, small populations, and geographical remoteness, SIDS struggle to sustain their economic growth and to remain resilient in the wake of global turbulences and natural disasters. As ocean temperatures and sea levels continue to rise at an alarming rate, the social and economic development of SIDS are threatened by coastal erosion, land loss, soil salinization, and damage to their ecosystems. These issues have a direct impact on tourism, which is one of the main pillars of their economy. The COVID-19 pandemic exacerbated the situation by forcing many countries to close their borders and impose international flight restrictions, thereby critically impacting the SIDS' tourism economy and dragging many inhabitants down into a spiral of poverty. More than ever, SIDS rely on sustainable development to contain the effects of global warming, foster social stability, and boost their economy.

Mauritius is one such small island. Located in the Indian Ocean, Mauritius covers a mere 2,040 km² of land with a population of 1.3 million. Its prominent tourism industry thrives on its unparalleled natural beauty and magnificent beaches. With hardly any other natural resources to rely on, the island is largely dependent on its human capital and has a strong focus on information technology both as a prime economic pillar as well as a productivity and sustainable development enabler. Currently, the information communications technology (ICT) sector is viewed as the third most important economic pillar of the island and includes both a Digital Mauritius and an Artificial Intelligence Strategy to support the country's vision of transforming itself into a knowledge economy. Although conversations about a green IT policy for Mauritius to capitalize on the use of technology for sustainable behaviours and production remain at a standstill, the Mauritian National Computer Board continues to promote green IT business and household practices through guidelines, tips, sustainable frameworks, and standards, including those advocated by the European Union (e.g., the EU Code of Conduct for Data Centres) and the International Telecommunication Union (ITU) Toolkit for Sustainable ICT.

Mauritius is aware if its constraints as a SIDS and its vulnerability to the dangers of climate change. The island has committed to a 30% reduction in greenhouse gas (GHG) emissions by 2030, as reinforced by its participation in the 2015 Paris Climate Conference. Despite a 2.9% rise in GHG emissions in 2019, attributed largely to the energy sector, the government remains determined to progress in a sustainable direction, as reflected in its 2020–2024 programme entitled 'Towards an Inclusive, High Income and Green Mauritius, Forging Ahead Together'. The programme is based on inclusivity, education, improved social well-being, the economy of the future, innovative public infrastructure, safety, strong governance, and a sustainable, green society. The vision for the country's future is clear and rests on a peaceful society where equality, human rights, sustainable development, technology, and innovation constitute the strong foundations of a high-income economy.

Even though the COVID-19 pandemic presented numerous social and economic challenges, the achievement of Sustainable Development Goals (SDGs) remains high on the Mauritian agenda and Mauritius continues to be a role model for many other SIDS.

References

Government Programme 2020–2024: *Towards an Inclusive, High Income and Green Mauritius, Forging Ahead Together*. Address by The President of the Republic of Mauritius. (2020). https://gis.govmu.org/Documents/Govt Programme 2020-2024.pdf

Statistics Mauritius. (2019). *Environment Statistics*. https://statsmauritius.govmu.org/Documents/Statistics/ESI/2020/EI1535/Env_Stats_Yr19.pdf

UNDP. (2020). *A Climate Promise: Mauritius' Response To Climate Change*. https://www.mu.undp.org/content/mauritius_and_seychelles/en/home/news-centre/news/a-climate-promise---mauritius-response-to-climate-change-.html

Questions

1   Why is sustainable development a priority for Small Island Developing States?
2   What is Mauritius doing right to meet SDGs?
3   What are the challenges faced by Mauritius along its sustainable development path?

Case Study: Decarbonizing Future Mining Operations

By Mrs Megha Bali, Specialist Risk and Capital, Rio Tinto, Perth, Australia

Over the course of time, technology has changed the way mining is done, although the fundamentals stay the same. The impact of sustainable methods of digging ore from the ground and practices for removing the minerals and metals is vital to carbon-free mining. Overall, carbon emissions are continuing to rise due to human activities. The mining industry adds tremendous value not only to their shareholders or their own country but also to global GDP.

Understanding the importance of decarbonization in future mining practices, each mining firm pledged to reduce the carbon emissions in its entire process chain and increase the utilization of renewable energy, which contributes to the global reduction targets of up to 30% by 2030 and net zero emissions by 2050 as a part of the 2015 Paris Agreement.

Some mining organizations are focusing mainly on two key areas: attracting new talent with that capability and driving decarbonization strategies in order to preserve their licence to operate. Investors, governments, and societies are applying intense pressure to reduce emissions and promote green mining technology, and all must align with the industry standards.

To accelerate progress towards lowering carbon emissions, the government is reducing technology costs dramatically, instituting carbon pricing schemes, and allocating significant capital funds to the carbon initiative. Carbon emission policies require constant review and tightening of standards, which will help achieve net zero carbon emissions by 2050.

In addition to this, bolder investment decisions require being fully embedded in a mining firm's climate plan. Proactive action on sustainable mining and green technology equipment in mining firms is growing in accordance with the Paris Agreement and as a way to protect the environment and the firms' long-term reputation.

The transition from rapid increases in technology in the hypothetical mining sector to greener technology in mining is purely based on reshaping the operational process (mine to market) and, of course, substantial efforts to reduce the intensity of carbon emissions. To meet all the external requirements to decarbonize the intensity of emissions, including those of the government, customers, and investors, is challenging due to heavy reliance on diesel fuel and very low accessibility to grid electricity.

To gain the trust and confidence of investors and governments for sustainable funding towards environmental, social, and governance (ESG) factors, it is necessary to understand the urgency of mine decarbonization and technology. It's time to put the ideas down on paper and start working on quick wins, which include shorter-term initiatives like on-site renewable energy or transport optimization. To meet the massive challenge of reducing carbon emissions in the mining process to zero, a transitional initiative such as replacing diesel vehicles with electric vehicles is required.

Mining companies are focusing on setting some baselines aligned with the Paris Agreement standards and country requirements, evaluating the progress rigorously, and sharing transparent decarbonization reporting. To succeed in the reduction of GHG emissions, every individual, firm, or industry needs to play the role of decarbonization champion and work on building decarbonization momentum to implement the necessary steps to achieve significant growth and mitigate the negative effects on the environment.

Questions

1   How can automation mitigate the impacts of a mining operation on climate?
2   How can mining industries maintain their level of production during electrification and the transition to decarbonization?

4.12 References

Ali, S., Green, P., Robb, A., & Masli, A. (2022). Governing information technology (IT) investment: A contingency perspective on organization's IT investment goals. *Australian Journal of Management*, *47*(1), 3–23.

Anand, S., & Sen, A. (2000). Human development and economic sustainability. *World Development*, *28*(12), 2029–2049. https://doi.org/10.4324/9781315241951-37

Benyon, D., Turner, P., & Turner, S. (2005). *Designing Interactive Systems: A Comprehensive Guide to HCI and Interaction Design* (2nd edition). Pearson Education Limited.

Bernstein, C. (2009). Green IT gains priority status. *Baseline 98*, 15–15.

Brundtland Commission. (1987). *Report of the World Commission on Environment and Development: Our Common Future*.

Chandrasiri, A., Collett, J., Fassbender, E., & De Foe, A. (2020). A virtual reality approach to mindfulness skills training. *Virtual Reality*, *24*(1), 143–149.

Chen, Y., Wang, Q., Chen, H., Song, X., Tang, H., & Tian, M. (2019). *An Overview of Augmented Reality Technology*. Paper presented at the Journal of Physics Conference Series.

Dastbaz, M., Pattinson, C., & Akhgar, B. (2015). *Green Information Technology: A Sustainable Approach*. Morgan Kaufmann.

Dempsey, N., Bramley, G., Power, S., & Brown, C. (2011). The social dimension of sustainable development: Defining urban social sustainability. *Sustainable Development*, *19*(5), 289–300. https://doi.org/10.1002/sd.417

Diesendorf, M. (2000). Sustainability and sustainable development. In D. Dunphy, J. Benviste, A. Griffiths, & P. Sutton (eds), *Sustainability: The Corporate Challenge of the 21st Century* (pp. 19–37). Allen & Unwin. https://doi.org/10.4324/9781315442044-11

DiSalvo, C., Sengers, P., & Hronn Brynjarsdottir, P. (2010). *Mapping the Landscape of Sustainable HCI*. Paper presented at the CHI 2010, Atlanta, GA, USA.

Dix, A., Finlay, J., Abowd, G., & Beale, R. (2004) *Human-Computer Interaction* (3rd edition). England Pearson Education Limited.

Dulebenets, M. A. (2016). Advantages and disadvantages from enforcing emission restrictions within emission control areas. *Maritime Business Review*, *1*(2), 107–132. https://doi.org/10.1108/mabr-05-2016-0011

Eizenberg, E., & Jabareen, Y. (2017). Social sustainability: A new conceptual framework. *Sustainability (Switzerland), 9*(1). https://doi.org/10.3390/su9010068

ElMassah, S., & Mohieldin, M. (2020). Digital transformation and localizing the Sustainable Development Goals (SDGs). *Ecological Economics, 169*(March 2020), 106490. https://doi.org/10.1016/j.ecolecon.2019.106490

Forti, V., Baldé, C. P, Kuehr, R., & Bel, G. (2020). The Global E-waste Monitor 2020: quantities, flows, and the circular economy potential. https://collections.unu.edu/view/UNU:7737#viewAttachments

Gauthier, G. (2015). A usability evaluation of a website focusing on the three initial steps of the conflict/resolution process for union members. http://scholarspace.manoa.hawaii.edu/bitstream/handle/10125/35855/Gauthier_Final_Paper_Scholarspace.pdf?sequence=1

Goddard, E. (2021). A68 iceberg that was once world's largest melts away. https://www.independent.co.uk/climate-change/news/a68-iceberg-melt-climate-crisis-b1833310.html

Goodland, R. (1995). The concept of environmental sustainability. *Annual Review of Ecology and Systematics.* https://doi.org/10.1146/annurev.es.26.110195.000245

Halkos, G., & Gkampoura, E. C. (2021). Where do we stand on the 17 Sustainable Development Goals? An overview on progress. *Economic Analysis and Policy, 70,* 94–122. https://doi.org/10.1016/j.eap.2021.02.001

Hardin, G. (1968). The tragedy of the commons: The population problem has no technical solution; it requires a fundamental extension in morality. *Science, 162*(3859), 1243–1248.

Harmon, R. R., & Auseklis, N. (2009). *Sustainable IT Services: Assessing the Impact of Green Computing Practices.* Paper presented at the PICMET'09-2009 Portland International Conference on Management of Engineering & Technology.

Hawkshaw, R. S., Hawkshaw, S., & Sumaila, U. R. (2012). The tragedy of the 'tragedy of the commons': Why coining too good a phrase can be dangerous. *Sustainability, 4*(11), 3141–3150. https://doi.org/10.3390/su4113141

Head, A. J. (1999) *Design Wise.* Thomas H Hogan Sr, Medford.

Hodgkins, S. (2020). Big data-driven decision-making processes for environmentally sustainable urban development: The design, planning, and operation of smart city infrastructure. *Geopolitics, History, and International Relations, 12*(1), 87–93. https://doi.org/10.22381/GHIR12120208

Ionescu, L. (2019). Climate policies, carbon pricing, and pollution tax: Do carbon taxes really lead to a reduction in emissions? *Geopolitics, History, and International Relations, 11*(1), 92–97. https://doi.org/10.22381/GHIR11120194

Intergovernmental Panel on Climate Change (IPCC). (2018). *Global Warming of 1.5°C. An IPCC Special Report on the Impacts of Global Warming of 1.5°C above Pre-industrial Levels and Related Global Greenhouse Gas Emission Pathways, in the Context of Strengthening the Global Response to the Threat of Climate Change, Sustainable Development, and Efforts to Eradicate Poverty* [Masson-Delmotte, V., P. Zhai, H.-O. Pörtner, D. Roberts, J. Skea, P.R. Shukla, A. Pirani, W. Moufouma-Okia, C. Péan, R. Pidcock, S. Connors, J.B.R. Matthews, Y. Chen, X. Zhou, M.I. Gomis, E. Lonnoy, T. Maycock, M. Tignor, and T. Waterfield (eds.)].

Issa, T. (2008). *Development and Evaluation of a Methodology for Developing Websites*. PhD thesis, Curtin University, Western Australia. Retrieved from https://espace.curtin.edu.au/handle/20.500.11937/2013

Issa, T. (Ed.) (2023) Sustainable design. In Haddad, B. M., & Solomon, B. D. (Eds.). (2023). *Dictionary of Ecological Economics: Terms for the New Millennium*. Edward Elgar Publishing

Issa, T., & Isaias, P. (2014). HCI and usability principles and guidelines in the website development process: An international perspective. In H. K. C. Ewelina Lacka & Y. Nick (eds), *E-commerce Platform Acceptance: Suppliers, Retailers, and Consumers* (pp. 169–189). Springer.

Issa, T., & Isaias, P. (2022). *Sustainable Design: HCI, Usability and Environmental Concerns*. Springer-Verlag London.

Issa, T., Isaias, P., & Issa, T. (2017). *Sustainability, Green IT and Education Strategies in the Twenty-first Century*. Springer.

Issa, T., & Issa, T. (2019). CSR, sustainability and green IT in higher education: An Australian perspective. In N. Capaldi et al. (eds), *Responsible Business in Uncertain Times and for a Sustainable Future. CSR, Sustainability, Ethics & Governance* (pp. 89–106). Springer.

Issa, T., Issa, T., & Issa, T. (2020). Awareness, opportunities and challenges of green IT: An Australian perspective. In T. Issa, T. Issa, T. Issa, & P. Isaias (eds), *Sustainability Awareness and Green Information Technologies* (pp. 443–462). Springer.

Jaffe, S. B., Fleming, R., Karlen, M., & Roberts, S. H. (2020). *Sustainable Design Basics*: John Wiley & Sons.

James, M. L. (2015). Accounting majors' perceptions of the advantages and disadvantages of sustainability and integrated reporting. *Journal of Legal, Ethical and Regulatory Issues, 18*(2), 107–123.

Kamble, S. S., Gunasekaran, A., & Gawankar, S. A. (2020). Achieving sustainable performance in a data-driven agriculture supply chain: A review for research and applications. *International Journal of Production Economics, 219*(January), 179–194. https://doi.org/10.1016/j.ijpe.2019.05.022

Kuik, O., & Mulder, M. (2004). Emissions trading and competitiveness: Pros and cons of relative and absolute schemes. *Energy Policy, 32*(6), 737–745. https://doi.org/10.1016/S0301-4215(02)00334-8

Lindsey, R., & Dahlman, L. (2021). Climate change: Global temperature. https://www.climate.gov/news-features/understanding-climate/climate-change-global-temperature

Ma, S., Zhang, Y., Liu, Y., Yang, H., Lv, J., & Ren, S. (2020). Data-driven sustainable intelligent manufacturing based on demand response for energy-intensive industries. *Journal of Cleaner Production, 274*, 123155. https://doi.org/10.1016/j.jclepro.2020.123155

McCabe, L. (2010). What is green it, and why should you care? https://www.smallbusinesscomputing.com/guides/what-is-green-it-and-why-should-you-care/

McGovern, G. (2003). Usability is good management. http://www.gerrymcgovern.com/nt/2003/nt_2003_04_07_usability.htm

Mensah, J. (2019). Sustainable development: Meaning, history, principles, pillars, and implications for human action: Literature review. *Cogent Social Sciences, 5*(1). https://doi.org/10.1080/23311886.2019.1653531

Molla, A., & Cooper, V. (2010). Green IT readiness: A framework and preliminary proof of concept. *Australasian Journal of Information Systems, 16*(2).

Morelli, J. (2011). Environmental sustainability: A definition for environmental professionals. *Journal of Environmental Sustainability, 1*(1), 1–10. https://doi.org/10.14448/jes.01.0002

Mouha, R. A. (2021). Internet of Things (IoT). *Journal of Data Analysis and Information Processing, 9*(2), 77–101.

Mozlin, R. (2007). Beyond Silent Spring. *Journal of Behavioral Optometry, 18*(4), 87, 93. http://dx.doi.org/10.1016/j.jaci.2012.05.050

Murugesan, S. (2008). Harnessing green IT: Principles and practices. *IT Professional, 10*(1), 24–33.

Murugesan, S., & Gangadharan, G. R. (2012). Green IT: An overview. *Harnessing Green IT: Principles and Practices*, 1–21.

Naeem, M., Jamal, T., Diaz-Martinez, J., Butt, S. A., Montesano, N., Tariq, M. I., … De-La-Hoz-Valdiris, E. (2022). Trends and future perspective challenges in big data *Advances in intelligent data analysis and applications* (pp. 309–325). Springer.

Nascimento, D. L. M., Alencastro, V., Quelhas, O. L. G., Caiado, R. G. G., Garza-Reyes, J. A., Lona, L. R., & Tortorella, G. (2019). Exploring Industry 4.0 technologies to enable circular economy practices in a manufacturing context: A business model proposal. *Journal of Manufacturing Technology Management, 30*(3), 607–627. https://doi.org/10.1108/JMTM-03-2018-0071

Newton, L. H. (2000). Millennial reservations. *Business Ethics Quarterly, 10*(1), 291–303.

Newton, L. H. (2003). *Ethics and Sustainability, Sustainable Development and the Moral Life*. Pearson Education.

Nielsen, J. (2003). Usability 101. http://www.useit.com/alertbox/20030825.html

NOAA. (2019). Climate change impacts. https://www.noaa.gov/education/resource-collections/climate/climate-change-impacts

Ogunbode, C. A., Doran, R., & Böhm, G. (2020). Exposure to the IPCC special report on 1.5 °C global warming is linked to perceived threat and increased concern about climate change. *Climatic Change, 158*(3–4), 361–375. https://doi.org/10.1007/s10584-019-02609-0

Pichlak, M., & Szromek, A. R. (2021). Eco-innovation, sustainability and business model innovation by open innovation dynamics. *Journal of Open Innovation: Technology, Market, and Complexity, 7*(2), 149.

Preece, J., Rogers, Y., Benyon, D., Holland, S., & Carey, T. (1994) *Human Computer Interaction*. England: Addison-Wesley.

Rahm-Skågeby, J., & Rahm, L. (2021). HCI and deep time: Toward deep time design thinking. *Human–Computer Interaction*, 1–14.

Reuters, T. (2020). Record 53.6 million tonnes of e-waste dumped globally last year, says UN report. https://www.cbc.ca/news/science/global-ewaste-monitor-2020-1.5634759

Rhodes, J. S. (2000). Usability can save your company. http://webword.com/moving/savecompany.html

Rowland, F. S. (1992). Failure at the Earth Summit. *Science, 256*(5060), 1109. https://doi.org/10.1126/science.256.5060.1109

Şeker, F., & Aydinli, B. (2023). A trial patch to sustainable development. *Science & Education, 32*(2), 421-446. doi:10.1007/s11191-021-00315-x

Silberman, M. S., & Tomlinson, B. (2010). *Toward an Ecological Sensibility: Tools for Evaluating Sustainable HCI*. Paper presented at the CHI 2010, Atlanta, GA, USA.

Smith, J. (2014). Green IT *Journal of Green IT, 16*(3), 1–10.

Smith, P., & Sharicz, C. (2011). The shift needed for sustainability. *The Learning Organization, 18*(1), 73–86.

Soden, R., Pathak, P., & Doggett, O. (2021). *What We Speculate About When We Speculate About Sustainable HCI*. Paper presented at the ACM SIGCAS Conference on Computing and Sustainable Societies (COMPASS).

Sony, M. (2020). Pros and cons of implementing Industry 4.0 for the organizations: A review and synthesis of evidence. *Production and Manufacturing Research, 8*(1), 244–272. https://doi.org/10.1080/21693277.2020.1781705

Steg, L. (2018). Limiting climate change requires research on climate action. *Nature Climate Change, 8*(9), 759–761. https://doi.org/10.1038/s41558-018-0269-8

Sulaksono, A., Astuti, E. S., & Almusadieq, M. (2020). *Strengthening Website Usability in the Pandemic Era*. Paper presented at the 2nd Annual International Conference on Business and Public Administration (AICoBPA 2019).

Thabit, T., Aissa, S. A. H., & Jasim, Y. (2021). The impact of green ICT adoption in organizations of developing countries. *Al-riyada for Business Economics Journal, 7*.

The World Bank. (2020). Atlas of Sustainable Development Goals from world development indicators. https://datatopics.worldbank.org/sdgatlas/

Tiseo, I. (2021). Outlook on global e-waste generation 2019-2030. https://www.statista.com/statistics/1067081/generation-electronic-waste-globally-forecast/

Tjoa, A. M., & Tjoa, S. (2016). The role of ICT to achieve the UN Sustainable Development Goals (SDG). In F. J. Mata & A. Pont (eds), *ICT for Promoting Human Development and Protecting the Environment* (Vol. *481*). Springer Nature.

Tsai, F. M., Bui, T. D., Tseng, M. L., Ali, M. H., Lim, M. K., & Chiu, A. S. (2021). Sustainable supply chain management trends in world regions: A data-driven analysis. *Resources, Conservation and Recycling, 167*(June 2020), 105421. https://doi.org/10.1016/j.resconrec.2021.105421

Tseng, S.-C., & Hung, S.-W. (2013). A framework identifying the gaps between customers' expectations and their perceptions in green products. *Journal of Cleaner Production, 59*, 174–184.

United Nations. (n.d.-a). *Sustainable Development Goals*. https://www.un.org/sustainabledevelopment/

United Nations. (n.d.-b). United Nations Conference on Environment and Development, Rio de Janeiro, Brazil, 3–14 June 1992. https://www.un.org/en/conferences/environment/rio1992

United Nations. (2015). *Transforming Our World: The 2030 Agenda for Sustainable Development*. https://sdgs.un.org/2030agenda

United Nations. (2021). *The Sustainable Development Goals Report 2020*. https://doi.org/10.4324/9781003099680-3

United Nations Development Programme. (UNDP). (2015). World leaders adopt Sustainable Development Goals. https://www.undp.org/content/undp/en/home/

presscenter/pressreleases/2015/09/24/undp-welcomes-adoption-of-sustainable-development-goals-by-world-leaders.html

United Nations Development Programme. (UNDP). (2021). Millennium Development Goals. https://www.undp.org/content/undp/en/home/sdgoverview/mdg_goals.html

United Nations Framework Convention on Climate Change (UNFCCC). (2008). *Kyoto Protocol Reference Manual.* https://unfccc.int/sites/default/files/08_unfccc_kp_ref_manual.pdf

Verma, A. K., & Garg, A. (2017). Blockchain: An analysis on next-generation internet. *International Journal of Advanced Research in Computer Science, 8*(8), 429–432.

Wakefield, B., Pham, K., & Scherubel, M. (2015). Usability evaluation of a web-based symptom monitoring application for heart failure. *Western Journal of Nursing Research, 37*(7), 922–934.

Xiong, J., Hsiang, E.-L., He, Z., Zhan, T., & Wu, S.-T. (2021). Augmented reality and virtual reality displays: Emerging technologies and future perspectives. *Light: Science & Applications, 10*(1), 1–30.

Yoon, C. (2018). Extending the TAM for green IT: A normative perspective. *Computers in Human Behavior, 83,* 129–139.

Zhang, C., & Lu, Y. (2021). Study on artificial intelligence: The state of the art and future prospects. *Journal of Industrial Information Integration, 23,* 100224.

Zhang, H., & Song, M. (2020). Do first-movers in marketing sustainable products enjoy sustainable advantages? A seven-country comparative study. *Sustainability (Switzerland), 12*(2), 1–15. https://doi.org/10.3390/su12020450

PART II

ADVANCES IN DIGITAL INFORMATION TECHNOLOGY

5

COMPUTER NETWORKS AND INFORMATION SECURITY

5.1 Learning Outcomes

After reading this chapter, you will be able to:

- Define a computer and describe the components of computer networks
- Describe the different types of networks
- Describe the different types of communication media and channels
- Explain how computer networks and the Internet support communication and collaboration in business
- List and describe the security controls used to protect information resources
- Describe the organizational strategies for protecting information resources

5.2 Introduction

The evolution of computer networks and Internet technologies has revolutionized the way businesses operate and collaborate. The emergence of network technologies such as cloud computing and mobile communication has transformed business processes and supply chain activities. Today, Internet connectivity is essential to any business organization and drives businesses' communication and collaboration with suppliers, customers, and employees. In the first part of this chapter, we will look at the various computer networks, communication media and channels, network types, and network collaboration applications that facilitate communications and collaboration within organizations. The second part of this chapter will discuss the threats to information and technology and the measures and controls that can be implemented to protect information resources in business organizations. In the final part of this chapter, we will discuss information security threats and how to control them.

5.3 Computer Networks

What is a Computer Network?

Networking technology enables the discovery and exchange of information, communication, and collaboration between various entities within an organization. Computer networks enable networking technology. A computer network is a cluster of computing devices connected through wired or wireless communication media, such as laptops, desktops, servers, smartphones, and tablets. The primary objective of this interconnectivity is to facilitate seamless data and resource sharing among the devices. Moreover, the rapid expansion of the Internet of Things (IoT) has resulted in the inclusion of an array of smart devices, including cameras, home security systems, appliances, traffic control systems, and sensors, into the network, thereby establishing a highly connected network system (Cisco, n.d.-b). The IoT will be discussed in Chapter 11.

In a business organization, computer networks play an essential role in supporting business functions' communication, collaboration, and resource-sharing capabilities. Computer networks enable communication within and between organizations. Email, instant messaging, video conferencing, and other collaboration tools help employees communicate with each other in real time, regardless of their location. This improves communication, increases productivity, and helps employees stay connected and informed. Computer networks also facilitate collaboration by allowing employees to share information and resources efficiently. Documents, files, and other resources can be shared within the organization's network, making it easy for employees to work together on projects and tasks. Collaboration tools like project management software shared calendars, and virtual whiteboards help teams work together seamlessly. Computer networks allow organizations to share resources like printers, scanners, and databases. This makes it easy for employees to access the resources they need to do their jobs without purchasing equipment. An organization's computer network enables data and resource sharing, reducing the duplication of data and providing data security, making IT infrastructure management easier, improving internal communications and communications with external stakeholders, and enabling a better computer power distribution within and between business functions and the organization's stakeholders, such as employees, business partners, suppliers, and customers. Additionally, shared resources can help organizations save money on equipment costs and reduce waste. Later in this chapter, there will be further discussion of the various applications that support these functions.

Definition: Computer Network

A computer network is a collection of computing devices connected through communication media to share data and resources.

A computer network is built using hardware components such as computers, switches, routers, cables, and software such as operating systems and business applications. The simplest network is established by connecting two computing devices using communication media such as network cables. The network increases in size as more devices are attached to the network using communication media, covering a larger communication area.

Network Components

A computer network consists of computing devices used by network users, which are interconnected through various network-connecting devices and data transmission/communication media and channels. Computing devices use a network interface card (NIC) to communicate with each other.

A NIC, also referred to as a network adapter or network interface controller, is a crucial hardware component that allows a computing device, such as a PC, laptop, server, printer, or scanner, to establish network connectivity. It provides the physical interface facilitating communication over the network transmission media, such as Ethernet cables or Wi-Fi signals. In addition to enabling communication, a NIC contains a unique Media Access Control (MAC) address, which identifies the device on the network.

In modern networks, almost all networked devices come embedded with a NIC. When a device wants to exchange data with other devices on the network, it uses the NIC to transmit and receive data. The NIC sends digital signals to the network cable or wireless radio waves, which travel across the network media to reach the destination device. The NIC also processes incoming data and sends it to the device's CPU for further processing.

Network-connecting devices are hardware components that enable connections and interactions between computing devices in a network. These devices are essential for building and maintaining a functional network infrastructure. Examples of network-connecting devices include modems, switches, routers, access points, hubs, and gateways. Each of these devices serves a unique purpose in enabling communication and data transfer between devices within a network or between multiple networks.

A modem is a device that connects to your Internet Service Provider (ISP) and allows your computer or other devices to access the Internet. An ISP is a company that provides individuals, businesses, and other organizations with Internet access, usually for a fee. ISPs may offer various types of Internet connections, such as broadband, Digital Subscriber Line (DSL) cable, or satellite, and may also provide additional services such as email accounts, web hosting, and virtual private networks (VPNs).

An example of an ISP in the Australian context is Telstra, which is Australia's largest telecommunications and media company. Telstra provides a wide range of Internet services, including ADSL cable, mobile broadband, and NBN (National Broadband Network) connections. Other popular ISPs in Australia include Optus, TPG, iiNet, and Vodafone.

A modem connects the computer to the Internet through the ISP. The term 'modem' comes from 'modulate' and 'demodulate', which refers to the way that it converts digital signals from your computer into analogue signals that can be transmitted over telephone or cable lines and then converts analogue signals back into digital signals that your computer can understand.

Depending on the type of Internet connection you have, your modem may connect to your ISP through a telephone line (using DSL technology), a coaxial cable (using cable technology), or a fibre optic cable (using fibre technology). Once the modem is connected to your ISP, it establishes a connection and provides your devices with access to the Internet. Some modems also come with additional features, such as Wi-Fi routers or Ethernet ports, which allow you to connect multiple devices to the Internet at the same time.

Network-connecting devices are hardware components that enable connections and interactions between computing devices in a network. These devices are essential for building and maintaining a functional network infrastructure. Examples of network-connecting devices include modems, switches, routers, access points and hubs. Each of these devices serves a unique purpose in enabling communication and data transfer between devices within a network or between multiple networks. Table 5.1 summarizes the main components of a computer network.

Table 5.1 The Main Components of a Computer Network

Component	Description
Computing devices	Any devices users use on the network such as PCs, laptops, and tablets. They use a network interface card (NIC) to communicate with other devices on the network.
Modem	Connects a computer to the Internet via an Internet Service Provider (ISP) by transforming digital data into analogue signals transmitted via telephone lines.
Switch	Interconnects multiple end devices in the same LAN (local area network), such as computers, printers, and servers, to networks in homes or organizations.
Access points (APs)	A networking device that allows wireless devices to connect to a wired network. APs are commonly used to extend the range of a wireless network and provide additional coverage in areas where the wireless signal is weak or non-existent.
	APs are typically connected to a wired network, such as a router or switch, and they broadcast a wireless signal that wireless devices can connect to. When a wireless device connects to an AP, it can access the wired network and any resources, such as printers, servers, and other devices.
Router	Connects a network to other networks and interconnects multiple networks such as LANs (local area networks) and MANs (metropolitan area networks) to form a larger network called a wide area network (WAN), which is the Internet. Determines the optimum paths for data delivery through the network.

Example: Small Business Network

Consider a small business that operates out of office space and requires a network infrastructure to connect its devices to the Internet and to each other. Here's how the different networking components could come into play:

1 **ISP:** The business would need to sign up with an Internet Service Provider (ISP) to gain access to the Internet. The ISP would provide a modem that connects to the Internet and receives the data signal.
2 **Modem:** The modem is the device that receives the data signal from the ISP and translates it into a format that the local network can use. It typically connects to the ISP's network via a cable or DSL line.
3 **Switch hub:** The business may use a switch hub to connect its devices to each other. A switch hub is a networking device that allows multiple devices to communicate with each other on a local network. It does not provide Internet access but enables network devices to communicate with each other.
4 **Router:** A router is a device that connects multiple networks together. In the context of our example, the router would connect the business's local network (which includes the switch hub and all the devices connected to it) to the ISP's network (which provides access to the Internet). The router would handle traffic between the two networks and ensure that data gets sent to the right destination.

So, in summary, a small business would need to sign up with an ISP to gain access to the Internet and receive a modem from the ISP to translate the data signal. It could then use a switch hub to connect its devices to each other on a local network, and a router to connect the local network to the ISP's network and provide Internet access to all devices on the local network.

Client-Server and Peer-to-Peer Networks

Computer networks can generally be classified into two main types: peer-to-peer (P2P) networks and client/server networks.

A P2P network is a type of network where computers are connected to each other directly and have equal roles and privileges on the network. Each computer can share resources such as storage, printers, or information with other computers on the network without the need for a centralized computer or server. This type of network is easy to install and configure, and is an inexpensive solution, especially for small businesses and home environments (IBM, 2020).

One of the main advantages of a P2P network is its ease of use. Since there is no need for a centralized computer or server, the network can be set up quickly and easily with minimal technical expertise. This makes it an ideal solution for home users or small businesses that still need a dedicated IT department. Another advantage of a P2P network is its flexibility. Since each computer on the network has equal privileges, any computer can act as a server and share resources with other computers on the network. This means that users can easily access resources such as files or printers without having to rely on a centralized system.

For instance, a freelancer such as a graphic designer considers file sharing an essential part of their work. They may need to share design files with their clients for review and approval. By utilizing P2P networks and file-sharing software like BitTorrent, Dropbox, OneDrive, or Google Drive, they can efficiently share files with clients without depending on external storage devices or complex network configurations. This process would be more efficient and facilitate quick and easy file transfers between the designer and their clients.

However, it is important to note that P2P networks may not be suitable for businesses or situations where security is a top concern. Since each computer on the network has equal privileges, there is a risk that sensitive data could be accessed or shared by unauthorized users. Additionally, there is no centralized system to store and share resources, so if one computer shuts down, other computers cannot access the data stored in that computer. Another drawback of P2P networks is their limited functionality. Peer-to-peer networks offer limited functions, have weak data protection, and do not provide backups. This makes them less suitable for businesses or situations where security is a concern.

In sum, P2P networks can be a great solution for sharing resources between computers in a small business or home environment. However, they are only suitable for some situations and can pose security risks if properly configured and managed.

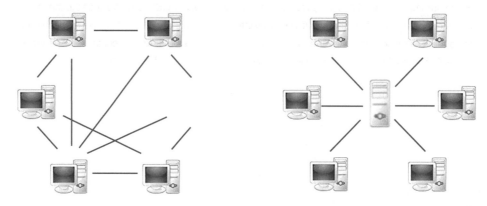

Figure 5.1 Peer-to-Peer Processing (Left) and Client-Server Processing (Right) (source: Mauro Bieg, https://commons.wikimedia.org/w/index.php?curid=2551723; https://commons.wikimedia.org/w/index.php?curid=2551745

In a client-server network, a centralized server is the main hub for managing and controlling access to resources on the network. This server provides various services, such as file sharing, printing, email, and web access to clients that request them. Clients, in this case, are computers that connect to the server to access these services (IBM, 2020).

Businesses and organizations that require high levels of security, data protection, and scalability commonly use this network type. The centralized control over resources and security in client-server networks makes it easier to manage and protect the network from unauthorized access. However, setting up and maintaining this network can be more complex and expensive compared to peer-to-peer networks.

In a client-server network configuration, all computers connect to a centralized computer system known as a server. The server stores and manages access to resources and services for clients on the network. Unlike the peer-to-peer model, client computers in a client-server system do not share resources with each other. Instead, all access and sharing of resources are channelled through the server computer.

To join the client-server network, any computer or device that wants to share or access a shared resource must connect to the network and receive permission from the server. A group password can be set to prevent unauthorized devices from joining the network, which improves security.

Overall, the choice between a P2P and a client-server network depends on the needs and resources of the organization or individual using the network. P2P networks are a good choice for small, informal environments where resources and data are not critical and cost is a significant factor. Client-server networks are better suited for larger business environments where resources and data are critical and security is a top priority.

Definition: P2P Network

In a peer-to-peer (P2P) network setup, computers are connected directly to one another and have equivalent roles and privileges on the network.

Definition: Client-Server Network

In a client-server network setup, all computers are linked to a centralized computer system known as a server.

Example: Client/Server network and MIS

Here's an example of how a small business might use a client-server network for their Management Information System (MIS).

(Continued)

Let's say a small business wants to set up an MIS to manage their inventory and sales. They could implement a client-server network by setting up a central server to manage the inventory and sales data, and installing client computers throughout the business for employees to access and update that data. The server could be configured to provide specific levels of access and security to different employees based on their roles and responsibilities.

By using a client-server network, the business can ensure that their inventory and sales data is securely stored and easily accessible to all employees who need it. It can also use the network to run reports and analyses on the data, helping the business to make informed decisions about its inventory and sales strategy.

In this scenario, a P2P network might not be the best choice because it would not provide the same level of centralized control and security as a client-server network. Additionally, as the business grows and more employees are added to the network, a P2P network would likely become less efficient and more difficult to manage.

Types of Networks

Computer networks can span various geographic locations and are commonly categorized based on their size and the range of their coverage. The two most widely used network types are local area networks (LANs) and wide area networks (WANs).

A local area network (LAN) is a privately owned and managed network that connects devices in a single, limited area to share data, files, and resources. For example, a LAN may connect all the computing devices in an office building, school, restaurant, coffee shop, or hospital. In a large office with multiple departments, each department's computers could be connected to the same switch but segmented to operate as if they were separate networks. This segmentation helps control access and secure the network.

Another type of LAN is a wireless LAN (WLAN), which employs wireless communication to connect devices in limited areas such as homes, schools, computer laboratories, campuses, or office buildings. WLANs provide flexibility and convenience by eliminating the need for physical cables, enabling users to connect to the network from any location within the coverage area. However, WLANs can pose security risks if not adequately secured, and the coverage area is limited compared to a wired LAN.

Computer networks are essential for managing information systems within an organization, relying on them to handle data and enable communication across different departments and locations. For instance, a company may use a LAN to link its employees' computers within a single building or department, allowing them to share files and collaborate on projects. Simultaneously, the company may use a WAN to connect its branches worldwide, allowing employees in various locations to access the same information.

An example of how computer networks are used in organizations are Enterprise Resource Planning (ERP) systems, which are integrated software systems that manage various business functions such as finance, accounting, human resources, and supply chain management. ERP systems depend on computer networks to provide real-time information to different departments, enabling them to make informed decisions and streamline processes.

Another example is Customer Relationship Management (CRM) systems, which help businesses manage customer interactions. CRM systems rely on computer networks to store customer data and provide it to different departments, enabling them to personalize interactions and improve customer satisfaction.

Definition: LAN

A local area network (LAN) is a privately owned and managed network that connects devices within a single, limited area, allowing them to share data, files, and resources.

Definition: WAN

A wide area network (WAN) facilitates communication between devices located on different networks spanning a large geographic area, such as cities, states, or even countries.

Table 5.2 lists the different types of networks based on their size and geographic scope (IBM Cloud Education, 2022).

A **wide-area network (WAN)** is a network that connects local-area networks (LANs) or other networks, enabling devices on different networks to communicate with each other over a large geographic area such as cities, states, or countries. Essentially, a WAN is a network of networks, which includes the Internet.

Wi-Fi is a wireless network technology that allows computing and mobile devices, such as desktops, laptops, smartphones, and printers, to connect with each other and to the Internet. **Wireless LAN** and **wireless WAN** are similar to their wired counterparts, but the network connections are made wirelessly.

Traditionally, network components such as routers and switches consist of two parts: the network control logic that decides how to handle network traffic and the data control devices such as routers and switches that control the movement of information in the network based on the decisions made by the control logic. Any changes to the network require manual configuration of network devices, such as routers and switches. This makes traditional networks inflexible and unable to meet the evolving networking requirements of businesses.

Table 5.2 Types of Networks based on Size and Geographic Scope (compiled from: IBM, 2020a)

Network Type	Characteristics	Examples
Local Area Network (LAN)	Connects network devices within a limited area or short distance, between 100 and 1,000 metres	Office building, home, school
Personal Area Network (PAN)	Covers small physical space less than 10 metres – connects devices close to a person	Laptop, smartphone, printer, tablets
Campus Area Network (CAN)	Covers multiple LANs but is smaller than a MAN	University campus
Metropolitan Area Network (MAN)	Usually spans a city or a large campus – the network size is between LAN and WAN and covers an area between 5 and 50 kilometres.	A single large city, multiple small cities
Wide Area Network (WAN)	Covers a large geographic area, interconnects multiple LANs, MANs and other smaller networks	Internet, regional areas
Software-Defined WAN (SD-WAN)	Software-defined wide-area networks use software to control the network hardware, connectivity, management and services, and direct network traffic across the WAN over the Internet or cloud-based private networks. This makes it simpler to manage and operate the network, as equipment can be controlled and configured from afar through software – without the need to send engineers to the site.	Large organizations, business enterprises
Storage Area Network (SAN)	A specialized network that provides access to a shared storage device on a network (or cloud). This shared cloud storage space is used to consolidate storage and for situations requiring fast, efficient, and reliable data transportation. To the user, the storage space looks and works like a storage drive physically attached to a computer. Each computer on the network can access the storage space on the SAN as though they were local disks connected directly to the computer (Cisco 2023.; IBM Cloud Education, 2021a).	Large organizations, business enterprises

A **software-defined network (SDN)** is a network that uses centralized software to manage network traffic in an organization's computer network, eliminating the need for manual configuration of physical devices. The software can dynamically modify data flows to match the needs of the business and applications (Kreutz et al., 2015; IBM Cloud Education, 2021a).

SDNs can be implemented in both LAN (local area network) and WAN (wide area network) environments in an organization. SDNs can provide numerous benefits for organizations deploying LAN and WAN networks, including simplified network management, increased visibility and control, and improved network performance and scalability.

In a LAN environment, SDNs can be used to simplify network management, improve network visibility, and optimize network performance. By centralizing the control plane in software, administrators can easily configure and manage network policies and services for all devices on the LAN (Cisco 2023.; IBM Cloud Education, 2021a).

In a WAN environment, SDN can be used to provide network-wide visibility and control, allowing administrators to manage traffic flows and prioritize applications across the entire WAN. SDNs can also help optimize network performance by dynamically routing traffic based on network conditions, such as congestion or latency.

Consider a large retail chain that operates hundreds of stores across the country. Each store has a local network connecting point-of-sale terminals, inventory systems, and other devices. Traditionally, managing and configuring these networks would be a time-consuming and error-prone task for the IT department.

However, by implementing an SDN solution, the retail chain can centralize network management and configuration in software, making monitoring and managing the entire network from a single location easier. The IT department can use SDN controllers to simultaneously deploy network policies and security measures across all stores, reducing the risk of security breaches and improving network performance.

Overall, SDNs can significantly benefit businesses in various industries, making it easier to manage and optimize complex network infrastructures. For example, a retail chain could use SDNs to prioritize network traffic from point-of-sale terminals during peak hours, ensuring that customers can complete their transactions quickly and efficiently. SDNs can also be used to optimize the network performance for inventory systems, which often generate large amounts of data that must be transmitted to a central location for analysis.

5.4 The Internet

The Advanced Research Project Agency (ARPA) of the US Department of Defence spearheaded an experimental project that gave birth to the Internet. The project, called ARPANet, launched on 30 August 1969. It involved a network of computers stationed in universities, government agencies, and research facilities. The goal was to examine the feasibility of a WAN that researchers, educators, military personnel, and government agencies could use to share data, exchange messages, and transfer files. The ARPANet project's tech team designed numerous protocols that are still relevant for the Internet today. As ARPANet linked with other computer networks, the Internet was born (Strickland, 2008).

No single entity owns the Internet. Instead, it is collectively owned, distributed, and managed by a range of organizations. These groups oversee the Internet infrastructure, develop rules and protocols that govern data exchange, and recommend standards and technology. Some of the key organizations involved in the Internet's management are IANA (Internet Assigned Numbers Authority), ICANN (Internet Corporation for Assigned Names and Numbers), IETF (Internet Engineering Task Force), IRTF (Internet Research Task Force), and W3C (World Wide Web Consortium) (Wikipedia, 2022).

To connect to the Internet, people and businesses must subscribe to an Internet Service Provider (ISP). An ISP is a company that provides Internet connections for a fee. In Australia, some of the significant ISPs include Telstra, Optus, and the TPG Group. ISPs connect to each other through network access points (NAPs), which are exchange points for Internet traffic. These access points determine how traffic flows through the Internet backbone, which comprises the primary data transmission routes that carry Internet traffic between large, interconnected computer networks.

Intranet, Extranet, Virtual Private Networks (VPNs), Software-Defined Networks (SDNs)

Internet technologies have become ubiquitous both within and between organizations. In a business setting, these technologies enable a company's headquarters to connect with its branch offices located in various cities and countries, cloud services, and other facilities. Enterprise networks, comprising LANs and WANs, allow users located at different sites to collaborate and share access to centrally located resources, eliminating the need to install the same application server, firewall, or other resources in multiple locations. Companies employ Internet-based technologies to provide secure access to company resources via intranets and grant authorized customers, vendors, partners, or others outside the company access via extranets.

An **intranet** is an internal network that consists of LANs or WANs and uses the same technologies and protocols as the Internet. Organizations utilize intranets to store and share company information with employees and users, improving internal communications and increasing collaboration between employees in a secure environment. Through intranets, organizations can ensure that only authorized users have access to information and services. For example, colleges and universities use intranets to provide services to students, faculty, and staff. Microsoft Office 365 and SharePoint online allow team members to share materials, and online productivity applications such as Word, Excel, or PowerPoint facilitate online engagement and collaboration in real-time.

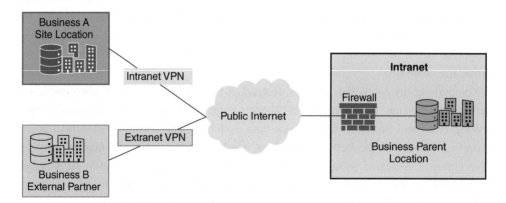

Figure 5.2　Intranet and Extranet VPNs

Extranets are intranets extended to authorized external users, such as customers, vendors, partners, or others outside the organization. Extranets enable business partners to share information and communicate securely over the Internet using *virtual private networks (VPNs)*. They are widely used in the areas of business-to-business (B2B) electronic commerce and supply chain management (SCM). Extranets enable companies to communicate and collaborate more effectively with their partners, customers, and vendors over a secure network, integrating supply chains, reducing costs, enhancing business relationships, improving customer service, and securing communications.

Network security is always a concern when sharing and communicating over the Internet. Information shared over the public Internet can be intercepted or compromised. VPN companies can create a secure channel for communication with their external partners. A **virtual private network (VPN)** is a network that creates a private network from a public Internet connection that encrypts the packets before they are transferred over the network. A VPN facilitates a company's connectivity and the security of WANs.

Definition: Intranet

An **intranet** is a type of internal network that is composed of local area networks (LANs) or wide area networks (WANs) and employs similar technologies and protocols to those used on the Internet. It enables companies to store and share information with their employees and authorized users, which can improve internal communication and collaboration while providing a secure environment to safeguard sensitive information.

Definition: Extranet

An extranet is an extension of an intranet that is accessible to authorized external users such as customers, vendors, partners, or other individuals outside the organization. It enables companies to share information and communicate securely with external parties using VPNs. Extranets are commonly used in supply chain management and business-to-business (B2B) electronic commerce.

Definition: Virtual Private Network (VPN)

A Virtual Private Network (VPN) is a type of network that establishes a private network from a public Internet connection. VPNs encrypt packets before transferring them over the network, providing secure connectivity and enhancing the security of WANs. VPNs can be used to facilitate a company's connectivity with external partners and to safeguard sensitive information.

Example: Networking Technologies for Efficient Operations: A Case Study of Thread & Co.

Thread & Co. is a clothing retailer with multiple store locations across Australia, as well as an online store. To streamline their business operations, they use a variety of networking technologies, including LAN, WAN, intranet, extranet with VPN. At each of their store locations, Thread & Co. uses a local area network (LAN) to connect their computers, printers, and other devices. This enables employees to efficiently communicate and share data, such as inventory levels and customer information. To connect their retail locations to their central headquarters in Sydney, Thread & Co. uses a wide area network (WAN). This allows for the centralized management of operations, including supply chain management and distribution logistics.

Within the organization, Thread & Co. uses an intranet to facilitate internal communication and the sharing of information. The intranet serves as a hub for company announcements, employee directories, training materials, and other resources that are essential for the efficient functioning of the business. To share information securely with external parties, such as suppliers and distributors, Thread & Co. uses an extranet. The extranet allows authorized external parties to access real-time information about inventory levels, the status of orders, and delivery schedules. To ensure secure access to the extranet, Thread & Co. employs a virtual private network (VPN) that encrypts data transmissions between the extranet and external parties.

Overall, Thread & Co.'s use of LAN, WAN, intranet, and extranet with VPN allows for efficient communication and data sharing across their retail locations, central headquarters, and external partners. This facilitates streamlined operations, improved decision-making, and, ultimately, a better customer experience.

Internet Communication Protocol

The transmission of information over the Internet is governed by a set of rules and procedures called network communication protocols. Devices connected to a network communicate with each other by following these protocols. The most widely used network communication protocol is the Transmission Control Protocol/Internet Protocol (TCP/IP).

TCP/IP is a suite of protocols that enables network devices to communicate with each other. It includes two main protocols: the TCP (Transmission Control Protocol) and the IP (Internet Protocol). These protocols work together to ensure that data is transmitted to its intended destination within a network (Figure 5.3).

Figure 5.3 Internet Communication using TCP/IP Protocol

Definition: TCP/IP

TCP/IP is a communication protocol consisting of the TCP (Transmission Control Protocol) and the IP (Internet Protocol), which work together to enable network devices to effectively communicate with each other and ensure the delivery of data to its intended destination.

The TCP/IP protocol is designed with a layered approach, where each layer performs a specific function and provides a specific set of services to the layer above it. The TCP/IP protocol is divided into four layers, each with its own set of functions and protocols. The layered approach ensures that data is transmitted efficiently and reliably across networks, and enables devices with different hardware and software to communicate effectively with each other. The four layers of the TCP/IP model (Figure 5.4) are:

1 **Application layer:** This layer is responsible for managing network applications and communication services, including email, file transfer, and remote access. Examples of protocols that operate at this layer include HTTP, FTP, SMTP, and Telnet.
2 **Transport layer:** This layer is responsible for managing the end-to-end delivery of data between applications running on different devices. It ensures that data is transmitted reliably and efficiently, and provides mechanisms for error recovery and flow control. The two main protocols that operate at this layer are **Transmission Control Protocol** (TCP) User Datagram Protocol (UDP).
3 **Internet layer:** This layer is responsible for managing the routing of data packets across multiple networks. It provides a mechanism for addressing and identifying devices on the network, and ensures that data is delivered to the correct destination. The IP protocol operates at this layer.
4 **Network interface layer:** This layer is responsible for managing the physical transmission of data between devices on the same network. It provides a mechanism for sending and receiving data using network-specific protocols and hardware, such as Ethernet, Wi-Fi, or Token Ring.

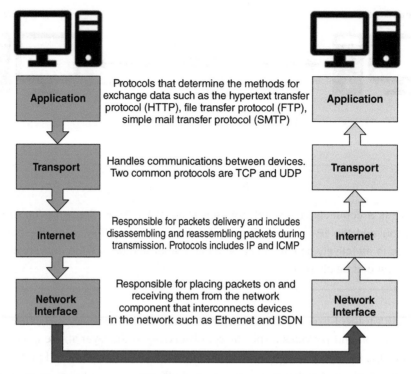

Figure 5.4 TCP/IP Layers

ICMP: The Internet Control Message Protocol; ISDN: Integrated Services Digital Network.

Packet Switching

In the TCP/IP protocol, the transmission of messages over the network is carried out through packet switching, where messages are divided into smaller packets and assigned a unique number for identification upon receipt. Each packet consists of a segment of data, the sender's IP address, and the destination IP address, which uniquely identifies and locates the device on the network. Network switches and routers are used to route these packets from the source to the destination. Due to different network paths, the packets may arrive at the destination out of order. The packets are then reassembled before being delivered to the user applications at the receiving end (Figure 5.5).

5.5 Transmission Media

In computer networks, transmission media or communication channels are essential components that allow devices to connect and transmit data. These media can be wired, using, for example, twisted-pair wires, cables, or fibre-optic cables, or wireless, using microwave, satellite, radio, or infrared technology. The bandwidth of each transmission media varies, which determines the amount of data that can be transmitted at a given time and is typically measured in Mbps. Due to business demands for greater bandwidth,

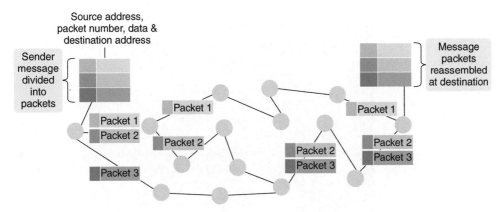

Figure 5.5   Packet Switching Network

faster and more reliable transmission media are needed. Therefore, businesses must understand the different types of network transmission media available to select the most efficient transmission media that meets their organizational needs (Verizon, 2022b).

Transmission media can be classified into two types: wired and wireless. Wired media refers to physical cables that transmit data, while wireless media transmits data using radio waves or light. The choice of transmission media depends on factors such as network size, layout, and distance between devices.

Wired Transmission Media

Wired transmission media consists of twisted pair cables, coaxial cables, and fibre optic cables. **Twisted pair cables** are the most commonly used and are relatively inexpensive and easy to install. They are ideal for LANs that cover short to medium distances. However, twisted pair cables are susceptible to noise and have lower bandwidth compared to coaxial and fibre optic cables. Their typical bandwidth is 10-10Gbps and covers distances up to 100m.

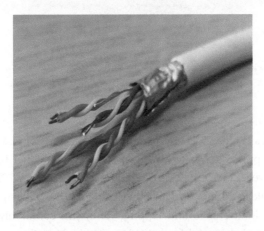

Figure 5.6   Twisted Pair Cable (source: https://commons.wikimedia.org/w/index.hp?search=Twisted+pair+cable+with+connector+&title=Special:MediaSearch&go=Go&type=image)

Figure 5.7 Twisted Pair Cable with Connector (source: Johan Braeken, https://commons.wikimedia.org/w/index.php?search=Twisted+pair+cable+with+connector+&title=Special:MediaSearch&go=Go&type=image)

Coaxial cables (Figure 5.8) are popular in the cable television industry because they are less susceptible to electrical interference, can carry more data, and can support longer cable lengths. They typically cover distances of 200–500m and have a bandwidth of up to 1 Gbps. However, they are more expensive and difficult to install and manage than twisted pair cables.

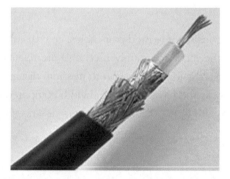

Figure 5.8 Coaxial Cable (Source: 10 FDominec, CC BY-SA 3.0,) https://commons.wikimedia.org/w/index.php?search=Coaxial+Cable&title=Special:MediaSearch&go=Go&type=image

Fibre optic cables (Figure 5.9) are made up of thousands of glass fibres that transmit information via light pulses generated by lasers. They offer higher bandwidth and transmission speeds of over 1,000Gbps (Tbps) and cover distances of 2km to 100km. Fibre optic cables are smaller and lighter than other cable media, transmit more data, and are more secure against interference and tapping. They are commonly used as backbone cables for networks and designed for long-distance, high-performance data networking and telecommunications applications.

Figure 5.9 Fibre Optic Cable – Cross-Section View (https://commons.wikimedia. org/w/index.php?curid=7029445)

Figure 5.10 Fibre Optic Cable on the Ocean Floor

Thus, understanding the different types of transmission media available is crucial for businesses looking to support their operations. By selecting the most efficient network transmission media that suits their organizational needs, businesses can achieve faster and more reliable network communication.

Wireless Transmission Media

Wireless transmission media, or Wi-Fi, has become an essential part of home and business networks. There are several types of wireless media, including infrared, Bluetooth, radio waves, microwaves, and satellites (see Figure 5.11).

Infrared (IR) is a wireless technology that transmits signals using infrared light waves. It has a limited transmission range of 1–5 metres and requires line-of-sight communication. IR is used mainly for short-range communication, such as remote controls, wireless mice, and keyboards.

Bluetooth is a wireless technology that uses radio wave frequencies to transmit and receive data over short distances, typically less than 10 metres, and does not require direct line-of-sight. It creates personal area networks (PANs) between multiple devices, such as mobile phones, laptops, and printers.

Radio transmission (RF) uses radio wave frequencies to transmit data between devices. RF has a wider signal range, covering up to 30 metres, and can carry data over long distances. RF can go through walls, and there is no need to point the remote controller at the device as it does not require line-of-sight. However, radio waves cannot transmit large volumes of data simultaneously because they operate at relatively low frequencies.

Microwaves are high-frequency radio waves used for high-volume and long-distance communication. Like infrared, microwave transmissions occur in line-of-sight. To maintain the microwave signal over long distances, microwave relay towers are placed within sight of one another, not exceeding a distance of 60 km.

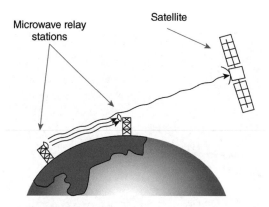

Figure 5.11 Wireless Transmission Media (Source: Decora – own work 14 May 2011 (UTC), Public Domain, https://commons.wikimedia.org/w/index.php?curid=18258823)

Satellite transmission systems use communication satellites for TV, telephone, radio, Internet, and GPS. Communication with satellites requires line-of-sight transmission. There are three types of satellites: geostationary-Earth-orbit (GEO), medium-Earth-orbit (MEO), and low-Earth-orbit (LEO). GEO is the farthest from the earth, MEO is closer to the earth, and LEO is closest to the earth.

Stop and Reflect: Communication Network for the New Warehouse

Imagine you are a project manager for a small start-up company that specializes in the online retailing of handmade crafts. Your company has been growing steadily and you recently decided to expand by opening a new warehouse in a different city. The new warehouse has allowed you to store more inventory and increase your shipping capacity to customers across the country. As the project manager, you were responsible for coordinating the move and ensuring that all systems were up and running smoothly. One of the major tasks in this project was setting up a communication network between the new warehouse and the main office. You had to choose the right transmission media to ensure that the network is reliable, fast, and secure. After careful consideration, you decided to use fibre optic cables as they offer high bandwidth, fast transmission speeds, and are secure against interference and tapping. However, the cost of installing the fibre optic cables was higher compared to other transmission media. You also had to ensure that all devices in the new warehouse were connected to the network and that the network was compatible with the existing network in the main office.

Questions

1   What challenges did you face as the project manager in setting up the communication network for the new warehouse?
2   What factors did you consider when choosing the transmission media for the new network?
3   What risks did you consider in choosing fibre optic cables for the new network?
4   How did you ensure that the new network was compatible with the existing network in the main office?
5   What steps did you take to ensure that all devices in the new warehouse were connected to the network?
6   What did you learn from this project and how will you apply this knowledge in future projects?

5.6 Networking Business Applications – Business Functions Supported by Computer Networks

In today's business landscape, computer networks and the Internet are critical components in supporting business operations. The emergence of cloud computing has further facilitated communication and collaboration, allowing businesses to access computing infrastructure and applications via digital platforms, using various channels and devices. Under this section, several applications are discussed in detail to give the reader an idea of the importance of each application and where it can be used.

Business productivity applications, such as project management and accounting software, can help streamline operations, increase efficiency, and reduce costs.

Communication and collaboration applications like Microsoft 365, Google Workspace, Slack, Webex, Zoom, Skype, Asana, Jira, Trello, and Basecamp enable people to connect and work together online.

Project management applications like Asana, Jira, Trello, and Basecamp help teams plan and manage their work.

Cloud storage and sharing applications like OneDrive, SharePoint, and Google Drive enable users to share documents and resources collaboratively.

Customer engagement applications, such as Salesforce, Dynamics 365, Zoho CRM, and Hubspot, help businesses improve their customer service, increase consumer satisfaction, and build stronger relationships with their customers.

Supplier management applications like Donesafe, Gatekeeper, and ShippingEasy enable businesses to manage and engage their vendors and suppliers for streamlined supply chain operations.

By using these applications, businesses can improve productivity, customer satisfaction, and supplier relationships, which can ultimately help them grow and succeed in today's competitive marketplace (see Table 5.3).

Table 5.3 List of Popular Productivity, Collaboration, Project Management, Customer Engagement, and Supplier Management Applications Used by Businesses

Productivity and Collaboration Applications	
Microsoft 365 Suite	A cloud-based productivity and collaboration suite that includes popular applications such as Microsoft Outlook Email, Calendar, and Microsoft Teams for communication, chat, and meetings, as well as the popular office productivity applications, Word, Excel, and PowerPoint. https://www.microsoft.com/en-us/microsoft-365
Google Workspace	An application suite for online productivity and collaboration that provides enterprise versions of Gmail, Google Meet, Calendar, and Chat for communication and collaboration. https://workspace.google.com/
Slack	A messaging application that includes instant messaging, voice and video calls, and a suite of tools to help groups share information and work together. https://slack.com/
Webex	Cisco's communication and collaboration platform that provides capabilities for online meetings, team messaging, and file sharing. https://www.webex.com/
Zoom	A video communication platform that enables meetings, chat, phone calls, webinars, and online events. https://zoom.us/
Skype	Communication software that enables individuals and businesses to make free video and voice one-to-one and group calls, send instant messages, and share files with other people on Skype. https://www.skype.com/
Project Management Applications	
Asana	A project management platform that provides task management, collaboration, document, workflow, and project portfolio management features to help teams organize, track, and manage their work. https://asana.com/
Jira	A software application used for issue tracking and project management. https://www.atlassian.com/software/jira
Trello	A collaborative project management application for teams to collaborate and manage projects. https://trello.com/

Project Management Applications	
Basecamp	A collaboration and project management application that provides capabilities for keeping track of tasks, deadlines, files, discussions, and announcements related to work and projects. Features include message boards, to-dos, schedules, file storage, real-time group chat, and automatic check-in questions. https://basecamp.com/

File Sharing and Collaboration Applications	
OneDrive	Included in the Microsoft 365 suite, it allows users to share their files with others and organizes files based on type, making it easy for users to locate their files and collaboratively work on different file formats. https://www.microsoft.com/en-us/microsoft-365/onedrive/online-cloud-storage
SharePoint	Also part of the Microsoft 365 suite, it is designed for collaboration. It allows businesses to provide their employees with cloud storage that can be managed through a central location. Users share and collaborate on stored files. Site collection administration in the organization can manage and control what users can do when accessing the central repository. https://www.microsoft.com/en-us/microsoft-365/sharepoint/collaboration
Google Drive	Part of the Google Workspace, it enables teams to work collaboratively using Google Drive as a single place to store, access, and share files. https://www.google.com/drive/

Customer Engagement Applications	
Salesforce	One of the most popular cloud-based customer relationship management (CRM) software solutions for support, sales, and marketing, enabling businesses to better connect with their partners, current customers, and potential customers. https://www.salesforce.com/
Dynamics 365	A cloud-based solution for CRM and ERP. Dynamics 365 provides tools for sales, customer service, field service management, talent acquisition, finance and operations, retail, project service automation, marketing, artificial intelligence, mixed reality, and more. https://dynamics.microsoft.com/
Zoho CRM	A CRM tool that functions as a single repository for marketing, sales, and customer support activities. It is an excellent tool to use for streamlining policies, processes, and people on one platform. https://www.zoho.com/crm/
Hubspot	A cloud-based marketing CRM platform that allows businesses to build automated workflows, track and create email and social media campaigns, automate social media publishing, and even build websites and landing pages. https://www.hubspot.com/

Supplier Management Applications	
Donesafe	A cloud-based supplier management system that helps companies to track supplier (vendor) performance and to manage relationships with suppliers. https://donesafe.com/
Gatekeeper	A cloud-based supplier, vendors, and contract management solution for businesses. https://www.gatekeeperhq.com/
ShippingEasy	A cloud-based shipping and inventory management solution suitable for small to medium-sized e-commerce businesses. Key features include order management, label customization, integration with multiple seller channels, rate comparison, and returns management. ShippingEasy streamlines the entire shipping process, from order fulfilment to label printing and shipment tracking, helping businesses save time and money while improving customer satisfaction. https://shippingeasy.com/

Stop and Reflect: Monster Inc

Monster Inc a medium-sized IT company providing software development services to clients, is struggling with managing its development processes efficiently, which is negatively impacting its productivity. One solution the company has considered is implementing a project management tool to automate and streamline their development processes. However, the company also recognizes the importance of communication and collaboration in improving productivity.

Questions

1   Which project management tool would you recommend for Monster Inc. and why?
2   How can the chosen project management tool improve Monster Inc.'s productivity?
3   Are there any potential drawbacks or limitations to using the chosen project management tool? If so, how can they be addressed?
4   Are there any alternative project management tools that could be used to address Monster Inc.'s challenges? If so, how do they compare to the chosen project management tool?
5   What other factors should be considered before implementing the chosen project management tool at Monster Inc.?

5.7 Information Security

Technological advancements like cloud and social computing, big data, and IoT have allowed companies to collect and analyse massive amounts of data, leading to more informed strategic decisions. However, the increased reliance on cloud technologies and the growing need for interconnected organizational information systems for fast access and the processing of big data has also made businesses' IT systems more susceptible to various threats.

When we talk about IT assets, we refer to organizational data, hardware, software, databases, and other information systems used within an organization. These assets are crucial for businesses to operate smoothly, and any potential weakness or vulnerability can lead to significant harm if a threat is carried out.

A threat, commonly called a cybersecurity threat, is any danger or risk that an IT resource may be exposed to, potentially leading to the loss or damage of that resource. According to a data breach investigation conducted by Verizon (Verizon, 2022a), the most common threats are hacking, malware, errors and misuse, social engineering, physical damage, and environmental damage.

Hacking involves gaining unauthorized access to IT systems, usually with malicious intent. For example, in 2013, Target was the victim of a massive hack that compromised the personal data of over 110 million customers. The attackers gained access through a third-party vendor and installed malware on Target's payment system (Eversley, 2013; Isidore, 2014).

Malware is any software designed to harm a computer system or network. It can be spread through email attachments, malicious websites, or software downloads. In 2017, the WannaCry ransomware attack affected hundreds of thousands of computers worldwide, encrypting users' files and demanding payment in exchange for the decryption key (Larson, 2017).

Errors and misuse are typically accidental, but they can still lead to significant harm. For instance, in 2020, the New York State Department of Labor mistakenly revealed tens of thousands of unemployment insurance claimants' personal information, including social security numbers, due to a technical issue (Biron, 2022).

Social engineering involves manipulating individuals to divulge confidential information or perform actions that can lead to data breaches. Phishing is a common social engineering attack where attackers send fraudulent emails to trick recipients into revealing sensitive information. For example, in 2013, a phishing attack targeting Yahoo led to the compromise of 3 billion user accounts (Perlroth, 2017).

Physical and environmental damage refer to the physical destruction of IT assets, usually caused by natural disasters or human error. For instance, in 2011, a massive earthquake and tsunami in Japan caused significant damage to the country's IT infrastructure, leading to widespread disruption of businesses and public services (Dignan, 2011; Niccolai, 2011).

Organizations must protect their IT assets and resources, given the potential risks associated with cyber threats. Companies can implement various security measures such as firewalls, antivirus software, data encryption, and regular employee training to mitigate the risks of cyber threats.

Definition: Cyber Security Threat

A cyber security threat refers to any potential danger or risk that can compromise an IT resource, resulting in potential loss of or damage to the said resource.

Threats to Information and Technology Resources

Changes in the social, economic, and political realms have an impact on cyber security and cybercrimes. In 2020–2021, the COVID-19 pandemic brought about significant changes in the way businesses operate, with many companies adopting remote working arrangements, cloud technologies, and bring-your-own-device (BYOD) policies. While these changes have brought about many benefits, they have also created new cybersecurity challenges for organizations. Remote working and BYOD policies can expand the attack surface for cyber criminals, making it easier for them to exploit vulnerabilities in an organization's IT systems. Additionally, the rapid adoption of cloud technologies has led to a proliferation of cloud-based applications and services, which can also be exploited by cybercriminals.

According to the ACSC Annual Cyber Threat Report for 2020–2021 (Australian Cyber Security Centre, 2021), fraud-related cybercrime remained a significant threat to Australians in this period, accounting for nearly 23% of all cybercrime reports. The cybercrime categories with the highest number of reports were primarily cyber-enabled crimes, such as online fraud, online shopping scams, and online banking scams. While ransomware-related cybercrime reports were relatively low in number, they remained the most serious threat due to their high financial impact and disruptive effects. Self-reported financial losses due to cybercrime in Australia totalled more than AU$33 billion, with small businesses reporting a higher number of cybercrime incidents than in the previous year, while medium-sized businesses suffered the highest average financial loss per cybercrime report (Australian Cyber Security Centre, 2021).

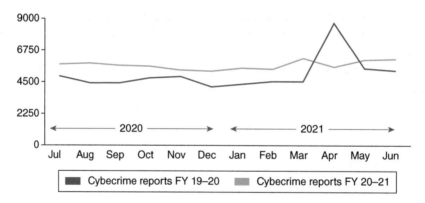

Figure 5.12 Cybercrime Reports by Month for Financial Year 2020–21 Compared with Financial Year 2019–20 (ACSC Annual Cyber Threat Report – 1 July 2020 to 30 June 2021)

During the 2021–22 financial year, Australia experienced a rise in the number and complexity of cyber threats, enabling crimes such as extortion, espionage, and fraud to be replicated on a larger scale. Cyberspace has become a battleground, as demonstrated by Russia's use of malware to destroy data and prevent computers from booting in Ukraine, and China and Iran's exploitation of Microsoft Exchange vulnerabilities to pursue their strategic interests. The regional dynamics in the Indo-Pacific are heightening the risk of a crisis, and Australia's prosperity is attracting cybercriminals. Although cybercrimes directed at individuals remained prevalent in 2021–22, ransomware was the most destructive form of cybercrime. Critical infrastructure networks were increasingly targeted, but effective cyber defences such as network segregation and collaborative incident response prevented any disruption to essential services (Australian Cyber Security Centre, 2022a).

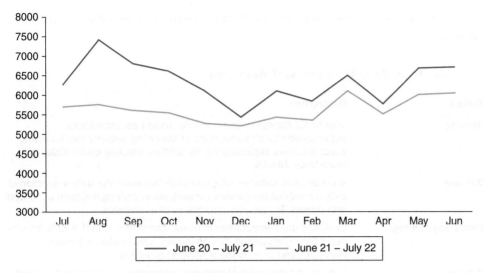

Figure 5.13 Cybercrime Reports by Month for 2021–22 Financial Year Compared with 2020–21 financial year (ACSC, 2022a)

Over the financial year, there were over 76,000 reports of Business Email Compromise (BEC), resulting in a loss of over $98 million, with an average loss of $64,000 per report. The most frequently reported cybercrimes were cyber-enabled crimes, with online fraud (27%), online shopping (14%), and online banking (13%) being the top three reported cybercrimes. Although cyber-dependent crimes, such as ransomware, constituted a small percentage of total cybercrime reports, the ACSC considers ransomware to be the most destructive cybercrime threat. This is because it impacts victim organizations twice: their business is disrupted by the data encryption, and they may face reputational damage if stolen data is released or sold (Australian Cyber Security Centre, 2022b).

The public can also be affected by disruptions and data breaches resulting from ransomware. For example, if a company's IT systems are disrupted by ransomware, it may not be able to provide services to its customers or clients. This can cause inconvenience and frustration for the public, especially if the company provides essential services. Data breaches resulting from ransomware can also compromise sensitive information about the public, such as personal identifying information (PII), financial data, or healthcare records. This information can be sold on the black market or used for identity theft or other fraudulent activities. This can lead to financial losses, reputational damage, and other harm to the public.

In response to these threats, organizations must take steps to ensure the security of their IT systems and data. This includes implementing robust cybersecurity policies and procedures, educating employees on best practices for working remotely and using personal devices for work purposes, and investing in security technologies such as firewalls, antivirus software, and intrusion detection systems.

Table 5.4 discuss the major security threats to IT resources classified into a number of categories.

Table 5.4   Major Security Threats to IT Resources

Threats	Description
Hacking	Intentional access or harm to information assets without authorization by circumventing or thwarting security mechanisms, which includes exploiting vulnerabilities, stealing credentials, or brute force attacks.
Malware	Any malicious software, script, or code that alters the state or function of a device without the owner's consent, compromising a system or network with viruses, Trojans, ransomware, or other malware.
Social engineering	Exploiting the vulnerabilities of users, information, and IT assets through deception, manipulation, or intimidation, which includes phishing, pretexting, and other forms of social engineering.
Misuse	The use of organizational resources or privileges in a way that was not intended or for a different purpose.
Physical threats	Deliberate threats that involve proximity, possession, or force.
Human error	Mistakes made by individuals or systems that lead to a security incident or breach, such as sending sensitive data to the wrong person, misconfiguring a system, or failing to update software in a timely manner. According to Verizon (2022) estimated 80% of breaches were driven by human factors.
Environmental threats	Hazards are associated with the immediate environment or infrastructure where assets are located, including natural disasters such as earthquakes and floods.

There are various types of cybersecurity threats, broadly classified into unintentional and intentional threats. **Unintentional threats** are introduced without any malicious intent, often caused by human error, technological failures or errors, and environmental hazards.

Within an organization, human errors can be caused by employees, contractors, and vendors, and are mostly due to negligence, inattention, or lack of awareness. Such errors include predictable passwords, password changes, failing to log off before leaving a workstation, careless discarding of sensitive information, not updating software security patches, and poor training. Workers who are usually reliable can expose the company to external risks due to low morale or carelessness (Bailey et al., 2018; Jouini et al., 2014). According to Verizon's Data Breach Investigations Report of 2022 (Verizon, 2022a), 85% of data breaches involve attempts to exploit human weaknesses.

Technological errors include hardware and software failures or errors. Software issues can be caused by bugs, code problems, accidental modification of software, and corruption of data resulting from programming mistakes or operator error. Programming errors, improper installation, or unauthorized changes can cause computer software to fail and compromise security, leaving the Information System (IS) vulnerable to attacks from external perpetrators. Natural disasters such as power failures, floods, fires, or other environmental hazards can also disrupt computer systems, causing serious damage such as the destruction and corruption of data and resources (Jouini et al., 2014).

Bring-your-own-device (BYOD) policies allow employees to use their personal devices for work-related purposes, reducing hardware costs and improving organizational productivity and flexibility. However, this policy is not without security implications. Corporate information stored in employees' devices may not be entirely protected, exposing it to the possibility of being lost, corrupted, or stolen. Employees might also access or store their company's information via unauthorized applications and cloud services for convenience. Furthermore, employees frequently lack the expertise and incentive to mitigate risks associated with personal devices, and organizations have less certainty about the integrity and security status of devices that are not corporately controlled (Australian Cyber Security Centre, 2012).

Even though these threats are unintentional, they still have the potential to cause significant disruption and financial costs to an organization. The security breaches involving Facebook and JustDial are stark reminders of the risks associated with the handling and storage of personal information in the digital age. In the case of Facebook, more than half a billion user records were exposed due to inadequate security measures on third-party app developer servers. This data included sensitive personal information such as email addresses, phone numbers, and photos. The exposed datasets were left unsecured and were freely accessible to anyone who had access to the unsecured servers. This breach was a significant blow to Facebook's reputation and raised questions about its ability to protect the privacy of its users (Romm and Dwoskin, 2019).

Similarly, the JustDial breach resulted in the exposure of personal data of over 100 million users due to an unprotected database that was discovered online. The exposed data included usernames, email addresses, mobile numbers, physical addresses, occupation details, and even photos. The fact that the database was accessible in real-time from any device that connected to JustDial's services made the breach even more serious. The scale of this breach was enormous and had far-reaching implications for the affected users (CISOMAG, 2019).

Both of these cases highlight the importance of implementing robust security measures to protect sensitive information from unauthorized access and unintended disclosures. It is imperative for companies to take proactive measures to safeguard their customers' data, including secure data storage, encryption, access controls, and user education on data handling best practices. Failure to do so can result in reputational damage, financial loss, and legal repercussions. It is crucial for organizations to remain vigilant and proactive in their approach to data security to protect their customers and their business.

Companies should implement measures to mitigate these risks, such as providing regular cybersecurity training to employees, enforcing strong password policies, conducting regular software updates and security patches, and implementing policies and procedures for BYOD usage. A comprehensive cybersecurity plan should include both proactive and reactive measures to address the threats posed by unintentional threats.

Intentional threats refer to purposeful and deliberate actions taken to harm an information system's resources or disrupt its operations by exploiting vulnerabilities within an organization. These attacks are often launched by attackers with malicious intent, either for personal gratification or financial gain. Attackers utilize various tools and techniques to achieve their goals.

Cybercrime involves illegal activities or attacks that are conducted through computer networks or systems. Attackers exploit vulnerabilities in information systems, including both technical and human weaknesses, to steal valuable data or intentionally cause damage. With the growing popularity of public cloud environments, there has been a significant increase in cyberattacks targeting resources and sensitive data residing within these platforms. Many organizations are unaware that they are still responsible for the security of their data when using cloud services (Check Point Research, 2020).

As businesses invest in technologies to support remote work and enhance customer experiences, new vulnerabilities are emerging, leading to increased cyber threats. These trends inadvertently create opportunities for attackers to exploit weaknesses in systems and networks, causing significant damage to organizations. Figure 5.14 shows the various cybercrimes reported between the years 2021 and 2022 in Australia (Australian Cyber Security Centre, 2022b).

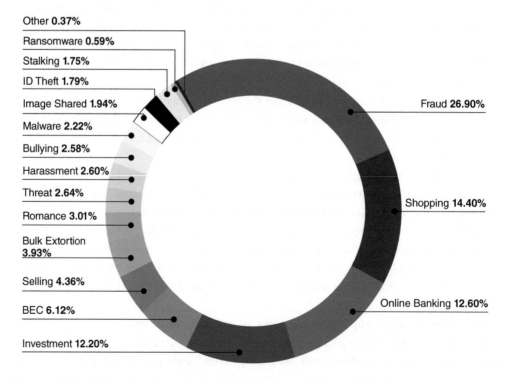

Figure 5.14 Cybercrime Reports by Type for Financial Year 2021–22

> ## Definition: Cybercrime
>
> Cybercrime involves exploiting vulnerabilities in computer networks and information systems through illegal activities or attacks, with the intention of stealing valuable data for financial gain or causing deliberate harm to property or information.

Cyber threats can range from simple theft of equipment and information to more sophisticated and malicious attacks such as cyberwarfare and cyberterrorism. Some of the common types of cyber threats include theft of equipment or information, dumpster diving, identity theft, various types of malwares such as viruses, worms, spyware, and ransomware, social engineering such as phishing and spear phishing, denial-of-service attacks, man-in-the-middle attacks, sniffing, cyber warfare, and cyberterrorism. All of these threats can cause significant harm and disruption to computer and information systems, leading to financial loss, data breaches, and compromised privacy.

Table 5.5 lists some of the most common types of cyber threats.

Table 5.5 Common Types of Cyber Threats (Australian Cyber Security Centre, n.d.-a; n.d.-b; 2018; Cisco, n.d.-a and -b; Microsoft, 2023)

Cyber Threat	Description	Example
Theft of Equipment or Information	The stealing of computing devices and storage devices to access and steal information	Stealing a laptop that contains sensitive company information
Dumpster Diving	Rummaging through trash to find discarded information	Going through a company's garbage to find sensitive documents
Identity Theft	The deliberate assumption of another person's identity to obtain personal information and financial gain	Using stolen credit card information to make unauthorized purchases
Malware	Malicious software that runs undetected in the background, causing damage and disrupting the normal use of devices	A virus that infects a computer system and corrupts important files
Virus	A rogue software program that attaches itself to other software programs or data files to be executed	A virus that spreads through email attachments and corrupts files
Worms	Independent computer programs that replicate themselves from one computer to others over a network	A worm that spreads through a vulnerability in a software program
Ransomware	A cyberattack that takes control of computers and blocks access to files, encrypted data, and folders, demanding payment in exchange for a key to unlock the data	A ransomware attack that locks up a company's important files and demands payment for access
Cryptomining Malware	Malware that uses a computer's processing power to mine cryptocurrency without the user's knowledge	Malware that slows down a computer's performance while mining cryptocurrency

(Continued)

Table 5.5   (Continued)

Cyber Threat	Description	Example
Social Engineering	The use of deception or manipulation of human errors and vulnerabilities to gain access to unauthorized information resources	Phishing emails that ask users for their login credentials to a fake website
Phishing	Deceptive action that involves setting up fake websites or sending email messages that look like those of legitimate businesses in order to ask users for confidential personal data	A phishing email that appears to be from a bank and asks for login credentials
Spear Phishing	A targeted form of phishing messages that appear to come from a trusted source, such as an individual within the recipient's own company or a friend	A spear phishing email that appears to come from a company's CEO and asks for sensitive information
Denial-of-Service Attack (DoS)	An attack that sends so many information requests to a target computer system that it ceases to function	An attacker sending a large volume of traffic to a company's website, causing it to crash
Distributed Denial-of-Service Attack (DDoS)	An attack that uses a botnet of computers to send a coordinated stream of information requests to a target computer, causing it to crash	An attacker using a botnet of compromised computers to overwhelm a company's server
Man-in-the-Middle (Spoofing) Attack	An attack that impersonates another person or redirects a web link to a different address, with the site masquerading as the intended destination	An attacker redirecting users to a fake website that looks like a legitimate one to steal sensitive information
Sniffing	An eavesdropping program that monitors information travelling over a network, enabling hackers to steal proprietary information	A sniffer that intercepts unencrypted emails and reads confidential company information
Cyberwarfare	A malicious attack launched against the IT network systems of an institution or a country to cause harm and disruption	A cyberattack against a country's power grid
Cyberterrorism	A premeditated, politically-motivated attack against computer and information systems to achieve political or ideological gains through threat or intimidation	A cyberattack against a government's computer systems to cause widespread chaos

Information Security Controls

It is crucial for organizations to prioritize and implement security measures to respond to and defend against developing threats and risks to their information and IT resources. Business and government organizations continuously collect and store valuable and sensitive information about their employees, customers, and partners, which often includes an individual's credit card, tax and financial details, medical details, address, and other contact details. Unauthorized access to this confidential information can result in the organization facing serious legal liabilities and harm the company's reputation for not taking adequate protective measures to prevent the loss of confidential information, data corruption, or privacy breaches. Thus, organizations have legal and moral obligations to protect their information assets, including their customers, employees, and business partners. To avoid data breaches and safeguard IT resources, organizations should invest in developing, implementing, and managing security policies and risk management plans.

Cybersecurity is associated with the protection of an organization's information and IT resources from security threats such as hacking, software and malware attacks, theft of intellectual property, equipment, and information theft. Organizations establish policies, plans, and control measures to ensure the security of their data, software applications, hardware, networks, and any organizational IT resources. These measures govern the design, security, and use of data and IT resources throughout the organization's information technology infrastructure. Security control measures are put in place to prevent accidental hazards, intentional threats, and early detection of problems, as well as damage recovery and problem correction plans. There are three main types of security control: physical controls, access controls, and communication controls (Figure 5.15).

Definition: Cyber Security

Cyber security involves safeguarding an organization's information and IT resources against security threats such as hacking, software and malware attacks, and the theft of intellectual property, equipment, and information.

Physical Controls	Access Controls	Network Communication Controls
• Locks • Alarm systems • ID cards and scanners • CCTV survellince	• Authemtication • Authorization	• Firewalls • Anti-malware Software • Encryptions & Virtual private networks (VPNS) • Network Access Controls

Figure 5.15   Types of Security Controls

Physical security controls

Physical security controls are critical in safeguarding IT systems and preventing unauthorized access to a company's physical IT assets, facilities, and resources. These controls protect against various threats, including human-generated risks, accidental damage, and natural disasters. Human-generated risks can come from insiders or outsiders attempting to gain access to restricted areas. Accidental damage can occur from electrical surges, extreme temperatures, or even spilled coffee. Natural disasters such as floods or earthquakes can also cause significant damage to IT systems and equipment.

Physical security controls are put in place to secure the physical environment. These controls include physical barriers such as walls, doors, fencing, gates, and locks, which restrict access to sensitive areas. Alarm systems such as motion detectors are also utilized to detect physical intrusion, alerting security personnel to potential breaches. Identification badges for authorized personnel, ID card scanners, and near-field communication (NFC) ID cards are used to verify individuals' right to access facilities, preventing unauthorized entry.

Closed-circuit television (CCTV) cameras are also essential physical security controls used for surveillance. These cameras provide a visual record of activities within the premises and can deter potential intruders. They can also be used to identify individuals who have gained unauthorized access and assist in investigations.

Access controls

Access controls are employed to regulate access to IT resources and prevent unauthorized individuals from gaining access to information resources. The two crucial components of access controls are authentication and authorization. **Authentication** is the process of confirming a user's identity, while **authorization** determines the user's access rights once their identity has been verified.

For example, when you log on to your bank account online, you are asked for your login and password details. If you use a new device to log on to your online account, the bank will ask for further verification by sending a confirmation code to your phone or email account. You then enter the confirmation code before you can log in to your account. In this case, there are three authentication factors: login information (username and password), device, and phone number or email address. Even if one piece of the evidence fails, there are still other hurdles to overcome. For example, if a user's computer password is stolen, the perpetrator will still need further information to obtain access to the account. Similarly, if you have turned on multifactor authentication (MFA) for your Google account, you will need both your password and an additional authentication method to log in to your Google account. This could be a security code from an authenticator app, SMS, or phone call. Alternatively, you could receive a notification via the Google app on your smartphone (Australian Cyber Security Centre, 2020a; 2020b).

Multifactor authentication (MFA) creates a multi-layered protection system to ensure that only authorized individuals can access information systems. MFA is becoming increasingly popular and requires users to provide multiple pieces of evidence, such as a passcode, ID card, or fingerprint, to confirm their identity.

After verifying a user's identity, the authorization process determines the user's access rights based on their role in the organization. Access rights specify the information and IT resources that a user is allowed to access and what they can do with those resources. Access rights are granted and monitored by the organization. Access rights are often granted on a need-to-know basis, meaning employees only have access to the information necessary to perform their job duties. This helps to minimize the risk of unauthorized access and data breaches. The organization may also have policies requiring employees to protect sensitive information and report suspicious activity.

In addition to implementing technical security measures, organizations may also establish policies and procedures to ensure that their employees are aware of the importance of maintaining the security and confidentiality of sensitive information and report any suspicious activity. These policies could include circulating guidelines on the handling of confidential data, password management, and reporting procedures in the event of a security breach or suspected breach, as well as training employees on best practices for protecting sensitive data and providing guidance on how to identify potential security threats.

Moreover, these policies can help to establish a culture of security within the organization. When employees understand that security is a priority for the organization, they are more likely to take responsibility for safeguarding sensitive information and reporting suspicious activity. This can help mitigate the risk of security breaches and minimize the potential impact of any security incidents.

Example: Authentication and Authorization

Let's say you work for a large e-commerce company that handles sensitive customer information such as credit card details, shipping addresses, and purchase history. As a responsible business, your company takes the security of this information seriously and implements strict access controls to ensure that only authorized individuals can access it.

Authentication is a crucial component of this security strategy. When you log in to your company's database, you are required to provide your username and password to verify your identity. Additionally, the company may require you to use multifactor authentication, such as a one-time passcode or fingerprint scan, to provide an extra layer of security.

Once your identity has been authenticated, the authorization process determines what data you are allowed to access based on your job role and responsibilities. For example, if you are part of the customer service team, you may be authorized to view customer records and shipping addresses. However, you may not be authorized to access sensitive information such as credit card numbers or purchase history.

Access rights are often granted on a need-to-know basis, which means that you are only given access to the information necessary to perform your job duties. This helps to minimize the risk of unauthorized access and data breaches.

By implementing strong authentication and authorization controls, your company can protect sensitive customer information from unauthorized access, which can lead to costly data breaches and damage to the company's reputation.

Network communication controls

Network communication controls are essential measures that organizations implement to ensure the security and accessibility of their computer networks and data. These controls include a variety of tools such as firewalls, anti-malware software, encryption, virtual private networks (VPNs), and network access controls (Cisco, n.d.-b).

A **firewall** is a network security system that serves as a protective barrier between an organization's trusted internal network and the untrusted external network such as the

Internet. It monitors and controls the data flow in and out of the network, using a set of predefined rules to allow or block traffic into the internal network. In addition to traffic filtering, firewalls also offer intrusion detection and prevention, as well as malware detection capabilities.

Anti-malware software is another critical tool organizations use to protect themselves from various malicious software types such as computer viruses, worms, spyware, and ransomware. This software can scan the system regularly to detect any signs of malicious activity, and it can also prevent infections from spreading further by isolating infected devices from the rest of the network. Suppose, for example, that an employee clicks on a malicious link in an email that introduces a virus into the organization's network. In that case, anti-malware software can detect and contain the infection before it spreads to other devices on the network.

Encryption and **virtual private networks (VPNs)** are technologies that provide secure communication links for users/devices over the public Internet. VPNs utilize security protocols such as IPsec or SSL/TLS to authenticate users/devices and establish encrypted communication channels. This ensures that the transmitted data is protected from unauthorized access or interception by hackers. For example, imagine you're working from home and need to access sensitive data stored on your company's server. By connecting to the company's VPN, your device will be authenticated and data transmitted between your device and the server will be encrypted, making it much more difficult for anyone to intercept or eavesdrop on your communication.

Network access control is another important security measure that helps to limit access to network resources by implementing policies and procedures to authenticate and authorize users/devices. This can include processes such as user authentication, device registration, and network segmentation.

Blockchain technology, which will be discussed in detail in Chapter 11, is gaining popularity as an alternative approach to secure transactions and establish trust among multiple parties. It uses cryptography to secure the records in a distributed ledger, and once a transaction is recorded, it cannot be altered. This makes blockchain a tamper-proof and secure way to conduct transactions without the need for intermediaries or centralized authorities.

Stop and Reflect: Under information security

When the COVID-19 pandemic hit, businesses were forced to accelerate their digital transformation and there was increase in remote working which often necessitated access to company's data. Companies were unprepared to completely secure the potential vulnerabilities in their systems arising from new business and work environments. Malicious perpetrators took advantage of these vulnerabilities to attack businesses. One security approach is the Zero Trust security strategy that continuously verifies and validates every staff member and device trying to access their network.

- Research the strategies that a zero-trust network model uses and how it can help to secure organizations' information resources.

Organizational Strategies for Protecting Information Resources

Nowadays, the reliance of organizations on their IT infrastructures for daily operations is high. However, with the increasing sophistication and frequency of cyberattacks in the evolving digital economy, protecting information and IT resources has become challenging. Consequently, organizations must develop and manage effective cybersecurity strategies and risk management plans to prevent data breaches, safeguard IT resources, and ensure the backup or continuity of operations in the event of security attacks or potential disasters.

In the digital economy, cyber resilience and security are fundamental to all organizations. **Cyber resilience** is the ability of an organization's IT systems to adapt to disruptions caused by cyberattacks while maintaining uninterrupted business operations. This includes detecting, managing, and recovering from incidents (Australian Securities and Investments Commission (ASIC), n.d.).

To safeguard their IT assets and resources from security risks, organizations must conduct risk assessments and then implement risk mitigation strategies to protect them from potential threats. **Cybersecurity risk** refers to the probability of IT resources and system vulnerabilities being exposed to cyber threats and being negatively affected by those threats.

The process of **cyber security risk management (CSRM)** involves identifying, assessing, and prioritizing current and potential risks, and implementing strategies to minimize the impact of attacks and reduce the risks to acceptable levels. This enables organizations to address vulnerabilities that expose them to risks, and to monitor risk control and financial resources to minimize any adverse effects of loss.

However, before investing in organization-wide security controls, it is important to perform a risk assessment to determine the vulnerabilities in IT assets and the level of protection needed. For instance, a financial institution that offers online banking services may conduct a risk assessment to identify potential security risks associated with their online banking systems. Based on the results of the assessment, the institution may implement strategies such as two-factor authentication and regular system updates to protect their customers' sensitive information.

Risk assessment is critical for identifying, analysing, and prioritizing IT security risks. Risk assessment involves gathering and evaluating risk information to enable the organization to adopt risk mitigation strategies (Liu et al., 2009).

Cyber security risk assessment involves two main tasks: analysis and evaluation. *Risk assessment analysis* involves identifying threats and estimating associated risks using available information, while *risk assessment evaluation* involves comparing the estimate against a set of criteria to determine the risk's significance and impact (Liu et al., 2009).

The following are the key elements of risk assessment as described by Liu et al. (2009):

1 **Identify at-risk assets:** The first step in risk assessment is to identify the most critical assets that could be affected should a threat materialize. This involves ranking the value, sensitivity, and criticality of the business's operations and assets. By doing so, it helps determine which operations and assets are the most important and need to be protected.

2 **Identify potential threats**: Once the at-risk assets are identified, the next step is to identify potential threats that could harm them. These threats could include intruders, criminals, disgruntled employees, terrorists, and natural disasters. It is important to identify all possible threats to assess the risk associated with each of them.

3 **Estimate the possibility:** The likelihood that a threat will materialize needs to be estimated based on historical information and expert judgment. Knowledgeable individuals in the organization or hired consultants can provide valuable insights into the likelihood of a threat materializing.

4 **Determine the impact:** The potential losses or damage that could occur if a threat materializes need to be determined. This includes not only direct financial losses but also indirect losses such as reputation damage and recovery costs.

5 **Develop mitigation options:** Once the risks have been identified and assessed, cost-effective actions need to be identified to mitigate or reduce the risk. This can include implementing new organizational policies and procedures as well as technical or physical controls.

6 **Document the results and develop an action plan:** After conducting the analysis, the results need to be documented, and an action plan developed. A 'lessons learned' summary can help put priorities into perspective and provide insights into future risk assessments.

Organizations can use the outcomes of risk assessments to develop effective strategies for mitigating risks and ensuring cyber-security resilience. **Risk mitigation** refers to the implementation of security policies, processes, and controls aimed at reducing the impact of cybersecurity threats, as well as developing plans to recover from these threats if they occur.

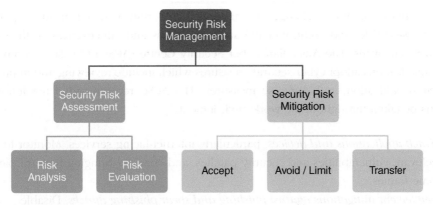

Figure 5.16 Risk Management Strategies

In essence, risk mitigation involves taking steps to prevent or minimize identified threats and developing a contingency plan for responding to such threats. There are three main strategies that organizations can use to mitigate risks:

1 **Risk acceptance:** This strategy involves accepting the potential risk, continuing to operate without implementing any controls, and absorbing any damages that may occur as a result of the risk. For instance, a company may choose to accept the risk of a data breach if the cost of implementing security controls outweighs the potential loss from the breach.

2 **Risk limitation or prevention:** This strategy aims to limit or prevent the risk by implementing controls that minimize the impact of the threat. For example, an organization may implement firewalls, antivirus software, or access controls to reduce the risk of a cyberattack.

3 **Risk transference:** This strategy involves transferring the risk to another entity, such as an insurance provider. Organizations can purchase insurance policies that cover the potential losses associated with cybersecurity threats, effectively transferring the risk to the insurance provider.

Definition: Cyber Security Risk Management

Cyber Security Risk Management is a process that involves the identification, assessment and prioritization of current and potential risks, as well as implementing strategies to minimize the impact of risks and possibly reduce them to acceptable levels.

Because risks and threats change over time, it is important that organizations periodically reassess risks and reconsider the appropriateness and effectiveness of their mitigation mechanisms. The Australian Cyber Security Centre (ACSC) (2022a) recommends that organizations adopt cyber security measures which include reviewing and improving detection, mitigation, and response measures. The ACSC recommended the following actions be taken throughout the work environment:

1   *Patch applications and devices*, particularly internet-facing services. Monitor for relevant vulnerabilities and security patches, and consider bringing forward patch time frames.
2   *Implement mitigations against phishing and spear phishing attacks*. Disable Microsoft Office macros by default and limit user privileges. Ensure that staff report all suspicious emails received, links clicked, or documents opened.
3   *Ensure that logging and detection systems are fully updated and functioning*. Prioritize internet-facing and critical network services, and ensure that logs are centrally stored.
4   *Review incident response and business continuity plans*. Plan responses to network compromise as well as disruptive or destructive activity such as ransomware. Ensure that these plans are known to and actionable by staff, and are accessible even when systems are down. (Australian Cyber Security Centre (ACSC), 2022a).

Example: The SolarWinds Hack

In December 2020, SolarWinds, a Texas-based software company that provides IT management services to over 425 companies in the US Fortune 500, was compromised in a sophisticated supply chain attack. The attackers gained access to SolarWinds' software build system and inserted a malicious code into an update for its Orion product. This code was then signed with SolarWinds' own digital certificate, making it appear legitimate and trustworthy to its customers. As a result, thousands of SolarWinds customers unknowingly downloaded the compromised update, which allowed the attackers to gain unauthorized access to their networks.

The SolarWinds hack was a serious threat to information resources and information security controls. The attackers were able to access and exfiltrate data, move laterally across networks, and establish backdoors for continued access. The hack exposed vulnerabilities in many organizations' IT infrastructure, highlighting the importance of strong supply chain security measures. The compromised data included sensitive information such as financial data, intellectual property, and government secrets. The attackers were able to maintain their access to the compromised networks for an extended period of time, giving them ample opportunity to move laterally and exfiltrate data.

In the aftermath of the hack, SolarWinds representatives claimed that the password "solarwinds123," was discovered in 2019 by an independent security researcher on the Internet, and this leak had exposed a SolarWinds file server.. US lawmakers criticized SolarWinds for the password issue in a joint hearing. SolarWinds is investigating three possible avenues of attack, including stolen credentials, brute-force password guessing, and third-party software compromise. The former CEO blamed an intern for the password issue but neither he nor the current CEO explained why such weak passwords were allowed in the first place.

The SolarWinds hack served as a wake-up call for many organizations, highlighting the need for robust supply chain security measures and stronger information security controls. In response to the attack, SolarWinds released a hotfix that removed the malicious code from the Orion product, and the company has been working to improve its security measures to prevent future attacks. Many organizations affected by the SolarWinds hack have also taken steps to improve their own security measures. The threat of future attacks remains a concern, and it is critical that organizations remain vigilant and proactive in their approach to cybersecurity. (Compiled from: B. Fung. and G. Sands (2021, February 26), 'Former SolarWinds CEO blames intern for "solarwinds123" password leak', CNN, https://edition.cnn.com/2021/02/26/politics/solarwinds123-password-intern/index.html; J. Tidy (2020, December 16), 'SolarWinds: why the sunburst hack is so serious', BBC News, https://www.bbc.com/news/technology-55321643; B. Fung (2020, December 16), 'Why the US government hack is literally keeping security experts awake at night', CNN, https://edition.cnn.com/2020/12/16/tech/solarwinds-orion-hack-explained/index.html)

Question

What are the key takeaways from the SolarWinds hack and what measures can organizations take to prevent similar attacks in the future?

One of the most critical elements of any security system is having a business continuity plan and a disaster recovery plan. The aim of a **business continuity plan** is to restore normal business operations as quickly as possible following an attack, and to ensure that critical business operations continue after a disaster occurs. Employees use this plan to prepare for, respond to, and recover from events that affect the security of information assets. The focus of a business continuity plan is on maintaining business functions or restoring them quickly when there has been a major disruption to business processes, assets, human resources, business partners, and more.

Disaster recovery planning devises plans for the restoration of disrupted computing and communications services. **Disaster recovery plans** focus primarily on the technical issues involved in keeping systems up and running, such as which files to back up and the maintenance of backup computer systems or disaster recovery services.

To ensure business continuity, it is essential for organizations to have an off-site recovery site in case of a major disaster and this should be a key element of any disaster recovery plan. These off-site recovery locations can help recover data, prevent further data loss, and ensure the continuity of critical business operations. Three types of off-site recovery sites are hot sites, warm sites, and cold sites.

A *hot site* is a fully-functional site, configured with all the necessary equipment, including office space, furniture, communications capabilities and computer equipment, which enables immediate recovery from a disaster. It also includes staffing to manage and monitor the equipment. For example, a financial institution might have a hot site that is fully equipped with computers, servers, and backup power systems, and is staffed with trained personnel who can immediately take over operations if the main site is hit by a disaster, such as a hurricane or earthquake. The hot site will have the same technology and resources as the primary site, so that the transition is as seamless as possible.

A *warm site* provides a fully equipped physical data centre, but it has no customer data. The warm site is a less expensive option than the hot site and is typically used when primary data centres are attacked. After a disruption at the primary data centre, an organization introduces its own customer data to restore normal business operations. A warm site takes longer to deploy than a hot site, but less time than a cold site. For example, a hospital might have a warm site that is equipped with the necessary hardware and software, but does not have any patient data. In case of an emergency, the hospital can quickly transfer its data to the warm site and continue operations. This is a more cost-effective option compared to a hot site, as it does not require constant maintenance and monitoring.

A *cold site* provides office space but requires the customer to provide and install the equipment needed to continue operations. It is the least expensive option, but it takes longer to get an organization back up to full operation. A cold site is a good option when the time to recovery is not critical. For example, a small business might have a cold site that provides office space and utilities, but does not have any hardware or software in place. If the main site experiences a disruption, the business can move its operations to the cold site and install the necessary equipment to resume operations. While it takes longer to get back up to full operation, a cold site is a good option for businesses that cannot afford the expense of a hot or warm site.

Companies can build their own disaster recovery sites, which can be expensive, or they can engage the services of a third-party commercial disaster recovery company to protect them against major business disruptions. Hot sites reduce risk to the greatest extent, but they are the most expensive option. Conversely, cold sites are the least effective in reducing risk, but they are the cheapest option.

Stop and Reflect: Cyber Security

Cyber Security is not just an IT problem; it is also a business issue.

●   Do you agree? Give reasons for your answer.

5.8 Chapter Summary

This chapter provides an overview of computer networks, including a discussion of their components, types, and communication media. Additionally, it examines the significance of computer networks and the Internet in facilitating communication and collaboration in business. The advancements in Internet technologies have allowed businesses to expand their reach and access new markets through e-commerce and digital marketing. They have also provided businesses with access to a wealth of information and resources, which has empowered them to make informed decisions and gain a competitive advantage.

However, the increasing complexity and frequency of cyber threats require the implementation of appropriate security measures to safeguard information resources. The latter part of this chapter focuses on the significant threats to information resources within an organization and outlines security controls that can be implemented to mitigate risks. It highlights the importance of cyber security risk management as a process for identifying, assessing, and minimizing risks to information resources. Staying current with the latest security technologies and practices is critical for organizations to protect their information resources from potential cyberattacks.

Discussion Questions

(Suggested answers are provided in the teaching guide.)

1   Describe the functions of a company's computer network and Internet connectivity.
2   How does Internet technology support communication and collaboration in education?
3   The terms World Wide Web (WWW), commonly known as the Web, and Internet, are often used interchangeably. What is the difference between the Internet and WWW? How are the Internet, intranet and extranet related to each other?
4   Explain the impact that communication network applications have had on business and everyday life. Describe how communication technologies and applications have transformed today's workplaces.
5   Define social engineering. Describe two ways in which social engineering could be used to obtain a user's credentials in order to gain access to an account or network.
6   Discuss how social networks and cloud computing increase IT security risks. How can these risks be minimized?
7   Why are employees the biggest threats to an organization? What can be done to protect a company's assets?

Case Study: Light Fidelity (Li-Fi)

Compiled by the author based on information from Dale Walker (July 2021), 'What is Li-Fi?', https://www.itpro.co.uk/network-internet/33293/what-is-li-fi; LiFi.co (2022) https://lifi.co/lifi-vs-wifi/; Closing the digital divide (The University of Edinburgh, 2018)

One of the emerging wireless communications technologies is Light Fidelity (Li-Fi). Unlike Wi-Fi which uses radio waves for data transmission, Li-Fi uses light to transmit and receive data. Professor Harald Haas from the University of Edinburgh, UK, first demonstrated the Li-Fi concept at a TED presentation in 2011 (Walker, 2021). Li-Fi uses light-emitting diodes (LEDs) that are present in homes and offices for data transmission using the LEDs as wireless routers. Thus, LED lights can be used to both light a space and transmit and receive data (LiFi.co, 2022).

While Wi-Fi technology enabled users to connect to the Internet and other devices from anywhere, it does have some shortcomings. It is inherently slower than wired connections, and its radio signals are susceptible to external interferences causing a variety of connection problems such as weak signals, poor reception, or even loss of connection, making Wi-Fi signals unreliable. In addition, since radio waves can penetrate walls, Wi-Fi is vulnerable to hackers.

Li-Fi, which uses visible light for transmission, offers several advantages over Wi-Fi, two being its availability and efficiency. Since homes and offices already have LED bulbs for lighting purposes, the same source of light can be used to transmit data. Moreover, there is no need for a router, making Li-Fi energy-efficient and cost-effective. Since, Li-Fi signals cannot pass through walls, they cannot be accessed or hacked by users from outside the room, thus enhancing security. Li-Fi is more effective in areas susceptible to electromagnetic interference, such as aircraft cabins and hospitals.

Li-Fi will not replace Wi-Fi, 5G, or 6G, although it has the potential to provide Internet connectivity to areas with poor or restricted Internet access, thereby helping to reduce the digital divide. Professor Haas noted that 'LiFi data communication can be built around existing infrastructures, with ordinary solar panels doubling up as LiFi receivers. With effective long-distance data transmission possible using lasers and self-powered relay stations, LiFi will enable affordable high-bandwidth internet access, particularly in remote and resource poor areas' (The University of Edinburgh, 2008; Haas, n.d.).

Two villages in Gujarat, India, became India's first smart villages with LiFi-based Internet connectivity, schools, hospitals, post offices, and government offices. These two villages will have faster and safer Internet connection through existing electricity lines (Smart Cities Council, 2021). Similarly, around 80 villages on the Ivory Coast, Africa, are equipped with solar energy systems that give rural areas access to economical and sustainable lighting and Internet connection using Li-Fi (Light Fidelity).

References

Diallo, B. (2018). LIFILED: Internet in Africa thanks to the light. *AfrikaTech*. https://www.afrikatech.com/start-business/lifiled-internet-in-africa-thanks-to-the-light/

Haas, H. (n.d.). Closing the digital divide with LiFi. https://youtu.be/adrLYxXUM5c

LiFi.co (2022). LiFi vs WiFi. https://lifi.co/lifi-vs-wifi/

Smart Cities Council (2021). Creating smart villages: Ahmedabad startup powers 2 villages with LiFi tech. https://www.smartcitiescouncil.com/article/creating-smart-villages-ahmedabad-startup-powers-2-villages-lifi-tech

The University of Edinburgh (2018). Closing the digital divide. https://www.ed.ac.uk/edinburgh-friends/supplements/closing-digital-divide

Questions

1 List and describe the possible applications of Li-Fi.
2 What are the limitations of Li-FI?
3 Discuss how Li-Fi technology could be used to support SDG goals.

(Refer to the teaching guide for suggested answers.)

5.9 References

Australian Cyber Security Centre. (ACSC). (n.d.-a). Threats. Cyber.gov.au. https://www.cyber.gov.au/taxonomy/term/5

Australian Cyber Security Centre. (ACSC). (n.d.-b). Watch out for threats. Cyber.gov.au. https://www.cyber.gov.au/learn/threats

Australian Cyber Security Centre. (ACSC). (n.d.-c) Common cyber threats. Retrieved from https://www.asd.gov.au/cyber-security

Australian Cyber Security Centre. (2012, November 1). Bring your own device for executives. Cyber.gov.au. https://www.cyber.gov.au/resources-business-and-government/maintaining-devices-and-systems/remote-working-and-secure-mobility/secure-mobility/bring-your-own-device-executives

Australian Cyber Security Centre (ACSC). (2022a) Australian organisations encouraged to urgently adopt an enhanced cyber security posture. Cyber.gov.au. www.cyber.gov.au. https://www.cyber.gov.au/about-us/alerts/australian-organisations-encouraged-urgently-adopt-enhanced-cyber-security-posture

Australian Cyber Security Centre. (2018). Cryptomining. Cyber.gov.au. https://www.cyber.gov.au/threats/type-threats/system-and-network-attacks/cryptomining

Australian Cyber Security Centre. (2020a). Multi-factor authentication. Cyber.gov.au. https://www.cyber.gov.au/protect-yourself/securing-your-accounts/multi-factor-authentication

Australian Cyber Security Centre. (2020b). Securing Google accounts. Cyber.gov.au. https://www.cyber.gov.au/sites/default/files/2023-03/Step-by-Step-Guide-Email-account-security-Gmail.pdf

Australian Cyber Security Centre. (2021). *ACSC Annual Cyber Threat Report, July 2020 to June 2021*. Cyber.gov.au. https://www.cyber.gov.au/about-us/reports-and-statistics/acsc-annual-cyber-threat-report-july-2020-june-2021

Australian Cyber Security Centre. (ACSC). (2022a). *ACSC Annual Cyber Threat Report, July 2021 to June 2022*. Cyber.gov.au. ACSC. https://www.cyber.gov.au/about-us/reports-and-statistics/acsc-annual-cyber-threat-report-july-2021-june-2022

Australian Cyber Security Centre (ACSC). (2022b, April 28). Australian organisations encouraged to urgently adopt an enhanced cyber security posture. Cyber.gov.au. https://www.cyber.gov.au/about-us/alerts/australian-organisations-encouraged-urgently-adopt-enhanced-cyber-security-posture

Australian Securities and Investments Commission (ASIC). (n.d.). Cyber resilience. Asic.gov.au. https://asic.gov.au/regulatory-resources/digital-transformation/cyber-resilience/

Bailey, T., Kolo, B., Rajagopalan, K., & Ware, D. (2018, September 24). Insider threat: The human element of cyberrisk. McKinsey. https://www.mckinsey.com/capabilities/risk-and-resilience/our-insights/insider-threat-the-human-element-of-cyberrisk

Bieg, M. (2007a) Peer to Peer processing. https://commons.wikimedia.org/w/index.php?curid=2551723

Bieg, M. (2007b) Client-server processing. https://commons.wikimedia.org/w/index.php?curid=2551745

Biron, B. (2022, May 2). At least 200 unemployed New Yorkers had their personal information leaked by the Department of Labor as a result of an 'unacceptable' printing error. *Business Insider*. https://www.businessinsider.com/at-least-200-unemployed-new-yorkers-had-personal-information-leaked-2020-5

Borgini, J. (2022, 29 March). Top advantages and disadvantages of IoT in business. https://www.techtarget.com/iotagenda/tip/Top-advantages-and-disadvantages-of-IoT-in-business

Brous, P., Janssen, M., & Herder, P. (2020). The dual effects of the Internet of Things (IoT): a systematic review of the benefits and risks of IoT adoption by

Check Point Research. (2020). *Cyber Security Report 2020*. Check Point Software Technologies Ltd. https://www.ntsc.org/assets/pdfs/cyber-security-report-2020.pdf

Cisco. (n.d.-a). What are the most common cyber attacks? Cisco. https://www.cisco.com/c/en_au/products/security/common-cyberattacks.html

Cisco. (n.d.-b). What is network security? Cisco. https://www.cisco.com/c/en_au/products/security/what-is-network-security.html

Cisco. (2023). SD-WAN – software-defined WAN. Cisco. https://www.cisco.com/c/en_au/solutions/enterprise-networks/sd-wan/index.html

CISOMAG. (2019, October 11). Security bug exposes personal data of 156 million JustDial users. *CISOMAG: Cyber Security Magazine*. https://cisomag.com/security-bug-exposes-personal-data-of-156-million-justdial-users/

Deloitte Insights, *Deloitte's 2021 Global Blockchain Survey: A New Age of Digital Assets*. Retrieved from https://www2.deloitte.com/xe/en/insights/topics/understanding-blockchain-potential/global-blockchain-survey.html

Dignan, L. (2011, March 10). Tokyo earthquake, tsunami puts data centers, cloud services at risk. *ZDNET*. https://www.zdnet.com/article/tokyo-earthquake-tsunami-puts-data-centers-cloud-services-at-risk/

Eversley, M. (2013, December 19). Target confirms massive credit-card data breach. *USA Today*. https://www.usatoday.com/story/news/nation/2013/12/18/secret-service-target-data-breach/4119337/

Fung, B. (2020, December 16). Why the US government hack is literally keeping security experts awake at night. CNN. https://edition.cnn.com/2020/12/16/tech/solarwinds-orion-hack-explained/index.html

Fung, B. and Sands, G. (2021, February 26). Former SolarWinds CEO blames intern for 'solarwinds123' password leak. CNN. https://edition.cnn.com/2021/02/26/politics/solarwinds123-password-intern/index.html

Geroni, D. (2021). Top 5 benefits of blockchain. Retrieved from https://101blockchains.com/benefits-of-blockchain-technology/

IBM. (2015, August). IBM Food Trust. Retrieved from https://www.ibm.com/au-en/products/supply-chain-intelligence suite/food trust

IBM. (2020a). What is networking? *The Fundamentals of Networking*. https://www.ibm.com/topics/networking

IBM. (2020b, November). IBM Food Trust: A new era in the world's food supply. https://www.ibm.com/blockchain/solutions/food-trust

IBM. (2022a). What is blockchain technology? Retrieved from https://www.ibm.com/topics/what-is-blockchain

IBM. (2022b). What is IoT? Retrieved from https://www.oracle.com/au/internet-of-things/what-is-iot/#technologies-iot-

IBM Cloud Education. (2021a, 17 March). Networking. https://www.ibm.com/cloud/learn/networking-a-complete-guide

IBM Cloud Education. (2021b, April 15). What is Software-Defined Networking (SDN)? https://www.ibm.com/cloud/blog/software-defined-networking

IBM Cloud Education (2022, April). 'What is networking?' https://www.ibm.com/cloud/learn/networking-a-complete-guide

Isidore, C. (2014, January 10). Target: Hacking hit up to 110 million customers. CNNMoney. https://money.cnn.com/2014/01/10/news/companies/target-hacking/

Jouini, M., Rabai, L. B. A., & Aissa, A. B. (2014). Classification of security threats in information systems. *Procedia Computer Science*, *32*(2014), 489–496. https://doi.org/10.1016/j.procs.2014.05.452

Kreutz, D., Ramos, F. M. V., Veríssimo, P. E., Rothenberg, C. E., Azodolmolky, S., & Uhlig, S. (2015). Software-defined networking: A comprehensive survey. *Proceedings of the IEEE*, *103*(1), 14–76. doi:10.1109/JPROC.2014.2371999.

Larson, S. (2017, May 12). Massive cyberattack targeting 99 countries causes sweeping havoc. CNNMoney. https://money.cnn.com/2017/05/12/technology/ransomware-attack-nsa-microsoft/

Liu, S., Kuhn, R., & Rossman, H. (2009). Understanding insecure IT: Practical risk assessment, *IT Professional*, *11*(3), 57–59, doi: 10.1109/MITP.2009.62.productivity

Niccolai, J. (2011, June 30). How Japan's data centers survived the earthquake. *Computerworld*. https://www.computerworld.com/article/2741389/how-japan-s-data-centers-survived-the-earthquake.html

Perlroth, N. (2017, October 3). All 3 billion Yahoo accounts were affected by 2013 attack. *The New York Times*. https://www.nytimes.com/2017/10/03/technology/yahoo-hack-3-billion-users.html

Romm, T., & Dwoskin, E. (2019, April 3). Millions of sensitive Facebook user records were left exposed on public web, security researchers say. *Washington Post*. https://www.washingtonpost.com/technology/2019/04/03/millions-sensitive-facebook-user-records-were-left-exposed-public-web-security-researchers-say/

Strickland, J. (2008, March 3). Who owns the Internet? *HowStuffWorks*. https://computer.howstuffworks.com/internet/basics/who-owns-internet.htm

The University of Edinburgh. (2018). Closing the digital divide https://www.ed.ac.uk/edinburgh-friends/supplements/closing-digital-divide

Tidy, J. (2020, December 16). SolarWinds: Why the Sunburst hack is so serious. BBC News. https://www.bbc.com/news/technology-55321643insights/insider-threat-the-human-element-of-cyberrisk.

Verizon. (2022a). *2022 Data Breach Investigations Report*. Verizon Business. http://www.verizonenterprise.com/verizon-insights-lab/dbir/

Verizon. (2022b). What is bandwidth? Definition, meaning & explanation. *Verizon*. https://www.verizon.com/info/definitions/bandwidth/

Walker, D. (2021). What is Li-Fi? https://www.itpro.co.uk/network-internet/33293/what-is-li-fi

Wikipedia. (2022). List of Internet organizations. https://en.wikipedia.org/wiki/List_of_Internet_organizations

6

MOBILE TECHNOLOGIES

6.1 Learning Outcomes

After reading this chapter, you will be able to

- Describe the features of the different mobile standards
- Identify and understand the different mobile wireless networks
- Describe wireless communication technologies
- Explain the role and application of mobile technologies in commerce
- Explain the challenges associated with mobile technologies and how these can be mitigated

6.2 Introduction

This chapter provides an overview of mobile technologies, discusses the history of mobile phones, and traces the evolution of mobile standards or network generations. The chapter describes several wireless networks and discusses the application of mobile computing as well as the challenges associated with mobile technologies.

Mobile technologies have come a long way in the last 50 years. The first handheld cellular mobile phone was demonstrated in 1973 by John F. Mitchell and Martin Cooper, with the handset weighing 2 kilograms (Anjarwalla, 2010). Over the years, mobile technologies have become ubiquitous and have gone beyond being units for verbal and text communication only. Mobile technologies have various capabilities and functionalities that are fast expanding, with applications becoming increasingly broad over time. However, although mobile technologies offer several benefits, there are security concerns associated with these technologies, with the portability of these technologies making them more vulnerable to security breaches.

6.3 Cellular or Mobile Network

Definitions

Cell Tower

Also known as a cell site, this has electronic equipment such as antennas transmitters, receivers and amplifiers that receive signals to and from wireless communication devices like cell phones and radios.

Cellular Channel

A cellular channel is a specific frequency band that is allocated for communication between a mobile device and a base station. Each channel is a portion of the overall radio frequency spectrum.

Mobile or cellular phones enable communication via a cellular network. A cellular network is a radio network made up of a number of radio cells, each served by a fixed transceiver known as a base station (Farley, 2005). The use of numerous cells means that when a mobile device moves from one cell to another, it communicates with different base stations. Each cell is served by at least one fixed-location transceiver (typically three cell sites or base transceiver stations). The base stations provide each cell with network coverage, which can be used for the transmission of data, voice and other types of content (Miao et al., 2016). In a cellular network, each cell uses a different set of frequencies from neighbouring cells to avoid interference and provide guaranteed bandwidth in each cell.

Currently mobile phone networks rely on a terrestrial connection. In each network each cell has its own tower, each tower is equipped with antennas and other electronic equipment which transmits and receives signals to and from mobile devices within that cell. A cellular channel is a specific frequency band that is allocated for communication between a mobile device and a base station. Each channel is a portion of the overall radio frequency spectrum.

6.4 Satellite Technology

Satellite technology plays a critical role in mobile infrastructure. In remote locations, beyond the reach of terrestrial cell towers, there is no reception. Satellites solve that problem by removing the need for a terrestrial connection (Hall, 2022). There are plans to use SpaceX's Starlink constellation of satellites in collaboration with T-Mobile to provide near complete coverage even in the most remote locations in the USA, which could solve the problem of over half a million square miles of the US that are completely unreachable by cellular signals from any provider (Baker, 2022). While satellite phones are already available and expensive they are designed for working in remote areas with no consumer features. Other companies that may be involved in powering the satellite technology include Globalstar for Apple's system and Snapdagon Satellite, which is likely to be a dominant player for Android devices (Hall, 2022).

6.5 History of Mobile Phones

The cellular concept emerged in 1947 when D. H. Ring wrote an internal technical memorandum in his capacity as a technician for Bell Labs, suggesting that the re-use of frequencies could improve call quality and network capacity. Moving from theory to technological implementation was somewhat slow, with the communications industry not supporting cellular research until the 1970s (Jessop, 2006). The first generation networks were in operation in developed countries in the 1980s (Huurdeman, 2003), with Japan leading the way in 1979 and Australia having a delayed launch in 1987. Table 6.1 lists the years when first generation networks were introduced in developed countries.

Table 6.1   Older Mobile Phones before 2002

Country	Introduction of First Commercial Analogue Network
Japan	1979
Germany	1981
Scandinavia*	1981
South Africa	1981
Spain	1982
United States	1983
Austria	1984
Britain	1985
Italy	1985
France	1985
Australia	1987

Note: *Scandinavia includes Sweden, Denmark, Norway, and Finland

The 1990s saw mobile phones become widely available, with the 2000s seeing advanced features such as cameras and Internet access. Mobile phones are now an integral part of life, used for communication and also perceived as a vital business tool.

6.6 The Evolution of Mobile Standards

Over the last five decades, mobile wireless technologies have experienced five generations of technological revolution and evolution. Mobile technologies continue to evolve with the aim of improving performance and efficiency to address the demands of increased communication. A mobile technology generation refers to a change in the nature of the system, in terms of speed, technology, and frequency, with each generation having specific capacities, techniques, and applications.

Definitions

Frequency Division Multiple Access (FDMA)

FDMA is the process of dividing one channel or bandwidth into multiple individual bands, each for use by a single user. Therefore, the channel is closed to other conversations until the initial call is finished, or until it is handed off to a different channel.

Time Division Multiple Access (TDMA)

TDMA is a digital technique that divides a single channel or band into time slots. Each time slot is used to transmit one byte or another digital segment of each signal in sequential serial data format.

Code Division Multiple Access (CDMA)

CDMA is a channel-access method or multiple-access method which allows more than two terminals connected to the same transmission medium to transmit over it and share its capacity. CDMA uses a spread spectrum technique to transmit data, and the technology allows several phones to send and receive data through a single channel.

Orthogonal Frequency Division Multiple (OFDM)

OFDM is a modulation method that divides a channel into multiple narrow orthogonal bands that are spaced so that they do not interfere with one another. OFDM is a method of encoding data on multiple carrier frequvencies.

Internet Protocol (IP)

The Internet Protocol (IP) is a set of rules established for routing and addressing packets of data so that they can travel across networks and arrive at the correct destination (Postel, 1981).

Voice over Internet Protocol (VoIP)

Voice-over-Internet protocol (VoIP) is communications technology that allows users to interact by audio through an Internet connection, rather than through an analogue connection (Collins, 2003).

6.7 First Generation

The first generation (1G) of wireless telecommunication technology comprised mobile phones that had only a voice facility. 1G phones were based on the analogue system, using frequencies of around 900MHz (Pereira & Sousa, 2004). 1G used a technique called Frequency Division Multiple Access (FDMA) to modulate a voice call to a higher frequency as the call is transmitted between radio towers (Bhalla & Bhalla, 2010). FDMA refers to the process whereby one channel or bandwidth is divided into multiple individual bands, each for use by a single user. This closes the channel to other conversations until the initial call is finished, or until it is handed off to a different channel. FDMA allows multiple users to send data through a single communication channel such as a coaxial cable or microwave beam, and the individual bands have non-overlapping frequency. With the introduction of 1G phones, the mobile market increased to 20 million subscribers by 1990 (Ashiho, 2003).

6.8 Second Generation

The second generation (2G) of the wireless mobile network was based on low-band digital data signalling (Pereira & Sousa, 2004). The most popular 2G wireless technology is the Global Systems for Mobile communications (GSM). 2G technologies can handle data capabilities such as fax (facsimile) and short message service (SMS), but are not suitable for web browsing and multimedia applications. A fax machine is an electronic device designed to scan printed textual and graphic material and then transmit printed documents over a telephone line. GSM uses Time Division Multiple Access (TDMA) technology to support multiple users and Code Division Multiple Access (CDMA) technology to break speech into small digitized segments, and encodes them to identify each call (Agrawal et al., 2015). TDMA is a digital technique that divides a single channel or band into time slots. Each time slot is used to transmit one byte or another digital segment of each signal in sequential serial data format. TDMA allows each user to access the entire radio frequency channel for the short period of a call. Other users share this same frequency channel at different time slots. CDMA is a channel-access method or multiple-access method which allows more than two terminals connected to the same transmission medium to transmit over it and share its capacity. CDMA uses a broad spectrum technique to transmit data, and the technology allows several phones to send and receive data through a single channel (Wu et al., 2014). CDMA is suitable for encrypted transmissions and has long been used for military purposes. CDMA increases spectrum capacity by allowing all users to occupy all channels at the same time. Transmissions are spread over the whole radio band, and each voice or data call is assigned a unique code to differentiate it from the other calls transmitted over the same spectrum.

2G cannot normally transfer data such as email or software (Bhalla & Bhalla, 2010). The pervasiveness of the GSM standard makes international roaming very common between mobile operators, enabling subscribers to use their phones in many parts of the world. 2G mobile phones are able to deal with issues of system capacity and coverage (Sood & Garg, 2014).

The 2.5G and 2.75G lie between 2G and 3G. 2.5G provides a data rate of 144–200Kbps and implements a packet switched domain in addition to the circuit switched domain (Gawas, 2015). Packet switching is a method of transmitting data over a network. To transfer the data in a fast and efficient manner, the data is broken into small pieces of variable length called packets (Roberts, 1978). 2.75G utilizes the Enhanced Data rates for GSM Evolution (EDGE) technology, with data rates of up to 236.8Kbps (Lamba et al., 2012). 2.5G is an informal term invented solely for marketing purposes while 2G and 3G are officially defined standards based on those established by the International Telecommunication Union (ITU) (Bhalla & Bhalla, 2010).

6.9 Third Generation

Definitions

Narrowband

Refers to data communication and telecommunications tools, technologies, and services that utilize a narrower set or band of frequencies in the communication channel (Hagen, 2009). A typical example is a dial-up internet connection.

Wideband System

Is a broad frequency communication channel that uses a relatively wide range of frequencies. Examples of wideband systems are Wi-Fi and Long-term Evolution (LTE).

The 3G technology added multimedia functions to 2G phones, permitting video, audio and graphic applications. 3G is a big step up from the 2G bandwidth, affording stationary users up to 2 MB/s data rates (Pereira & Sousa, 2004). 3G utilizes TDMA and CDMA. 3G was developed to provide universal roaming capability. 3G services include broadband wireless data and value-added services such as mobile television, global positioning system (GPS), and video conferencing. 3G finds an application in wireless voice telephony, mobile internet access, video calls and mobile TV. However, it is being phased out because 3G handsets and base stations operate on a wideband system which uses the entire cellular spectrum, unlike the 4G/5G which operate on narrowband systems. The wideband and narrowband systems require different sets of hardware and it is financially uneconomical to run both systems.

6.10 Fourth Generation

As data requirements increased, 4G was introduced. 4G is Internet Protocol (IP) based, which means it uses a standard communications protocol to send and receive data packets for both voice and data. The main goal of 4G technology was to provide high speed, high capacity, high quality, secure, and low cost voice and data services as well as multimedia and Internet over IP (Gawas, 2015). Some applications of 4G include IP telephony also known as Voice over Internet Protocol (VoIP), gaming services, HD mobile TV, video conferencing and 3D TV. 4G gives more integrity through Orthogonal Frequency Division Multiple (OFDM) access with Wi-Max, delivering up to 70Mbps over wireless technology and can reach up to 1Gbps indoors (Ezhilarasan & Dinakaran, 2017). OFDM is a modulation method that divides a channel into multiple narrow orthogonal bands that are spaced so that they do not interfere with one another (Frenzel, 2013). OFDM is a method of encoding data on multiple carrier frequencies. The main advantage of OFDM over single-carrier schemes is its ability to cope with severe channel disruptions. 4G offers network interoperability as well as personalized multimedia communication tools.

6.11 Fifth Generation

The fifth generation is up to 100 times faster than 4G. 5G has the potential to significantly impact businesses across a range of industries. It is designed to deliver peak data rates of up to 20Gbps based on IMT-2020 requirements. 5G uses radio waves using the three different ranges: low, mid, and high frequency (Shafique et al., 2020). New antennas will incorporate massive MIMO (multiple input, multiple output), which enables multiple transmitters and receivers to transfer data simultaneously. 5G is designed to support the new radio spectrum as well as heterogeneous networks which combine licensed and unlicensed wireless technologies. 5G architectures are software-defined platforms so that the networking functionality is managed through software rather than hardware. 5G utilizes advanced technology such as virtualization, cloud-based technologies and business automation, which enable 5G networks to be agile and flexible. 5G utilizes machine learning to enhance digital experiences by providing greater realism in virtual reality (VR), augmented reality (AR), and extended reality (XR), stable connectivity in crowded spaces, and the use of drones in activities such as the delivery of retail goods (Baratè et al., 2019). Downloads take seconds, providing seamless streaming and real-time gaming. 5G use cases include the use of

VR for media and entertainment, while the combination of 5G with Artificial Intelligence has revolutionized manufacturing. Other 5G use cases are given in Table 6.2.

Table 6.2 5G Use Cases

5G Use cases	Application
Driverless vehicles	• Vehicle-2-Infractucture (V2I) communication – communication between the vehicle and road infrastructure. Lane markings, road signs and traffic lights provide information to the vehicle and vice versa • Vehicle-2-Vehicle (V2V) communication will enable two vehicles approaching from directions that are perpendicular to determine which vehicle will yield for the other one when their paths cross • Vehicle-to-everything V2X communication will enable vehicles to communicate with objects, pedestrians, and traffic management systems (Qualcomm, 2017)
Retail	• Immersive commerce e.g. virtual fitting room and virtual shopping experience • Automatic checkout
Smart cities	• City management, energy management, enhanced services, and infrastructure for citizens, improving security (Wigginton & Greenberg, 2022) • Automotive security, infrastructure and entertainment (Qualcomm, 2017)
VR and AR	• Immersive gaming and immersive experiences with AR in sports arenas • In industry 5G AR goggles could be used by technicians to see an overlay of a machine and identify parts, provide repair instructions, or show parts not safe to touch • AR, interactive 3D meetings moving from phone or 2D video conferences • Increased hologram entertainers (Rajiv, 2018)
Drone operation	• Drones will be used during natural disasters to reach out and collect useful information
IoT	• IoT will connect every object, appliance, sensor, device and application to the Internet • Industrial IoT will lead to the efficient automation of equipment, predictive maintenance, safety, process tracking, and energy management (Ericsson, 2020; Rajiv, 2018)
Healthcare	• Remote diagnosis (Ericsson, 2020) • Wearable devices alerting healthcare providers when a patient is experiencing symptoms
Agriculture	• Farms in the future using more data and less chemicals • Farmers precisely pinpointing which areas need water, have disease, or require pest management using data from sensors

A summary of the applications of the various network generations is given in Figure 6.1. The first two network generations 1G and 2G offer voice capability, with 3G expanding to offer mobile broadband in addition to voice. 4G sees the introduction of IoT, and 5G offers more potential use cases that include Voice, Mobile Broadband, IoT, Broadband IoT, Critical IoT (e.g., wireless control of industrial manufacturing and production, remote medical surgery), and Industrial Automation IoT (e.g., smart autonomous guided vehicles, safer mining environments, etc.).

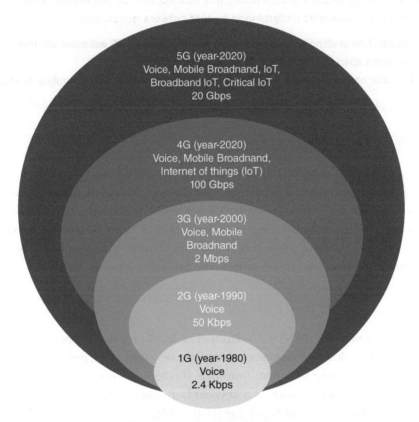

Figure 6.1 Summary of Applications of the Various Network Generations

6.12 Sixth Generation

Samsung has released a white paper on 6G (Samsung, 2022), and although it is an exciting prospect, it does not exist at the moment. Samsung predicts that the widespread deployment of 6G will occur in 2028. Huawei perceive 6G as going beyond communication, serving as a distributed neural network providing communication links to bring together physical, cyber, and biological worlds (Huawei 6G Research Team, 2021). It is anticipated that 6G will be shaped by cloud computing, big data, Artificial Intelligence, blockchain, edge computing, heterogeneous computing, and intrinsic security. To date, a new mobile generation has been introduced every decade, so it is likely that 6G will be on the market in 2030 at the earliest (Businesswire, 2022).

> ### Stop and Reflect: Network Generations
>
> As a network generation is shut down, this has impacts on the mobile devices and a variety of technologies underpinned by that network generation.
>
> * Discuss how shutting down a technology as ubiquitous as 3G will affect different industries apart from upgrading smartphones.
> * Consider how shutting down a network generation has an impact on wireless solutions.

6.13 Wireless Networks

The previous sections discussed the history of mobile phones and the network generations. It is important to understand the role of wireless networks in mobile technologies. Wireless networks are computer networks that enable communication to take place between two devices without of the need for cables or wires (Cisco, 2019). Although there is a range of different wireless networks, this chapter starts by discussing the cellular or mobile network and will now examine two other wireless networks.

Personal Area Network (PAN)

A personal area network (PAN) is a collection of fixed or wireless devices, which may comprise laptop or desktop computers, a smartphone, tablet, iPad, printer, etc. Typically, the devices are not more than 30m from one another and form a personal or private network. Fixed PAN devices such as a keyboard or mouse may be connected to a personal computer via a Universal Serial Bus (USB) cable.

Wireless PAN (WPAN) is often used to characterize the number of short-range radio technologies that enable PAN to interconnect such as Bluetooth, Wireless Home Digital Interface (WHDI), and ZigBee (Gratton, 2013). PAN represents the topology, while WPAN refers to the ability of the topology to interconnect wirelessly.

Mobile Ad-Hoc Network (MANET)

This is an infrastructure-less wireless network made up of an autonomous collection of mobile nodes (smartphones, laptops, iPads, tablets, etc.). The flexibility and openness of MANETs make them attractive for several applications, such as military communication, automated battlefields, emergency search and rescue operations, firefighting, and policing (Kumar & Dutta, 2016). A Mobile Ad-Hoc Network (MANET) consists of mobile hosts without the support of base stations. The network can freely and dynamically self-configure to reconstruct its topology and routing table information for the exchange of data packets joining and leaving each node on an ad-hoc basis (Raza et al., 2016). This allows people and devices to seamlessly internetwork in areas without any pre-existing communication infrastructure (Ilyas, 2017).

MANETs are susceptible to a variety of active and passive attacks that can be launched with relative ease as all communication is over a wireless medium. Wireless communication facilitates eavesdropping because of continuous monitoring of the shared medium, also known as a promiscuous mode, that is required by many MANET protocols (Papadimitratos & Haas, 2002). Some inherent features of MANETs make them vulnerable to a variety of security threats, for example: the wireless medium (is free to access by everyone – making the network susceptible to attacks such as eavesdropping and active interference); the lack of infrastructure (no specific infrastructure to address security issues); the dynamic topology (this is prone to both internal and external attacks) (Kumar & Dutta, 2016).

6.14 Wireless Communication Technologies

There are a variety of wireless communication technologies. Mobile communication technologies allow transmissions via a mobile device without being connected to any physical or fixed link. Some commonly used examples of wireless network technologies are Bluetooth and Wi-Fi, described in Table 6.3.

Table 6.3 Bluetooth and Wi-Fi Technologies

Mobile Communication Technology	Features	Applications
Bluetooth	• A short-range wireless technology used for exchanging data between fixed and mobile devices • Initially the range for most devices was about 10 metres • Key features of Bluetooth are robustness, low power consumption and low cost • Compatibility with most modern devices such as smartphones, tablets, laptops, and smartwatches • Multiple device connections	• Used to allow hands-free calls using mobile devices and a headset or speaker phone in vehicles • Bluetooth is also used for wireless headphones. Other audio hardware include wireless keyboards, mice, speakers, trackers, and game controllers • Bluetooth version 5.0 allows devices to do data transfer at speeds of up to 2Mbps, and devices can communicate within a range of up to 240m. • Used in medical healthcare, sports and fitness devices, e.g. pedometers, heart rate monitors • Used in smart home devices, e.g. smart lights, thermostats, security cameras linked to smartphones • Vehicle connectivity, connecting smartphones to car audio system, enabling hands-free phone calls on mobile phones and streaming music • Wearable technology, e.g. smartwatches

(Continued)

Table 6.3 (Continued)

Mobile Communication Technology	Features	Applications
Wi-Fi	• Based on IEEE 802.11 standards that define communications of wireless LANs • Designed to work seamlessly with Ethernet • Walls, pillars, home appliances can be obstructions that reduce range • Wi-Fi's wavebands work best for line-of-sight use	Wi-Fi is used in home settings, offices and some cities. Cities offering the largest Wi-Fi networks are Moscow, New York, Tel Aviv, Hong Kong, Seoul and Perth

Definitions

Personal Area Network (PAN)

A personal area network (PAN) is a collection of fixed or wireless devices, which may comprise laptop or desktop computers, a smartphone, tablet, iPad, printer, etc.

Wireless PAN (WPAN)

WPAN often used to characterize the number of short-range radio technologies that enable PAN to interconnect such as Bluetooth, Wireless Home Digital Interface (WHDI) and ZigBee (Gratton, 2013).

Mobile Ad-Hoc Network (MANET)

This is an infrastructureless wireless network comprising an autonomous collection of mobile nodes (smartphones, laptops, iPads, tablets, etc.). The network can dynamically self-configure to reconstruct its topology and routing table information for the exchange of data packets arriving at and leaving each node on an ad-hoc basis.

Cellular Network or Mobile Network

This is a radio network distributed over land areas called cells, with the link to and from end nodes being wireless. Each cell is served by at least one fixed-location transceiver (typically three cell sites or base transceiver stations).

6.15 Wireless Security

> ## Definitions
>
> ### Encryption
>
> Encryption is a method whereby users can securely share data over an insecure network or storage site.
>
> ### Jamming
>
> The disruption of existing wireless communications by decreasing the signal-to-noise ratio at the receiver end through the transmission of interfering wireless signals.
>
> ### Direct-Sequence Spread Spectrum (DSSS)
>
> DSSS is a modulation technique used in telecommunications to reduce signal interference during transmission. It is a spread spectrum technique which means that the frequency of the signal generated with a particular bandwidth is deliberately increased (spread), resulting in a signal with a wider bandwidth.
>
> ### Frequency-Hopping Spread Spectrum (FHSS)
>
> FHSS is a method of transmitting radio signals by rapidly changing the carrier frequency among many distinct frequencies occupying a large spectral band. The changes are controlled by a code known to both transmitter and receiver.
>
> ### Man-in-the-Middle (MITM) Attack
>
> The attacker secretly takes control of the communication channel between legitimate parties. The attacker intercepts the physical addresses of the legitimate parties, impersonates the two victims, and then establishes a connection with them.

Access to the Internet and opportunities to connect computers and mobile devices anywhere globally has increased the vulnerability of business assets and data transmitted through the networks. Losses to security breaches can be huge for individuals and organizations. In Australia, a company called Optus put up AU$140million to cover the cost of a data breach in 2022 (Tan, 2022). Data breaches can be a result of stolen or weak credentials, application vulnerabilities, malware, malicious insiders, and internal errors (Irwin, 2022). Apart from financial losses for organizations, other repercussions may include loss of trust, legal consequences, and disruption of operations during breach response and investigation. For individuals, data breaches may lead to identity theft, emotional stress, and financial loss through fraud. Individuals can protect themselves from major data breaches by not sharing accounts and maintaining strong passwords. Individuals and organizations need to be trained on data breaches, and how these occur. Other approaches can be prioritizing security actions throughout the organization.

Because wireless networks are pervasive in a wide range of applications, their security is of critical societal interest. Wireless networks are prone to malicious attacks because of the broadcast nature of the wireless medium. Encryption has been the main method used to secure data confidentiality, although this falls short in some of the current network architectures. Encryption is a method for a user to securely share data over an insecure network or storage site (Boneh et al., 2011). Ad-hoc networks in which messages pass through various intermediary terminals and Radio Frequency Identification (RFID) networks that involve IoT in which end devices have little complexity are examples where data encryption is complex (Poor & Schaefer, 2017). According to Netscout, users of IoT devices might have only five minutes to change settings in a factory to avoid the risk of hackers taking over. In 2019, refrigeration systems made by Resource Data Management were exposed to remote attacks because they were using default passwords and had failed to implement other security measures. Malicious attacks on wireless networks can be passive or they can completely disrupt communication.

Passive Attacks

Wireless networks generally adapt the 7-layer Open Systems Interconnection (OSI) protocol architecture. The lowest layer, which is the physical layer (with resources such as network hubs, cabling, repeaters, and network adapters), has emerged as a promising means of protecting wireless communications. Physical layer security (Phy-security) explores the random characteristics of wireless channels (e.g. fading, noise, and interference) to make the information transmission greater than the capacity of an eavesdropping channel (Qi et al., 2020). This means the eavesdropper cannot decode the interception signal. Phys-security provides secure communications for several cellular IoT devices (Qi et al., 2020).

Apart from eavesdropping, another passive attack on wireless networks is by means of traffic analysis. Traffic analysis is an attack in which an unintended receiver intercepts information such as the location or identity of the communicating parties by analysing the traffic of the received signal. Traffic analysis can be used for encrypted signals, to reveal patterns of the communication parties. Traffic analysis does not impact the legitimate communication (Fang et al., 2017).

Attacks that Disrupt Communication

Other attacks on wireless networks can completely disrupt communication between legitimate users, through malicious nodes that generate intentional interference. Jamming disrupts the environment with noise, interference, or collision. Some techniques that can be used to combat jamming in the physical layer of the OSI model are spectrum techniques, namely Direct-Sequence Spread Spectrum (DSSS) and Frequency-Hopping Spread Spectrum (FHSS). The spectrum techniques make it difficult for the jamming attacks to disrupt legitimate transmission (Zou et al., 2016). Another serious attack to wireless networks is the Man in the Middle (MITM). In an MITM attack, the attacker secretly takes control of the communication channel between legitimate parties. The attacker intercepts the physical addresses of the legitimate parties, impersonates the two victims and then establishes a connection with them (Zou et al., 2016). MITM attacks act as a relay between legitimate parties, with victims under the impression they are communicating directly over a private connection. Unencrypted Wi-Fi connections are easy to eavesdrop and are prone to MITM attacks. In addition, a hacker can create a Wi-Fi hotspot called an 'Evil Twin', making the connection look like the authentic one; then users may connect to the 'evil twin', thereby allowing the hacker to snoop on their activities. A solution to MITM attacks on mobile technologies may rest in encryption and good network hygiene such as security protocols.

Stop and Reflect: Wireless Security

As computers and mobile devices connected to Internet become increasingly pervasive, individuals and organizations become more vulnerable to security breaches. What steps can be taken to avoid security breaches by:

1   Individuals?
2   Organizations?

Wireless networks are prone to malicious attacks.

1   How can a user prevent some of these malicious attacks?
2   How can organizations prevent malicious attacks?

6.16 Mobile Computing

Mobile computing is a technology that provides an environment enabling users to transmit data from one device to another without the need for any physical cables or links. Mobile computing involves mobile communication, mobile hardware, and mobile software. The technology is based on the use of battery powered, portable and wireless computing and communication devices. There are a variety of technologies involved in mobile computing.

Barcodes

Barcodes encode product information into bars and alphanumeric characters, making it faster and easier to ring up items in a store or track inventory. Bar-coding is an AIDC

(Automatic Identification and Data Collection) technology that reduces the need for human intervention in data entry and collection, reducing error and time. Barcodes are used to quickly and accurately identify a product or item by scanning the code with a barcode scanner. Other advantages of barcode technology are that it is versatile and can be used in a wide range of industries and applications. Barcode technology offers real-time data which helps businesses make informed decisions on inventory and purchases. Some disadvantages of using barcodes is that barcode scanners need a clear line of sight to the barcode to read it properly. So items may need to be repositioned or manipulated for the barcode to be visible to the scanner. The information a barcode can store is limited. Barcodes can be damaged or become distorted making them unreadable. Barcode technology heavily relies on the reliability of the equipment and software used to interpret the barcodes, which means a failure of either equipment or software can disrupt business operations.

Optical Character Recognition (OCR)

This technology automatically recognizes characters through an optical medium. It is a process of classification of optical patterns contained in a digital image corresponding to alphanumeric or other characters (Arica & Yarman-Vural, 2001). OCR systems have several functions which include optical scanning, location segmentation, pre-processing, segmentation, representation, feature extraction, recognition and post-processing (Chaudhuri et al., 2017). OCR has been used for mail sorting, bank cheque reading, and signature verification (Shen & Coughlan, 2012). OCR is also used for utility bills, passport validation, automated number plate recognition, and helping blind and visually impaired people to read text (Bhammar & Mehta, 2012; Bhavani & Thanushkodi, 2010).

There were some disadvantages associated with OCR before the introduction of Artificial Intelligence (AI), such as accuracy, being time consuming, and limited OCR software. AI-based technologies have caused OCR to jump from traditional systems managed by humans to fully automated systems that can merge with innovative technology to solve complex problems, such as the use of Google Translate OCR technology that allows users to read in any language or digitizing data containing x-rays. The use of AI-based technologies with OCR has enhanced benefits such as increased accuracy, greater efficiency, and lowering costs in document processing, storage and retrieval associated with paper documents.

Finally, a biometric system is a pattern recognition system that confirms personal identity by establishing the authenticity of a specific physiological or behavioural characteristic of the user (Jain, 2000). There are various biometric identification technologies: finger print, face recognition, iris, hand geometry, retina geometry, speaker recognition, and speaker verification technology (Bhattacharyya et al., 2009).

Radio Frequency Identification (RFID)

Radio Frequency Identification (RFID) is a technology used for the automated identification of objects and people (Juels, 2006). RFID helps machines and computers to identify objects and record metadata (Jia et al., 2012). This is information carried by radio waves. There are a variety of automatic identification systems. Barcoding is the most common ID technology and is used extensively on most commodities (Youssef & Salem, 2007). However, although the barcode was a revolutionary concept, systems have low storage capacity and cannot be reprogrammed, which is a significant stumbling block (Finkenzeller, 2010).

Other automatic identification systems are the optical character recognition (OCR), biometric procedures and smart cards. Smart cards are placed in a reader, which makes a galvanic connection with the contact surfaces of the smart card using contact springs. A smart card is supplied with energy and a clock pulse from the reader via the contact surfaces. The smart card can be equipped with memory only (memory card), or with a memory and a small microprocessor to execute pre-programmed tasks (Pelletier et al., 2011).

RFID systems are closely related to smart cards as data is stored on an electronic data-carrying device known as the transponder. RFID can be either active or passive. Active tags require a power source. The energy source can be integrated in a battery, or the tag can be connected to a powered infrastructure. Passive RFID does not require batteries or maintenance, with tags having an indefinite operational life. A passive RFID consists of three parts: an antenna, a semiconductor chip attached to an antenna and some form of encapsulation (Want, 2006). The power supply to the data-carrying device and the data exchange between the data-carrying device and the reader uses magnetic or electromagnetic fields. An RFID system is made up of two components:

- The transponder, which is located on the object to be identified.
- The interrogator or reader, which may be a read or write/read device depending on the design and technology used.

The data-capture device is known as the reader, whether it can only read data or is also capable of writing. A reader typically has a radio frequency module (transmitter and receiver), a control unit and a coupling element to the transponder. A transponder usually consists of a coupling element and an electronic microchip.

RFID has a wide range of applications, as indicated by Table 6.4.

Table 6.4 Applications of RFID

Manufacturing and Supply Chain	• Manufacturing – Management of inventory, tracking, quality control and resources
	• Warehousing – Management of picking, receiving and shipping
	• Transportation – Management of distribution, material processing and safety
	• Retail – Management of inventory, smart shelf operations and checkout

(Continued)

Table 6.4   (Continued)

Transport and ticketing	• Public transport tickets
	• Entertainment and events
	• Toll fee collection
	• Smart car key
	• Automatic vehicle location
Monitoring and tracking	• Parcels, mailbags, laundry management
	• Luggage handling
	• Library inventory
	• Animal tracking
	• Tracking golf balls
Healthcare	• Pharmaceutics
	• Patient monitoring
	• Patient medical history
	• Implants and prostheses
	• Animal diagnostics

RFID are also used for smart bankcards and bank note identification. Sport event timing and gaming chips also make use of RFID. The RFID technology enables contactless payments to be made, although this carries some risk. Fraudsters can scan another person's card and steal the victim's money or identity. As a safety precaution, these cards should be treated as cash and not let out of the owner's sight. It is essential that card holders report any unauthorized or suspicious transactions on bankcards, and safeguard RFID chipped cards and documents from skimming.

RFID technology helps reduce waste and increase recycling. RFID technology aids the waste and recycling industry through tracking, work order management, and maintenance of waste containers. RFID tags attached to recycling containers keep track of the container's fullness and can alert the hauler to deploy a vehicle to transfer waste when the container is full.

Definitions

Barcodes

These provide a method of representing data in a visual, machine-readable form.

Optical Character Recognition (OCR)

OCR is a process of classification of optical patterns contained in a digital image corresponding to alphanumeric or other characters.

Radio Frequency Identification (RFID)

RFID is a technology used for the automated identification of objects and people. RFID aids machines and computers to identify objects and record metadata.

6.17 Mobile Commerce

Mobile technology has become a game-changer in various industries, improving customer service and engagement. Mobile commerce refers to the buying and selling of goods and services via wireless devices. The term 'mobile commerce' was originally coined in 1997 by Kevin Duffey at the launch of the Global Mobile Commerce Forum, to mean 'the delivery of electronic commerce capabilities directly into the consumer's hand, anywhere, via wireless technology' (Market Business News, 2023).

Mobile apps have sparked a revolution across all industries, as most apps would fit into one of the following categories: lifestyle, social media, utility, entertainment and games, productivity, and news/information outlets (Reacher, 2021). The main mobile commerce technologies include SMS, USSD, and Sim Toolkit (STK).

SMS users can receive one-way push messages such as news, alerts, and offers. Two-way interaction is also supported, which allows users to message call centres. The main advantage of SMS is its ubiquity and ease of use, while a major drawback is the lack of encryption.

Unstructured Supplementary Services Data (USSD)

Similar to SMS, USSD has been used in the operations of a majority of large-scale mobile financial services in a limited number of markets such as Bangladesh, Cambodia, Pakistan, Tanzania, and Zimbabwe (Sutherl, 2021). The African market generally uses USSD for activities such as the transfer of money and the buying of data bundles, with 90% of mobile transactions in sub-Saharan Africa conducted through USSD (Quadri, 2022). USSD is used for mobile money transfers, prepaid call-back services, soliciting feedback from customers, confirming the delivery orders, and sending virtual coupons. Unlike SMS, USSD establishes real-time connections. SMS and USSD are similar in terms of their ease of use and accessibility from almost all mobile phones. USSD can incorporate secure password or mobile pin protection, thereby making it more secure than SMS.

Applications of Mobile Commerce

Mobile applications have disrupted several business models in a variety of industries like e-commerce, hospitality, travel, dating, photography, and entertainment.

Shopping

Online purchasing is prevalent across different age groups using various social media platforms (e.g., Facebook marketplace, Instagram shopping). Other selling platforms include Amazon, eBay, Alibaba, and Etsy. The use of mobile devices for online shopping continues to increase because of convenience, competitive prices, and the consumer's ability to compare prices. Excluding groceries, 75% of Australians shop online (Young, 2022), with statistics showing that the USA ($1,804), UK ($1,629), Sweden ($1,446),

France ($1,228) and Germany ($1,064) are leaders in terms of the average expenditure per online shopper (Taheer, 2023). Online shopping and e-commerce have become subsidiaries of the traditional bricks and mortar stores and services.

Mobile payments

Financial technology (fintech) uses mobile devices, particularly smartphones. The payment systems incorporated in the design of mobile devices have become drivers of socio-economic development (Karsen et al., 2019). Mobile payment is payment made for a product or service via mobile devices. Mobile payment technology can be used to send money to friends and family. Examples of mobile payment apps include PayPal, Apple Pay, Google Pay, Samsung Pay, WorldRemit, M-Pesa, MyZaka, and Ecocash. Initially, mobile payments were popular in Asia and Europe; however, they have now become a global phenomenon. One benefit of mobile payments is that no physical presence or contact is required when making a purchase, which boosted the popularity of mobile payments during the COVID-19 pandemic. Other benefits are convenience, security through encryption, faster payments, and the ease of tracking each transaction as it leaves a digital record. However, mobile-facilitated payments have several disadvantages which hinder their universal acceptance. For instance, the variety of mobile payment systems means some stores may accept only specific mobile payments and not all the available mobile payments, for example some retailers accept Visa but do not accept American Express. This means that sometimes customers may be asked for cash even though the retailer accepts digital payment. Mobile payments are tied to the device, so battery failure or loss of the device means that one cannot make payments.

Contactless payment methods, such as Apple Pay, Google Pay and Android Pay, have become more popular because of near-field communication (NFC) technology. NFC allows devices like smartphones, tablets and smartwatches to exchange small bits of data with other devices. Other applications of NFC technology is mobile ticketing, access control in buildings and facilities, public transportation, marketing and advertising. While mobile and contactless payments are convenient, security threats are likely to increase with these type of payments.

Ridesharing

The integration of smartphones, global position systems (GPS), and electronic payments have greatly contributed to the increasing popularity of real-time ridesharing services like Uber, Ola, Didi, LYFT, GoJek, and Careem. This is very convenient for riders as they can book a ride, receive an indication of when the ride will arrive, and obtain details about the vehicle and the driver. Besides being convenient for riders, ridesharing has environmental benefits, such as reducing road traffic and emissions (Caulfield, 2009; Cici et al., 2014). Moreover, rideshare apps support the development of social and cultural capital. Social capital refers to the benefits people can draw from their social network (Putnam, 2000). Cultural capital refers to the inherent qualities and skills of an individual, as well as their academic qualifications and knowledge that result in an understanding of cultural meaning and references (Bourdieu & Richardson, 1986). The rideshare technology connects riders and drivers in a shared space, affording interactions between riders and drivers which fosters social and cultural capital (Kameswaran et al., 2018).

Entertainment

Streaming services for music, podcasts, movies, TV shows, anime and documentaries have provided affordable and accessible access to entertainment databases, reinforced by the emergence and development of mobile technologies (Bentley & Lottridge, 2019). Spotify and Apple Music allow up to six devices on premium accounts under a single subscription. Some top video streaming apps are Hulu, YouTube, Netflix, Amazon Prime, and Disney+ (Minor & Moore, 2022). In Q1, 2020 Netflix secured 16 million new subscribers, widely attributed to the lockdowns as a result of the COVID-19 pandemic (Spangler, 2020).

Mobile Gaming

Technological advances in mobile devices have attracted millions of people to subscribe to mobile gaming. The advances have led to the incorporation of new features such as touch screen, motion sensor, heavy storage, enhanced display and ubiquitous connection, and application stores. Moreover, users can play online while on the move (Feijoo et al., 2012). Demand for mobile gaming can be attributed to three main factors (Soh & Tan, 2008):

- Increased penetration rates of mobile devices.
- The ability of mobile devices to deliver high quality video and audio.
- Improved Internet connectivity through wireless networks.

The mobile games market generated about $7.1 billion from players spending in the App Store and Google Play in November 2021. According to Sensor Tower (Orr 2022), European spending on mobile games reached $11.2 billion in 2021. The COVID-19 pandemic increased demand for mobile gaming as consumers were in lockdown and sought online resources for entertainment, with mobile game spending reaching $1.7 billion per week in Q1 2021 (Perez, 2021). While the growth of mobile gaming has been accelerated by the pandemic, mobile gaming will likely outpace the uptake of other types of digital games. The dangers associated with mobile gaming include addiction, which can be damaging to individuals' physical and mental health (Feng, 2022). However some games, such as Pokémon GO, involve physical activity and have been reported to increase exercise levels for players. The gaming industry has adopted AR technology to bring virtual creatures and characters to life. Major companies such as Nintendo, Microsoft, and Sony have heavily invested in AR technology in the gaming industry.

Stop and Reflect: Mobile Commerce

Online shopping and mobile gaming mean that people do not need to go to a specific location to fulfil their needs, which can be convenient.

- Discuss the advantages and disadvantages of mobile technologies in terms of their impact on society.

6.18 Mobile Health (M-Health)

Mobile wireless technologies have the potential to revolutionize the way that people interact with national health services. M-health makes use of mobile and wireless technologies to support the achievement of health objectives (Burke et al., 2015). Mobile phone text messaging has been proven to increase adherence to antiretroviral therapy for HIV patients, monitor depression and increase attendance at healthcare appointments. A wide range of mobile technology applications in the healthcare sector have been approved by EU and US regulatory authorities. Wearable technology is a key element of mobile health technology. The increase in the number of smartphone users, and the rise in popularity of health apps coupled with wearable technology will likely lead to greater use of M-health.

Wearable Devices (Wearables)

Wearable technologies offer innovative solutions for healthcare problems. Wearable technologies enable the continuous monitoring of human physical activities and behaviours as well as physiological and biochemical parameters (see Table 6.5). According to Qian & Long (2018), the five main features of wearable devices as a standard healthcare intervention are:

- wireless mobility
- interactivity and intelligence
- sustainability and durability
- simple operation and miniaturization
- wearability and portability.

Table 6.5 Applications of Wearable Technologies (Wu & Luo, 2019)

Category	Use	Application & Results
Prevention of diseases and maintenance of health	Fall identification and prevention	Fall prevention and fall detection in the elderly population. Falls occur in 30–60% of older adults annually and can produce severe health consequences. Fall-detecting sensors and associated electronics can be attached to clothing or worn on the body. To date, research has reported good results.

Category	Use	Application & Results
	Physical activity and interaction monitoring	Vibration reminders are sent through a wearable device. This is an effective means of producing behavioural change.
	Mental status monitoring	Wearable devices are equipped with sensors to detect human physiology status such as heartbeat, blood pressure, and body temperature, or other complex vital signs. Signals from these devices are used to monitor mental conditions.
	Weight control and monitoring	Wearable devices such as Fitbit, Apple Watch, and Garmin have been used as stimulus mechanisms to increase user activities which can lead to behavioural changes such as increased physical activity and healthy eating.
	Sports medicine	Wearable devices can assist athletes and coaches to manage athletic training and matches by monitoring functional movements, workloads and heart rates to maximize performance and reduce injury.
Patient management	Cancer survivors	Physical inactivity and sedentary behaviour are common amongst cancer survivors, as side effects of treatment can make it challenging to exercise. Wearable activity trackers (WATs) have been used to provide effective, intensive, home-based rehabilitation.
Disease management	Heart disorders	Cardiovascular disease can be monitored using the Holter monitor, which is a wearable medical device used in hospitals for dynamic monitoring (which is not possible with a conventional electrocardiogram (ECG)). A sports vest made from nanofibres has been developed for long-term ECG data collection, with the data uploaded to the cloud and analysed by physicians (Tsukada et al., 2019).
		Apple Watch Series 4 combines the functions of an ECG and a watch.

Issues with wearable devices

Ethical issues associated with wearables include unanticipated access to personal information, which is related to specific methodologies and concerns about data conceptualization and interpretation (e.g., the ethics of monitoring low-income youth of colour).

Privacy issues, security and informed consent

One of the biggest privacy threats from mobile devices is location tracking. There are a variety of ways of location tracking through mobile devices that include Wi-Fi and Bluetooth tracking, mobile signal tracking, triangulation and location information leaks from web browsing and apps. A weather app on a phone can be used to track a person's movements and sold to third parties (Banaschik, 2020). The EU's General Data Protection

Regulation (GDPR), treats location data as personal data, which means users must specifically agree to location tracking rather than opting out.

Many wearable devices store data locally without encryption. This could result in the loss of confidential and personal health data. Most wearable devices are usually connected to a smartphone using Bluetooth or Wi-Fi, which can be unsecured channels. Wearable sensors are always synchronized with smartphones for data transfer, and third-party apps installed on smartphones can increase the susceptibility to data hacking.

There is also a general lack of knowledge about information security issues surrounding data from wearable devices. An example of a security threat is the fitness app, Strava, as the 'heatmap' feature revealed the location of the US military in Syria and other conflict zones as well as some troop movements in 2017 Strava also allowed users to de-anonymize user-share data to reveal a recorded user's name, speed and heart rate (Drape, 2018).

Data accuracy from wearables

Wearables promise a myriad of health-related information such as low heart rate alerts, sleep tracking and pulse pressure. Some health constructs have been reported to be inaccurate for a population with darker skin tones. Apple 6 watch pulse oximeters have increased error rates depending on skin tones (Sjoding et al., 2020).

Technological barriers

There are a variety of bottlenecks in the application of wearable medical devices. Some wearable devices have poor compatibility and do not integrate with other functions, and while the main function is health monitoring, there can be slow progress to clinical treatment. Also, most wearables have poor battery life (Lu et al., 2020).

Stop and Reflect: Wearable Devices

As more consumers purchase wearable devices, they may expose themselves to both potential security breaches and various ways in which their data may be legally used by companies without the consumer ever knowing.

- Discuss how the awareness of privacy and security issues can be increased when using wearables.
- What happens to consumer data if a company files for bankruptcy and decides to sell all its consumer data?
- What harm can be done to the customer if personal data falls in to the wrong hands?

Definitions

Direct-Sequence Spread Spectrum (DSSS)

DSSS is a modulation technique used in telecommunications to reduce interference in signals during transmission. It is a spread spectrum technique which means that the frequency of the signal generated with a particular bandwidth is deliberately increased (spreading), resulting in a signal with a wider bandwidth.

Frequency-Hopping Spread Spectrum (FHSS)

FHSS is a method of transmitting radio signals by rapidly changing the carrier frequency among many distinct frequencies occupying a large spectral band. The changes are controlled by a code known to both transmitter and receiver.

Man-in-the-Middle (MITM) Attack

The attacker secretly takes control of the communication channel between legitimate parties. The attacker intercepts the physical addresses of the legitimate parties, impersonates the two victims and then establishes a connection with them.

6.19 The Challenges of Mobile Technologies

Although this chapter has discussed several benefits of mobile technologies, these technologies are not without challenges arising from their inherent nature.

Security Issues

Security issues are a major challenge with mobile technologies, these have been discussed earlier under 'Wireless Security'.

Technostress

The compulsive use of mobile devices is associated with technostress. While the ubiquity of mobile devices can be beneficial, there is the risk that mobile technologies will produce technostress. Interruptions on mobile devices during non-work hours may result in the active use of mobile devices for work during non-work hours. This can lead to work–life conflict. Mobile technologies have led to the expectation that workers will be accessible at all times, with assumed short response times, leading to work–life conflict, which can have a negative impact on individuals and organizations (Tams et al., 2020).

Work–Life Balance with Mobile Devices

Mobile phones impact our work and personal lives. Some statistics from Cell Phones at Workplace and Qualtrics (Elad, 2022; Qualtrics, 2023) in Table 6.6, give an indication of how mobile phones are intertwined with people's work and personal lives and the impact mobile devices have on work productivity and private lives. With mobile phones constantly connected to Internet, it is important to take into account how one can achieve a work–life balance. While mobile devices may be one reason people do not have a good work–life balance, the same devices can be used to achieve work–life balance.

Table 6.6 Statistics on Work–Life Balance when Using Mobile Devices

28% of workers use social media at work.

34% of employees find it difficult to resist work notifications while at home, while 29% employees find it difficult to resist checking personal notifications while at work.

39% of surveyed companies had suffered a data security breach due to lost or stolen devices.

50% of people who work more than 50 hours a week find it difficult to resist the urge to check on work outside work hours.

51% of workers conduct work on their phones while using the restroom.

55% of workers believe that the mobile phone is the greatest obstacle to office productivity.

55% of workers prefer using their mobile phones over desk phones for work purposes.

62% of employees use their phone for work while not at work.

70% of employees would prefer greater separation between their work and personal life on their phones.

75% of American workers use their cell phones for work purposes.

83% of millennials open a text message within 90 seconds of receiving the text message.

Work–life balance could be achieved by establishing clear boundaries between work and personal life. Other approaches can include tracking phone usage and having a limit for daily usage and use of apps that helps reduce connectivity, such as Flipd. Work–life balance improves productivity and is important for mental well-being.

Adoption by the Young Elderly

Some of the aforementioned benefits of mobile technology might not be available to the 'young elderly', who are people aged between 60 and 75. This generation has experienced significant technological and social changes and has a large representation in developed countries. While M-health offers practical advantages to ageing adults, and potentially may be a solution to the health-related problems of ageing adults, the young-elderly may find it difficult to adopt mobile technology. The young-elderly tend to be conservative when it comes to innovative mobile technology and have varying levels of commitment, familiarity, and competencies when it comes to utilizing it (Nikou, 2015). Some young elderly consider themselves 'too old' to learn new technology.

Mobile Scams

Mobile-facilitated scams and malware are on the rise. In 2021, Australians lost AU\$63.6 million to scams involving unsolicited calls or text messages (Williams, 2021). Copycat apps are increasing on official app stores and are a problem for developers and app users. Some unique features of the mobile app market have contributed to an increase in copycat apps. Some developers are limited by budget constraints, making it difficult for them to spend money identifying copycats. Also, although the source code of apps can be protected under intellectual property laws, the concept is not. Copycat apps are not necessarily poor quality, so consumers might not care whether the app is an original or a copycat (Wang et al., 2018).

Example: Wordle

A browser-based game, Wordle, inspired the development of many copycat mobile apps which attempted to become as popular as Wordle, either by copying the name, mechanics or both. The founder of Wordle, Josh Wardle, developed the game as a unique gift for his partner. It was released in October 2021 and rapidly became a viral sensation, spreading throughout the USA, New Zealand and Australia (Sebo, 2022). Wordle has almost 3 million players worldwide. The original Wordle game is free and played solely through a web browser, which gave copycats the opportunity to monetize it on the App Store (Lunden & Silberling, 2022), although Apple removed the Wordle clones from the App Store (Jacob, 2022). One Wordle copycat creator monetized the game and later apologised for exploiting the popular free word game.

Example: FluBot

FluBot is a sophisticated type of malware that sends text messages or notifications to both Androids and iPhones, with Androids being more vulnerable. Although the text messages vary, they will contain a link which often will ask the user to download an app in order to organize a time delivery, hear a voice mail message, or view photos that have been uploaded, after which the FluBot will install malware onto the device. A FluBot can attack mobile banking apps, users' contact lists, personal information, credit card details, and any sort of information (Salsabila et al., 2022).

(Continued)

FluBot spreads fast because it uploads contact numbers to a command-and-control server, then sends messages to each of those numbers. It also adds the numbers to the device's blacklist and disables the operating system's built-in security, making it easier to wreak havoc undetected. In many cases, a link to download FluBot will arrive on a device via one of the user's contacts. An unusual message with a URL which urges the user to click it is likely a message generated by FluBot.

Stop and Reflect: Mobile Technologies

- Discuss some positive aspects of mobile technologies.
- Discuss some of the threats posed by mobile technologies.
- How do mobile technologies impact work–life balance?
- How can mobile technologies be used to promote work–life balance in organizations and for individual users?

6.20 Chapter Summary

This chapter provides an overview of the history of mobile technologies and the current use of mobile technologies. Mobile technology applications have been discussed together with current issues associated with the use of mobile technologies, such as security, technostress, and scams. The use and application of mobile technologies continues to expand with, in the future, the predicted 6G anticipated to offer intrinsic security, shaped by cloud computing, big data, Artificial Intelligence, blockchain, edge computing, and heterogeneous computing.

Discussion Questions

1. Phasing out a network technology or adopting a newer network generation does not happen simultaneously and globally. However, what are the eventual global effects of this phasing out?
2. Discuss the current benefits of mobile technologies in society.
3. Discuss issues associated with current mobile technologies.
4. Discuss the approaches that can be taken by individuals and organizations to improve security when using mobile technologies.

Case Study: Mobile Technologies Impact on GDP and SDGs

Adapted from Adeputun (2022) and Wamola (2021).

In 2021, mobile technologies and services generated $4.5 trillion, which is 5% of global Gross Domestic Product (GDP). This figure is likely to rise to nearly $5 trillion by 2025.

According to the Mobile Economy Report Sub-Saharan Africa 2021, mobile technologies and services generated more than $130 billion of economic value added (8% of GDP) in sub-Saharan Africa in 2020. This will reach $155 billion by 2025 as countries increasingly benefit from the improvements in productivity and efficiency brought about by the increased take-up of mobile services.

The 2022 Mobile Economy Report (GSMA, 2022) noted that by the end of 2021, 5.3 billion people would have subscribed to mobile services, representing almost 70% of the global population. By the end of 2020, 495 million people had subscribed to mobile services in sub-Saharan Africa, representing 46% of the region's population – an increase of almost 20 million since 2019. With more than 40% of the region's population under the age of 15, young consumers owning a mobile phone for the first time will remain the primary source of growth for the foreseeable future. There will be around 120 million new subscribers by 2025, taking the total number of subscribers to 615 million (50% of the region's population).

It is anticipated that by 2025, there will be an additional 400 million new mobile subscribers, most of them from the Asia Pacific and sub-Saharan Africa, taking the total number of subscribers to 5.7 billion (70% of the global population).

The Global System for Mobile Telecommunications Association (GSMA) (GSMA, 2023) noted that a new wave of 5G roll-outs in large markets with modest income levels (such as Brazil, Indonesia and India) could further incentivize the mass production of more inexpensive 5G devices, which in turn could boost subscriber growth. The GSMA predicts that, by the end of 2025, 5G will account for around 25% of total mobile connections, and more than 40% people around the world will live within reach of a 5G network. The GSMA stated that 4G still has room for expansion in most developing markets, particularly in sub-Saharan Africa where 4G adoption is still below a fifth of total connections and operators are stepping up efforts to migrate existing 2G and 3G customers to 4G networks. However, GSMA observed that increasing uptake of 5G in leading markets, such as China, South Korea, and the US, means that 4G adoption on a global level is beginning to decline.

The GSMA asserted that mobile technology would be at the centre of efforts to achieve the United Nations Sustainable Development Goals (SDGs). According to the GSMA, the COVID-19 pandemic slowed progress on the SDGs around the world, with the pandemic exacerbating existing social and economic inequalities. With only eight years until the deadline for the SDGs, stakeholders are renewing their efforts to achieve them. Mobile technology will play a central role in those efforts, from improving access to education and healthcare to addressing issues with poverty and inequality.

In 2021, the GSMA celebrated a major milestone, having impacted over 100 million lives globally through its Mobile for Development (M4D) activities. In Africa alone, M4D initiatives have reached over 45 million people across 128 projects. M4D helps drive innovation in digital technology to reduce inequalities by forming partnerships between the mobile industry, tech innovators, governments, and the development sector. The programme has impacted the lives of over 126 million people by empowering underserved populations to build a better future and supporting the drive for sustainable business and large-scale socio-economic improvement. Almost all 17 of the

(Continued)

UN Sustainable Development Goals (SDGs) have benefitted, with the greatest number of lives impacted by some achievement of the SDGs related to Hunger, Gender Equality, Industry Innovation and Infrastructure, and Decent Work & Economic Growth.

Mobile money in particular is leading productivity. International transactions increased by 65% during 2020 as a result of the COVID-19 pandemic. According to the GSMA's 2022 State of the Industry Report on Mobile Money, (Awanis et al., 2022) there were significant increases in the adoption and use of mobile services since the start of the Covid-19 pandemic. Mobile data and mobile money indicate the value of utilizing mobile technology in challenging times. According to the report, the number of registered accounts rose by 12% globally in 2020 to more than 1.2 billion – double the forecast. The fastest growth was observed in markets where governments provided significant pandemic relief to their citizens.

With economies recovering, mobile technology will be even more fundamental to the way that people live, and businesses are run. Mobile technologies offer new digital solutions for small and large enterprises and will encourage the increasing use of online channels by consumers. The pandemic has highlighted the importance of digital technology as a means of responding effectively to crises and planning for recovery. At the same time, the pandemic has the potential to accelerate the continent's digital transformation and create resilient digital jobs in sub-Saharan Africa.

The continued rollout of 4G and the first stages of the 5G era have opened up opportunities in areas such as healthcare, digital commerce, industrial automation, and smart city infrastructure. The GSMA encourages sector-wide dialogue with governments and policymakers to help encourage mobile adoption, usage, and digital inclusion, which in turn will help drive economic growth across African countries.

Governments and policymakers should implement policies that improve access to connectivity and drive investment in more resilient digital infrastructure for the future. For example, governments and regulators in sub-Saharan Africa should adopt forward-looking spectrum management and fiscal policies. Mobile sector taxation is a barrier to digital inclusion in sub-Sahara Africa, where mobile services are subject to a high level of sector-specific taxes. Hence, the affordability of services and smartphones is one of the current key barriers to connectivity. A reduction of other mobile sector taxes such as airtime tax and mobile money transactions would encourage more people to become connected and get online.

According to the GSMA's State of Mobile Internet Connectivity Report (2023), 2022 ended with more than half of the world's population using mobile Internet. This translates to over 4 billion people connected to the Internet via mobile devices. Even with this impressive growth in mobile Internet connectivity, in terms of both mobile Internet coverage and usage, the digital divide still exists, and more work needs to be done to bridge it. Around 3.4 billion people, or 43% of the world's population, are still not utilizing mobile Internet despite living in areas with mobile broadband coverage.

1   Discuss how mobile technologies have been used globally during the COVID-19 pandemic, using examples from both developed and developing countries.

2   Discuss how mobile technologies can be used in healthcare, digital commerce, industrial automation, and smart city infrastructure.

3   How can mobile technologies be used for sustainability? Discuss how individuals and organizations can strengthen their commitment to sustainability and the UN Sustainable Development goals.

4   Does the advancement of mobile technology increase the risk of inequality? Discuss. What measures could be taken to reduce the mobile technology digital divide.

6.20 References

Adeputun, A. (2022, March 10). Mobile technologies generated $4.5tr in 2021, target 400m new subscribers. *The Guardian Nigeria News – Nigeria and World News.* https://guardian.ng/business-services/mobile-technologies-generated-4-5tr-in-2021-target-400m-new-subscribers/

Agrawal, J., Patel, R., Mor, P., Dubey, P., & Keller, J. (2015). Evolution of mobile communication network: From 1G to 4G. *International Journal of Multidisciplinary and Current Research, 3,* 1100–1103.

Anjarwalla, T. (2010, July 9). Inventor of cell phone: We knew someday everybody would have one. CNN.com. http://edition.cnn.com/2010/TECH/mobile/07/09/cooper.cell.phone.inventor/

Arica, N., & Yarman-Vural, F. T. (2001). An overview of character recognition focused on off-line handwriting. *IEEE Transactions on Systems, Man, and Cybernetics, Part C (Applications and Reviews), 31*(2), 216–233.

Ashiho, L. (2003). Mobile technology: Evolution from 1G to 4G. *Electronics for You, 6,* 968–976.

Awanis, A., Lowe, C., Andersson-Manjang, S. and Lindsey, D. (2022) *State of the Industry Report on Mobile Money 2022.* https://www.gsma.com/sotir/wp-content/uploads/2022/03/GSMA_State_of_the_Industry_2022_English.pdf

Baker, L. (2022, August 26). Elon Musk and T-Mobile announce plans to provide the whole of the US with mobile coverage. *Pocket-Lint.* https://www.pocket-lint.com/phones/news/162397-elon-musk-and-t-mobile-plans-to-provide-the-whole-us-with-mobile-coverage/

Banaschik, M. (2020, September 18). How location tracking is raising the stakes on privacy protection. www.ey.com. https://www.ey.com/en_gl/forensic-integrity-services/how-location-tracking-is-raising-the-stakes-on-privacy-protection

Baratè, A., Haus, G., Ludovico, L. A., Pagani, E., & Scarabottolo, N. (2019). *5G Technology for Augmented and Virtual Reality in Education.* Paper presented at the Proceedings of the International Conference on Education and New Developments.

Bentley, F., & Lottridge, D. (2019). *Understanding Mass-market Mobile TV Behaviors in the Streaming Era.* Paper presented at the Proceedings of the 2019 CHI Conference on Human Factors in Computing Systems.

Bhalla, M. R., & Bhalla, A. V. (2010). Generations of mobile wireless technology: A survey. *International Journal of Computer Applications, 5*(4), 26–32.

Bhammar, M., & Mehta, K. (2012). Survey of various image compression techniques. *International Journal on Darshan Institute of Engineering Research & Emerging Technologies, 1*(1), 85–90.

Bhattacharyya, D., Ranjan, R., Alisherov, F., & Choi, M. (2009). Biometric authentication: A review. *International Journal of u- and e-Service, Science and Technology, 2*(3), 13–28.

Bhavani, S., & Thanushkodi, K. (2010). A survey on coding algorithms in medical image compression. *International Journal on Computer Science and Engineering, 2*(5), 1429–1434.

Boneh, D., Sahai, A., & Waters, B. (2011). *Functional Encryption: Definitions and Challenges*. In Theory of Cryptography: 8th Theory of Cryptography Conference, TCC 2011, Providence, RI, USA, March 28-30, 2011. Proceedings 8 (pp. 253–273). Springer.

Bourdieu, P., & Richardson, J. G. (1986). *Handbook of Theory and Research for the Sociology of Education*. Greenwood Press.

Burke, L. E., Ma, J., Azar, K. M., Bennett, G. G., Peterson, E. D., Zheng, Y., … Suffoletto, B. (2015). Current science on consumer use of mobile health for cardiovascular disease prevention: A scientific statement from the American Heart Association. *Circulation, 132*(12), 1157–1213.

Businesswire. (2022, March 30). *Global Sixth Generation (6G) Wireless Market Report 2022–2030: Technology Developments, Market Commercialization, Use Cases and Industry Verticals – ResearchAndMarkets.com*. https://www.businesswire.com/news/home/20220330005643/en/Global-Sixth-Generation-6G-Wireless-Market-Report-2022-2030-Technology-Developments-Market-Commercialization-Use-Cases-and-Industry-Verticals---ResearchAndMarkets.com

Caulfield, B. (2009). Estimating the environmental benefits of ride-sharing: A case study of Dublin. *Transportation Research Part D: Transport and Environment, 14*(7), 527–531.

Chaudhuri, A., Mandaviya, K., Badelia, P., & Ghosh, S. K. (2017). Optical character recognition systems. In *Optical Character Recognition Systems for Different Languages with Soft Computing* (pp. 9–41). Springer.

Cici, B., Markopoulou, A., Frias-Martinez, E., & Laoutaris, N. (2014). *Assessing the Potential of Ride-sharing Using Mobile and Social Data: A Tale of Four Cities*. Paper presented at the Proceedings of the 2014 ACM International Joint Conference on Pervasive and Ubiquitous Computing.

Cisco. (2019). *What Is a Wireless Network? Cisco*. https://www.cisco.com/c/en/us/solutions/small-business/resource-center/networking/wireless-network.html

Collins, D. (2003). *Carrier Grade Voice Over IP* (Vol. 2). McGraw-Hill.

Drape, S. (2018) How data breach is inevitable in wearable devices. https://wt-obk.wearable-technologies.com/2018/10/how-data-breach-is-inevitable-in-wearable-devices/

Elad, B. (2022, October 11). 30+ Cell phones at workplace statistics and facts 2022. *Enterprise Apps Today*. https://www.enterpriseappstoday.com/stats/cell-phones-at-workplace-statistics.html

Ericsson. (2020, September 30). The 5G connected ambulance: Leading the UK's first remote diagnosis. Ericsson.com. https://www.ericsson.com/en/cases/2020/the-5g-connected-ambulance

Ezhilarasan, E., & Dinakaran, M. (2017). *A Review on Mobile Technologies: 3G, 4G and 5G.* Paper presented at the 2017 Second International Conference on Recent Trends and Challenges in Computational Models (ICRTCCM).

Fang, D., Qian, Y., & Hu, R. Q. (2017). Security for 5G mobile wireless networks. *Ieee Access, 6*, 4850–4874.

Farley, T. (2005). Mobile telephone history. *Telektronikk, 101*(3/4), 22.

Feijoo, C., Gómez-Barroso, J.-L., Aguado, J.-M., & Ramos, S. (2012). Mobile gaming: Industry challenges and policy implications. *Telecommunications Policy, 36*(3), 212–221.

Feng, S. (2022). The detrimental effects of mobile game addiction on Chinese primary school students and possible interventions. *Science Insights Education Frontiers, 13*(2), 1911–1922.

Finkenzeller, K. (2010). *RFID Handbook: Fundamentals and Applications in Contactless Smart Cards, Radio Frequency Identification and Near-field Communication.* John Wiley & sons.

Frenzel, L. (2013). Fundamentals of communications access technologies: FDMA, TDMA, CDMA, OFDMA, and SDMA. *Electronic Design.* https://www.electronicdesign.com/technologies/communications/article/21802209/electronic-design-fundamentals-of-communications-access-technologies-fdma-tdma-cdma-ofdma-and-sdma

Gawas, A. U. (2015). An overview on evolution of mobile wireless communication networks: 1G–6G. *International Journal on Recent and Innovation Trends in Computing and Communication, 3*(5), 3130–3133.

Gratton, D. A. (2013). *The Handbook of Personal Area Networking Technologies and Protocols.* Cambridge University Press.

GSMA (2021) The mobile economy Sub-Saharan Africa 2021. https://www.gsma.com/mobileeconomy/wp-content/uploads/2021/09/GSMA_ME_SSA_2021_English_Web_Singles.pdf

GSMA (2023). Second wave of 5G: 30 countries to launch services in 2023. https://www.gsma.com/newsroom/press-release/second-wave-of-5g-30-countries-to-launch-services-in-2023/

Hagen, J. B. (2009). *Radio-frequency Electronics: Circuits and Applications.* Cambridge University Press.

Hall, C. (2022, September 2). Satellite to cellular: Everything you need to know about satellite communication on smartphones, including iPhone 14. *Pocket-Lint.* https://www.pocket-lint.com/satellite-communication-smartphones-ntn-availability-specs-details/

Huawei 6G Research Team. (2021, November). *6G: The Next Horizon.* https://www.huawei.com/en/huaweitech/future-technologies/6g-the-next-horizon

Huurdeman, A. A. (2003). *The Worldwide History of Telecommunications.* John Wiley & Sons.

Ilyas, M. (2017). *The Handbook of Ad Hoc Wireless Networks.* CRC Press.

Irwin, L. (2022, April 9). The most common causes of data breaches and how you can spot them. *IT Governance Blog.* https://www.itgovernance.eu/blog/en/the-most-common-causes-of-data-breaches-and-how-you-can-spot-them

Jacob. (2022, January 12). Wordle clones are off of the Apple App Store. *Video Game News.* https://game-news24.com/2022/01/12/wordle-clones-are-off-of-the-apple-app-store/

Jain, A., Hong, L., & Pankanti, S. (2000). Biometric identification. *Communications of the ACM, 43*(2), 90–98.

Jessop, G. (2006). A brief history of mobile telephony: The story of phones and cars. *Southern Review: Communication, Politics & Culture, 38*(3), 43–60.

Jia, X., Feng, Q., Fan, T., & Lei, Q. (2012). *RFID technology and its Applications in Internet of Things (IoT)*. Paper presented at the 2012 2nd International Conference on Consumer Electronics, Communications and Networks (CECNet).

Juels, A. (2006). RFID security and privacy: A research survey. *IEEE Journal on Selected Areas in Communications, 24*(2), 381–394.

Kameswaran, V., Cameron, L., & Dillahunt, T. R. (2018). *Support for Social and Cultural Capital Development in Real-time Ridesharing Services*. Paper presented at the Proceedings of the 2018 CHI conference on human factors in computing systems.

Karsen, M., Chandra, Y. U., & Juwitasary, H. (2019). Technological factors of mobile payment: A systematic literature review. *Procedia Computer Science, 157*, 489–498.

Kumar, S., & Dutta, K. (2016). Securing mobile ad hoc networks: Challenges and solutions. *International Journal of Handheld Computing Research, 7*(1), 26–76.

Lamba, A., Yadav, J., & Devi, G. U. (2012). *Analysis of Technologies in 3G and 3.5 G Mobile Networks*. Paper presented at the 2012 International Conference on Communication Systems and Network Technologies.

Lu, L., Zhang, J., Xie, Y., Gao, F., Xu, S., Wu, X., & Ye, Z. (2020). Wearable health devices in health care: Narrative systematic review. *Jmir Mhealth and Uhealth, 8*(11), e18907.

Lunden, I., & Silberling, A. (2022, January 13). Wordle founder Josh Wardle on going viral and what comes next. https://techcrunch.com/2022/01/12/josh-wardle-interview-wordle/

Market Business News (2023). What is M-Commerce? *Definition and examples*. https://marketbusinessnews.com/financial-glossary/m-commerce/

Miao, G., Zander, J., Sung, K. W., & Slimane, S. B. (2016). *Fundamentals of Mobile Data Networks*. Cambridge University Press.

Minor, J., & Moore, B. (2022, 4 June). The best video streaming services for 2022. *PC Mag Australia*.

Nikou, S. (2015). Mobile technology and forgotten consumers: The young-elderly. *International Journal of Consumer Studies, 39*(4), 294–304.

Orr, A. (2022). Europeans spent $11.2 billion on mobile games in 2021. https://www.pocketgamer.biz/news/77849/europeans-spent-11-billion-on-mobile-games-in-2021/

Papadimitratos, P. and Haas, Z. (2002). Securing mobile ad hoc networks. In M. Ilyas (ed.), *The Handbook of Ad Hoc Wireless Networks*. CRC Press.

Pelletier, M.-P., Trépanier, M., & Morency, C. (2011). Smart card data use in public transit: A literature review. *Transportation Research Part C: Emerging Technologies, 19*(4), 557–568.

Pereira, V., & Sousa, T. (2004). Evolution of mobile communications: From 1G to 4G. Department of Informatics Engineering of the University of Coimbra, Portugal.

Perez, S. (2021, June 15). Mobile game spending hits record $1.7B per week in Q1 2021, up 40% from pre-pandemic levels. https://techcrunch.com/2021/06/15/mobile-game-spending-hits-record-1-7b-per-week-in-q1-2021-up-40-from-pre-pandemic-levels/

Poor, H. V., & Schaefer, R. F. (2017). Wireless physical layer security. *Proceedings of the National Academy of Sciences, 114*(1), 19–26.

Postel, J. (1981). *Internet Protocol, STD 5, RFC 791*, DOI 10.17487/RFC0791, September 1981, https://www.rfc-editor.org/info/rfc791.

Putnam, R. D. (2000). Bowling alone: America's declining social capital: Originally published in *Journal of Democracy, 6*(1), 1995. *Culture and Politics: A Reader*, 223-234.

Qi, Q., Chen, X., Zhong, C., & Zhang, Z. (2020). Physical layer security for massive access in cellular Internet of Things. *Science China Information Sciences, 63*(2), 1–12.

Qian, R. C., & Long, Y. T. (2018). Wearable chemosensors: A review of recent progress. *ChemistryOpen, 7*(2), 118–130.

Quadri, S. (2022, April 19). The next wave: USSD needs more disruption in Africa. *TechCabal.* https://techcabal.com/2022/04/19/the-next-wave-ussd-needs-more-disruption-in-africa/

Qualcomm. (2017, July 25). What is 5G? Everything you need to know about 5G. 5G FAQ. Qualcomm. https://www.qualcomm.com/5g/what-is-5g

Qualtrics (2023) How our phones affect our work-life balance. https://www.qualtrics.com/blog/phones-affect-work-life-balance/

Rajiv. (2018, February 10). *Applications of 5G Technology*. RF Page. https://www.rfpage.com/applications-5g-technology/

Raza, N., Aftab, M. U., Akbar, M. Q., Ashraf, O., & Irfan, M. (2016). Mobile ad-hoc networks applications and its challenges. *Communications and Network, 8*(3), 131–136.

Reacher, J. (2021, May 25). The six main types of mobile apps. *The Industries and Functionalities.* https://medium.com/technosols/the-six-main-types-of-mobile-apps-the-industries-and-functionalities-f74b0ca6d9fd

Roberts, L. G. (1978). The evolution of packet switching. *Proceedings of the IEEE, 66*(11), 1307–1313.

Salsabila, H., Mardhiyah, S., & Budiarto Hadiprakoso, R. (2022, November 1). Flubot malware hybrid analysis on android operating system. *IEEE Xplore.* https://doi.org/10.1109/ICIMCIS56303.2022.10017486

Samsung. (2022, May 8). Samsung unveils 6G spectrum white paper and 6G research findings. https://news.samsung.com/global/samsung-unveils-6g-spectrum-white-paper-and-6g-research-findings

Sebo, E. (2022, January 26). Why the word puzzle Wordle has become a new global online obsession. https://7news.com.au/technology/why-the-word-puzzle-wordle-has-become-a-new-online-obsession-c-5458930

Shafique, K., Khawaja, B. A., Sabir, F., Qazi, S., & Mustaqim, M. (2020). Internet of things (IoT) for next-generation smart systems: A review of current challenges, future trends and prospects for emerging 5G-IoT scenarios. *IEEE Access, 8*, 23022–23040.

Shen, H., & Coughlan, J. M. (2012). *Towards a Real-time System for Finding and Reading Signs for Visually Impaired Users.* Paper presented at the International Conference on Computers for Handicapped Persons.

Sjoding, M. W., Dickson, R. P., Iwashyna, T. J., Gay, S. E., & Valley, T. S. (2020). Racial bias in pulse oximetry measurement. *New England Journal of Medicine, 383*(25), 2477–2478.

Soh, J. O., & Tan, B. C. (2008). Mobile gaming. *Communications of the ACM, 51*(3), 35–39.

Sood, R., & Garg, A. (2014). Digital society from 1G to 5G: A comparative study. *International Journal of Application or Innovation in Engineering & Management (IJAIEM), 3*(2), 186–193.

Spangler, T. (2020). Netflix packs on record 16 million subscribers in Q1, getting huge lift from coronavirus lockdowns. *Variety*. https://variety.com/2020/digital/news/netflix-record-16-million-subscribers-q1-2020-coronavirus-1234586125/

Sutherl, S. (2021, November 22). What is USSD & how does it benefit businesses? *Adapt IT Telecoms*. https://telecoms.adaptit.tech/blog/what-is-ussd/

Taheer, F. (2023, January 17). Online shopping statistics you need to know in 2023. *Optinmonster.com*. https://optinmonster.com/online-shopping-statistics/#:~:text=General%20Online%20Shopping%20Statistics&text=And%20in%20th

Tan, A. (2022, November 10). Optus earmarks A$140m to cover cost of data breach. *ComputerWeekly.com*. https://www.computerweekly.com/news/252527126/Optus-earmarks-A140m-to-cover-cost-of-data-breach#:~:text=Optus%20sets%20aside%20A%24140

Tams, S., Ahuja, M., Thatcher, J., & Grover, V. (2020). Worker stress in the age of mobile technology: The combined effects of perceived interruption overload and worker control. *The Journal of Strategic Information Systems, 29*(1), 101595.

Tsukada, Y. T., Tokita, M., Murata, H., Hirasawa, Y., Yodogawa, K., Iwasaki, Y.-K., … Tsukada, S. (2019). Validation of wearable textile electrodes for ECG monitoring. *Heart and Vessels, 34*(7), 1203–1211. doi:10.1007/s00380-019-01347-8

Wamola, A. (2021, December 1). The mobile economy: How growth is positively impacting lives in Africa. www.forbesafrica.com. https://www.forbesafrica.com/brand-voice/2021/12/01/the-mobile-economy-how-growth-is-positively-impacting-lives-in-africa/

Wang, Q., Li, B., & Singh, P. V. (2018). Copycats vs. original mobile apps: A machine learning copycat-detection method and empirical analysis. *Information Systems Research, 29*(2), 273–291.

Want, R. (2006). An introduction to RFID technology. *IEEE Pervasive Computing, 5*(1), 25–33.

Wigginton, C., & Greenberg, B. (2022, November 15). Smart cities and 5G: Taking it to the next level. *Forbes*. https://www.forbes.com/sites/deloitte/2022/11/15/smart-cities-and-5g-taking-it-to-the-next-level/?sh=527038921e49

Williams, T. (2021, September 28). Phone scams are 'exploding' and costing vulnerable Australians millions, new data shows. ABC News. https://www.abc.net.au/news/2021-09-28/phone-scams-exploding-vulnerable-australians-new-data/100496496

Wu, B., Shastri, B. J., & Prucnal, P. R. (2014). Chapter 11: Secure communication in fiber-optic networks. In B. Akhgar & H. R. Arabnia (eds), *Emerging Trends in ICT Security* (pp. 173–183). Morgan Kaufmann.

Wu, M., & Luo, J. (2019). Wearable technology applications in healthcare: A literature review. *Online Journal Nursing Informatics, 23*(3).

Young, A. (2022, March 2). E-commerce is harming the planet. Here's why smart retailers need to find a balance. *SmartCompany*. https://www.smartcompany.com.au/industries/retail/retail-online-sustainability-planet/

Youssef, S. M., & Salem, R. M. (2007). Automated barcode recognition for smart identification and inspection automation. *Expert Systems with Applications, 33*(4), 968–977.

Zou, Y., Zhu, J., Wang, X., & Hanzo, L. (2016). A survey on wireless security: Technical challenges, recent advances, and future trends. *Proceedings of the IEEE, 104*(9), 1727–1765.

7

SOCIAL COMPUTING AND SOCIAL COMMERCE

7.1 Learning Outcomes

After reading this chapter, you will be able to:

- Define and explain social computing and its dimensions
- Differentiate between the various generations of the World Wide Web (WWW)
- Discuss the most popular tools for social computing and user-generated content
- Identify key components of social computing in the business sector
- Understand the concept of social commerce, its types, and its benefits and challenges
- Critically distinguish between social commerce and traditional e-commerce platforms
- Understand the key components of the social commerce conceptual model and be able to apply this model to real-life social commerce applications

7.2 Introduction

This chapter provides an overview of social computing and social commerce. It explains the evolution of the Web with a particular emphasis on Web 2.0. It describes the conceptual model for both social computing and social commerce and discusses various relevant definitions, components, types, and tools. It critically differentiates between social commerce and traditional electronic commerce, and examines certain benefits and challenges by using social commerce tools and applications.

7.3 Social Computing

This section introduces the concept of social computing, presents a definition of the term and its overall conceptual model, and describes the tools currently being used in this domain. It also discusses several generations of the Web including Web 2.0 technology, which has revolutionized social computing in various ways.

Introduction to Social Computing

The Internet has opened up new horizons for commerce and communication, and is now impacting on many aspects of daily life, seeing a dramatic rise in uptake since the emergence of the earliest version of the Web. The interest in the Internet continues to increase with each more sophisticated version of the Web. With Web 2.0, for example, online social networks (OSNs) have opened the door wide for people and communities to exchange ideas, thoughts, and beliefs, utilizing virtual platforms with different norms, orientations, and functions (Abu-Salih et al., 2021). The use of these platforms and their various applications has also expanded to include non-profitable sectors in addition to industrial and commercial sectors. It has become evident that social media plays a vital role in transforming business activities. For example, OSNs have consolidated marketing tools by establishing new dialogues whereby companies communicate with their customers, listen to their voices, and respond to their concerns promptly and effectively (Abu-Salih et al., 2018).

In this new era, *social computing* – although not new in relative terms – has emerged as a significant discipline that has driven the scientific community to frame this interaction between people and communication technology by conceptualizing social computing terminology in different ways. One perspective perceives social computing as the software medium (social software) that is used to facilitate social interaction (Schuler, 1994).

Definition: Social Computing

Social computing refers to the dynamic relationship between individuals' social actions and their engagement with computerized technologies (Dryer et al., 1999).

The definition of social computing comprises three core dimensions that can be used to conceptualize the terminology: the IT infrastructure, the human factor, and the technology that facilitates digital self-representation (Ali-Hassan & Nevo, 2009). Figure 7.1 depicts these dimensions which conceptualize the notion of social computing and are interrelated. The figure shows the technology (i.e., Web 2.0) that enables people to receive and generate content through the Internet. It is important to understand the difference between Web 2.0 technology and the technologies of both its forerunners and descendants. Therefore, the next section will briefly discuss the evolutionary journey of the World Wide Web, starting with the Web 1.0 technology and proceeding to subsequent Web developments.

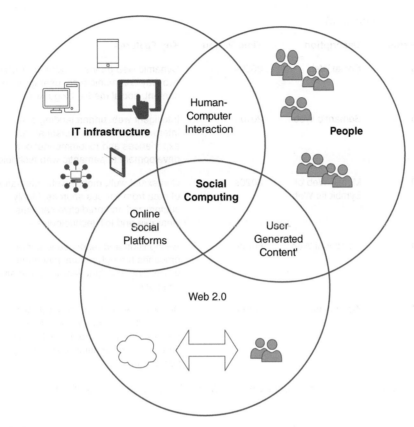

Figure 7.1 Social Computing – a Conceptual Model (based on the social computing dimensions proposed in Ali-Hassan & Nevo (2009)

Evolution of the World Wide Web – Web 1.0 to Web 6.0

The World Wide Web (a.k.a. WWW or the Web) was invented in 1989 by Sir Tim Berners-Lee (a.k.a. TimBL) after he noticed the difficulty of sharing information when working at the European Organization for Nuclear Research (CERN, https://home.web.cern.ch/). Since then, the Web has witnessed various advances which have revolutionized the way that we interact with the Internet.

Table 7.1 shows the generations of the Web which have been introduced to date.

Table 7.1 Generations of the WWW*

Web Version	Description	Time Period	Key Features
Web 1.0	Static Web	1990s	Static web pages, limited interactivity, one-way communication, focus on information consumption rather than creation

(Continued)

Table 7.1   (Continued)

Web Version	Description	Time Period	Key Features
Web 2.0	Social Web	2000s	Dynamic web pages, greater interactivity, two-way communication, user-generated content, social media, blogs, wikis
Web 3.0	Semantic Web	2010s	Intelligent web, understanding and interpretation of data, personalized experiences and recommendations, development of semantic web technologies
Web 4.0	Mobile Web or Symbiotic Web	2020s	Contextual web, mobile web, integration of data from various sources, highly customized and predictive services, wearable and IoT technologies
Web 5.0	Emotional Web	Future	Recognition and response to human emotions through natural language processing, machine learning, and affective computing
Web 6.0	Web Online	Future	Biological web, integration with human biology, direct neural connections between humans and the web, potential for enhanced cognition and sensory perception

Note: * Prepared by the authors based on the discussion provided in Król (2020).

As can be seen, the Web has undergone a series of developments which have influenced various facets of our lives. Because this chapter focuses on the social computing domain, in the next section, we discuss only those tools that are relevant to Web 2.0.

Social Computing Tools

As discussed previously and illustrated in Figure 7.1, social computing comprises a set of interrelated components. Social computing tools are web-enabled platforms that allow the proliferation of user-generated content (UGC) (Meneghello et al., 2020). These tools facilitate creating, editing, sharing, commenting on, and disseminating various UGC. The following are some of the most popular social computing tools:

- **Online social networks (OSNs):** These platforms have opened wide the door for people to make public their thoughts, ideas, and feelings. By leveraging the easy and free access provided by these tools, people are now able to establish dialogues with others by sharing content instantly in the form of textual content, photos, videos, and other files. The use of these platforms is dramatically increasing in all areas of society; more than 4.3 billion people worldwide were active on social media as of April 2021 (> 55% of the global population) (Datareportal, 2021). Businesses have also been using these tools to establish relationships with their customers, run marketing campaigns, run advertising, and obtain insights from the analysis of social and personal data. Examples of OSNs are Facebook™, Twitter™, YouTube™, WhatsApp™, Instagram™, Snapchat™, WeChat™, LinkedIn™, Tumblr™, and Flickr™.

- **Social review sites:** These sites offer their users a space wherein they can convey their attitudes and opinions on products, services, businesses, and even people. In fact, these sites are becoming much more critical for customers; 93% of customers check online review sites before purchasing a product or service (Kaemingk, 2020). Further, these sites empower customers by providing them with a word-of-mouth[1] podium where they can discuss their purchase experiences. Therefore, businesses rely on statistics provided by these platforms to improve their brand image and compete to provide the best customer experience. Although some of the OSNs, such as Facebook, provide a social review service to their connected users, various stand-alone social review sites are available, including Amazon, Yelp, Trip Advisor, BBB, and YellowPages.
- **Discussion forums:** These are the most primitive and traditional forms of OSNs. Users of these sites can contribute by posting or replying to a discussion post in an asynchronous fashion. Forums are commonly categorized into several sections, each one on a specific or high-level topic. Hence, all discussions conducted in each section are relevant to the designated topic. Question and answer (Q&A) sites are examples of these sites as they offer users the opportunity to ask questions and let other users provide their answers in threaded conversational sequences (Boh, 2014). Examples of online discussion forums are: Nexopia, Quora, Stack Overflow, eCommerceFuel, and The Education Forum.
- **Wikis:** These are online platforms that allow people to create and modify content pertaining to specific topics. One of the interesting features of Wikis is that they provide an area where members of a team can collaborate and work on a shared report and documentation simultaneously and effectively. This consolidates efforts to achieve the organization's goal as well as facilitating the creation and dissemination of knowledge. Wikipedia, WikiBooks, Wikispecies, Wiktionary, Wikitravel, and WikiHow are all examples of Wikis.
- **Blogs:** Blogs or weblogs are online journal sites where contents are displayed in reverse chronological order; thus, the latest published posts appear first. This kind of website is commonly managed and moderated by either an individual (e.g., maintaining a personal diary) or perhaps a group of people (e.g., discussing a small business, community blog, etc.). The subjects discussed in blogs can be

---

[1]Word-of-mouth: In marketing this terminology refers to positive dialogues established by consumers to convey their satisfaction with a product, service, or brand.

relevant to a specific theme or can be generic and relevant to various themes and topics. Blogs allow members and visitors to interact with the published content by giving feedback in the form of replies, likes, etc. The verb 'blogging' implies that the user has the skills set to publish and share content, and to manage and moderate published content. A vlog (video blog) belongs to a special category of blogs that comprises published posts that are broadcast as videos and multimedia content. The backbone of the software system that is used to operate blogs is called the Content Management System (CMS). Examples of such CMSs are Wordpress™, TypePad™, and Tumblr™.

- **Video hosting and sharing sites**: These sites facilitate the creation, uploading, managing, storing, and broadcasting of personal as well as business-related videos. These websites (a.k.a. online video platforms (OVPs)) have been adopted by several organizations, government agencies, educational institutions, and other categories of society as alternative media. OVPs are an effective marketing tool and usually provide advanced analytical solutions to obtain a greater understanding of audience behaviour. Further, several video hosting sites offer users an opportunity to monetize their videos and live streams by turning on ads and other venues/platforms. Similar to other Web 2.0 and social computing tools, OVPs allow users to comment, reply, and interact with published videos. YouTube, Vimeo, Kaltura, and JW Player are all examples of OVPs.

- **Sharing economy sites:** The idea of a 'sharing economy', while not new, has evolved to become an economic phenomenon that relies on the sophisticated improvements to ICT of late, particularly easy Internet access and the ubiquity of smartphones. The *Oxford English Dictionary* describes it as 'an economic system in which assets or services are shared between private individuals, either for free or for a fee, typically by means of the Internet'. The propagation of sharing economy networks (a.k.a. peer-to-peer models/apps) has reduced the costs of services, while at the same time allowing people to better utilize their idle assets. Various industries, including accommodation, transportation, and food production have been disrupted by this new socio-economic system. Examples of sharing economy apps are Airbnb, Uber, and Seed Exchange.

Stop and Reflect: Social Computing Tools

Discuss examples of social computing tools that you have experienced and answer the following questions:

- How do you evaluate your experience with these tools?
- What are the benefits and drawbacks of using these tools?
- How can social computing technologies benefit domains/fields/sectors that have not yet adopted them?

Business is one of the core sectors benefitting from social computing technologies. The next section will discuss the effect of social computing, particularly online commerce, on the business sector. It will show how social computing and the subsequent emergence of social commerce have revolutionized commerce activities.

7.4 Social Computing in the Business Sector

The previous section presented the background of social computing. Social computing technologies have become increasingly prevalent in the business sector over the past decade, transforming the way companies interact with customers, collaborate with employees, and operate their businesses. This section examines the business domain and various aspects of business operations that have been affected by social computing.

An Overview of Social Computing Components in Business

The business sector is one of the key areas that has felt the massive impact of the extensive use of social computing. As demonstrated in Figure 7.2, social computing affects not only business-to-consumer relationships (Parameswaran & Whinston, 2007); it also influences a businesses' relationships with their employees (Kim et al., 2013), suppliers (Chae et al., 2020), and competitors (Vannoy & Medlin, 2012).

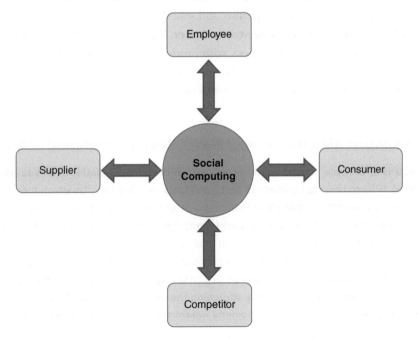

Figure 7.2 Businesses' Internal and External Interactions with Social Computing (based on the discussions in Chae et al. (2020), Kim et al. (2013), Parameswaran & Whinston (2007) and Vannoy & Medlin (2012))

The interaction between business and social computing as depicted in Figure 7.2 can also be perceived as the interactional relationship between businesses themselves and between businesses and their consumers and employees.

- **Social computing in business-to-business (B2B):** OSNs have established a new means by which businesses are now able to collaborate with partners, distributors, and other third-party entities to a broader extent. OSNs provide valuable marketing insights by allowing businesses to track and monitor the best social marketing strategy applied by them or their competitors. Adobe is one example of a company that has increased its revenue by successfully incorporating B2B advertising solutions using social networks (Adobe, 2020).
- **Social computing in business-to-consumer (B2C):** B2C activities have flourished, as evidenced by the dramatic increase in the usage of OSNs. Businesses have found OSNs to be a fertile medium for promoting various features of B2C practices to their customers. The technology incorporated in social computing has provided better-tailored personalized services, reduced customers' waiting time, increased revenue, and enhanced the image of companies (Chamoso et al., 2019).
- **Social computing in business-to-employee (B2E):** With social computing, employees are now able to communicate easily and actively via formal social means – such as corporate social networks[2] – as well as other informal OSNs. In particular, a corporate social network allows the company to disseminate information and services to their employees, exchange expertise, and solve problems efficiently.
- **Social computing in customer-to-customer (C2C):** Customers can use these platforms to share their experiences with products and services, ask questions, and get advice from other customers. They can also leave reviews and ratings, which can influence the purchasing decisions of other customers.

Example: Alibaba – a Successful Social Computing Story

Alibaba is a Chinese company with a leading B2B and B2C platform. It was established in 1999 to provide businesses and individuals with a means by which they could open online retail stores that cater to customers worldwide (Tan et al., 2016). Alibaba has incorporated two distinguished social-computing-based platforms into its ecosystem. Firstly, the Juhuasuan social app has been established to add new social computing values by preventing environmental catastrophes as well as protecting and supporting disadvantaged rural groups in China. Juhuasuan also facilitates sharing the value of a good product, thereby improving the experiences of both producers and consumers. Secondly, the giant company established an open platform for logistics

---

[2]Socialcase (https://www.vmware.com/) is an example of a corporate social network application that delivers an electronic workspace to track and integrate corporate data.

firms across China, the aim of which is to assist socially vulnerable groups to participate in the social distribution platform (Yun et al., 2020).

7.5 Social Commerce and Electronic Commerce

The definition of social computing comprises the incorporation of technology so as to enhance the relationships between people and businesses. In business, social computing is generally referred to as social commerce (s-commerce). This section provides an overview of s-commerce and explains how it differs from traditional e-commerce.

Social Commerce: A Definition

In the previous section, an overview was given of the internal and external interactions of business with social computing. S-commerce is a new stream in electronic commerce (e-commerce) that has reshaped online commercial activities, shopping experience, and information accessibility (Bugshan & Attar, 2020).

Definition: Social Commerce

S-commerce refers to e-commerce activities conducted via social media and Web 2.0 tools as a means of facilitating online purchases (Hajli, 2013; Liang et al., 2011).

This notion was initially established by Yahoo™ to indicate the online social collaborative shopping experiences in B2B and B2C by using what was called the 'Yahoo Shoposphere',[3] which consisted of a pick list of the most popular products. Since then, companies have been incorporating OSNs as an effective arena in which to promote products and services through, for example, social commerce campaigns.

S-Commerce vs E-Commerce

E-commerce (a.k.a. Internet commerce) essentially means the buying and selling of products and services online. Generally, a buyer may purchase an item after seeing its online description (text, image, or video). The purchase occurs once the buyer pays for the item

---

[3]Yahoo Shoposphere was the first platform that enabled users to share their opinions on the products listed. More on this can be found in: https://socialcommercetoday.com/steve-rubels-original-2005-social-commerce-post/ (accessed: 07/06/2021).

which is shipped or delivered to the buyer depending on what it is. S-commerce is considered an extension of e-commerce and comprises the same activities, albeit via OSNs. Nevertheless, the two models cross and differ in various features and aspects. Table 7.2 demonstrates some of these aspects and how they are tackled in each commerce model (Huang & Benyoucef, 2013).

Table 7.2   E-Commerce vs S-Commerce*

Feature	E-commerce	S-commerce
Definition	Commercial transactions via the Internet	Commercial transactions by means of OSNs
Platform usage and design	Designated for commerce (catalogued and search-supported)	Not fully designated and partially designed for commerce
Technology	Web 1.0	Web 2.0
Business model	Mainly B2C	B2C and C2C
Customer base	Long track to establish a customer base	Fast track to establish a customer base
Group shopping	Limited	Friends on OSNs can conduct a purchase together
Reviews and recommendation	Can be provided, mainly anonymously	Users can share their recommendation and reviews with friends
Tailored shopping	Limited and mainly based on previous purchase transactions	Personalized shopping experience based on user's expertise and domain of interest
Customer Power	Less powered	Empowered customers – Voice of the Market (VoM) and Voice of the Customer (VOC)
Interaction with vendor	Limited	High

Note: Prepared by the authors based on the discussions in Huang & Benyoucef (2013).

Stop and Reflect: E-Commerce vs S-Commerce

Discuss an example of both an e-commerce and an s-commerce application/platform, then articulate the variations in both applications in regard to the features listed in Table 7.2.

Types of S-Commerce

As discussed previously, s-commerce is an extension of e-commerce whereby the buying and selling activities are conducted mainly via social media. Various studies have attempted to categorize s-commerce activities based on the nature of these activities or based on the incorporated technology, community, or platform (Cui et al., 2018; Han et al., 2018). Figure 7.3 demonstrates various types of s-commerce, which can be described as follows:

- **Social shopping:** Online shopping sites that provide embedded chat and forum plug-ins to allow their community members to discuss and exchange information about their products and services, and to share them using social networks. Examples of social shopping business applications are Wanelo, Pinterest, and GoTryItOn.
- **Flash sale:** A time-limited discount or online offering on a product that is promoted using social media. Examples of private sites offering flash sales are Gilt, The Clymb, and Jetsetter.
- **Group purchase:** A limited-time discount that can be given only to a group of people. Among others, Groupon and LivingSocial are two well-known group purchasing sites.
- **Social shopping apps:** Applications that reward consumers who share their e-shopping experiences with other shoppers. An example of a social shopping app is Shopkick, which rewards its affiliated members with kicks (points), which can be redeemed with gift cards when users visit participating online stores and scan the barcodes of the purchased products.
- **Purchase sharing:** In this type of social computing, consumers' purchasing behaviour is collected by tracking their credit card transactions. The collected data are passed on to business firms for analysis, and are used as marketing tools. The purchasing of this information can also benefit the designated consumers who receive a financial reward. Upserve is an example of a purchase sharing site that sells purchase transactions and their analytics to local merchants.
- **Social peer-to-peer:** Social P2P s-commerce promotes the consumer-to-consumer (C2C) model by means of OSNs. In this type of s-commerce, people within a limited geographical area can undertake commercial activities with each other using well-established social networks. P2P s-commerce does not necessarily involve money; bartering – exchanging products and services via social media – is another form of P2P s-commerce. Facebook Marketplace is an example of a social service that supports P2P social transactions.
- **Participatory commerce:** This type of s-commerce empowers customers by engaging them with one or several phases of the manufacturing and production process. This participation involves feedback, voting, funding, and collaborative design. Threadless, Kickstarter, and Nike are examples of sites and companies that adopt participatory commerce.

Figure 7.3   Types of S-Commerce (based on Cui et al. (2018) and Han et al. (2018))

Besides the types depicted in Figure 7.3, s-commerce can also be categorized into two groups (Huang & Benyoucef, 2013): (i) OSNs sites that provide an integrated e-commerce component to enable commercial transactions and advertisements; and (ii) conventional e-commerce sites that incorporate social tools in order to facilitate the social interaction of visitors and members.

S-commerce Framework Model

S-commerce is a phenomenon consisting of various components that interplay to achieve the overall objective. Therefore, it is important to describe the core elements of s-commerce and explain their interconnectivity. S-commerce consists of four key components: *people, technology, information,* and *business* (Wang & Zhang, 2012). The interrelation between these components and dimensions is demonstrated in Figure 7.4.

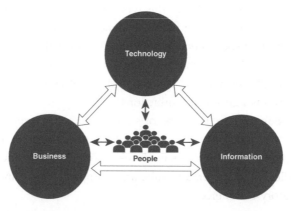

Figure 7.4   S-Commerce Framework Model (based on the dimensions discussed in Wang & Zhang (2012))

The following explains each of the key dimensions of this model:

- **People:** In this model, 'People' is used as an abstract term which refers to more than just a particular group of people. Instead, it might represent one individual, a community of individuals, or small or large organizations. The term can also refer to consumers, service providers, or mediators (those involved in delivering the service from the provider to the consumer). People are the central element of the s-commerce framework, the generators of social content, and the operators of the entire s-commerce process. Further, various assumptions relating to people are also identified and utilized to give a better understanding of the s-commerce framework. These assumptions include, but are not limited, to: the view of the empowered consumers; social heuristics and psychology; gender orientation and overall social demographics, and their effect on consumer social behaviour; and cultural and economic factors.

- **Technology infrastructure:** This is the backbone of the infrastructure that is required for s-commerce activities. Here, technology refers to the overall ICT (hardware and software) which expedites two-way communication in the realm of social digital commerce. Technology infrastructure is usually either conventional infrastructure or cloud-based infrastructure. In conventional technology, s-commerce requires a well-designed hardware infrastructure that is scalable to accommodate high-volume social commercial transactions. This infrastructure comprises server machines, networking platforms, personal computers, mobile devices, and other required electronic devices. Technology also includes the software systems and applications which are operated on the physical hardware. Software systems include operating systems, Web servers, and various s-commerce platforms, tools, and functionalities (Web-based and mobile-based). The aforementioned hardware and software components and resources for s-commerce can also be operated on the cloud by using a cloud-based infrastructure.[4]

- **Business:** The integration of business and social media gave rise to the term *social commerce*. In s-commerce, business involves more than just buying and selling via online social platforms. It also embraces objectives, strategies, frameworks, and models to enhance and consolidate s-commerce practices. Business in the s-commerce framework also comprises policies and procedures which are constantly being improved to provide the best s-commerce regulations and guidelines.

   Various management aspects are considered in the business dimension of the s-commerce framework:

   o *Supply Chain Management (SCM):* This en compasses a chain of several activities and drivers which are undertaken by various levels of suppliers and consumers. These activities include: the acquisition of raw materials; manufacturing, coordination, warehousing and inventory management; and

---

[4]Further discussion on cloud computing in general and its components will be presented in Chapter 11.

product transportation and delivery. Currently, social media are incorporated in SCM. This is an effective tool that has led to the emergence of Social SCM. Social SCM has proven ability to facilitate collaboration and reduce SCM costs. Also, using social media, problems throughout the supply chain can be promptly shared and resolved (Sung-Min, 2012).

    o   *Customer Relationship Management (CRM)*: This company department manages all of a company's interactions with its customers and potential customers mainly via a software system. Like SCM, CRM and all embedded activities have witnessed a significant shift since the emergence of social media, thus Social CRM has evolved to depict the incorporation of social media to establish new touchpoints with customers.

    o   *Other functional areas*: The business dimension in an s-commerce framework also consists of other management areas, including social marketing, business intelligence, accounting and finance, and operations management.

- **Information:** As discussed previously, the advent of Web 2.0 technology has encouraged people to contribute to the Internet by enabling them to generate user-generated content (UGC) using various means. As the information is generated by people who have different interests and agendas, the information creates a content-driven environment produced by various s-commerce stakeholders, including consumers and businesses. In regard to consumers, s-commerce information includes various self-representative data which consist of customers' purchasing details, profiling and personalization data, social contents (can be multimodal), and opinions and feedback (including reviews and recommendations with associated emotions and sentiments).

For businesses, s-commerce information also comprises businesses' self-representative data, such as the company's profile and products' descriptions, which can be shared and advertised on s-commerce platforms. Contents that are generated by dialogues established with customers (e.g., through chat platforms, CRM, SCM, and customer service and support) are also examples of business-related s-commerce information.

As can be inferred from the above, each component of the s-commerce framework cannot be isolated from the other components; they are correlated and integrated to provide cohesion to s-commerce and facilitate its functions. Hence, various benefits can be derived from using an s-commerce framework, although challenges also exist and hamper the adoption of an s-commerce framework. The next section elaborates on the benefits and challenges of s-commerce.

Benefits and Challenges of S-Commerce

The integration of social media and e-commerce has brought various benefits and challenges to customers and businesses (Han et al., 2018; Zhou et al., 2013).

Benefits

- **Competitive pricing:** The cost of a product or service is considered an important factor that influences the purchase decision, and competitive pricing is one of the strategies used by businesses to obtain or strengthen their competitive advantage. Therefore, companies compete to deliver a low-cost but high-quality product or service. With social media having become an essential means of promoting products and services, another arena of competitiveness has been established which generally results in cheaper pricing. Via social media, customers are now able to compare prices – by themselves or using price comparison sites[5] – and share and recommend designated products or services.

- **Brand awareness:** The ever-increasing utilization of social media has created an opportunity for businesses to target and reach new customers. This is intensified by the word-of-mouth phenomenon, purchase intentions, ability to share and discuss brands' products, and the application of various social media marketing strategies, thereby expanding the audience base and influencing customers' purchase decisions.

- **Greater profits:** Successful investment in s-commerce results in an increase in sales volume and profits. With appropriate social media marketing strategies, companies can now reach more customers who can benefit from the flexibility of s-commerce platforms that provide an easy and prompt checkout process. Nevertheless, to achieve success in s-commerce, companies must adopt smart advertising strategies and select those social media platforms that seem to be favoured by the targeted customers.

- **Consolidation of customer engagement and loyalty:** Customer engagement is one of the key factors that optimizes commerce activities conducted via social media. In fact, by using sophisticated social analytics, companies are now able to understand their customers' behaviours, and they compete to provide the best transaction experience. To this end, companies have established various social touchpoints with their customers, thereby augmenting their engagement. These include messaging, commenting, replying, live chatting, chatbots, rating, recommending, etc. However, customer touchpoints that provide poor customer service would have a negative effect. Hence, the key to success in the s-commerce sphere is to give customers a responsive, seamless, timely, omni-channel, and personalized service (such as Facebook retargeting[6]).

- **Better business opportunities:** In addition to the aforementioned benefits of s-commerce, s-commerce assists companies to improve their products and services by listening closely to the VoC and VoM, and examining and understanding customers' attitudes and emotions. S-commerce also can increase traffic to companies' websites and optimize their search engine capability. In terms of marketing, s-commerce offers companies a dynamic venue for promoting their products and services using multimodal advertising methods.

---

[5]Price comparison sites are online tools that are used to compare the price of a certain product or service provided by various vendors and brands (e.g., Google Shopping: https://www.google.com/shopping).

[6]Facebook retargeting is a mechanism used by Facebook to reach people who have visited a certain website and then deliver targeted advertisements to them to encourage them to revisit website.

Challenges

- **S-commerce data acquisition and integration:** The ever-increasing volume of social data that is generated by various social media platforms poses a challenge to the means used to collect and manage such a massive data island. Social media data constitutes most of social *big data*.[7] This necessitates the development of sophisticated technical solutions that can handle and analyse vast amounts of social activities and transactions that are generated by s-commerce platforms. Moreover, it is challenging for companies to integrate these data silos with their internal corporate databases. This is particularly important since a 360-degree view of customers is obtained from both internal and external data sources, which should be aggregated in one place.

Definition: Customer 360-Degree View

A 360-degree view of the customer is obtained by having a comprehensive and unified view of all explicit and implicit interactive customer touchpoints with the company.

- **Trust and privacy:** The acquisition of customers' social data might comprise certain information that is personal and sensitive. It is the company's responsibility to maintain the security and privacy of this sensitive data, and by doing so it will gain its customers' trust. To ensure the protection of consumers' sensitive data, rigorous policies and procedures should be established so that the collection, management, storage, and utilization of consumers' data are undertaken using the best privacy and security practices.
- **Responsive interaction with customers' opinions:** The open environment of social media platforms has encouraged people to reveal attitudes towards, and their opinions on, various issues that affect some aspect of their lives. Products and services are no exception; consumers perceive social media as an ideal medium through which they can discuss their experiences and express their sentiments and emotions. Hence, companies must take this into account, and take measures to ensure that they listen to customers' feedback, problems, and complaints, respond promptly, and address negative issues. At the same time, positive comments and reviews are important word-of-mouth marketing manifestations that should be incentivized to enhance the company's reputation.
- **Fierce competition:** The power of s-commerce to boost sales and expand the customer base has produced a fiercely competitive arena. Therefore, businesses should respond to the social market pressures and handle the competitive forces by

---

[7]Big data will be discussed further in Chapter 11.

exploring new opportunities. This can be tackled, for example, by applying strategies that will give a competitive advantage (Turban et al., 2016). These include: (i) cost leadership (lowest price); (ii) differentiation (variety in products, services, or features); (iii) establishing a niche (narrow scope with best operation); (iv) growth (increase consumer base and market share); (v) alliances (collaboration with businesses partners); (vi) innovation (new products, services, or features); (vii) operational effectiveness (enhance overall business processes); (viii) customer orientation (customer satisfaction); (ix) timeliness (prompt and responsive service); and (x) entry barriers (discouraging other potential competitors from entering the market by offering innovative products, exceptional service, etc.).

- Difficulty in assessing s-commerce performance: It is difficult to measure the financial benefits obtained from s-commerce. For example, although a company website may receive a great number of visits, there is no guarantee that the visitors will become buyers. Further, user interaction and engagement is relatively hard to quantify when e-commerce activities are transformed into s-commerce platforms (Kumar et al., 2019).

Stop and Reflect: Benefits and Challenges of S-Commerce

Refer to the examples you provided in the last **Stop and Reflect** box and answer the following questions:

- What are the benefits and challenges associated with both applications?
- How would you describe the advertising landscape in both applications?
- How have social content creators and influencers transformed conventional advertising?
- To what extent do friends' recommendations about products and services offered on social media influence your purchasing decisions?

7.6 Chapter Summary

With the emergence of Web 2.0, information is no longer monopolized; people are now able to access, produce, retrieve, store, manipulate, and exchange information interactively at an unprecedented pace. Therefore, the notion of social computing has drawn much attention from both academia and industry, and various attempts have been made to ensure its optimal utilization. Hence, the business sector is one of the key sectors that has witnessed a qualitative leap in several respects. E-commerce is one of the vital areas affected by this revolution, particularly with the emergence of social commerce.

S-commerce is a natural phenomenon resulting from the implicit or explicit integration of online commerce activities with social media tools.

This chapter has shed the light on social computing as a generic paradigm that encompasses the new advances and generations of the Web as well as the technologies, infrastructure, tools, platforms, and applications that facilitate the human–computer interaction by which user contents are generated. Then, the implications of social computing for the business sector were discussed. This chapter also introduced and explained s-commerce, and discussed the differences between s-commerce and e-commerce. Also, an overview of types, a conceptual model, and the benefits and challenges of s-commerce were presented to offer students a solid foundation prior to tackling this important topic more comprehensively.

Overall, social commerce is an emerging trend that has the potential to transform the way that businesses engage with customers and sell products online. By understanding the opportunities and challenges presented by social commerce, businesses can develop effective strategies for leveraging this growing trend.

7.7 Further Reading

Busalim, A. H., & Ghabban, F. (2021). Customer engagement behaviour on social commerce platforms: An empirical study. *Technology in Society, 64*, 101437. doi: 10.1016/j.techsoc.2020.101437.

Customer engagement is one of the crucial aspects of any business as it is the emotional interconnection between the customer and the brand. This article developed a customer engagement model for s-commerce. The authors leveraged various scientific theories including social support, social presence, and uses and gratifications theories to indicate the factors that positively influence the customers' engagement behaviour in s-commerce.

Zhang, K. Z. K., & Benyoucef, M. (2016). Consumer behavior in social commerce: A literature review. *Decision Support Systems, 86*, 95–108. doi: 10.1016/j.dss.2016.04.001.

Customer behaviour studies examine those factors that affect customers' purchasing decision process. The authors of this article carried out a comprehensive literature review of customer behaviour in the context of s-commerce. They reported the theories and research methods adopted in the reviewed studies, and proposed a conceptual framework – the stimulus–organism–response model – comprising the factors affecting consumers' decision-making processes. The model gives a comprehensive understanding of consumer behaviour in social commerce.

Bugshan, H., & Attar, R. W. (2020). Social commerce information sharing and their impact on consumers. *Technological Forecasting and Social Change, 153*, 119875. doi: 10.1016/j.techfore.2019.119875.

Trust is a critical aspect of successful s-commerce, playing a significant role in customers' engagement, and it influences purchase intentions. The authors examined the notion of trust in sharing commerce – i.e., collaborative business activities undertaken by consumers, businesses, and involved stakeholders. The article reported that trust, the sharing of social commerce information, perceived privacy risks, and the intention to buy are crucial constructs for social commerce research in emerging markets.

Discussion Questions

1   How has the evolution of the WWW boosted s-commerce and its activities?
2   Why have OSNs taken the place of the traditional online forums, and what direct impact has this had on s-commerce?
3   Why do you think it takes less time to establish a customer base using an s-commerce platform than an e-commerce platform?
4   What distinguishes participatory commerce from other types of s-commerce?
5   Besides those discussed in this chapter, what other benefits and challenges confront s-commerce?

Case Study: OpenSooq™ – A Social Commerce Perspective

OpenSooq™ is a well-established online marketplace brand with its head office in Amman, Jordan, and regional offices in four other countries in the Middle East and North Africa (MENA). Its core business is the classifieds web portal and app that connects sellers and buyers who wish to list their products and search for their specific requirements, respectively. The company started operations in 2012 and has since grown into a group with over 250 employees with rapid plans for expansion and growth. In this endeavour, they have secured multiple financing rounds recently and the firm plans to expand its digital footprint in classifieds as well as related businesses.

What Are Classifieds?

Classifieds are the section of a newspaper or magazine that contains advertisements for products or services, which are paid for by the seller. With the dawn of the Internet era, classifieds published in magazines and newspapers have taken a back seat as a form of advertising following the launch of .com portals across the globe, each with different business models. Businesses promoting themselves via the Internet have continued to innovate and improve on their business operations and have introduced terrific, augmented features such as vertical integration with the supply chain, along with their core product offering: classifieds. OpenSooq.com enables consumers and SMEs across the Middle East and North Africa to trade

(Continued)

across all key economic sectors including real estate, automotive, electronics, furniture, and fashion. It also connects consumers with service providers in areas such as education, training, and home repair and maintenance services.

Every 13 seconds, an item is sold on OpenSooq and, in an average month, customers browse over 2.7 billion pages looking for products and services. OpenSooq had a reach in excess of 65 million customers in 2020 and the gross market value of goods and services listed was $30 billion. This creates a chain effect that has an impact on economic growth, new employment, and an improvement in the lifestyles of the relevant stakeholders.

How is S-Commerce Incorporated in OpenSooq?

OpenSooq incorporates the notion of s-commerce using different means:

1   OpenSooq allows users to create profiles and make them publicly available to both buyers and sellers. This lets the buyer observe, track, and obtain insights about the seller. The profiles on OpenSooq can be linked to the users' social media profiles. This enables sellers to share their advertisements in standardized form across all social media platforms, creating a multiplier effect in generating leads for the advertisement, as well as building buyers' trust in a seller, as they are buying from a person rather than a machine.

2   In its endeavour to enhance communication with their customers and provide a secure and reliable approach to verifying users' accounts, OpenSooq has incorporated WhatsApp™ to manage account updates and verification, as well as communication about the delivery process. This has been achieved by working with Infobip,[8] an IT and telecommunications company, to set up and launch WhatsApp Business API in 19 countries. OpenSooq uses WhatsApp to create an automated customer onboarding experience, seamless sign-up process, and account verification process instead of using traditional SMS. Also, OpenSooq uses WhatsApp to establish new dialogues with their current and potential users, thereby resolving issues pertaining to account access and authentication as well as selling and buying products and services using the platform. The WhatsApp service of OpenSooq has demonstrated proven effectiveness and customer satisfaction. In particular, the company has witnessed the following outcomes: (i) 82% increase in customer satisfaction (CSAT) score; (ii) 78% increase in agent productivity; (iii) 65% increase in first-contact resolution; (iv) 44% decrease in agent handling time; and (v) 60% decrease in verification and password reset complaints.

3   Within different categories, consumer behaviour depends largely on the product's sophistication and complexity. Consumers are likely to describe their experience by commenting, reviewing, and rating products and services. OpenSooq, being a classifieds platform, has the ability and massive potential to grow using direct social commerce and employing these technologies to further increase its reach and exploit its potential. Through the OpenSooq platform, users are able to interactively

[8]https://www.infobip.com/

communicate by means of direct calls, direct chat via OpenSooq's chat system, and comments, and share posted items with friends on social media.

4 The traffic between several OSNs and the OpenSooq platform has been increasing. To obtain further insights on how the OpenSooq platform is accessed via OSNs, an analysis of the traffic coming to OpenSooq listings from OSNs was undertaken.

5 The communication between users (buyers and sellers) reports an augmented interest in the chat messaging service provided by the OpenSooq platform.

Questions

1 How has OpenSooq benefited from the Internet and Web 2.0 technology in promoting its business activities?
2 How does OpenSooq utilize social commerce and its touchpoints with the OSNs?
3 How does OpenSooq apply the s-commerce framework model?
4 How has its partnership with Infobip helped OpenSooq to be successful?
5 Why do people tend to use the Chat messaging service rather than phone calls? Do you think this applies to other similar platforms?

Links

- OpenSooq: https://www.opensooq.com/
- OpenSooq: WhatsApp Business API case study | Facebook for Business (2021). https://www.facebook.com/OpenSooq.Jordan/

7.8 References

Abu-Salih, B., Wongthongtham, P., & Chan, K. Y. (2018). Twitter mining for ontology-based domain discovery incorporating machine learning. *Journal of Knowledge Management, 22*(5).

Abu-Salih, B., Wongthongtham, P., Zhu, D., Chan, K. Y., & Rudra, A. (2021). *Social Big Data Analytics*. Springer.

Adobe. (2020). How Adobe achieves alignment and ABM success with LinkedIn. https://business.linkedin.com/marketing-solutions/case-studies/how-adobe-achieves-alignment-and-abm-success-with-linkedin

Ali-Hassan, H., & Nevo, D. (2009). Identifying social computing dimensions: A multidimensional scaling study. *ICIS 2009 Proceedings*, 148.

Boh, W. F. (2014). Knowledge sharing in communities of practice: Examining usefulness of knowledge from discussion forums versus repositories. *ACM SIGMIS Database: The DATABASE for Advances in Information Systems, 45*(2), 8–31.

Bugshan, H., & Attar, R. W. (2020). Social commerce information sharing and their impact on consumers. *Technological Forecasting and Social Change, 153*, 119875.

Chae, B. K., McHaney, R., & Sheu, C. (2020). Exploring social media use in B2B supply chain operations. *Business Horizons, 63*(1), 73–84.

Chamoso, P., González-Briones, A., Rivas, A., De La Prieta, F., & Corchado, J. M. (2019). Social computing in currency exchange. *Knowledge and Information Systems, 61*(2), 733–753.

Cui, Y., Mou, J., & Liu, Y. (2018). Knowledge mapping of social commerce research: A visual analysis using CiteSpace. *Electronic Commerce Research, 18*(4), 837–868.

Datareportal. (2021). Global social media stats. https://datareportal.com/social-media-users

Dryer, D. C., Eisbach, C., & Ark, W. S. (1999). At what cost pervasive? A social computing view of mobile computing systems. *IBM Systems Journal, 38*(4), 652–676.

Hajli, M. (2013). A research framework for social commerce adoption. *Information Management & Computer Security, 21*(3).

Han, H., Xu, H., & Chen, H. (2018). Social commerce: A systematic review and data synthesis. *Electronic Commerce Research and Applications, 30*, 38–50.

Huang, Z., & Benyoucef, M. (2013). From e-commerce to social commerce: A close look at design features. *Electronic Commerce Research and Applications, 12*(4), 246–259.

Kaemingk, D. (2020). Online reviews statistics to know in 2021. https://www.qualtrics.com/blog/online-review-stats/

Kim, H. D., Lee, I., & Lee, C. K. (2013). Building Web 2.0 enterprises: A study of small and medium enterprises in the United States. *International Small Business Journal, 31*(2), 15–174.

Król, K. (2020). Evolution of online mapping: From Web 1.0 to Web 6.0. *Geomatics, Landmanagement and Landscape, 1*, 33–51.

Kumar, A., Salo, J., & Li, H. (2019). Stages of user engagement on social commerce platforms: Analysis with the navigational clickstream data. *International Journal of Electronic Commerce, 23*(2), 179–211.

Liang, T.-P., Ho, Y.-T., Li, Y.-W., & Turban, E. (2011). What drives social commerce: The role of social support and relationship quality. *International Journal of Electronic Commerce, 16*(2), 69–90.

Meneghello, J., Thompson, N., Lee, K., Wong, K. W., & Abu-Salih, B. (2020). Unlocking social media and user generated content as a data source for knowledge management. *International Journal of Knowledge Management (IJKM), 16*(1), 101–122.

Parameswaran, M., & Whinston, A. B. (2007). Social computing: An overview. *Communications of the Association for Information Systems, 19*(1), 37.

Schuler, D. (1994). Social computing. *Communications of the ACM, 37*(1), 28–29.

Sung-Min, P. (2012). New business applications for social networking. *SERI Quarterly, 5*(1), 121–125.

Tan, F. T. C., Tan, B., & Pan, S. L. (2016). Developing a leading digital multi-sided platform: Examining IT affordances and competitive actions in Alibaba.com. *Communications of the Association for Information Systems, 38*(1), 36.

Turban, E., Strauss, J., & Lai, L. (2016). Strategy and performance management in social commerce. In *Social Commerce: Marketing, Technology and Management* (pp. 233–263). Springer International Publishing.

Vannoy, S. A., & Medlin, B. D. (2012). *Investigating Social Computing in Competitive Dynamics*. Paper presented at the 2012 45th Hawaii International Conference on System Sciences.

Wang, C., & Zhang, P. (2012). The evolution of social commerce: The people, management, technology, and information dimensions. *Communications of the Association for Information Systems, 31*(1), 5.

Yun, J. J., Zhao, X., Park, K., & Shi, L. (2020). Sustainability condition of open innovation: Dynamic growth of Alibaba from SME to large enterprise. *Sustainability, 12*(11), 4379.

Zhou, L., Zhang, P., & Zimmermann, H.-D. (2013). Social commerce research: An integrated view. *Electronic Commerce Research and Applications, 12*(2), 61–68.

8

SMART
TECHNOLOGIES

8.1 Learning Outcomes

After reading this chapter, you will be able to:

- Discuss the differences between reality and virtuality
- Answer the question, 'What is virtual reality?'
- Explain the applications of virtual reality
- Understand what augmented reality (AR) is and when it emerged
- Discuss the use of AR applications by various sectors
- Discuss what the metaverse is

8.2 Introduction

In the 21st century, technology plays an important role in specific sectors as a means of improving job performance, providing faster and more effective communication, facilitating the development of new and innovative approaches, increasing profit and, most importantly, decreasing waste and carbon footprints. In particular, technologies such as augmented reality (AR) and virtual reality (VR) have received much attention from individuals, industries, and scholars. These technologies involve computer programming for modelling, simulation, and augmentation that allow people to interact to achieve their goals and aspirations. These technologies are used in various sectors, including education, health, marketing, design, and gaming, among others, and the beauty of these technologies is that people can accomplish their tasks in virtual reality without creating a specific device. This chapter will explain these technologies and describe their application in specific sectors that use them to improve job performance, acquire new knowledge and, most importantly, detect life-threatening diseases or conditions.

8.3 Reality and Virtuality

The world has experienced several waves of technological innovation which have driven changes in lifestyle, social interactions, and preferred modes of communication. The first wave brought personal computers, the second offered users the immense power of the Internet, while the third defied the limitations of cable connection with the introduction of mobile Internet. The fourth wave has pushed the boundaries of innovation with the emergence of immersive or enhancement technologies such as virtual reality (VR), augmented reality (AR), and the metaverse. While VR offers a means of simulating an alternate reality, AR enhances the natural environment by adding digital/virtual elements to it (Mystakidis, 2022). The difference between AR and VR is clearly illustrated in Milgram et al.'s (1994) reality–virtuality (RV) continuum (Figure 8.1), which presents natural and virtual environments at two opposite ends of a straight line (continuum), with AR being closer to the actual world. Figure 8.1 also depicts the mixed reality (MR) spectrum which straddles the real and virtual worlds and is seen as any combination of AR and VR or augmented virtuality (AV) where a virtual experience is enhanced with the inclusion of real-life elements. Moreover, in 2021 users were brought to the cusp of the metaverse – a collection of immersive three-dimensional (3D) spaces spearheaded by VR technology that allows users to navigate from one space to the other while feeling as close as possible to reality (Rospigliosi, 2022).

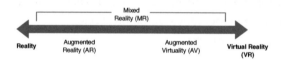

Figure 8.1   The Reality-Virtuality Continuum – adapted from Milgram et al. (1994) by the authors

All these various degrees of realities can be grouped under the umbrella term, 'extended reality' (Floridi, 2022). A timeline of key milestones of extended reality is shown in Figure 8.2.

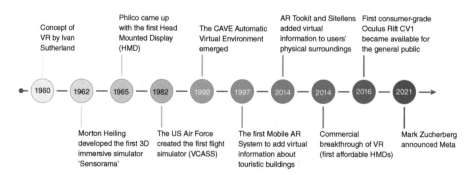

Figure 8.2   Timeline of Key Extended Reality Milestones (adapted from Cipresso et al. (2018), Moro et al. (2017), and Zuckerberg (2021), and designed by Nikhil Toolsee, Curtin University Mauritius, illustrations from https://slidesgo.com/ and https://www.freepik.com/)

8.4 What is Virtual Reality?

In its literal sense, and quite paradoxically, virtual reality means 'fake true world'. In practice, VR provides an experience of reality without the individual being in the real world. For example, in VR vehicle simulations, users experience driving a vehicle and facing risky scenarios without actually being in danger (Tsaramirsis et al., 2022). Today, users of VR technology are immersed in a 3D virtual space complete with sensations such as sight, sound, and touch as they interact with virtual objects which mimic reality (Hite, 2022).

> ### Definition: Virtual Reality
>
> VR provides an experience of reality without being in the real world.

VR experiences are characterized by three elements: presence, interaction, and immersion.

- 'Presence' refers to the individual's feeling of being in one environment while physically being in another;
- 'Interaction' is linked to the degree of engagement with characters or objects within the virtual environment;
- 'Immersion' is the extent to which the illusion of reality is as close to real life as possible (Radianti et al., 2020).

Depending on the technology used, VR systems can be non-immersive (desktop VR), semi-immersive or totally immersive (Makransky & Mayer, 2022). While the last two categories provide a full (immersive) or partial (semi-immersive) illusion of reality and presence, a non-immersive experience delivers the impression of looking at a situation from the outside (Cabero-Almenara et al., 2022). For example, computer-generated, networked 'virtual worlds' that provide users with a common space within which to communicate can be non-immersive.

CAVE Automatic Virtual Environments, where images are projected onto the walls of a room for a partial illusion of depth without the need for specialized wearable equipment, are semi-immersive. Wireless, stand-alone head-mounted displays (HMDs), on the other hand, are capable of providing fully-immersive experiences (Mystakidis, 2022) (see Table 8.1).

Table 8.1   VR Types

VR Type	What it offers	Example
Non-Immersive	Delivers the impression of looking at a situation from the outside	Computer game, i.e. Dota 2

(Continued)

Table 8.1 (Continued)

VR Type	What it offers	Example
Semi-Immersive	Enables a virtual tour while maintaining a connection to the real world.	Flight simulator
Totally Immersive	Users receive the most lifelike simulation experiences through simulations which include both sight and sound.	Virtual gaming

Early VR prototypes can be traced as far back as the 1950s, with one of the first designs of HMDs surfacing in 1966 (Sutherland et al., 2019). As technology evolved, particularly within the game and entertainment spheres, other peripherals capable of delivering haptic experiences emerged in the 1990s; however, their performance did not always justify their high cost. Nonetheless, academic and medical institutions continued to value VR as the technology progressed and reached new heights (Hite, 2022; Zhang et al., 2022). In 2014, the appearance of the first affordable HMDs with 3D vision and surround-sound brought about the long-awaited commercial breakthrough of VR (Dzardanova et al., 2022). Video game companies consistently improved the technology, and headsets such as the Oculus Rift and Quest 2 provided even higher quality immersive experiences. Figure 8.3 shows some of the input and output devices used in VR. By means of gloves capturing hand and finger movements, eye and motion trackers, HMDs, VR glasses, and auditory and haptic output devices to stimulate body senses, the virtual experience becomes even more real (Cipresso et al., 2018).

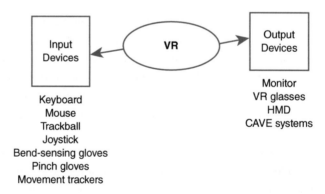

Figure 8.3 Examples of VR Input and Output Devices (adapted from Cipresso et al. (2018))

Stop and Reflect: Virtual Reality

List some of the VR input and output devices.

8.5 Applications of Virtual Reality

With advanced VR technology taking the market by storm, the popularity of VR not only soared within the gaming realm, but also in other areas, such as education, remote work, entertainment, and medicine. For example, Hite (2022) considers VR to be a safe and accessible means of learning science, particularly where experiments can be reset for repeated attempts to ensure learning, or where the required materials are difficult to access, too expensive or hazardous. Through VR, students can experience scientific phenomena which are microscopic, big (e.g., possible impacts of global warming), or difficult to trace in the past or future. Taking the example of a virtual field trip, Makransky and Mayer (2022) add that such immersive lessons stimulate greater interest in the material covered as student enjoyment and the resulting learning engagement increase.

The application of social VR for remote but face-to-face, web-based collaborations and interactions within virtual environments (VE) has also become more popular. Termed the 'second generation of social networking', social VR uses immersive technologies such as HMDs, avatars (3D representations of users), and data gloves to mimic real-life interactions within Web-based 3D VEs set up for shared activities, such as playing games or even attending social events virtually (Dzardanova et al., 2022). This application can be extended to include the workplace where VR is an invaluable asset for virtual collaborations within the remote workforce, particularly as the world has been scrambling to find alternative ways of working since the COVID-19 pandemic and its resulting lockdowns. Ranging from immersive, virtual meeting platforms to collaborative spaces, VR tools can be used to optimize business operations and maintain social workplace interactions even from a distance (Bennett, 2022). Further, Hawkins (2022) discusses the adoption of worker avatars for employee training, skills development, and remote collaboration to maximize team performance within a 3D virtual environment much improved by wearable VR technology.

The COVID-19 pandemic also resulted in innovations within the tourism sector. Technology enabled people to satisfy and sustain their need to travel within the safe and often less expensive confines of a VR space. Virtual tourism can provide a vivid, customized tour of countries and spectacular natural landscapes through immersive, 3D VR technology, and can considerably promote real-world tourism (Lee, 2022).

VR has also found its place within immersive journalism – a term used for the generation of news in a way that allows its consumers to experience the event or situation as if they were really present there (Slater & Sanchez-Vives, 2016). Such immersion elicits empathy and a greater understanding of another person's plight, thus generating a better emotional connection with the news, although its high cost, technological requirements, and innovative nature act as deterrents (Herrera Damas & Benítez de Gracia, 2022). The ethics of immersive journalism is also subject to debate, regarding the extent to which transporting the viewer to tragic or violent situations can be emotionally damaging. Posting such content on public platforms also raises the issue of how the data can be used and for what means (Herrera Damas & Benítez de Gracia, 2022). Consequently, despite its promises, the novelty of immersive journalism appears to have worn off as its popularity has taken a downward turn (Hidalgo et al., 2022).

The applications of VR in the medical field have long preceded its commercial success. In their review of the literature, Cipresso et al. (2018) identify multiple applications of VR in medical practices, such as: surgical procedures; the rehabilitation of motor functions through VR games; the treatment of psychological disorders; including phobias, anxiety, and stress; through Virtual Reality Exposure Therapy (VRET) to combat emotional problems in a therapist-controlled space; and even episodic memory training for the elderly. VR has the advantages of: enabling multiple task repetition, thereby facilitating and reducing the cost of medical training; providing the possibility of home treatment through wearable VR technology, thus decreasing the need to commute to hospitals; facilitating the collection and sharing of data for patient monitoring; and considerably reducing the risks posed to patient safety due to surgical errors (Kan Yeung et al., 2021).

As opposed to more conventional treatments, VR-enabled therapies can be customized to better stimulate patient response, and can eliminate the need for patients to be physically present – an often desirable advantage in the context of pandemics such as COVID-19 (Z. Liu et al., 2022).

On the other hand, the use of VR technology itself may cause several health issues, such as motion sickness, dizziness, and nausea. Head and neck pain can also result from prolonged use of HMDs owing to their weight. In addition, VR can cause psychological issues such as antisocial behaviour due to an over-reliance on virtual experiences to the detriment of real ones, or trauma resulting from exposure to violent immersive realities (Mystakidis, 2022). Therefore, awareness and caution are critical to prevent such issues.

Stop and Reflect: Virtual Reality

List two virtual reality applications.

8.6 What Is Augmented Reality (AR) and When Did this Technology Emerge?

In general, AR is seen as being the next step after virtual reality (VR). AR is a technology that enhances the real world with Artificial Intelligence and objects by means of computer-generated sensory input, such as video sound, graphics, or a global positioning system (GPS). AR has the ability to present information by merging live images with virtual layers (Mekni & Lemieux, 2014; Rauschnabel et al., 2015; 2022). An increasing number of AR use cases are emerging, illustrating just how far this technology has come in terms of variety and applications. From NASA simulations to commercial interactions, augmented technology makes work easier and no doubt more pleasurable in some instances. Real examples of AR are: Pokémon GO, Snapchat, and Google Glass.

Definition: Augmented Reality

AR is defined as a system that enhances the real world with AI and objects by means of computer-generated sensory input such as video sound, graphics, or a global positioning system (GPS), and AR has the ability to present information by merging live images with virtual layers.

Here follows a description of how AR has been used by people and industries from its inception in 1960 when numerous industries began to implement it in their operations. The first head-mounted display device, developed by Ivan Sutherland in 1968, heralded the arrival of augmented reality technology. In 1974, computer scientist and artist Myron Kruger established the 'Videoplace' lab at the University of Connecticut, which was devoted solely to virtual reality (Kumar, 2022; Leone et al., 2022).

However, the term 'augmented reality' did not appear until 1990, when it was used by Boeing researcher Tim Caudell. In her 1994 theatrical performance, *Dancing in Cyberspace*, Julie Martin, a writer and producer, introduced augmented reality to the entertainment sector for the first time. Furthermore, the first live NFL (National Football League) game with the virtual 1st & Ten visual technology, sometimes known as the 'yellow yard marker', was televised by Sportsvision in 1998. The technology overlays a yellow line across the video so viewers can see where one team recently made a move to grab a first down. In 1999, NASA developed a hybrid synthetic vision system for its X-38 spacecraft. During the spacecraft's test flights, the system used AR technology to improve navigation (Vertucci et al., 2023).

The twenty-first century saw an increase in the application of AR. For instance, in 2000, Hirokazu Kato created the ARToolKit, an open-source software library. This package helps other developers to create augmented reality software. The library applies virtual graphics to the actual world via video tracking. Additionally, when the new Skycam technology was introduced in 2003, Sportvision improved the 1st and Ten graphics to incorporate it, giving spectators an aerial perspective of the field with graphics superimposed on it. In 2009, *Esquire* magazine attempted to bring its pages to life by utilizing augmented reality for the first time in print media. Furthermore, The MARTA app (Mobile Augmented Reality Technical Assistance), introduced by Volkswagen in 2013, primarily provided technicians with the step-by-step repair instructions found in the service handbook (Sharma et al., 2022; Yung & Khoo-Lattimore, 2019).

In addition, a set of augmented reality glasses (Google Glass) that users can wear for immersive experiences was first seen in 2014. Wearable AR technology allowed users to interact with the Internet using natural language commands. Users of this device had access to several applications, including Google Maps, Google+, Gmail, and others. As of 2016, Microsoft released the HoloLens, a wearable augmented reality device that is more sophisticated than Google Glass but more expensive. It is undeniably not the kind of item you wear every day. Also, IKEA Place, an augmented reality software, was released in 2017 by the Swedish IKEA corporation. With this application, clients can digitally sample their home decor options before making a purchase (Alves & Luís Reis, 2020; Sandu & Scarlat, 2018). Finally, the Web-based platform Designhubz, which has been demonstrated to improve conversion rates and decrease returns, was introduced in 2019. It allows retailers to turn their actual inventory into immersive 3D and AR visuals (Designhubz, 2021).

Stop and Reflect: Augmented Reality

Discuss the history of AR as summarized in Figure 8.4.

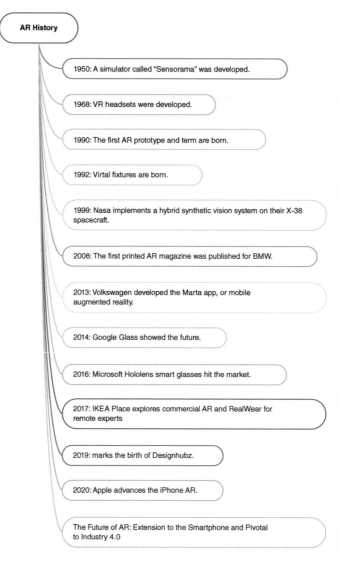

Figure 8.4 AR History (adapted from Designhubz (2021) and Gogou & Kasvikis (2022))

8.7 Applications of AR by Various Sectors

These days, AR is utilized in many different fields, including marketing, public safety, healthcare, education, gas and oil, and public health. A variety of phone headsets, including Google Glass, Oculus Rift, Meta 2 headset, Microsoft HoloLens, CastAR, and windscreen head-up displays, have been introduced to the market. At the moment, the addition of data in many forms (text, photos, video, music, and more) to the actual environment is made possible by using small mobile devices like smartphones or tablets. Google created an AR project dubbed Bridge, a new headgear that combines the actual environment with virtual items and lets iPhone users engage in the novel experience.

As AR increasingly becomes a critical tool in the healthcare industry, it makes training more accessible to medical students and assists future physicians in visualizing illnesses. In the field of medicine, augmented reality has seven practical applications: medical teaching; educating doctors on innovative treatments; virtualizing procedures; accurate symptom detection; patient self-care; vein visualization; and medical imaging. Hence, smart technology and appropriate training should be made available in hospitals to fulfil the hospitals' goals i.e., scope, cost, time and quality. (Andrews, 2022; Quqandi et al., 2022).

Because AR has the potential to transform businesses' consumer engagement strategies, it has become a crucial tool in the marketing industry. Customers can now use a smartphone to virtually test and evaluate business products in the comfort of their own homes. For instance, Ray-Ban has used AR to create a virtual webcam mirror application that enables customers to try on several pairs of sunglasses and move their heads around to see how they appear from various angles. Customers can also choose their preferred optical frames and alter the colour. Finally, in the future, AR technology can make shopping more fun and relaxing since it will enable more intimate, engaging encounters that will permanently alter the way we shop (Du et al., 2022; Rauschnabel et al., 2022).

Stop and Reflect: Augmented Reality

Discuss the various applications of AR in the healthcare and business sectors.

Apart from its application in healthcare and marketing, AR is used in design and construction projects to display details and elements on the construction plan. By visualizing working models, the project team, stakeholders, and clients can better understand the project and identify any potential risks before proceeding with the project. By using augmented reality for construction purposes, it is also possible to take virtual tours before construction begins. Finally, the application of AR in the design and construction sectors will reduce the need to rework design and construction and will improve project management and teamwork. Nevertheless, to achieve these benefits, smart technologies and support should be made available by the top management (Hajirasouli & Banihashemi, 2022; Hajirasouli et al., 2022; Jahn et al., 2022).

Stop and Reflect: Augmented Reality

Give an example of how AR applications are used in the design and construction sectors.

Additionally, AR is having a significant impact in the educational field since it has the potential to increase student interest and engagement, as well as improve the learning environment and the understanding of content, teamwork, memory, sensory development, and cost-effectiveness. In education, AR incorporates components that encourage the development of skills such as problem solving, collaboration, and creativity to better prepare students for the future. It is also advantageous for traditional education which places a strong emphasis on technical proficiency and knowledge. AR can take the place of textbooks and printed materials; this allows students to access the relevant learning materials whenever they want, from any place, and on any device; it also reduces the cost of learning and makes access simpler for everyone; it encourages greater student collaboration and communication; and it makes classes more engaging and appealing so that students can learn the necessary information more effectively. In order that students can benefit from these advantages, smart devices, training, support, and a digital curriculum should be made available by schools and universities (Y. Liu et al., 2022; Sandu & Scarlat, 2018).

Stop and Reflect: Augmented Reality

Give an example of how AR is used in the education sector.

In addition, AR is strongly evident in the gaming and digital entertainment industries since the younger generation relies on this technology to have fun and communicate with their peers locally and internationally. By means of AR, players can walk about and battle zombies or aliens, and bring Ghostbusters 'to life' in the real world. An example of AR in this field is Niantic's Pokémon GO app, which has quickly acquired popularity and allows users to venture outside, wander about, and capture virtual Pokémon outdoors (Lisowski et al., 2023; Ye & Li, 2022).

> ### Stop and Reflect: Augmented Reality
>
> Give an example of how AR is used in the digital gaming environment.

8.8 AR Challenges

AR is expensive, raises privacy and security concerns, encourages risky behaviour, and, finally, can cause harm in cases where people spend hours using AR and neglect other aspects of their lives. However, AR can increase people's knowledge and access to information. It is simple to use, enriches individuals' experiences, supports various sectors such as business and education, and improves technology (Ali et al., 2022; Markaryan et al., 2022; Marrahí-Gómez & Belda-Medina, 2022).

On the other hand, the application of AR in any industry may present difficulties due to the need for specialized equipment, training, infrastructure, support, and the acquisition of new skills. However, AR can reduce costs associated with design, production, and maintenance costs, and enables problems to be resolved more quickly and effectively while decreasing the need for research and the acquisition of new information. Finally, because it does not require physical presence, AR is regarded as a major technology innovation of the 21st century as it offers a virtual reality experience that has a long-term effect, and minimizes carbon footprints to a certain degree (AlQallaf et al., 2022; Zou et al., 2022). Finally, management and top management should be available and supportive to ensure the success of AR and VR use by individuals and industries. This will help the relevant parties acquire the necessary knowledge to improve decision-making and save costs.

8.9 The Metaverse

'Meta' is a Greek word which translates into English as 'post', 'after', or 'beyond'. Thus, metaverse refers to a 'post-reality universe' which merges reality with virtuality in a multi-user space (Mystakidis, 2022, p. 486). With VR at its core, the metaverse is intended to give user avatars access to an array of 3D spaces for the best possible extended experience through hardware such as AR/VR headsets (Floridi, 2022). While the term was coined in Stephenson's science fiction novel, *Snow Crash*, in 1992 (cited in Mystakidis, 2022, p. 492), it is only since 2021 that the metaverse gained popularity, with Facebook's highly publicized mutation to Meta, and sandbox games such as Roblox partnering with brands and celebrities to enable users to shape branded/celebrity-enhanced play environments.

Hirsch (2022) cites multiple such examples, ranging from Gucci's fashion and Hyundai's theme parks within the Roblox online game universe, to McDonald's Big Macs being ordered by avatars using virtual currency and resulting in users having an actual burger delivered to their doorstep, and celebrity Paris Hilton opening a virtual version of her Beverly Hills estate for users to explore as well as commercializing a virtual jet ski experience at her Ibiza home. Big retail firms such as Adidas and Samsung have also invested in the metaverse. Users can visit their virtual space to buy items which can either be delivered to the customer in real life or be used to accessorize an avatar. Unlike browser online shopping, metaverse users can move from shop to shop as avatars for an engaging experience akin to real-world shopping. The switch from visitor to consumer is facilitated by metaverse data analytics that track and predict customer patterns, behaviours, and preferences for enhanced, optimized, and personalised buying journeys (Dawson, 2022).

As real examples of using the metaverse by specific sectors, Gucci has developed 'Gucci Vault Land', which is a testing ground where users can play their way through the history of Gucci, while Samsung is opening its first metaverse store 'Samsung 837X', which gives users access to a groundbreaking digital experience connecting technology with art, music, fashion, and sustainability.

The metaverse is also finding its way into the workplace. With increasing focus on authentic, engaging, and interactive remote methods of work, the metaverse provides multiple alternatives. For example, the NextMeet Indian metaverse platform offers dedicated 3D spaces enabling workers to collaborate and work remotely. According to Purdy (2022), employees can access NextMeet's immersive platform via their computer or mobile device, choose or customize their own avatars and, through these, move in and out of offices within the 3D office space, attend meetings, give presentations, and even take a lounge break with other employees. Through NextMeet, remote work still maintains some of the social connections of the workplace and meetings are a lot more interactive and 'real'. Work and home boundaries are also clearer as employee avatars walk into the virtual workplace in the morning and leave it once work is over.

This demarcation is useful in preventing fatigue, inability to switch off, and burnout, which often result from blurred distinctions between work and home times. PixelMax, originating from a UK start-up, is another example of an immersive workplace solution aimed at improving employee cohesion, wellness, and collaboration (Purdy, 2022). This platform allows employee avatars to 'bump into' each other within the virtual workplace and stop for informal chats, which are an essential component of business communications. PixelMax also provides dedicated wellness spaces which can be customized for relaxation, meditation and even exercise. Additionally, extending its gaming origins to the workplace, the metaverse can optimize employee training. For example, employee avatars can learn from their experiences within real-world work simulations with AI bots coaching, training, and advising them as they go along.

Despite the giant leaps made in terms of its realism, the metaverse continues to lag behind the richness of the analogue universe. Floridi (2022) describes many of the challenges and risks yet to be addressed. For example, the metaverse does not easily provide sensations of smell, heat, cold, texture, or even flavours. While the same objects can be used in multiple places in the real word (for example, the same pen can be used at work, at home or anywhere else), metaverses are mostly closed and their objects are not transferrable from one metaverse to another.

Risks of addiction, data privacy breaches, cyber-crimes (including cyber bullying and sexual violations) and hacker attacks continue to loom over virtual worlds. Social backlash could also arise from a lack of or inability to access the numerous opportunities offered by the metaverse in multiple spheres such as education, the workplace, health services, and even entertainment.

Future metaverses will also welcome digital colleagues – AI-based bots – with increasingly human-like looks, emotions, and capacity. The potential is enormous, especially for repetitive or hazardous work, but the risks are also numerous. Low-skilled workers might easily be replaced by their digital counterparts, leaving them with little to no job alternatives, while automation could take over, leaving less space for human interactions, and behavioural issues between man and machine could lead to an erosion of values in real life (Purdy, 2022).

Stop and Reflect: The Metaverse

Define the metaverse

Give an example of how the metaverse can be employed by users.

8.10 Chapter Summary

This chapter addresses the definitions, applications, potential, and difficulties of AR and VR technology. These technologies include modelling, simulation, and augmenting computer programmes that enable users to collaborate to achieve their objectives. These technologies are used to improve work performance, acquire new information, and identify significant issues in a number of industries, including health, education, marketing, design, gaming, and others. Unlike VR, which is entirely virtual and controlled by the system, AR employs a real-world context and allows people to manage their presence there. AR can be evaluated with a smartphone, while VR needs an additional headgear device. Finally, while VR simply improves an imagined reality, AR improves both the virtual and actual worlds.

Discussion Questions

1   What is the difference between VR and AR?
2   List three types of VR and provide an example.
3   Give an example how AR has transformed business.
4   What is the metaverse and provide an example?

Case Study: Augmented Reality (AR) in Education

By Rodney Roche, Learning Technologies Developer and IT Projects Officer, AISWA (*Association of Independent Schools of Western Australia*)

AR, or augmented reality, provides a plethora of simulated or digital environments that integrate with the user's real-life environment in real time and can help enhance the user's understanding of the environment without needing to experience it in real life. This comes with advantages and disadvantages for the user. A local school in Australia was looking to improve its methods of tutoring students. Parents had complained that the school lacked a technological edge in terms of teaching tools when compared to other schools. Furthermore, many students had complained that the school and its teachers were not very confident in their teaching skills and lacked a practical approach to tutoring the students, and that, most importantly, this had been reflected in the students' grades, affecting the overall school's pass rates. Taking into account the students' and parents' complaints and the pass rate of the school, the management explored various technologies that could cater to the issues faced.

The school conducted interviews and surveys with students, parents, and teachers to further understand the issues and receive recommendations on how best to tackle them. Once the interviews and survey were completed and the school collated the data, the management deduced from the report the project produced that the school should invest in smart technologies in order to support and increase the quality of teaching. A number of smart technologies were recommended, and one such prominent smart technology that the management had previously looked at was augmented reality (AR). This was one of the top smart technologies recommended by both students and parents that could potentially enhance student learning at school. The management of the school decided to implement a pilot phase for using the said technology in the humanities and social sciences classes, particularly in geography.

The school purchased AR headsets, tablets, and apps that support educational learning in a classroom setting. In addition, the school then implemented the technology for Year 9 students' geography lessons. The students were then able to view landscapes, natural calamities, and the diverse types of biomes within the reach of their classroom and easily define and interpret them. This greatly pleased the parents, students, teachers, and management as a whole. The school was then approached by another school in the local area and asked for a report on why they had implemented AR, the advantages and disadvantages, as well as the cost of the program.

Questions

1 What other smart technologies could have been recommended to the school or for an education setting?
2 What types of apps help support such learning?
3 Why was the school not yet able to harness the full potential of VR technology?
4 What are the advantages of using AR in education?
5 Develop a cost-benefit analysis of using such technology in a school of 100 students.
6 What are the disadvantages of using AR in education?
7 From your perspective, what are the advantages and disadvantages of using AR in education contexts?
8 Explain and provide examples of how AR could be beneficial in other sectors or industries, such as manufacturing and/or primary sectors such as farming.

Case Study: Meta

In October 2021, the parent company of Facebook changed its name from Facebook, Inc. to Meta in an attempt to project its users into the metaverse. In his founder's letter (2021) marking that change, Mark Zuckerberg traced the journey of Facebook from typed text to more visual, richer forms of communication, such as photos and videos accessible anytime and anywhere through advancements in mobile Internet. Zuckerberg (2021) added that through Meta, the company has taken the plunge into its next defining phase – the metaverse. With Facebook's core mission of 'bringing people together' unchanged, Meta promises immersive, social connections where users feel 'present' with others and even in other places without being physically there. Zuckerberg (2021) describes a future with users instantly teleporting to work or social gatherings as a hologram through their phone or computer. Through Meta and as holograms, one can expect to attend a concert, enjoy a game with friends, 'be' at work, in a shop, or even in someone else's living room without the need to commute. Meta holograms or avatars can also transform learning by enabling repeated or hazardous experiments, transporting learners into historical or actual places, and even facilitating employee training. For creators and developers, virtual reality (VR) technology is at the heart of immersions, and augmented reality (AR) glasses will maintain the connection with the real world. For example, Meta's VR-meeting platform, Horizon Workrooms, is equipped with an array of business-related VR tools (Rospigliosi, 2022).

Meta's functionalities provide numerous advantages. Not having to physically commute from one place to another not only brings down travelling costs, reduces traffic, and leaves time for doing other things, but it also helps reduce one's carbon footprint and facilitates the lives of people who are physically incapable of travelling or have difficulties doing so. Learning also becomes much more engaging through immersive, virtually hands-on, and near-real

(Continued)

experiences. Work or 'the office' no longer needs to be constrained by physical and geo-graphical barriers. In times of pandemic and lockdowns, Meta provides a one-stop platform for people to remain better connected and for the world to keep going – both economically and socially.

Nonetheless, several questions emerge. How does Meta intend to prevent 'simulacra' or a disconnection from reality? Cultural theorist, Baudrillard (cited in Rospigliosi, 2022, p. 3) warns users about distinguishing 'the map from the territory' – in other words, blurring the lines between simulations and the real world. Will the user data collected by Meta be safe from unauthorized use? Facebook's reputation in this regard was seriously shaken after the 2018 Cambridge Analytica scandal, where Facebook was accused of partnering with the consulting firm to provide user data for voter profiling during Donald Trump's election cam-paign (Paul & Milmo, 2022). Will Meta be different? Will the real connection between teachers and learners disappear with virtual learning communities (Rospigliosi, 2022)? Despite its promise of an exciting entry into the metaverse, Meta needs to demonstrate strong ethical responsibility towards its users and tread carefully as it begins this new tech-nological chapter.

References

Paul, K., & Milmo, D. (2022, July 20). Mark Zuckerberg to face deposition over Cambridge Analytica scandal. *The Guardian*. https://www.theguardian.com/technology/2022/jul/20/mark-zuckerberg-deposition-cambridge-analytica-facebook

Rospigliosi, P. 'asher' (2022). Metaverse or simulacra? Roblox, Minecraft, Meta and the turn to virtual reality for education, socialisation and work. *Interactive Learning Environments, 30*(1), 1–3. https://doi.org/10.1080/10494820.2022.2022899

Zuckerberg, M. (2021). Founder's letter. https://about.fb.com/news/2021/10/founders-letter/

Questions

1   What are the main characteristics of Meta's metaverse experience?
2   In your opinion, what are the advantages and disadvantages of using Meta?

8.11 References

Ali, N. A., Sadiq, M. H., Albabawat, A. A., & Salah, R. M. (2022). *Methods and Applications of Augmented Reality in Education: A Review*. Paper presented at the 2022 International Conference on Computer Science and Software Engineering (CSASE).

AlQallaf, N., Bhatti, S., Suett, R., Aly, S. G., Khalil, A. S., & Ghannam, R. (2022). *Visualising Climate Change using Extended Reality: A Review*. Paper presented at the 2022 29th IEEE International Conference on Electronics, Circuits and Systems (ICECS).

Alves, C., & Luís Reis, J. (2020). *The Intention to Use E-Commerce using Augmented Reality – The Case of IKEA Place*. Paper presented at the Information Technology and Systems: Proceedings of ICITS 2020.

Andrews, A. (2022). Integration of augmented reality and brain-computer interface technologies for health care applications: Exploratory and prototyping study. *JMIR Formative Research, 6*(4), e18222.

Bennett, D. (2022). Remote workforce, virtual team tasks, and employee engagement tools in a real-time interoperable decentralized metaverse. *Psychosociological Issues in Human Resource Management, 10*(1), 78–91. https://doi.org/10.22381/pihrm10120226

Cabero-Almenara, J., Llorente-Cejudo, C., & Martinez-Roig, R. (2022). The use of mixed, augmented and virtual reality in history of art teaching: A case study. *Applied System Innovation, 5*(3). https://doi.org/10.3390/asi5030044

Cipresso, P., Giglioli, I. A. C., Raya, M. A., & Riva, G. (2018). The past, present, and future of virtual and augmented reality research: A network and cluster analysis of the literature. *Frontiers in Psychology, 9*(Nov), 1–20. https://doi.org/10.3389/fpsyg.2018.02086

Dawson, A. (2022). Data-driven consumer engagement, virtual immersive shopping experiences, and blockchain-based digital assets in the retail metaverse. *Journal of Self-Governance and Management Economics, 10*(2), 52–66. https://doi.org/10.22381/jsme10220224

Designhubz. (2021). History of AR 10 Feb 2023. https://designhubz.com/history-of-ar/

Du, Z., Liu, J., & Wang, T. (2022). Augmented reality marketing: A systematic literature review and an agenda for future inquiry. *Frontiers in Psychology, 13.*

Dzardanova, E., Kasapakis, V., Gavalas, D., & Sylaiou, S. (2022). Virtual reality as a communication medium: A comparative study of forced compliance in virtual reality versus physical world. *Virtual Reality, 26*(2), 737–757. https://doi.org/10.1007/s10055-021-00564-9

Floridi, L. (2022). Metaverse: A matter of experience. *Philosophy & Technology, 35*(73), 1–7. https://doi.org/10.1007/s13347-022-00568-6

Gogou, A., & Kasvikis, K. (2022). 'Release Orpheus!': Understanding historical time in a mixed/augmented reality environment through embodied learning. *Education 3-13*, 1–20

Hajirasouli, A., & Banihashemi, S. (2022). Augmented reality in architecture and construction education: State of the field and opportunities. *International Journal of Educational Technology in Higher Education, 19*(1), 39.

Hajirasouli, A., Banihashemi, S., Drogemuller, R., Fazeli, A., & Mohandes, S. R. (2022). Augmented reality in design and construction: Thematic analysis and conceptual frameworks. *Construction Innovation* (ahead-of-print).

Hawkins, M. (2022). Virtual employee training and skill development, workplace technologies, and deep learning computer vision algorithms in the immersive metaverse environment. *Psychosociological Issues in Human Resource Management, 10*(1), 106–120. https://doi.org/10.22381/pihrm10120228

Herrera Damas, S., & Benítez de Gracia, M. J. (2022). Immersive journalism: Advantages, disadvantages and challenges from the perspective of experts. *Journalism and Media, 3*(2), 330–347. https://doi.org/10.3390/journalmedia3020024

Hidalgo, A. L., Majuelos, I. M., & Olivares-García, F. J. (2022). The decline of immersive journalism in Spain since 2018. *Revista Latina de Comunicacion Social, 80*, 15–27. https://doi.org/10.4185/RLCS-2022-1536

Hirsch, P. B. (2022). Adventures in the metaverse. *Journal of Business Strategy*, *43*(5), 332–336. https://doi.org/10.1108/jbs-06-2022-0101

Hite, R. (2022). Virtual reality: Flight of fancy or feasible? Ways to use virtual reality technologies to enhance students' science learning. *The American Biology Teacher*, *84*(2), 106–108.

Jahn, G., Newnham, C., & Berg, N. (2022). *Augmented Reality for Construction from Steam-Bent Timber*. Paper presented at POST-CARBON, Proceedings of the 27th International Conference of the Association for Computer-Aided Architectural Design Research in Asia (CAADRIA).

Kan Yeung, A. W., Tosevska, A., Klager, E., Eibensteiner, F., Laxar, D., Stoyanov, J., Glisic, M., Zeiner, S., Kulnik, S. T., Crutzen, R., Kimberger, O., Kletecka-Pulker, M., Atanasov, A. G., & Willschke, H. (2021). Virtual and augmented reality applications in medicine: Analysis of the scientific literature. *Journal of Medical Internet Research*, *23*(2). https://doi.org/10.2196/25499

Kumar, H. (2022). Augmented reality in online retailing: A systematic review and research agenda. *International Journal of Retail & Distribution Management*, *50*(4), 537–559.

Lee, U. K. (2022). Tourism using virtual reality: Media richness and information system successes. *Sustainability (Switzerland)*, *14*(7). https://doi.org/10.3390/su14073975

Leone, D., Pietronudo, M. C., & Dezi, L. (2022). Improving business models through augmented reality applications: Evidence from history, theory, and practice. *International Journal of Quality and Innovation*, *6*(1), 28–42.

Lisowski, D., Ponto, K., Fan, S., Probst, C., & Sprecher, B. (2023). Augmented reality into live theatrical performance. In *Springer Handbook of Augmented Reality* (pp. 433–450). Springer.

Liu, Y., Sathishkumar, V., & Manickam, A. (2022). Augmented reality technology based on school physical education training. *Computers and Electrical Engineering*, *99*, 107807.

Liu, Z., Ren, L., Xiao, C., Zhang, K., & Demian, P. (2022). Virtual reality aided therapy towards Health 4.0: A two-decade bibliometric analysis. *International Journal of Environmental Research and Public Health*, *19*(3). https://doi.org/10.3390/ijerph19031525

Makransky, G., & Mayer, R. E. (2022). Benefits of taking a virtual field trip in immersive virtual reality: Evidence for the immersion principle in multimedia learning. *Educational Psychology Review, 0123456789*. https://doi.org/10.1007/s10648-022-09675-4

Markaryan, I. N., Datsun, N. A., & Chakryan, V. R. (2022). *The Use of Virtual and Augmented Reality Technologies in Industrial Training*. Paper presented at the Computer Applications for Management and Sustainable Development of Production and Industry (CMSD2021).

Marrahí-Gómez, V., & Belda-Medina, J. (2022). The application of augmented reality (AR) to language learning and its impact on student motivation. *International Journal of Linguistics Studies*, *2*(2), 07–14.

Mekni, M., & Lemieux, A. (2014). Augmented reality: Applications, challenges and future trends. *Applied Computational Science*, *20*, 205–214.

Milgram, P., Takemura, H., Utsumi, A., & Kishino, F. (1994). Augmented reality: A class of displays on the reality-virtuality continuum. *SPIE – The International Society for Opticak, January*. https://doi.org/10.1117/12.197321

Moro, C., Stromberga, Z., & Stirling, A. (2017). Virtualisation devices for student learning: Comparison between desktop-based (Oculus Rift) and mobile-based (Gear VR) virtual reality in medical and health science education. *Australasian Journal of Educational Technology, 33*(6), 1–10. https://doi.org/10.14742/ajet.3840

Mystakidis, S. (2022). Metaverse. *Encyclopedia, 2*, 486–497.

Purdy, M. (2022). How the metaverse could change work. *Harvard Business Review.* https://hbr.org/2022/04/how-the-metaverse-could-change-work

Quqandi, E., Joy, M., Drumm, I., & Rushton, M. (2022). Augmented reality in supporting healthcare and nursing independent learning: Narrative review. *CIN: Computers, Informatics, Nursing, 10.*1097.

Radianti, J., Majchrzak, T. A., Fromm, J., & Wohlgenannt, I. (2020). A systematic review of immersive virtual reality applications for higher education: Design elements, lessons learned, and research agenda. *Computers & Education, 147*(2020). https://doi.org/10.1016/j.compedu.2019.103778

Rauschnabel, P. A., Babin, B. J., tom Dieck, M. C., Krey, N., & Jung, T. (2022). *What is augmented reality marketing? Its definition, complexity, and future, 142*, 1140–1150.

Rauschnabel, P. A., Brem, A., & Ro, Y. (2015). *Augmented Reality Smart Glasses: Definition, Conceptual Insights, and Managerial Importance.* Unpublished Working Paper, The University of Michigan-Dearborn, College of Business.

Rospigliosi, P. 'asher.' (2022). Metaverse or simulacra? Roblox, Minecraft, Meta and the turn to virtual reality for education, socialisation and work. *Interactive Learning Environments, 30*(1), 1–3. https://doi.org/10.1080/10494820.2022.2022899

Sandu, M., & Scarlat, I. S. (2018). Augmented reality uses in interior design. *Informatica Economica, 22*(3).

Sharma, A., Mehtab, R., Mohan, S., & Mohd Shah, M. K. (2022). Augmented reality – an important aspect of Industry 4.0. *Industrial Robot: The International Journal of Robotics Research and Application, 49*(3), 428–441.

Slater, M., & Sanchez-Vives, M. V. (2016). Enhancing our lives with immersive virtual reality. *Frontiers in Robotics and AI, 3*, 1–47. https://doi.org/10.3389/frobt.2016.00074

Sutherland, J., Belec, J., Sheikh, A., Chepelev, L., Althobaity, W., Chow, B. J. W., Mitsouras, D., Christensen, A., Rybicki, F. J., & La Russa, D. J. (2019). Applying modern virtual and augmented reality technologies to medical images and models. *Journal of Digital Imaging, 32*(1), 38–53. https://doi.org/10.1007/s10278-018-0122-7

Tsaramirsis, G., Kantaros, A., Al-Darraji, I., Piromalis, D., Apostolopoulos, C., Pavlopoulou, A., Alrammal, M., Ismail, Z., Buhari, S. M., Stojmenovic, M., Tamimi, H., Randhawa, P., Patel, A., & Khan, F. Q. (2022). A modern approach towards an Industry 4.0 model: From driving technologies to management. *Journal of Sensors, 2022*, 1–18. https://doi.org/10.1155/2022/5023011

Vertucci, R., D'Onofrio, S., Ricciardi, S., & De Nino, M. (2023). History of augmented reality. In *Springer Handbook of Augmented Reality* (pp. 35–50). Springer.

Ye, W., & Li, Y. (2022). Design and research of digital media art display based on virtual reality and augmented reality. *Mobile Information Systems, 2022.*

Yung, R., & Khoo-Lattimore, C. (2019). New realities: A systematic literature review on virtual reality and augmented reality in tourism research. *Current Issues in Tourism, 22*(17), 2056–2081.

Zhang, J., Yu, N., Wang, B., & Lv, X. (2022). Trends in the use of augmented reality, virtual reality, and mixed reality in surgical research: A global bibliometric and visualized analysis. *Indian Journal of Surgery, 84*(April), 52–69. https://doi.org/10.1007/s12262-021-03243-w

Zou, S., Zhang, Y., Tao, B., & Yang, X. (2022). *Research on the Augmented Reality (AR) Technology to Optimize Humanized Design of Carbon-Neutral Urban Landscapes.* Paper presented at the 2022 Global Conference on Robotics, Artificial Intelligence and Information Technology (GCRAIT).

Zuckerberg, M. (2021). Founder's letter. https://about.fb.com/news/2021/10/founders-letter/

PART III

KNOWLEDGE AND DATA MANAGEMENT TECHNOLOGIES

9

ARTIFICIAL INTELLIGENCE AND KNOWLEDGE GRAPHS

9.1 Learning Outcomes

After reading this chapter, you will be able to:

- Define, explain, and differentiate between Artificial Intelligence (AI) and Machine Learning (ML)
- Discuss the importance of AI and ML in our daily lives, and explain why they are so successful
- Identify and critically segregate the main types of ML
- Identify the limitations and challenges of AI
- Understand knowledge graphs and their abstract structure
- Distinguish between generic and domain-specific knowledge graphs
- Understand and apply techniques for knowledge graph construction
- Examine and discuss various real-life applications of knowledge graphs

9.2 Introduction

We live in the era of big data in which data is generated at a surprising speed. These large-scale and heterogeneous datasets require advanced and sophisticated technologies that can produce hoped-for added value as well as derive knowledge from data that can benefit several industrial applications and business domains. This chapter provides an overview of two powerful technologies that are currently being incorporated in business and other operations to offer insights on obtained data, namely Artificial Intelligence (AI) and its branch Machine Learning (ML). Both AI and ML are described, and then their relationship and importance are explained. Following this, knowledge graphs (KGs) are introduced, specifically generic and domain-specific KGs, followed by an explanation of one of the techniques used to construct a KG, and examples of real-life applications that have benefited from KGs.

9.3 Artificial Intelligence and Machine Learning

This section gives the reader an overview of a well-known technology, namely AI, its definition, and its importance. The focus then shifts to the other essential technology, Machine Learning (ML), including its definition, types, and how it is different from AI. The section closes with an examination of the factors that make AI and ML successful.

What is Artificial Intelligence?

There has been an ongoing effort to develop a means of mimicking the human mind and its thinking pattern throughout history. Artists, writers, filmmakers, and game developers have attempted to portray the notion of *intelligence* using different approaches. The term *Artificial Intelligence* was officially coined in 1956 by John McCarthy, the father of AI, who defined it as 'The science and engineering of making intelligent machines' (Andresen, 2002). Since then, various attempts have been made towards better understanding, conceptualizing, and framing this term, in order to determine and clarify its potential applications. The definition of AI has also evolved to address its theoretical results or practical applications and to determine whether to offer computers conscious (strong) AI or not conscious (weak) AI (Russell & Norvig, 2002).

Definition: Artificial Intelligence

Artificial intelligence is the branch of computer science concerned with the automation of intelligent behaviour so that machines can act intelligently (Jackson, 1986; Luger, 2005).

AI refers to the simulation of intelligent behaviour in machines that are programmed to perform tasks that typically require human intelligence, such as visual perception, speech recognition, decision-making, and natural language processing. The term 'intelligent behaviour' in this context means the ability of a machine or system to learn from experience, adapt to new situations, reason, understand complex concepts, and generalize knowledge. The goal of AI is to create machines that can perform tasks autonomously and improve their performance over time, without explicit programming (Russell, 2010).

Why Artificial Intelligence?

AI has emerged from research labs and from the pages of science fiction novels to become an integral part of our daily lives, from helping us navigate cities and avoid traffic to using virtual assistants and allowing us to perform various tasks more easily and quickly. AI has the potential to significantly improve our lives by making tasks easier, faster, and more personalized, while also driving progress and innovation in various industries. Table 9.1 demonstrates the importance of AI through several applications.

Table 9.1 Importance of AI*

Importance	Description
Automation and robotics	AI can automate tasks that are repetitive and mundane, freeing up humans to focus on more creative and strategic work. With AI, robots can perceive, reason, learn, and act intelligently in real time, allowing them to perform tasks more efficiently and effectively than ever before.
Efficiency	AI can process and analyse large amounts of data much faster than humans, resulting in increased efficiency and productivity in various industries.
Personalization	AI can learn about individual preferences and behaviours, enabling personalized recommendations and experiences in areas such as e-commerce, healthcare, and entertainment.
Decision-making	AI can help businesses and organizations make better decisions by providing insights and predictions based on data analysis.
Innovation	AI has the potential to drive innovation and breakthroughs in fields such as healthcare, transportation, and energy, leading to new products, services, and industries.

Note: *Prepared by the authors based on the discussions in Chugh et al. (2022), Macrorie et al. (2021), and Russell (2010).

Real-world problems are complex because they often involve multiple variables, dependencies, and interactions that are not easily observable or understood. These problems can be influenced by a range of factors, including social, cultural, economic, environmental, and technological factors, which can create nonlinear and dynamic relationships that are difficult to predict or control. In addition, real-world problems often require decision-making under uncertainty, which further adds to their complexity. The complexity of these problems can make it challenging to identify and develop effective solutions, which is where AI can play a crucial role in providing insights and optimizing decision-making (Davenport & Ronanki, 2018).

Today, our use of AI is rooted in the common good of society. For example, AI and expertise applied in the domains of environmental sciences and humanitarian aid will help save lives and alleviate suffering by improving predictive methods and the means of dealing with disasters before or after they occur (Smith, 2018).

Example: AI for Humanitarian Action

Microsoft has launched the 'AI for Earth' program, which is intended to protect our planet through AI. In particular, this initiative aims to support non-profit and humanitarian organizations which focus on four different priorities: (i) assisting the world to recover from disasters; (ii) tackling the needs of children; (iii) protecting refugees and evacuated people; and (iv) promoting human rights as well as preventing their violations. This is done by developing open-source tools and applications that can accelerate technology development for environmental sustainability[1] (Ferres et al., 2020).

Moreover, we live in the era of big data, where conventional means of obtaining insights from such massive amounts of data are no longer applicable (Abu-Salih et al., 2021a). The complexity of real-life problems has driven industrial sectors to develop intelligent solutions incorporating AI to enable them to take prompt, automated, and effective decisions. AI has brought enormous opportunities for economic development (West & Allen, 2018). A project commenced by PriceWaterhouseCoopers[2] estimated that 'AI technologies could increase global GDP by $15.7 trillion, a full 14%, by 2030' (Anand & Verweij, 2019).

Data analytics and dashboards are essential tools for measuring and tracking performance indicators. AI systems require accurate and up-to-date data to make informed decisions and generate useful insights. Data analytics allows businesses and organizations to identify patterns and trends in their data, while dashboards provide a visual representation of the data to make it easier to understand and interpret.

Definition: Key Performance Indicators

Key Performance Indicators (KPIs) are measurable values that indicate how well an organization, business unit, project, or individual is achieving specific objectives (Parmenter, 2015).

By setting KPIs and monitoring progress using data analytics and dashboards, businesses can improve their performance, identify areas for improvement, and make data-driven

---

[1]More on the 'AI for Earth' initiative can be found at: https://www.microsoft.com/en-us/ai/ai-for-earth

[2]PricewaterhouseCoopers is a multinational professional services network of firms, delivering quality in assurance, tax and advisory services under the PwC brand (https://www.pwc.com/).

decisions. AI systems can use these KPIs and data analytics to automate and optimize decision-making processes. For example, an e-commerce business may use data analytics to track customer behaviour and identify trends in their purchasing habits. They can use this data to set KPIs for customer acquisition, retention, and sales, and use a dashboard/ Kanban to monitor their progress in real time. An AI system can then use this data to personalize recommendations for each customer based on their individual preferences and behaviour. See also the discussion on data analytics in Chapter 10.

What is Machine Learning?

The discussions of AI generally include the term *Machine Learning* (ML). There is evidence of ML in several areas of our lives: in ride-sharing apps, email spam filtering, fraud prevention, online shopping, personalized advertisements, and many other use cases (some of which will be discussed later in this chapter). ML is the most prominent branch of AI. It has been integrated firmly within various disciplines in past years due to its ability to design and develop algorithms and techniques that enable the computer to 'learn'.

Definition: Machine Learning

Machine Learning (ML) is a sub-field of AI which involves various statistical techniques designed and implemented to enable applications to learn and make predictions without explicit programming (Samuel, 1959).

What Are the Differences between AI and ML?

Although the terms AI and ML are sometimes used interchangeably, they differ, and both terms are used in different contexts Ahuja, 2019; Marr, 2016; Pati, 2021):

1   AI is a broader concept that is applied to develop smart computer systems that can simulate human behaviour, thereby enabling machines to perform complex tasks which a human generally performs. On the other hand, ML is a subset of AI, the aim of which is to develop and implement computer programs that can learn and improve from experience.
2   AI can be categorized into weak AI, general AI, and strong AI, while ML can be classified as supervised learning, semi-supervised learning, unsupervised learning, and reinforcement learning.
3   AI systems are designed to maximize the chances of success, while ML applications are developed to ensure the accuracy of the output.

4   Siri, chatbots, expert systems, robots, etc. are examples of AI systems.
     Recommender systems, search engines, auto-translation, weather forecasting, etc.,
     are examples of ML applications.

Figure 9.1 illustrates the relationship between AI and ML, and the different types of ML
and their applications. This will be discussed in more detail in the next section.

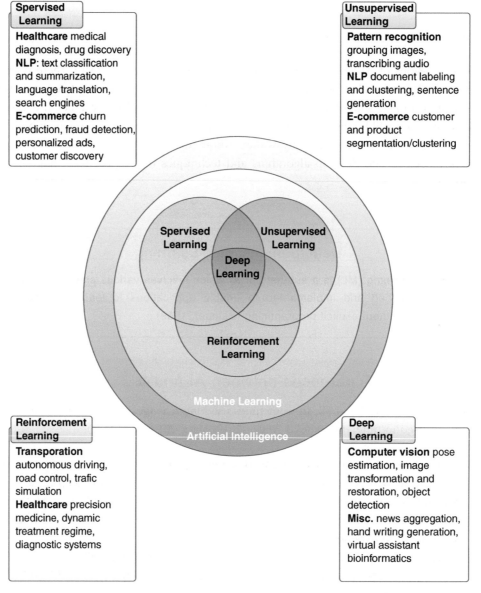

Spervised Learning
Healthcare medical diagnosis, drug discovery
NLP: text classification and summarization, language translation, search engines
E-commerce churn prediction, fraud detection, personalized ads, customer discovery

Unsupervised Learning
Pattern recognition grouping images, transcribing audio
NLP document labeling and clustering, sentence generation
E-commerce customer and product segmentation/clustering

Reinforcement Learning
Transporation autonomous driving, road control, trafic simulation
Healthcare precision medicine, dynamic treatment regime, diagnostic systems

Deep Learning
Computer vision pose estimation, image transformation and restoration, object detection
Misc. news aggregation, hand writing generation, virtual assistant bioinformatics

Figure 9.1   Types of ML, their Relationships, and Examples of their Real-life
Applications (based on the discussions in Bertolini et al. (2021), Coronato et al.
(2020), Goodfellow et al. (2016), Haydari & Yilmaz (2020), and Khan & Yairi (2018))

What are the Main Types of ML?

The various types of ML are categorized according to the intended outcome of the learning algorithm. Table 9.2 gives the types of ML, a brief description, the type of dataset used in each category, some examples of embedded algorithms, and examples of generic tasks that can be performed using a particular type of ML.

Table 9.2 Types of ML Learning*

Type	Description	Type of Data	Algorithms	Type of Problems
Supervised Learning	The algorithms of supervised learning receive a labelled dataset as training data and map an input to an output so as to make predictions on unseen data	Labelled dataset	Support vector machine, decision tree, linear regression, K-nearest neighbour, etc.	Classification, regression, and ranking problems
Unsupervised Learning	The algorithms of this category receive an unlabelled dataset and attempt to make predictions on all unseen observations	Unlabelled dataset	K-means, hierarchal clustering, principal component analysis, a priori algorithm, etc.	Clustering, segmentation, association, and dimensionality reduction
Reinforcement Learning	In this model, the intelligent agent makes predictions sequentially by actively interacting with the environment where each output depends on the state of the previous input	No predefined dataset	A2C/A3C, proximal policy optimization, AlphZero, CS1, etc.	Reward-based and planning tasks
Deep Learning	The algorithms of this model use artificial neural network architectures to learn an adequate representation of data	Both labelled and unlabelled datasets	Convolutional neural network, recurrent neural networks, long-short-term memory networks, etc.	Both supervised and unsupervised learning tasks

To gain a better understanding of how supervised learning works, let's say we want to build a model that predicts the price of a house based on its location, size, and number of bedrooms. We would start by collecting a dataset of houses with their corresponding prices, where each house is described by its location, size, and number of bedrooms. This is our labelled data. We would then train a supervised learning algorithm, such as a linear regression or a decision tree, on this dataset. The algorithm would learn the relationship between the input variables (size and number of bedrooms) and the output variable (price) and use this to make predictions on new, unseen data. We can then use this model to predict the price of a new house based on its location, size, and number of bedrooms.

Unsupervised learning can be used in marketing, whereby clustering can be incorporated to group together customers with similar purchase patterns or preferences, which can help businesses tailor their marketing strategies accordingly. Another example is anomaly detection, which involves identifying unusual or rare data points or patterns that deviate from the norm. This can be used in various fields such as fraud detection, network intrusion detection, and predictive maintenance.

One example of reinforcement learning is the use of AI in game playing. AlphaGo, developed by Google DeepMind, is a well-known example of reinforcement learning. AlphaGo is a computer program that was designed to play the ancient Chinese board game, Go. The game is known for its complexity, and until the development of AlphaGo, it was thought to be too difficult for computers to master due to the vast number of possible moves. The program uses a form of reinforcement learning called deep reinforcement learning to learn from experience and improve its performance over time. It was trained on a dataset of expert moves, and then it played millions of games against itself, improving its performance with each game. In 2016, AlphaGo defeated Lee Sedol, a world champion in the game, in a five-game match, demonstrating the capabilities of reinforcement learning in AI (Silver et al., 2016; 2018).

Example: ChatGPT

ChatGPT[3] uses sophisticated machine learning algorithms to generate responses to user inputs by analysng patterns in large amounts of text data, such as online articles and books, and using those patterns to make predictions about which words and phrases are likely to follow a given input. It has the ability to understand natural language and generate human-like responses in a conversational manner, making it a powerful tool for communication and automation.

It is worth noting that the classification of ML types might vary, and drawing a line between them is somewhat arbitrary. For example, reinforcement learning can also be considered as supervised learning, albeit with a less informative feedback signal (Russell & Norvig, 2002). Further, the underlying structure of deep learning algorithms can also be applied to supervised learning, unsupervised learning, and reinforcement learning tasks. This can be perceived in Figure 9.1 which shows that deep learning intersects with other types of ML.

---

[3]https://chat.openai.com/

Stop and Reflect: AI in real life

Discuss examples of applications that integrate an AI functionality (e.g., mimicking humans such as chatbots, personalized ads such as those you find on social media, etc.) and answer the following questions:

- What are the pros and cons of these applications?
- Do you think AI can entirely replace humans? If not, what are the human aspects/features that AI cannot replace?
- Think of domains/fields/sectors have yet to incorporate AI and ML in their operations, and how could AI benefit them?

Why Are AI and ML So Successful?

AI and ML have brought breakthroughs to various industrial sectors, and these technologies continue to be applied in several aspects of our lives (Bertolini et al., 2021). Gartner™ reported that the business value of AI will reach $5.1 billion by 2025 (Gartner, 2017). The same report indicated the significance of using AI as the main driver for organizations to stay competitive, pursue new opportunities, improve their products and services, and provide customer satisfaction. For example, companies have started to incorporate intelligent virtual assistants (such as Apple's Siri, Amazon's Alexa, Google Assistant, and Microsoft Cortana) into their business practices to strengthen the collaboration between humans and AI as well as enable more natural open-ended conversation by means of sophisticated AI and Natural Language Processing (NLP) technologies (de Melo et al., 2020). Therefore, virtual assistants have been widely used in conversational marketing strategies to provide a better and more compelling customer interaction (Sotolongo & Copulsky, 2018). In fact, the combination of data availability, advancements in computing power, improved algorithms, cost-effectiveness, and scalability has made AI a powerful tool for businesses in the digital global economy (Brynjolfsson & McAfee, 2014; Varian, 2018).

Example: DoNut Talk

Mad Over Donuts™ was founded in Singapore and is known for its doughnuts, which are available in over 20 flavours.[4] The company initiated a conversational marketing campaign by establishing a new messaging system using AI technology (DoNut Talk)

(Continued)

---

[4]https://www.madoverdonuts.com/

to bridge the gap between online engagement and offline sales. DoNut Talk was implemented by Jumper.ai,[5] a company that provides omni-channel conversational commerce via an integrated Messenger API for consumer-to-business messaging across Facebook and Instagram. DoNut Talk was built upon the Messenger API, which was used to establish a dialogue with customers in geo-fenced locations by asking them questions to understand their interest in donuts, and subsequently offer them free in-store purchase coupons. This virtual assistant experience provided Mad Over Donuts with collective customer feedback that benefited them by increasing sales, refining their next campaign, and releasing new flavours (Chawla & Chakraborty, 2021; Jumperai, 2019).

Another important consideration is the proliferation of big data, where the conventional techniques used to process and analyse such massive data are inadequate and inferior. AI technologies offer an effective and practical means of tackling such massive and heterogeneous datasets by identifying patterns in data, solving complex problems, and achieving in-depth insights in an efficient and scalable manner (Abu-Salih et al., 2021b). See also the discussion on big data in Chapter 11.

One specific example of why AI and ML are so successful is the use of deep learning algorithms in image recognition. In the past, image recognition required hand-engineered features and complex algorithms to accurately identify objects in images. However, with the advent of deep learning algorithms and neural networks, computers are now able to learn and recognize objects in images with a high degree of accuracy. For example, the use of deep learning has allowed for the development of image recognition systems that can accurately identify objects in images with a performance that surpasses human capabilities. This has led to a range of applications, from self-driving cars that can recognize road signs and pedestrians, to facial recognition software used for security and identification purposes (LeCun et al., 2015).

The Limitations and Challenges of AI

Despite the many benefits of AI, there are also a number of limitations and challenges associated with this technology. Some of the limitations of AI are illustrated in Table 9.3.

9.4 Knowledge Graphs

This section offers an introduction to the knowledge graph (KG). First, a definition of the term is provided followed by a discussion of the differences between generic and domain-specific KGs. An important technique used to construct a KG is presented and discussed, followed by an examination of various applications can benefit from KGs.

---

[5]https://jumper.ai/

Table 9.3 Challenges of AI*

Challenge	Description
Limited Creativity	AI can be excellent at solving specific problems and tasks, but it lacks the creativity and innovation that humans possess. This means that AI may struggle with tasks that require thinking outside of the box or coming up with original ideas.
Data Dependence	AI algorithms rely heavily on large amounts of high-quality data to learn and make predictions. If the data is biased or incomplete, the AI models may produce inaccurate results.
Lack of Emotional Intelligence	AI lacks emotional intelligence, which means it may struggle with tasks that require understanding and managing human emotions, such as counselling or social work.
High Cost of Implementation	The development and implementation of AI technologies can be expensive, especially for smaller organizations or those operating on limited budgets.
Job Displacement	There are concerns that AI may replace certain jobs, particularly those that involve routine and repetitive tasks. This could lead to unemployment or underemployment in some industries.
Ethical Concerns	There are ethical concerns surrounding the use of AI, particularly with regard to privacy, bias, and accountability. AI can be programmed to perpetuate biases and stereotypes, and it can be challenging to hold machines accountable for their actions.

Note: * Prepared by the authors based on the discussions in Mukhamediev et al. (2022), Prentice et al. (2020), Russell (2010), Russia (2020), and Tegmark (2018).

What is a Knowledge Graph (KG)?

Have you ever wondered how Google understands the meaning of the words you search for through its search engine, and how it provides relevant search results? These words represent real-world entities.

Definition: Real-World Entity

A real-world entity refers to a specific person, movie, location, event, or other concepts and objects that exist in the physical or abstract world.

In the context of knowledge graphs, these entities are represented as nodes, and the relationships between them are represented as edges, forming a graph-like structure. For example, in a knowledge graph related to the film industry, real-world entities could include actors, directors, movie titles, genres, release dates, and production companies.

These entities are connected by relationships such as 'acted in', 'directed', 'belongs to genre', 'released on date', etc.

When you search Google, these entities and their relevant information are delivered in special information boxes known as knowledge panels that appear on Google's search results page when real-life entities are searched. Figure 9.2 shows an example of a knowledge panel related to the famous computer scientist, Alan Turing. The knowledge panel contains various facts about a particular entity, thus giving the user more in-depth details. These facts are collected from a giant knowledge base known as the Google Knowledge Graph (Singhal, 2012).

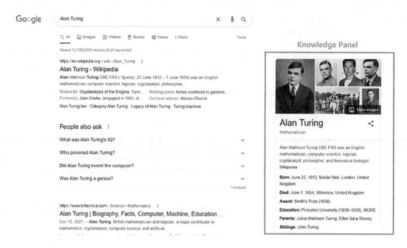

Figure 9.2 An Example of a Knowledge Panel

KGs are a new form of knowledge representation and one of the key trends driving the next wave of technologies (Bellomarini et al., 2020). The KG depicts an integrated collection of real-world entities which are linked by semantically-interrelated relations.

Definition: Semantic Interlinking

Semantic Interlinking is the process of interconnecting the descriptions of entities that exist in different datasets and vocabularies to extend the understanding of the real-world entities which belong to one or different domains (Ferraram et al., 2013).

The notion of semantic interlinking is leveraged by the use of Semantic Web technology introduced by Tim Berners-Lee,[6] who provided a new vision for the next Web generation whereby data can be given semantic meanings by annotating it (the data) in a

---

[6]Tim Berners-Lee is known for his invention of the World Wide Web (WWW).

machine-readable format (Berners-Lee et al.,). This is done by using ontologies[7] that model the knowledge about a specific domain knowledge by defining concepts (representing a set of entities), constraints, and the relationship between entities, thereby providing a formal and an explicit representation of that domain (Gruber, 1993; Stevens, 2001). KGs extend these endeavours by capturing a unified standard representation of semantically interconnected datasets through an abstract data model (i.e., a graph).

Definition: Knowledge Graph

A knowledge graph can be perceived as a multidimensional graph containing entities/ nodes and relations/edges which are relevant to one or more domains (Ehrlinger & Wöß, 2016).

A KG is described as a directed graph (G, where $G = (V, E)$. This notation illustrates the relationship between entities, and the relationships between these entities in terms of the vertices (V) of the graph and the edges (E) between these vertices. The vertices represent real-world entities and the edges correspond to the relationships between such entities. Vertices/entities/nodes are interlinked using relations which are the edges of the graph, and facts can be represented as an RDF[8] triple (*subjects, predicate, object* or *head, relation, tail*, which also is referred to as *<h, r, t>*. Hence, a relationship that connects two entities constitutes a fact in the KG.

Figure 9.3 depicts a KG representation in terms of entities and the relationships between these entities. The interesting thing about a KG is that we can semantically interlink different topics/domains when building this graph. For example, Figure 9.3 shows the information captured about three main entities: Alan Turing, Enigma Machine, and Princeton University. Various facts (triples) can be extracted from this KG. For example, the fact '*Alan Turing has cracked Enigma Machine*' comprises two entities/nodes, namely '*Alan Turing*' and '*Enigma Machine*', and the relationship '*has cracked*' forms the triple '*Alan Turing, has cracked, Enigma Machine*'. The other entities in this KG can also be extended and thus interlinked with additional real-life objects.

Generic and Domain-Specific KGs

KGs are either generic or domain-specific. Generic KGs (also known as domain-independent, cross-domain, or open-world) have been constructed continuously since the invention of the Semantic Web. Generic KGs have been associated with the

---

[7]The notion of ontology in computer science was firstly defined by Tom Gruber as 'an explicit specification of a conceptualisation' (Gruber, 1993).
[8]https://www.w3.org/TR/rdf11-concepts/

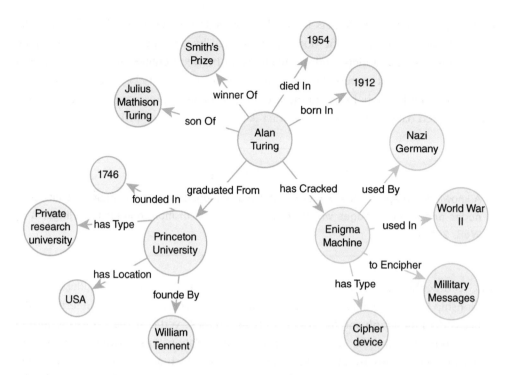

Figure 9.3 A Sample KG to Demonstrate Entities and Relationships between Those Entities (based on information extracted from Wikipedia, https://en.wikipedia.org/wiki/Knowledge_graph

linked data as a natural representation of interlinked entities (Ehrlinger & Wöß, 2016). Various generic KGs include the BabelNet, YAGO, Cyc, NELL, CliGraph, and DBPedia knowledge bases, and the number of such KGs is growing at an increasing rate. A domain-specific KG, on the other hand, is a special type of KG that is used to represent a specific and complex domain (Fan et al., 2017; Li et al., 2020; Yuan et al., 2020), such as health, sports, social science, engineering, travel, etc. Domain KGs are usually constructed based on a specific and predefined domain ontology so as to capture the domain of interest either in its high-level sense or in its specific subdomains (Abu-Salih, 2021). Examples of domain KGs include: HKGB (Zhang et al., 2020), K12EduKG (Chen et al., 2018), SoftwareKG (Schindler et al., 2020), ClaimsKG (Tchechmedjiev et al., 2019). Table 9.4 shows some of the differences between generic and domain-specific KGs.

Knowledge Graph Construction

The construction of a KG involves entities and the relationships between these entities. There are various approaches to the construction of a KG, and the choice of approach depends on

Table 9.4 Generic vs Domain-Specific KGs (based on the discussions in Abu-Salih (2021))

Criteria	Generic KG	Domain KG
Domain dependency	Domain-independent	Domain-dependent
Uses predefined ontology	Rarely	Mainly
Data sources	Vary	Limited
Data size	Massive	Limited
Examples	BabelNet, YAGO, Cyc, NELL, CliGraph, and DBPedia	HKGB, K12EduKG, ClaimsKG, and SoftwareKG

the knowledge extraction level, the type of knowledge base, and the incorporated technicalities (Abu-Salih, 2021). This chapter discusses the mechanism used to construct a KG based on the type of knowledge base. In this regard, the construction of a KG depends on whether a predefined schema is used (i.e., ontology), no predefined ontology is used (schema-free), or the KG construction involves a hybrid of schema-based and schema-free approaches (Dong et al., 2014; Heist, 2018; Nickel et al., 2015).

Figure 9.4 shows a taxonomy of KG construction approaches according to the types of knowledge bases. The first mechanism (i.e., schema-based) can be classified into two categories according to the data sources and ontology: (i) the bottom-up method where the ontology and its predefined structure are incorporated to build the KG (e.g. Wikipedia is elaborated by using the predefined ontology schema, i.e. DBpedia (Kuhn et al., 2016)); and (ii) the top-down method, by which the underlying structure of the data is used to infer the ontology schema (e.g. YAGO (Suchanek et al., 2007)). The second mechanism is based upon the openness of the Web and thus the approaches in this category are called schema-free approaches. In these approaches, no consideration is given to the ontology design; thus, the construction approach is mainly ad hoc and based on information collected using different knowledge extraction techniques (e.g. OpenIE (Fader et al., 2011)). The last mechanism is the hybrid approach in which the knowledge is obtained by both a predefined schema and the Web and other repositors (e.g. KnowledgeVault (Dong et al., 2014), NELL (Carlson et al., 2010)).

Stop and Reflect: Constructing a KG

Try to construct a simple KG for a certain topic/theme/domain. You can start with a particular entity and elaborate and augment the graph with other relevant entities and relationships between these entities, such as the sample we constructed for Alan Turing (i.e., Figure 9.3). Discuss the resultant KG with your lecturer.

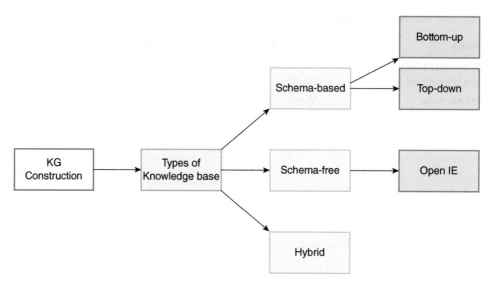

Figure 9.4 KG Construction Approaches Based on the Types of the Knowledge Base (based on Dong et al. (2014), Heist (2018), Nickel et al. (2015), and Zou (2020))

Knowledge Graph Applications

The ongoing and popular use of KGs has given rise to various applications that can benefit from the KG's abstract underlying structure, which machines can interpret. This intuitive and significant feature of KGs has driven both academia and industry to build consolidated intelligent systems that can benefit a variety of industrial applications (Zou, 2020). The number of pages and embedded contents available on the Web are already incredibly huge and continue to grow exponentially. This requires a smart approach to extract valuable and relevant information from such enormous volumes of data. KGs facilitate the interlinking of useful information that is captured from a variety of sources. To deal with this issue, Google embedded a KG in its search engine in 2012 as an intelligent and cognitive technology layer that has proven its utility in providing users with a better search experience (Singhal, 2012). By integrating KGs with AI-based technologies and ML algorithms such as deep learning, new insights can be gained by providing users with an engaged and relevant search experience, thus transforming a search engine into a knowledge engine (Lewis, 2020). Search engines are not the only beneficiary of KGs; the usage of KGs expands to a wide variety of use cases in different domains of knowledge. Figure 9.5 demonstrates some of these domains and gives examples of how KGs are used in them.

9.5 Chapter Summary

The rapid growth of sophisticated technologies such as AI, ML, and KGs have contributed to the Fourth Industrial Revolution and provided the means by which knowledge can be created and managed. The successful adoption of such technologies has propelled economies forward and created waves of innovations that have disrupted various industries.

Figure 9.5 Examples of KGs' Use Cases in Several Domains of Knowledge (based on the discussions in Abu-Salih (2021))

This chapter explains these technical terms and provides a theoretical background in order to better understand the landscape of these technologies. The chapter starts with an overview of AI including a brief historical view and a definition of the term. It also points to the importance of AI for people and societies. In the same context, the chapter also defines ML and explains how it differs from AI. Also, various types of ML are discussed, and the reasons for their success are given. Then, the chapter explains KGs and distinguishes two types of KGs, namely generic KGs and domain-specific KGs. This is followed by presenting approaches to KG construction approaches and the important applications of KGs.

9.6 Further Reading

Mitchell, M. (2019). *Artificial Intelligence: A Guide for Thinking Humans*. Penguin Books.

The application of AI has dominated several aspects of our lives. In this book, the author introduces several state-of-the-art AI systems and discusses their success and limitations. The author takes the reader on a journey to discover the actual essence of AI and the extent to which machines can act intelligently and do things that might require high levels of intelligence and affect our lives.

LeCun, Y., Bengio, Y., & Hinton, G. (2015). Deep learning. *Nature, 521*(7553), 436–444.

Deep learning has become a buzzword and has revolutionized several industrial applications for large-scale datasets. In this seminal article, the authors shed light on the deep learning area by examining the relevant technicalities behind it. In particular, the authors discuss the technical architectures of deep learning (including convolutional neural networks, recurrent neural networks, etc.) and discuss important applications that have benefited from them. Finally, the future of deep learning with regard to computer vision and natural language understanding are presented and discussed.

Abu-Salih, B. (2021). Domain-specific knowledge graphs: A survey. *Journal of Network and Computer Applications, 185*, 103076.

Knowledge graphs have become a cornerstone of several industrial domains. In this survey paper, the author provides a comprehensive definition of the notion of domain KG. This is followed by a comprehensive state-of-the-art review of recent advances in KGs in seven domains of knowledge, namely Healthcare, Education, ICT, Science and Engineering, Finance, Society and Politics, and Travel. Limitations and future research directions are also reported and discussed.

Discussion Questions

1. What is the difference between strong AI and weak AI?
2. What are some real-life examples of supervised learning and unsupervised learning?
3. How can AI infer insights and furnish a solution to the big data problem?
4. What are some of the benefits of constructing domain-specific KGs?
5. How can KGs and AI be integrated to provide better data analytics? Provide an example to justify your answer.

Case Study: Artificial Intelligence in Telemedicine – Altibbi™

Nowadays, telehealth and telemedicine are fuelled by advanced technologies that suit primary and professional care services, and allow medical professionals to treat patients whenever and wherever they are, as long as there is an Internet connection.

However, the COVID-19 pandemic has placed increasing pressure on healthcare systems worldwide, but especially in the Middle East and North Africa (MENA) region. Hence, it was envisaged that telemedicine services would play a role in alleviating the pressure on traditional healthcare systems. Altibbi™ is an end-to-end digital health platform in MENA that addresses the lack of medical services and medical content, and this is done in the Arabic language. The following sections discuss the applications of AI in healthcare and in telemedicine offered by Altibbi, a well-known telemedicine platform in the MENA region.

The Need for Telehealth and Telemedicine Platforms

In recent years, we have witnessed an immense rise in Internet usage, social media, and wearable and IoT devices that have produced high-dimensional and large-scale data. However, the emergence of COVID-19 has revolutionized the telehealth and telemedicine platforms, which attracted more people to use them as an alternative to physical clinic visits under pandemic and lockdown situations. Such platforms provide better access to healthcare services by allowing patients to communicate with their practitioners using dissimilar dialogue mediums, including interactive voice and video chats, in a low-cost and more convenient way. Telehealth and telemedicine platforms increase accessibility to healthcare, particularly for those who live in rural or remote areas, have mobility issues, or are unable to travel to a healthcare facility. These platforms can improve patient outcomes by allowing for more frequent monitoring and follow-up care, and by providing access to specialists who may not be available in person. To sum up, these platforms have become an essential tool for healthcare providers and patients alike, providing improved accessibility, convenience, cost-effectiveness, and patient outcomes, as well as reducing the risk of transmitting infectious diseases.

Altibbi – a Distinguished Platform

Altibbi is an integrated telemedicine platform with a long history of delivering primary healthcare services, medical content, bookings, and clinic management systems in the Arabic language in the MENA region. It started in Jordan and expanded to include Egypt, Saudi Arabia, UAE, and other countries such as Kuwait, Bahrain, Qatar, Oman, Iraq, and Palestine. The Altibbi website[9] contains millions of medical articles and diverse content, offering telemedicine consultations that permit patients to connect with doctors through audio and video calls and text chats. Altibbi has more than 600 doctors available online and conducts more than 150,000 consultations monthly. It has launched various applications, such as 'Altibbi Website', 'Altibbi

(Continued)

[9]https://altibbi.com/

User App', 'Altibbi Mama', 'Altibbi Clinic', 'Altibbi for Doctors', and others. Further, Altibbi supports research and development. The platform has published several academic research studies in different prestigious journals. Additionally, it strengthens and broadens its expertise by engaging in research collaborations with Harvard Business School, Granada University, and Lancaster University.

Healthcare Data as the Main Driver

The Altibbi platform is rich in diverse data that the company saves in its databases, which is a significant resource for AI-based applications. Since 2019, the platform has integrated ML in its applications to improve the quality of various processes and services at different levels using state-of-the-art data science and deep learning technologies. For example, the Patient Health Records (PHRs), including the diagnoses, medications, and treatments, can be used to extract essential data from which useful knowledge can be derived, which helps with making diagnoses. Figure 9.6 shows the different sources of data in Altibbi.

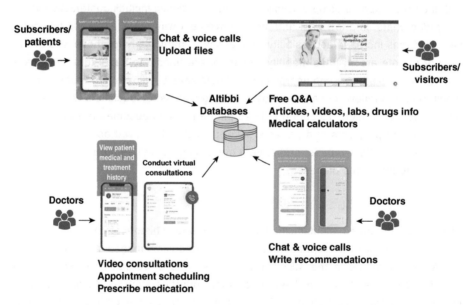

Figure 9.6 A Representation of the Different Data Sources at Altibbi (prepared by Altibbi)

How AI is incorporated into Altibbi?

Altibbi utilizes AI techniques, including machine learning and deep learning, in different modules, as explained below.

Supportive Diagnostic Module (SDM)

Although primary healthcare services aim to ensure the delivery of the correct treatment for common health conditions, diagnostic errors can lead to incorrect or late treatment, which may cause serious harm to patients. Computer-Aided Diagnostic (CAD) systems are computational approaches that can assist clinicians to make the right decisions, thereby reducing the possibility of cognitive errors. CAD systems utilize intelligent models to assist clinicians in different use cases, including the diagnosis. The SDM model was built to suggest different possible diagnoses so that telemedicine doctors can write appropriate recommendations. Medical recommendations contain complaints, symptoms, diagnoses, and treatments that also involve drugs, test labs, any medical imaging, free-text notes, and action plans. The data science team at Altibbi built a ML model to predict the various possible diagnoses of patients' conditions based on documented symptoms and medical consultations (Faris et al., 2021). Figure 9.7 shows how the SDM model operates: the input is a group of features in which the association rules are related to unpermitted combinations of diagnostic codes of the International Classification of Diseases (ICD-10). At the same time, the output is a set of diagnoses ranked by the probability function of the deep network model.

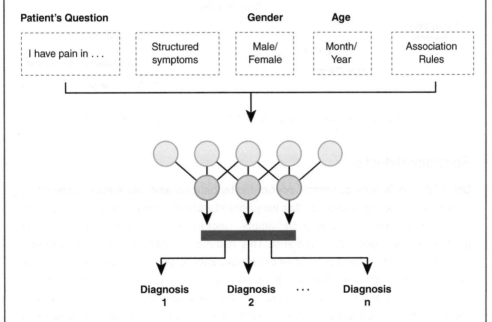

Figure 9.7   A Demonstration of the SDM Model (prepared by Altibbi)

(Continued)

Supportive Treatment Module (STM)

The STM model was developed to help doctors prescribe appropriate treatments; it can recommend drugs, lab tests, and imaging (e.g., x-rays) based on the consultations, the symptoms, and diagnosis.

AltibbiVec

AltibbiVec is the core NLP language model in Altibbi that assists most ML projects to understand the different Arabic dialects across the MENA region. Arabic is a low-resource language; thus, it is difficult to use NLP to process Arabic due to several limitations, such as the lack of linguistic resources, datasets, and analytical tools compared to other high-resource languages like English. AltibbiVec was developed to learn the complex relationships between Arabic words, and to capture their semantics. It was built using more than 5 million elements of Altibbi's content, including free Q&As (questions and answers), medical consultations, articles, news, and drug info, to name a few (Habib et al., 2021). As AltibbiVec provides semantically-based embedding, it is a core component of most of Altibbi's AI-based NLP-oriented projects. Figure 9.8 shows a schematic diagram of it.

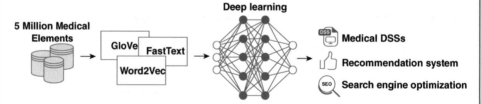

Figure 9.8   A Representative Diagram of AltibbiVec (prepared by Altibbi)

Specialty detection

One of the challenges commonly confronted by patients who use Altibbi's application is deciding which specialist doctor they should consult or visit. As primary care is an essential service provided by Altibbi, doctors are responsible for referring patients to the appropriate specialist. This is done manually by the general practitioner and immediately after a medical consultation with the patient. However, the medical doctor receives thousands of questions every day, making the process very time-consuming and imprecise. Therefore, the data science team at Altibbi developed an automated classification system that classifies medical consultations according to the medical specialty using a machine-learning-based classification system (Faris et al., 2020).

Questions

1   What are the key drivers of Altibbi's success in the MENA region?
2   Identify and discuss potential ML types used in Altibbi applications.
3   If Altibbi decided to build a KG, which KG construction approach would you recommend and why?
4   How can Altibbi's current telemedical services be improved?

Acknowledgements

Thanks to Hossam Faris and Maria Habib from Altibbi for drafting and developing the case study material.

9.7 References

Abu-Salih, B. (2021). Domain-specific knowledge graphs: A survey. *Journal of Network and Computer Applications, 185*, 103076.

Abu-Salih, B., Wongthongtham, P., Zhu, D., Chan, K. Y., & Rudra, A. (2021a). Introduction to Big Data Technology. In *Social Big Data Analytics* (pp. 15–59): Springer.

Abu-Salih, B., Wongthongtham, P., Zhu, D., Chan, K. Y., & Rudra, A. (2021b). *Social Big Data Analytics: Practices, Techniques, and Applications*. Springer Nature.

Ahuja, A. S. (2019). The impact of artificial intelligence in medicine on the future role of the physician. *PeerJ, 7*, e7702.

Anand, S., & Verweij, G. (2019). What's the real value of AI for your business and how can you capitalise. https://www.pwc.com/gx/en/issues/analytics/assets/pwc-ai-analysis-sizing-the-prize-report.pdf

Andresen, S. L. (2002). John McCarthy: Father of AI. *IEEE Intelligent Systems, 17*(5), 84–85.

Bellomarini, L., Sallinger, E., & Vahdati, S. (2020). Knowledge graphs: The layered perspective. In *Knowledge Graphs and Big Data Processing* (pp. 20–34): Springer, Cham.

Berners-Lee, T., Hendler, J., & Lassila, O. (2001). The semantic web. *Scientific American, 284*(5), 28–37.

Bertolini, M., Mezzogori, D., Neroni, M., & Zammori, F. (2021). Machine Learning for industrial applications: A comprehensive literature review. *Expert Systems with Applications, 175*, 114820.

Brynjolfsson, E., & McAfee, A. (2014). *The Second Machine Age: Work, Progress, and Prosperity in a Time of Brilliant Technologies*. WW Norton & Company.

Carlson, A., Betteridge, J., Kisiel, B., Settles, B., Hruschka Jr, E. R., & Mitchell, T. M. (2010). *Toward an Architecture for Never-ending Language Learning*. Paper presented at the AAAI.

Chawla, M., & Chakraborty, A. (2021). A success story. *Delhi Business Review, 22*(1), 103–109.

Chen, P., Lu, Y., Zheng, V. W., Chen, X., & Li, X. (2018). *An Automatic Knowledge Graph Construction System for K-12 Education*. Paper presented at the Proceedings of the fifth annual ACM conference on learning at scale.

Chugh, R., Macht, S., & Hossain, R. (2022). Robotic Process Automation: a review of organizational grey literature. *International Journal of Information Systems and Project Management, 10*(1), 5–26.

Coronato, A., Naeem, M., De Pietro, G., & Paragliola, G. (2020). Reinforcement learning for intelligent healthcare applications: A survey. *Artificial Intelligence in Medicine, 109*, 101964.

Davenport, T. H., & Ronanki, R. (2018). Artificial intelligence for the real world. *Harvard Business Review, 96*(1), 108–116.

de Melo, C. M., Kim, K., Norouzi, N., Bruder, G., & Welch, G. (2020). Reducing cognitive load and improving warfighter problem solving with intelligent virtual assistants. *Frontiers in Psychology, 11*, 3170.

Dong, X., Gabrilovich, E., Heitz, G., Horn, W., Lao, N., Murphy, K., ... Zhang, W. (2014). *Knowledge Vault: A Web-scale Approach to Probabilistic Knowledge Fusion*. Paper presented at the Proceedings of the 20th ACM SIGKDD International Conference on Knowledge Discovery and Data Mining.

Ehrlinger, L., & Wöß, W. (2016). Towards a definition of knowledge graphs. *SEMANTiCS (Posters, Demos, SuCCESS), 48*, 1–4.

Fader, A., Soderland, S., & Etzioni, O. (2011). *Identifying Relations for Open Information Extraction*. Paper presented at the Proceedings of the 2011 conference on empirical methods in natural language processing.

Fan, Y., Wang, C., Zhou, G., & He, X. (2017). *Dkgbuilder: An Architecture for Building a Domain Knowledge Graph from Scratch*. Paper presented at the International Conference on Database Systems for Advanced Applications.

Faris, H., Habib, M., Faris, M., Alomari, M., & Alomari, A. (2020). Medical speciality classification system based on binary particle swarms and ensemble of one vs. rest support vector machines. *Journal of Biomedical Informatics, 109*, 103525.

Faris, H., Habib, M., Faris, M., Elayan, H., & Alomari, A. (2021). An intelligent multimodal medical diagnosis system based on patients' medical questions and structured symptoms for telemedicine. *Informatics in Medicine Unlocked, 23*, 100513.

Ferraram, A., Nikolov, A., & Scharffe, F. (2013). Data linking for the semantic web. *Semantic Web: Ontology and Knowledge Base Enabled Tools, Services, and Applications, 169*, 326.

Ferres, J. L., Robinson, C., Yang, S., Ortiz, A., Nasir, M., Yu, Y., & Trivedi, A. (2020). *Lessons Learned from Our Investments in AI for Good at Microsoft*. Paper presented at the AGU Fall Meeting 2020.

Gartner. (2017). Reinforce your Artificial Intelligence (AI) ecosystem. https://www.gartner.com/en/information-technology/insights/artificial-intelligence

Goodfellow, I., Bengio, Y., & Courville, A. (2016). *Deep Learning*. MIT Press.

Gruber, T. R. (1993). *A Translation Approach to Portable Ontology Specification*. Paper presented at the Knowledge Acquisition.

Habib, M., Faris, M., Alomari, A., & Faris, H. (2021). AltibbiVec: A word embedding model for medical and health applications in the Arabic Language. *IEEE Access, 9*, 133875–133888.

Haydari, A., & Yilmaz, Y. (2020). Deep reinforcement learning for intelligent transportation systems: A survey. *IEEE Transactions on Intelligent Transportation Systems*.

Heist, N. (2018). *Towards Knowledge Graph Construction from Entity Co-Occurrence*. Paper presented at the EKAW (Doctoral Consortium).

Jackson, P. (1986) Introduction to expert systems. United States.

Jumperai. (2019). Mad Over Donuts: Literally. https://jumper.ai/success-stories/mad-over-donuts

Khan, S., & Yairi, T. (2018). A review on the application of deep learning in system health management. *Mechanical Systems and Signal Processing, 107*, 241–265.

Kuhn, P., Mischkewitz, S., Ring, N., & Windheuser, F. (2016). Type inference on Wikipedia list pages. *Informatik 2016*.

LeCun, Y., Bengio, Y., & Hinton, G. (2015). Deep learning. *Nature, 521*(7553), 436–444.

Lewis, P. (2020). Smarter enterprise search: Why knowledge graphs and NLP can provide all the right answers. https://www.accenture.com/us-en/blogs/search-and-content-analytics-blog/enterprise-search-knowledge-graphs

Li, Y., Zakhozhyi, V., Zhu, D., & Salazar, L. J. (2020). *Domain Specific Knowledge Graphs as a Service to the Public: Powering Social-Impact Funding in the US*. Paper presented at the Proceedings of the 26th ACM SIGKDD International Conference on Knowledge Discovery & Data Mining.

Luger, G. F. (2005). *Artificial Intelligence: Structures and Strategies for Complex Problem Solving*. Pearson Education.

Macrorie, R., Marvin, S., & While, A. (2021). Robotics and automation in the city: A research agenda. *Urban Geography, 42*(2), 197–217.

Marr, B. (2016). What is the difference between artificial intelligence and machine learning. *Forbes, December, 6*.

Mohri, M., Rostamizadeh, A., & Talwalkar, A. (2018). *Foundations of Machine Learning*. MIT Press.

Mukhamediev, R. I., Popova, Y., Kuchin, Y., Zaitseva, E., Kalimoldayev, A., Symagulov, A., … Yakunin, K. (2022). Review of Artificial Intelligence and Machine Learning technologies: Classification, restrictions, opportunities and challenges. *Mathematics, 10*(15), 2552.

Nickel, M., Murphy, K., Tresp, V., & Gabrilovich, E. (2015). A review of relational machine learning for knowledge graphs. *Proceedings of the IEEE, 104*(1), 11–33.

Parmenter, D. (2015). *Key Performance Indicators: Developing, Implementing, and Using Winning KPIs*. John Wiley & Sons.

Pati, S. (2021). The difference between Artificial intelligence and Machine Learning. https://www.analyticsinsight.net/the-difference-between-artificial-intelligence-and-machine-learning/

Prentice, C., Dominique Lopes, S., & Wang, X. (2020). Emotional intelligence or artificial intelligence – an employee perspective. *Journal of Hospitality Marketing & Management, 29*(4), 377–403.

Russell, S., & Norvig, P. (2002). *Artificial Intelligence: A Modern Approach*. Prentice Hall.

Russell, S. J. (2010). *Artificial Intelligence a Modern Approach*. Pearson Education, Inc.

Russia, E. B. (2020). Standardization of Artificial Intelligence for the development and use of intelligent systems. *Advances in Wireless Communications and Networks, 6*(1), 1.

Samuel, A. L. (1959). Some studies in machine learning using the game of checkers. *IBM Journal of Research and Development, 3*(3), 210–229.

Schindler, D., Zapilko, B., & Krüger, F. (2020). *Investigating Software Usage in the Social Sciences: A Knowledge Graph Approach*. Paper presented at the European Semantic Web Conference.

Silver, D., Huang, A., Maddison, C. J., Guez, A., Sifre, L., Van Den Driessche, G., ... Lanctot, M. (2016). Mastering the game of Go with deep neural networks and tree search. *Nature, 529*(7587), 484–489.

Silver, D., Hubert, T., Schrittwieser, J., Antonoglou, I., Lai, M., Guez, A., ... Graepel, T. (2018). A general reinforcement learning algorithm that masters chess, shogi, and Go through self-play. *Science, 362*(6419), 1140–1144.

Singhal, A. (2012). Introducing the Knowledge Graph: Things, not strings. https://blog. google/products/search/introducing-knowledge-graph-things-not/

Smith, B. (2018). Using AI to help save lives. https://blogs.microsoft.com/on-the-issues/2018/09/24/using-ai-to-help-save-lives/

Sotolongo, N., & Copulsky, J. (2018). Conversational marketing: Creating compelling customer connections. *Applied Marketing Analytics, 4*(1), 6–21.

Stevens, R. (2001). What is an ontology? http://www.cs.man.ac.uk/~stevensr/onto/node3. html

Suchanek, F. M., Kasneci, G., & Weikum, G. (2007). *Yago: A Core of Semantic Knowledge*. Paper presented at the Proceedings of the 16th International Conference on World Wide Web.

Tchechmedjiev, A., Fafalios, P., Boland, K., Gasquet, M., Zloch, M., Zapilko, B., ...Todorov, K. (2019). *ClaimsKG: A Knowledge Graph of Fact-Checked Claims*. Paper presented at the International Semantic Web Conference.

Tegmark, M. (2018). *Life 3.0: Being Human in the Age of Artificial Intelligence*. Vintage.

Varian, H. (2018). Artificial intelligence, economics, and industrial organization. In *The Economics of Artificial Intelligence: An Agenda* (pp. 399–419). University of Chicago Press.

West, D. M., & Allen, J. R. (2018). How artificial intelligence is transforming the world. *Report. April, 24*, 2018.

Yuan, J., Jin, Z., Guo, H., Jin, H., Zhang, X., Smith, T., & Luo, J. (2020). Constructing biomedical domain-specific knowledge graph with minimum supervision. *Knowledge and Information Systems, 62*(1), 317–336.

Zhang, Y., Sheng, M., Zhou, R., Wang, Y., Han, G., Zhang, H., ... Dong, J. (2020). HKGB: An inclusive, extensible, intelligent, semi-auto-constructed knowledge graph framework for healthcare with clinicians' expertise incorporated. *Information Processing & Management, 57*(6), 102324.

Zou, X. (2020). *A Survey on Application of Knowledge Graphs*. Paper presented at the Journal of Physics: Conference Series.

10

DATA
ANALYTICS

10.1 Learning Outcomes

By the end of this chapter, you will be able to:

- Define the term 'data analytics'
- Understand the various stages of the big data analytics process
- Explain the four ways in which data analytics can be used
- Understand the use of data analytics in various areas
- Explain the concept of visualization and its various types
- Define business intelligence
- Describe the five-layered business intelligence architecture
- Detail various types of business intelligence
- Discuss the various business intelligence techniques

10.2 Introduction

This chapter will discuss data analytics as a method of capturing the requirements of the systems and summarizing them. Different diagramming techniques are also covered, to allow students to understand how this data will be used for decision-making in business. In the fourth industrial revolution, known as Industry 4.0, production has been decentralized so that shared facilities can achieve on-demand manufacturing and resource efficiency. Data analytics has been expediting this fourth industrial revolution by providing the means for analysing massive amounts of data. The information and patterns derived from this analysis are used to inform subsequent business decisions. The sophisticated parallel and distributed systems in big data analytics enable us to harness the volume of data currently exceeding exabytes. The emerging landscape of cloud-based environments also allows us to access any data as required regardless of its volume, velocity, variety, veracity and location. Additionally, significant advancements in computing memory, storage, processing power, networking infrastructure and communication technologies have helped to increase the scope and scalability of data analytics. Evolving visualization technologies along with optimization techniques for resource utilization and parallel data processing also facilitate data analytics applications in various domains including business and commercial applications in the domains of public health, government, environmental management, etc.

10.3 Data Analytics

There are three different types of decisions – strategic decisions, tactical decisions, and operational decisions – that the management of any business or organization needs to make when planning, coordinating, organizing and leading their businesses or organization in order to improve performance.

1 Strategic decisions can impact the overall direction of an organization, where senior management makes strategic decisions for a time horizon of three to five years.
2 The focus of tactical decisions is on achieving goals and objectives derived from the strategic decisions. Tactical decisions are made by mid-level management personnel who set annual targets and revisit these decisions half-yearly or annually.
3 Operational decisions affect the day-to-day operations of businesses or organizations; these decisions are made by the operational managers. Data analytics have been used to ensure that this decision-making is more effective and efficient, particularly when managers are given many decision-making choices.

Data analytics has been defined by Camm et al. (2014, p.4) as 'the scientific process of transforming data into insight for making better decisions. Business analytics is used for data-driven or fact-based decision making, which is often seen as more objective than other alternatives for decision making'.

Stages in the Big Data Analytics Process

It is important that organizations can process large amounts of rapidly generated and diverse data, and transform these into meaningful insights to enable them to make evidence-based decisions. There are five stages in the big data analytics process: data acquisition/recording; extraction/cleaning/annotation; integration/aggregation/representation; analysis modelling; and interpretation (Figure 10.1) (Agrawal et al., 2011).

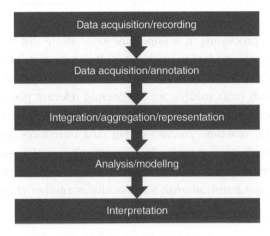

Figure 10.1   Stages of the Big Data Analytics Process

Generally, many people focus on the challenges which are expected to emerge from the analysis and modelling stage. It is important to understand the complexities of such challenges, which can be encountered starting from the data acquisition stage. Agrawal et al. (2011) stated that several difficulties may arise during every stage of the big data analytics process. These are explained below.

Data acquisition and recording

Nowadays, because of the abundant data being generated, one of the challenges is to establish filters for the data so that important information is identified and prioritized, and no useful information is discarded or ignored. Another challenge is to automatically generate the correct metadata to provide detailed descriptions of acquired data, together with the measurements and methods used to record them. The metadata is used for the correct and relevant interpretation of the findings from the analysis and modelling stage.

Extraction, cleaning, and annotation

The data acquired in the first stage will not be in the appropriate and consistent format necessary for processing and analysis because they will be unstructured, quasi-structured, semi-structured, or structured. Technically speaking, it is an ongoing challenge to extract the required information and then clean and transform it into the formats required for the data analysis stage.

Data integration, aggregation, and representation

All of the datasets acquired, extracted, and transformed in the previous stages are designed and recorded for various reasons and purposes. Having a large number of datasets in the repository does not mean that meaningful and insightful analysis can be conducted. It is still a challenge to integrate all of these datasets on the same temporal and spatial basis or any other common characteristics.

Analysis and modelling

Even in simple query processing, it is important to be aware that big data can be noisy, heterogeneous, dynamic, and highly interrelated. It is necessary to ensure sure that big data does not contain redundancies. Another challenge involves choosing the analysis and modelling methods most suitable for discovering relevant patterns and information in the big data, and identifying any correlations between the datasets of interest. The increasing demand for real-time analysis of big data introduces another challenge: to improve the interactive response time while processing complex queries. Querying the information from various databases, utilizing analytics packages for non-SQL processing, such as data mining and statistical analyses, introduces another challenge.

Interpretation

The assumptions which are made during data acquisition, transformation, and analysis have an impact on the relevance and accuracy of the interpretation of the findings from the analysis and modelling stage. Therefore, it is important to document all assumptions made during each stage of the data analytics process and to consider them in the interpretation of the findings so as to obtain more contextual insights.

What Are the Four Ways to Use Data Analytics?

The most commonly used big data analytic techniques for structured and unstructured data are: text analytics; audio analytics; video analytics; social media analytics; and predictive analytics. Data analytics methods can vary and can be anything from simple descriptive reports to the most sophisticated and complex optimization techniques. These methods can generally be categorized under descriptive analytics, diagnostic analytics, predictive analytics, and prescriptive analytics (see Table 10.1 and Figure 10.2).

Table 10.1 Types of Data Analytics (Banerjee et al., 2013) Prepared by the Authors

	Category	Definition
1	**Descriptive analytics**	Descriptive analytics comprises the techniques that we use to describe what happened in the past, such as data queries, reports, descriptive statistics (mean, measures of variation) and data visualization for the data dashboard. Data dashboards with collections of charts, maps, and summary statistics from both historical and real-time data are used to enable management to understand the business performance which will inform their decision-making. Some data mining techniques such as cluster analysis and sentiment analysis can also be used to understand the patterns showing what is happening in their business activities.

	Category	Definition
2	**Diagnostic analytics**	Diagnostic analytics enables us to determine the cause(s) of an occurrence. Exploratory analysis of the existing data or (sometimes) additional external data is used to discover the root causes of why something happened.
3	**Predictive analytics**	The techniques of predictive analytics use past data to predict what could happen in the future by considering the impact of one or more variable on another. Depending on the nature of the business and product(s), the growth trajectory and seasonality of past trends are taken into account. The predictive analytics techniques used to examine the impact of uncertainty on a business decision include linear regression, time series analysis, data mining methods, and simulations which involve probability analysis.
4	**Prescriptive analytics**	The techniques of prescriptive analytics are used to determine the best course of action to take to achieve the business's desired outcome(s). For example, in the financial market, prescriptive analytics is used for investment portfolio modelling to determine which mix of investments is expected to yield the highest return while minimizing or controlling the exposure to potential risks.
		It is also used in supply chain management to design a supply network with the widest possible coverage of plants and distribution centres while minimizing costs. These optimization models are also useful for marketing as a means of identifying the price markdown models that will maximize the revenue with the best possible discount along with the best timing of discount offers and the number of units sold.
		These simulation optimization techniques use probability and other statistical methods to model uncertainty in order to achieve the desired outcomes or business goals. Moreover, utility theory is also used in decision analysis techniques to identify the optimal strategy for making the best possible decision from several alternatives and in the presence of uncertainty.

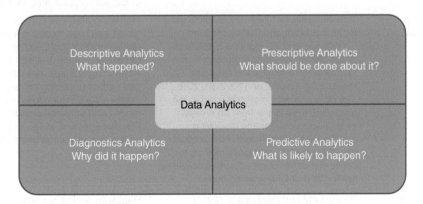

Figure 10.2 Types of Data Analytics (Banerjee et al., 2013)

Data Analytics Examples

Data analytics techniques have been applied in various areas of business operations. Table 10.2 lists some examples of data analytics applied in the financial, human resources, marketing, healthcare, supply chain, government and non-profit organizations, sports, and web analytics domains.

Table 10.2   Data Analytics Examples

Type of Data Analytics	Explanation	Example
Financial Analytics	Andriosopoulos et al. (2019) state that optimization models using linear, non-linear, dynamic, stochastic, fuzzy or multi-objective methods are applied to identify the maximum utilization of asset allocation, to create optimal capital financial planning and to develop the risk management plan. Data analytics and machine learning approaches are used to identify significant patterns in immense amounts of financial data which are in various structured and unstructured formats. Decision analysis and decision support systems are used to automate decision-making procedures by relying on domain knowledge and expertise.	One of the data analytics applications in financial services is portfolio management for asset screening, capital allocation, and trading. Other applications are credit risk modelling which includes credit scoring and rating, loss-given default, and loan portfolio management, investment and insurance modelling which consists of volatility modelling, asset pricing, operational and liquidity risk modelling, venture capital investment, and also mergers and acquisitions.
Human Resource Analytics	According to Camm et al. (2014), HR analytics has been used to manage and improve human capital to ensure that the organization has the right combination of skills sets to meet its goals by hiring and retaining the highest quality talent, and achieving diversity.	One of the applications of HR analytics is identifying the factors that influence the productivity of human capital in the organization and determining potential new employment opportunities, which can be very useful for predicting employee turnover and retention.
Marketing Analytics	Data analytics has been extensively used in the marketing area since the Ford Foundation and the Harvard Institute of Basic Mathematics for Applications in Business were founded in 1950 and 1960 respectively (Wedel and Kannan, 2016). The data analytics methods used in the marketing area range from an analysis of variance, econometric modelling, and Bayesian modelling to new product diffusion models, stochastic models for consumer behaviour and multidimensional scaling and unfolding techniques.	Marketing analytics applications have been used to obtain a better understanding of consumer behaviour, identify the best use of advertising budgets, develop the most effective pricing strategies, improve the demand forecasting model, and enhance product-line management, to increase customer satisfaction and loyalty.
Healthcare Analytics	Raghupathi and Raghupathi (2014) recognize that data analytics techniques have been used in healthcare in areas such as clinical operations, to determine more clinically relevant and cost-effective	Heathcare analytics applications can also be used to analyse a large amount of data in order to develop evidence-based medicine. Additionally, data analytics is

Type of Data Analytics	Explanation	Example
	ways for diagnosing and treating patients; research and development, to investigate improved clinical trial designs, and examine their adverse effects; and public health, to analyse disease patterns, track disease outbreaks, develop vaccines, and establish public health policies.	useful for: conducting genomic analytics for gene sequencing more efficiently and effectively; pre-adjudication fraud analysis for assessing a large number of claim requests to minimize fraudulent claims; and device/remote monitoring for collecting and analysing real-time data generated by in-hospital and in-home devices to monitor patients' safety and predict adverse events. Advanced analytics have been applied to patient profiling so that individual patients can benefit from proactive care for healthier living or preventive care by reducing the risk of developing a specific disease.
Supply Chain Analytics	Wang et al. (2016) state that data analytics has been applied in supply chain management at various decision-making levels.	At the logistics and supply chain strategy level, it has been used for: strategic sourcing for collaborative supplier relationship management to reduce operational costs, optimize financial performance and improve the suppliers' performance; supply chain network design to identify the optimized number, location, and size of manufacturing plants, distribution centres, and warehouses; optimizing logistics and transportation routes; product design and development to ensure high quality and reliability and to obtain a competitive advantage.

At the logistics and supply chain operations level, data analytics techniques are used for demand planning, procurement planning, production planning, inventory planning, and logistics planning. |
| **Analytics for Government and Non-profit Organizations** | Alongside progressive open data initiatives, data analytics have been used in government and non-profit organizations to reduce inefficiencies and increase the effectiveness and accountability of their operations and programmes, especially in the provision of utilities and transportation services. | Data analytics have been used to determine the educational needs of children and to provide quality education in recognition of the fact that children are a nation's valuable assets. Some of the government operations where data analytics are extensively |

(Continued)

Table 10.2   (Continued)

Type of Data Analytics	Explanation	Example
		applied are taxation, employment planning, urban and rural development planning, etc. Non-profit organizations are also using data analytics to allocate their relief resources or distribute them effectively and efficiently to those who are in need.
Sports Analytics	Morgulev et al. (2018) define sports analytics as the 'investigation and modelling of sports performance, implementing scientific techniques'.	At the field level, data analytics have been used since the 1960s in the USA for American football and basketball to improve the players' performance. With the availability of big data, data analytics have been improved to evaluate and forecast more accurately players' prospects at the professional level and also their rebound ability. Not only the performance of the individual player but also the overall performance of the team can be analysed, predicted, and prescribed by means of data analytics. Additionally, data analytics can be used to conduct a cost-benefit analysis of hosting mega-sport events for short-term and long-term benefits by applying the decision-oriented analysis of management and policymakers.
Web Analytics	This is based on the analysis of online activities on websites, social media sites such as Facebook, Twitter, and Instagram and professional networking sites like LinkedIn.	Web analytics was developed to examine user behaviour in online shopping for the purpose of promoting and selling products and services. It has expanded to include online experiments that examine the best possible way to configure websites to provide the best services, position ads and promote products and services based on the user's activities on social media. The number of visitors, page views, referring sites, bounce rates and exit pages, keywords and phrases are the parameters used in web analytics to gain insights into the behaviours of online users.

Definition: Data Analytics

Data analytics has been defined by Camm et al. (2014, p. 4) as 'the scientific process of transforming data into insight for making better decisions. Business analytics is used for data-driven or fact-based decision making, which is often seen as more objective than other alternatives for decision making'.

Definition: Descriptive Analytics

Descriptive analytics consists of the techniques that we use to describe what happened in the past, such as data queries, reports, descriptive statistics (mean, measures of variation), and data visualization for the data dashboard.

Definition: Diagnostic Analytics

Diagnostic analytics enables us to examine the cause(s) of a particular occurrence. Exploratory analysis of the existing data or (sometimes) additional external data are used to discover the root causes of an event.

Definition Box: Predictive Analytics

Predictive Analytics techniques use past data to predict what could happen in the future by considering the impact of one or more variable on another. Depending on the nature of the business and product(s), the growth trajectory and seasonality of past trends are taken into account.

Definition Box: Prescriptive Analytics

Prescriptive analytics techniques are used to discover the best course of action to take to achieve a business's desired outcome(s).

Stop and Reflect: Data Analytics

Businesses have been using data analytics to acquire a better understanding of consumers' behaviour and to predict their sales and business growth. Descriptive, diagnostics, predictive, and prescriptive analytics are four categories of big data analytic techniques. Which of these data analytics techniques is used to generate the products list which should be included in a businesses' special sales catalogues to increase their sales?

Stop and Reflect: Data Analytics

Big data analytics have been applied in the domains of finance, human resources, marketing, healthcare, supply chain management, sports, etc. by governments, non-profit organizations and businesses. Identify three data analytics applications which have impacted your daily life activities.

10.5 Visualization

What is Visualization and Why Is it Used?

Manovich (2011, p. 37) defines visualization as 'a mapping between discrete data and a visual representation'. Information visualization can be static, dynamic or interactive to enable us to understand the findings from the data analysis so that we will be able to solve specific problems. Another interesting definition offered by the Berkeley School of Information (2010) states that 'the goal of information visualization is the unveiling of the underlying structure of large or abstract datasets using visual representations that utilize the powerful processing capabilities of the human visual perceptual system'. There have been several definitions of visualization or information visualization since the 1980s, with Chen et al. (2014) asserting that the purposes of information visualization are to acquire insights, amplify the cognitive performance of abstract data, discover the unseen, answer the questions for decision-making, and solve problems by digesting a large amount of data with computer-supported, interactive visual representations. These visual representations include geometric, projection techniques, pixel-based techniques, icon-based, tree, and graph-based techniques (Chen and Floridi, 2013).

These visual representations are further comprised of geometric channels (e.g. size, orientation, shape, and curvature), optical channels (intensity, colour, opacity, texture, line styles, sharing, depth, and explicit motion), topological and relational channels (connection, node, intersection, depth order, closure, distance, density), and semantic channels (number, text, symbol, sign, and icon), and all of these features need to be considered when selecting the most suitable visual representation formats that will convey the message to the recipient more effectively (Figure 10.3).

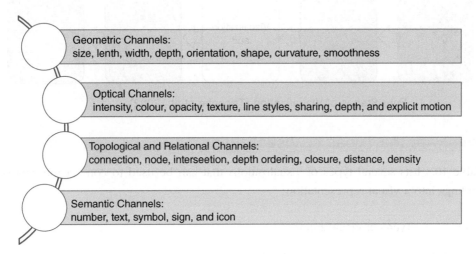

Figure 10.3   Features of the Four Channels of Visualization (Chen & Floridi, 2013)

One of the main reasons for using visualization is to save time in conveying the information and findings from massive data sources in a condensed form that and gives insightful illustrations. The other reasons for using visualization are to make an observation, facilitate external memorization, stimulate hypotheses, evaluate hypotheses, and disseminate knowledge and insights. These visual representations enable us to retain the information in both an accurate and timely manner for memory recall. Additionally, they assist us to focus our attention so that concepts and key messages are conveyed quickly in visual formats, facilitating analytical tasks that will provide insights (Chen et al., 2014).

What Are the Four Stages of Visualization?

Tricoche et al. (2002) describe the four stages of the visualization pipeline whereby data is transformed into images or visual representations (Figure 10.4). The first stage of the visualization process is the data generation stage, where data (numerical, textual, image, signal or geocoded) are generated and collected as measurements during business operations, transactions, experiments, or observations. The second stage is the data enrichment and improvement stage, where the collected data are re-formed to condense the amount or improve the richness of the information content by using domain transformations, interpolation, sampling, and noise filtering processes. Then the visualization and mapping step is applied to transform the application data including vector or tensor data into visual representations. The third stage involves the rendering process where computational and graphical operations are applied to create the visual representations. The final stage is the display stage, where these visual representations are illustrated on screen or printed on paper.

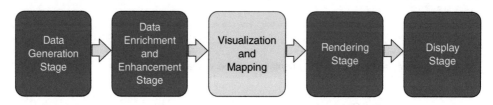

Figure 10.4　Four Stages of Visualization (Tricoche et al., 2002)

What Are the Types of Visualization?

Table 10.3 lists several types of visualizations that can be used to convert the data or findings into a visual representation.

Table 10.3　Types of Visualization

Type of Visualization	Explanation
1D/Linear data visualization	Presents a list of data items which are organized according to a single characteristic or feature
2D/Planar (including geospatial) data visualization	Used for geospatial mapping of location-based data to gain insights into geographical variation or dispersion
3D/Volumetric data visualization	Mainly used to render volume-based 3D molecular scientific visualization
Temporal visualization	Comprise a graphical representation of time series analysis on temporal data to discover the trends or patterns over time, including a Gantt chart on progress analysis
Multidimensional visualization	Useful for creating the visual representation of more than one variable, feature, or characteristic of a subject matter in the same graphical illustration to examine the situation or condition from various perspectives
Tree/Hierarchical visualization	Uses tree diagrams, tree maps, or hierarchical diagrams to demonstrate the hierarchical data existing in the principle of containment, along with the hierarchical relations among data points
Network visualization	The process of visually representing the networks of connected data points (entities), their centrality, connectivity, and relationships between data elements by applying the principle of connection

It is important to consider four design principles when choosing the most appropriate and relevant type of visualization to convey the required information to the recipients (Figure 10.5). These four design principles are:

1   Modularity: The structure should minimize overcrowding and allow different combinations of visual representations appropriate to different and different formats.
2   Context independence: Content should be kept context-free and abstract to enable reusability.
3   Clear graphics: Explanatory text is used together with graphics to facilitate recall and lookup.
4   Style neutrality: A consistent style should be adopted – one that is suitable for the targeted audience and is free of the implications produced by strong graphic styles or overly minimalist designs (Wang et al., 2020).

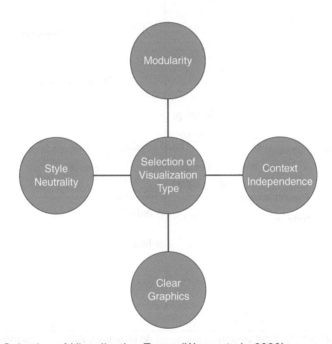

Figure 10.5   Selection of Visualization Types (Wang et al., 2020)

What Visualization Tools Are Available?

There are several visualization tools in the market that enable businesses and organizations to gather big data, acquire a better understanding of their operations, and make more effective and efficient strategic decisions to achieve their goals. Stobierski (2021) identifies the following top four visualization tools that are widely used by businesses:

1   Power BI and Microsoft Excel: Based on the user-friendliness and functionalities of 20 visualization types in Excel, Power BI was developed and introduced to provide more big data visualization capabilities to connect and integrate the various data sources.

More importantly, its powerful integrations with its various services in Azure and Power platforms, data science applications such as R, Python, ArcGIS and other applications such as Salesforce, and Google Analytics enable the user to conduct any data analytics and visualizations in any graphical and geospatial formats on one platform. Therefore, it was named the Magic Quadrant leader in analytics and business intelligence platforms in the Gartner 2022 report (Kronz et al., 2022) (Figure 10.6).

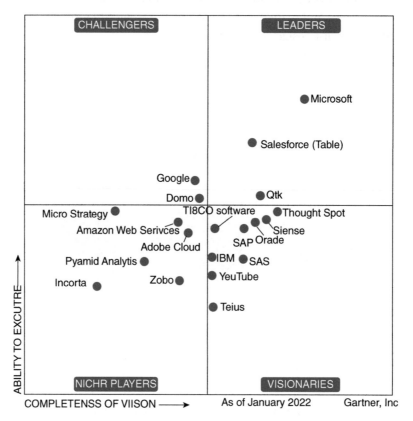

Figure 10.6 The Magic Quadrant for Analytics and Business Intelligence Platforms (Kronz et al., 2022)

2   Google Charts: This is a widely used, open-source data visualization tool which allows one to analyse and visualize the findings on an interactive dashboard by streamlining the static, dynamic, and real-time data from various data sources. It also enables the integration of the data from Salesforce, SQL databases, and Google sheets by using HTML5/SVG technology.

3   Tableau: This is another popular visualization tool and was named one of the market leaders in the Magic Quadrant in the Gartner report. This platform enables users to curate the importing, integrating, and analysing of any kind of data, and provides user-friendly features to deploy and utilise data very efficiently to create any required visual representation.

4   Zoho Analytics: This platform has been identified as a niche player in Gartner's Magic Quadrant report of 2022 (Kronz et al., 2022) as it focuses mainly on business sales and marketing by applying conversational analytics, what-if analysis, predictive analytics, and data alerts on the business sales and marketing data. Its pre-built analytics on business projects facilitates managing, monitoring, and controlling the project's progress in order to compete successfully.

Definition: Visualization

According to the Berkeley School of Information (2010), 'the goal of information visualization is the unveiling of the underlying structure of large or abstract datasets using visual representations that utilize the powerful processing capabilities of the human visual perceptual system'.

Definition: The Four Stages of Visualization

The four stages of visualization are: data generation; data enrichment and enhancement; rendering; and display (Tricoche et al., 2002).

Definition: Modularity

Modularity is a design principle of visualization and refers to a structure that minimizes overcrowding and enables different combinations of visual representations according to different situations and different formats (Wang et al., 2020).

Definition: Context Independence

Context independence is a design principle of visualization that maintains context-free and abstract content, enabling reusability (Wang et al., 2020).

Definition: Clear Graphics

Clear graphics is a design principle of visualization where explanatory text is used in combination with graphics to facilitate recall and lookup (Wang et al., 2020).

> ## Definition: Style Neutrality
>
> Style neutrality is a design principle of visualization where a consistent style is adopted that is suitable for the targeted audience, and which lacks the implications produced by strong graphic styles or overly minimalist designs (Wang et al., 2020).

> ## Stop and Reflect: Visualization
>
> Visualization is used to convey information and findings from massive data sources via condensed and insightful illustrations. What factors would you consider when choosing the type of visualization that you will use?

> ## Stop and Reflect: Visualization Tools
>
> There are several visualization tools that we can use. What factors would you consider when choosing the visualization tool(s) that you will use?

10.6 Business Intelligence and Applications

Nowadays, business organizations are facing intense competition, and intelligence capability is essential when dealing with critical business challenges. In the current highly competitive and knowledge-based economy, business intelligence systems have been used to generate the knowledge and foreknowledge of the internal and external environments of businesses to enable them to survive in the hypercompetitive environments of most industries.

Negash and Gray (2008, p. 175) define business intelligence as: 'a data-driven DSS [decision support system] that combines data gathering, data storage, and knowledge management with analysis to provide input to the decision process'. Similarly, business intelligence has also been defined as 'systems [that] combine data gathering, data storage and knowledge management with analytical tools to present complex internal and competitive information to planners and decision-makers' (Negash and Gray, 2008, p. 178). It is the most valuable asset of an organization as the raw transactional data are transformed into actionable and competitive information for strategic decision-making to improve the business's performance (Ong et al., 2011).

The steps comprising the business intelligence process are not new. Before computing technologies were utilized extensively for business intelligence, businesses were using five basic steps making up the internal intelligence process in order to understand the external environments and equip themselves to make strategic decisions in the hyper-competitive environment of most industries. According to Sawka (1996), the five basic steps are: (1) determining the intelligence needs; (2) gathering relevant information; (3) collecting human intelligence; (4) analysing the intelligence; and (5) disseminating the strategy. Nowadays in computing-based environments, business intelligence accumulates a large amount of data, stored in a data warehouse to generate insightful information for strategic decision-making by applying complex data modelling and analysis, but still following these five basic steps. Various data analysis methods, ranging from aggregated reporting, multidimensional analysis (slicing and dicing), drill down, and ad hoc queries, to predictive and prescriptive analytics, are applied in business intelligence. By means of these analysis methods, business intelligence measures business performance, monitors business activities, forecasts future performance, and prescribes the actions required in order to achieve the company's strategic goals.

The Five-layered Business Intelligence Architecture

It is very important to design and implement a business intelligence architecture which ensures that systems are being utilized effectively and efficiently. The components that must be included in the business intelligence framework are: data, people, processes, technology, and management. Ong et al. (2011) propose a business intelligence architecture comprising the following five layers (see also Figure 10.7):

1   Data source: This needs to include both internal and external data sources in order
    to acquire all the required unstructured, semi-structured, and structured data.
    Internal data are collected by operational and transactional systems such as sales
    and marketing, customer relationship management, supplier relationship
    management, enterprise resource planning, etc., which are process oriented.
    External data are collected from suppliers, government agencies, market research
    companies, etc., and are analysed to gain an understanding of the external
    environment factors that may impact on businesses. It is crucial to understand
    business issues and requirements so that internal and external data sources can be
    tapped for information when necessary.
2   ETL (Extract -Transform-Load) : This involves extraction, transformation, and
    loading processes. First, the required data are extracted from both internal and
    data external sources before being sent to the data staging area. Then the
    extracted data is cleaned and transformed into standardized formats where
    aggregation may be necessary based on the business rules. It is important to
    clearly define the business logic underlying data mapping and the data definitions
    to ensure consistency across the systems. When an error is identified in the
    transformation, the item may need to go back to the data extraction stage to be
    cleaned and then transformed. The transformed data is then loaded into the target

repository. This ETL process may require several iterations until a satisfactory level of data quality is reached prior to loading.

3   Data warehouse: This consists of an operational database, data warehouse, and data marts. All required data are extracted from operational databases and integrated with the ETL layer before being loaded into the data warehouse(s). Real-time or near-real-time data are stored in the operational databases and used for business operations or short-term tactical decision-making. Inmon (2005, p. 29) defines the data warehouse as a 'subject-oriented, integrated, time-variant and non-volatile collection of data in support of management's decision-making process'. Data from various data sources are extracted and grouped based on the common subject areas of the business operations or processes. After these subjected-oriented datasets are transformed into consistent formats and data structures, they are integrated into the data warehouse. As historical data are integrated and stored in the data warehouse, the time-variant attribute is the main dimension used to keep track of changes in the datasets and to analyse the trends and patterns in these datasets. One of the main characteristics of the data warehouse is its non-volatility. This means that data stored in the data warehouse are read-only and cannot be updated or deleted, even though new data are added periodically. To be able to support the specific analytical needs and requirements of each business area, the data marts are used as a subset of the data warehouse.

4   End user: This is the individual who really makes use of a certain product. Various users need different levels of information granularity and degrees of comprehensiveness, and it is important to provide customized information based on what end users require for their decision-making. Any query, reporting, or analytical processing tools should enable end users to:

o   roll up or drill up to increase the aggregation level;
o   drill-down to reduce the aggregation level for more detailed information;
o   slice and dice to analyse the information from a specific perspective or dimension; and
o   pivot to rotate the dimensions of data so that information can be viewed from different perspectives.

5   Metadata: These are the data about data and comprise the objectives of data analysis or usage, the origin or the structures of the data collection and storage process, the data custodian details, the data definitions, and how the data are disseminated and with whom they are shared. It is also important to maintain the metadata of the ETL process as log files reporting its usages. In addition, online analytical processing (OLAP) metadata maintains the descriptions (dimensions and hierarchies) of data cubes in analytical processes and any types of drill paths taken. Data mining metadata record detailed descriptions of algorithms and queries, while reporting metadata consist of XML-based reporting templates and the details of these reports.

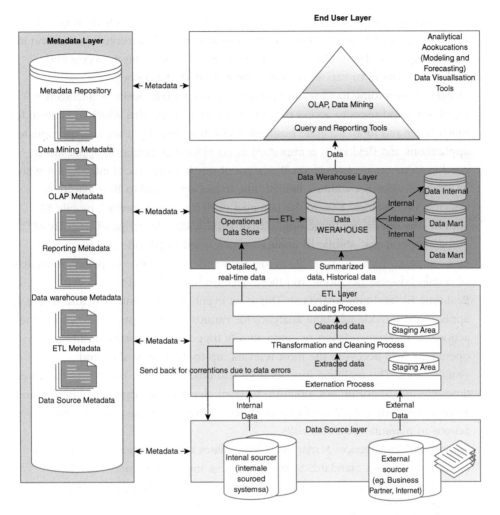

Figure 10.7   Five-layered Business Intelligence Architecture (Ong et al., 2011)

Business Intelligence Types

The types of business intelligence can be classified as:

- Ad hoc analysis: This responds to ad hoc queries by processing a large amount of data acquired from data sources in a low-latency manner. It is the basic function of all current business intelligence applications, and all insights derived from this analysis are visualized on dashboards to assist business decision-making.
- Online analytical processing (OLAP): The OLAP Council (1997) states that OLAP is 'characterised by dynamic multidimensional analysis of consolidated enterprise data supporting end-user analytical and navigational activities including calculations and modelling applied across dimensions, through hierarchies and/or across members,

trend analysis over sequential periods, slicing subsets for on-screen viewing, drill down to deeper levels of consolidation, rotation to new dimensional comparison in the viewing area'. The OLAP tools provide users with the ability to access and analyse the data from various multidimensional OLAP data cubes.

- Mobile BI: According to Stipić and Bronzin (2011), mobile business intelligence enables the end users to access data or information or insights which are critical for much faster and more accurate business decision-making by using the appropriate applications and devices. It is important to consider that mobile BI applications need to focus on a relatively small amount of much more crucial information with its practical value set within a limited time frame, compared to BI applications available on desktops. Due to the potential of being always 'online', mobile BI applications offer more usage opportunities and widen the scope of usability of mobile applications. Mobile BI applications are used to provide end users with targeted data which are available at the 'right' time to identify any potential impacts of certain business decisions, and these data are relatively real-time.

- Real-time BI (real-time analytics): This is an event-driven IT infrastructure where BI applications provide real-time analytics for various business processes, inform the actionable recommendation or automatically trigger the necessary business operations with access to the most relevant, up-to-the-minute data and visualizations. The real-time insights from real-time BI enable businesses to capture time-sensitive opportunities, optimize ways of changing management strategy, and assist in the early detection of critical issues so that businesses can take proactive actions to minimize potential risks.

- Operational intelligence: Marjanovic (2007) states that 'operational BI builds on existing technology standards to make business intelligence more flexible, transparent and cost-effective by tightly integrating BI with organisation's constantly evolving business processes'. To utilize the operational BI effectively and efficiently, it is essential that the right information be delivered to the right people in the right format at the right time (Sandu, 2008).

- Software-as-a-service BI (SaaS BI): Liyang et al. (2011) proposed a five-layered framework for Business Intelligence as a Service. This framework consists of the infrastructure layer, the data service layer, the business service layer (integration service, analysis service, knowledge discovery service, reporting service), the user interface service layer, and the operational service layer. It enables business users to obtain business insights by means of powerful tools and services without the need for costly in-house installation of the infrastructure and implementation of the applications. Small and medium-sized businesses can benefit from SaaS BI as it offers a reliable service at a lower cost, can integrate multiple data sources, and provides comprehensive data analytics solutions enabling users to scale up according to their business needs.

- Open source BI: Golfarelli (2009) mentions that open source BI platforms can provide a wide range of BI capabilities due to the significant expansion of features in open source solutions which have a high level of reliability and progression. It enables business users to utilize BI capabilities to obtain business insights without incurring high overheads for the development and management of BI applications. JasperSoft, Pentaho and SapgoBI are the most widely used open-source BI platforms. Golfarelli (2009) suggests being aware of the risks related to unexpected termination or adaptation of more restrictive licensing of OS BI, although OS BI platforms bring added value given their reliability and various functionalities.
- Location-Based Business Intelligence: Traditionally, this has been part of business decision-making such as choosing the store or factory location based on the traffic patterns and planning the logistics and transportation routes to minimize the operational costs. Nowadays, more location-based data have been collected and location-based business intelligence techniques such as geospatial analysis have been applied to generate location-based knowledge about the impacts of location on business performance.

Business Intelligence Techniques

Business intelligence applications have evolved over several decades from decision-support systems to those that add value to business decision-making processes. A large number of business intelligence applications have been implemented to increase efficiency within the organization, minimize the operational and overhead costs, and to understand and accurately forecast the trends in the market by using various analytical methods. Several business intelligence techniques have been applied to forecast the economic environment as well as the business operations. Some of these techniques are:

- Forecasting: This involves predicting the likely course of future conditions or events based on historical data. This technique includes univariate, multivariate and qualitative analysis. These techniques can be classified as forecasting with linear and non-linear regression models, forecasting with confidence intervals and forecasting with time series, and used to examine the patterns in how history repeats itself or how external factors determine future events (Kahraman et al., 2010).
- Artificial neural network analysis: Tayarani et al. (2013) define artificial neural network (ANN) analysis as a data analysis method that imitates the workings of the human brain in terms of the way that arrays of neurons function in biological learning and memory. This gives computing models the ability to learn or adapt, to categorize, or to generalize the findings with iterative

processing. This technique has been widely used for optimization, calibration and pattern recognition.

- Vector auto-regression: This has been widely used for forecasting purposes since the 1970s. It has been extended to include genetic-programming-based vector error correction models, co-integration and dynamic factor models. These methods are used to identify 'common trends' in a nonstationary dataset. For example, the genetic programming-based vector error correction model is used to forecast the US imports from China (Wang and Wang, 2010). Their forecasting model is based on the economic theory that imports increase when domestic consumption exceeds domestic production. Personal consumption expenditures and industrial production index data are used as indicators of total consumption and production. In addition, the trade-weighted exchange index is used to adjust the influences of relative costs on the trade.

- Logistic Analysis: This is used to predict the binomial response variable by considering more than one explanatory variable. It involves steps similar to those used in the multiple regression model. The impact of each explanatory variable is taken into account to predict the odd ratio of the response (observed) variable (Sperandei, 2014). This analysis has been used to generate insights into business cycles, economic bubbles, laws of diminishing returns, fluctuation in activities and their long-term trends.

- Clustering analysis: Sinharay (2010, p. 5) defines cluster analysis as 'a technique to group similar observations into several clusters based on the observed values of several variables for each individual'. In his study, cluster analysis was applied to examine the different levels of performance, their similarities, and differences in the patterns of change from reading and arithmetic test scores from the fourth to the sixth grades of 25 schools. Cluster analysis has been applied in business strategic management to determine key relationships between strategy, environment, leadership, and performance (Ketchen and Shook, 1996). In addition, this analysis method is used to identify consumer behaviour and data-driven market segmentation (Dolnicar, 2002).

- Fuzzy time series: Song and Chissom (1993, 1994), proposed the fuzzy time series approach for prediction based on the historical data with linguistic value, and introduced the first-order time-invariant and time-variant models. Later, Hwang and Chen (2000) developed the cross-over method (two-attribute time-variant model) to predict the circulations and eddies in the South China Sea. Since then, several fuzzy time series methods have been proposed and improved. For instance, Liu (2009) developed the integrated fuzzy time series forecasting system to overcome the challenge of single-point forecasted value from the rigid time series method, and to deal with stationary, trend, and seasonal time series datasets.

Definition: Business Intelligence

Business intelligence has also been defined as 'systems [that] combine data gathering, data storage and knowledge management with analytical tools to present complex internal and competitive information to planners and decision-makers' (Negash and Gray, 2008, p. 178).

Definition: The Five Layers of Business Intelligence Architecture

The five layers of business intelligence architecture are: data source, ETL, data warehouse, end user, and metadata (Ong et al., 2011).

Definition: Online Analytical Processing

Online analytical processing (OLAP) is 'characterised by dynamic multidimensional analysis of consolidated enterprise data supporting end-user analytical and navigational activities including calculations and modelling applied across dimensions, through hierarchies and/or across members, trend analysis over sequential periods, slicing subsets for on-screen viewing, drill down to deeper levels of consolidation, rotation to new dimensional comparison in the viewing area' (OLAP Council, 1997).

Definition: Artificial Neural Network Analysis

Artificial neural network analysis (ANN) is a data analysis method that imitates the workings of the human brain in terms of the way that arrays of neurons function in biological learning and memory. This gives computing models the ability to learn or adapt, to categorize, or to generalize the findings with iterative processing.

Definition: Cluster Analysis

Cluster analysis is 'a technique to group similar observations into several clusters based on the observed values of several variables for each individual' (Sinharay, 2010, p. 5).

Definition: Fuzzy Time Series

Fuzzy time series is a better time series approach for predictions derived from the historical data with linguistic value, and introduced the first-order time-invariant and time-variant models (Song and Chissom, 1993, 1994).

Stop and Reflect: Business Intelligence

Nowadays, business organizations are facing intense competition and intelligence capability is essential for dealing with critical business challenges. In the current highly competitive and knowledge-based economy, business intelligence systems have been used to generate knowledge and foreknowledge of businesses' internal and external environments to ensure their viability in the hypercompetitive environment of most industries.

How will you use the five layers of business intelligence architecture to assess your organization's readiness to implement business intelligence?

Stop and Reflect: Business Intelligence Techniques

There are several business intelligence techniques that can be applied so that informed decisions can be made by management. Which business intelligence technique is the best? What factors would you consider when choosing the most suitable technique for your business intelligence applications?

10.7 Chapter Summary

This chapter begins with a definition of data analytics, which is the scientific process used to transform the massive amount of internal and external data into insights which assist business management personnel to make better strategic decisions. The data analytics process consists of five stages: data acquisition/recording; extraction/cleaning/annotation; integration/aggregation/representation; analysis/modelling; and interpretation. There are four types of data analytics: descriptive analytics (identifying what happened); diagnostic analytics (investigating why it happened); predictive analytics (forecasting what is likely to happen); and prescriptive analytics (exploring what should be done to achieve the desirable outcomes). Data analytics is being widely applied in various domains such as finance, human resources, marketing, healthcare, supply chain management, sports and online user behaviour management, and also in government and non-profit organizations.

The findings from data analytics are translated into visual representation to utilize the powerful processing capabilities of human visual perception. The purposes of information visualization are to gain insights, amplify the cognitive performance of abstract data, discover the unseen, answer questions for decision-making and solve problems by digesting a large amount of data with computer-supported, interactive visual representations. Visualization has four visual channels: geometric, optical, topological and relational, and semantic channels. Data and findings from data analytics can be transformed into insightful visual representations by applying the four steps of the visualization pipeline: data generation, data enrichment and enhancement, rendering, and display. There are several types of visualizations programs, the most popular ones being 1D/linear, 2D/Planar (including geospatial), 3D/Volumetric, temporal, multidimensional, tree/hierarchical and network visualizations. It is important to consider the four design principles, namely, modularity, context independence, style neutrality, and clear graphics, while selecting the visualization types that will be effective in making an observation, facilitating external memorization, stimulating hypotheses, evaluating hypotheses, retaining the information, directing audience attention to a specific concept, and disseminating knowledge and insights.

After the discussion on data analytics and visualization techniques, the business intelligence concept was introduced. This is a 'data-driven DSS [decision support system] that combines data gathering, data storage, and knowledge management with analysis to provide input to the decision process' (Negash and Gray, 2008, p. 175). The five-layered business intelligence architecture is described, comprising the metadata layer, the end user layer, the data warehouse layer, the ETL layer and the data source layer. Various types of business intelligence are explained; these are: ad hoc analysis, online analytical processing, mobile BI, real-time BI, operation intelligence, software-as-a-service BI (SaaS BI), open-source BI, and location-based business intelligence. Several business intelligence techniques – forecasting, artificial neural network analysis, vector auto-regression, logistics analysis, clustering analysis and fuzzy time series – are also explained.

Discussion Questions

1 What are the four ways to use data analytics? How are they different from each other?
2 What are the stages in the data visualization process?
3 What are the components of business intelligence? How do they interact with other each other?
4 What are the main business intelligence techniques and how will you select the suitable technique(s) for your data analytics projects?

Case Study: Predictive Analytics for Big Data in Public Transport Planning

By the authors, drawing on Balbin et al. (2020).

Open data has become a trend in recent years, and more and more collections of big datasets have been made publicly available in science, government, and non-profit organizations with the aim of adding value such as transparency and accountability and also to gain insights and ensure data accessibility. Several countries, including members of the Organisation for Economic Co-operation and Development (OECD), have participated in open government initiatives and made their public sector data available and assessable by enabling data reusability.

In Canada, several cities and provinces have collaborated on the open data platform initiated by the Canada Open Government Working Group (COGWA). One of the significant open datasets relates to *transit open data*, which consists of service provision data such as bus stop numbers, route numbers, and timetables, and service performance data such as the scheduled and actual arrival and departure times. In terms of veracity, there are challenges as a result of transmission problems, data issues, GPS, and other geospatial location data errors. Other non-technical challenges to on-time performances are construction, emergencies, accidents, special events, traffic congestion, and weather events.

All the buses operated by the Winnipeg Transit (a public transit agency in the City of Winnipeg) are equipped with an on-board computer and global positioning systems (GPS), and log the arrival and departure times of public transport vehicles at each bus stop. Therefore, their big data sets contain not only the scheduled arrival and departure times, but also the actual arrival and departure times. Researchers at the University of Manitoba, Winnipeg, Canada, and the University of Calabria, Rende, Italy applied predictive analytics to this open big data set to examine frequently occurring patterns of bus on-time performance and to predict the bus performance in future based on their past history. Scheduled and actual arrival and departure times at each bus stop are taken into account in their predictive analytics by applying frequent pattern mining and decision-tree-based classification. They identified the routes and stops with frequently late, frequently on-time, and frequently early departures. Cross-checking the data with weather information, they found that weather conditions have a significant impact on late departures.

Questions

1   What other datasets would you consider integrating with this big data set to improve the accuracy of prediction?
2   What are the other data analytics methods that you would consider in order to acquire more insights into the on-time performance of public transport services.

10.8 References

Agrawal, D., Bernstein, P., Bertino, E., Davidson, S., Dayal, U., Franklin, M., ... & Widom, J. (2011). Challenges and opportunities with big data 2011-1. Cyber Center Technical Reports. Paper 1. http://docs.lib.purdue.edu/cctech/1

Andriosopoulos, D., Doumpos, M., Pardalos, P. M., & Zopounidis, C. (2019). Computational approaches and data analytics in financial services: A literature review. *Journal of the Operational Research Society, 70*, 1581–1599.

Balbin, P. P. F., Barker, J. C., Leung, C. K., Tran, M., Wall, R. P. & Cuzzocrea, A. (2020). Predictive analytics on open big data for supporting smart transportation services. *Procedia Computer Science, 176*, 3009–3018.

Banerjee, A., Bandyopadhyay, T., & Acharya, P. (2013). Data analytics: Hyped up aspirations or true potential? *Vikalpa, 38*, 1–12.

Berkeley School of Information. (2010). *Information Visualization Showcase* https://www.ischool.berkeley.edu/events/2010/information-visualization-showcase

Camm, J., Cochran, J., Fry, M., Ohlmann, J., Anderson, D., Sweeney, D., & Williams, T. (2014). *Essentials of Business Analytics*. Cengage Learning.

Chen, M. & Floridi, L. (2013). An analysis of information visualisation. *Synthese, 190*, 3421–3438.

Chen, M., Floridi, L., & Borgo, R. (2014). What is visualization really for? In L. Floridi & P. Illari (eds) *The Philosophy of Information Quality*. Springer.

Dolnicar, S. (2002). *A Review of Unquestioned Standards in Using Cluster Analysis for Data-Driven Market Segmentation 2002*. https://ro.uow.edu.au/commpapers/273

Golfarelli, M. (2009). Open Source BI platforms: A Functional and Architectural Comparison. International Conference on Data Warehousing and Knowledge Discovery. Springer, 287–297.

Hwang, C. & Chen, S. A. (2000). Circulations and eddies over the South China Sea derived from TOPEX/Poseidon altimetry. *Journal of Geophysical Research: Oceans, 105*, 23943–23965.

Inmon, W. H. (2005). *Building the Data Warehouse*. John Wiley & Sons.

Kahraman, C., Kaya, İ., Ulukan, H. Z. & Uçal, İ. (2010). Economic forecasting techniques and their applications. In J. Wang & S. Wang (eds), *Business Intelligence in Economic Forecasting: Technologies and Techniques*. IGI Global.

Ketchen, D. J. & Shook, C. L. (1996). The application of cluster analysis in strategic management research: An analysis and critique. *Strategic Management Journal, 17*, 441–458.

Kronz, A., Schlegel, K., Sun, J., Pidsley, D., & Ganeshan, A. (2022). Gartner Magic Quadrant for analytics and business intelligence platforms. Gartner Magic Quadrant for analytics and business intelligence platforms. https://www.gartner.com/en/documents/4012759

Howson, C., Sallam, R. L., Richardson, J. L., Tapadinhas, J., Idoine, C. J., & Woodward, A. (2018). Magic quadrant for analytics and business intelligence platforms. https://www.semanticscholar.org/paper/Magic-Quadrant-for-Business-Intelligence-and-Sallam-Howson/7c54d33d02485af6a81d1e598cc0ac9b45d07ad3

Liu, H.-T. (2009). An integrated fuzzy time series forecasting system. *Expert Systems with Applications, 36,* 10045–10053.

Liyang, T., Zhiwei, N., Zhangjun, W., & Li, W. (2011). *A Conceptual Framework for Business Intelligence as a Service (SaaS BI).* Fourth International Conference on Intelligent Computation Technology and Automation, 2011. IEEE, 1025–1028.

Manovich, L. (2011). What is visualisation? *Visual Studies, 26,* 36–49.

Marjanovic, O. (2007). *The Next Stage of Operational Business Intelligence: Creating New Challenges for Business Process Management.* 40th Annual Hawaii International Conference on System Sciences (HICSS'07), 2007. IEEE, 215c–215c.

Morgulev, E., Azar, O. H., & Lidor, R. (2018). Sports analytics and the big-data era. *International Journal of Data Science and Analytics, 5,* 213–222.

Negash, S. & Gray, P. (2008). Business Intelligence. In F. Burstein & C. W. Holsapple (eds), *Handbook on Decision Support Systems 2.* Springer.

OLAP Council (1997). *OLAP Council White Paper.* http://www.olapcouncil.org/research/whtpaply.htm

Ong, I. L., Siew, P. H. & Wong, S. F. (2011). A five-layered business intelligence architecture. *Communications of the IBIMA.*

Raghupathi, W. & Raghupathi, V. (2014). Big data analytics in healthcare: Promise and potential. *Health Information Science and Systems, 2,* 1–10.

Sandu, D. I. (2008). Operational and real-time Business Intelligence. *Revista Informatica Economică, 3,* 33–36.

Sawka, K. A. (1996). Demystifying business intelligence. *Management Review, 85,* 47.

Sinharay, S. (2010) An overview of statistics in education. In: Peterson, P., et al., (eds) *International Encyclopedia of Education,* 3rd Edition, Elsevier Ltd. https://doi.org/10.1016/B978-0-08-044894-7.01719-X

Song, Q. & Chissom, B. S. (1993). Forecasting enrollments with fuzzy time series – Part I. *Fuzzy Sets and Systems, 54,* 1–9.

Song, Q. & Chissom, B. S. (1994). Forecasting enrollments with fuzzy time series – Part II. *Fuzzy Sets and Systems, 62,* 1–8.

Sperandei, S. (2014). Understanding logistic regression analysis. *Biochemia Medica, 24,* 12–18.

Stipić, A. & Bronzin, T. (2011). Mobile BI: the past, the present and the future. *Proceedings of the 34th International Convention MIPRO, 2011.* IEEE, 1560–1564.

Stobierski, T. (2021). Top data visualisation tools for business professionals: https://online.hbs.edu/blog/post/data-visualization-tools

Tayarani, A., Baratian, A., Sistani, M.-B. N., Saberi, M. R. & Tehranizadeh, Z. (2013). Artificial neural networks analysis used to evaluate the molecular interactions between selected drugs and human cyclooxygenase2 receptor. *Iranian Journal of Basic Medical Sciences, 16,* 1196.

Tricoche, X., Scheuermann, G., Hagen, H. & Clauss, S. (2002). *Vector and Tensor Field Topology Simplification, Tracking, and Visualization.* PhD thesis, Schriftenreihe Fachbereich Informatik (3), Universität. Citeseer.

Wang, G., Gunasekaran, A., Ngai, E. W., & Papadopoulos, T. (2016). Big data analytics in logistics and supply chain management: Certain investigations for research and applications. *International Journal of Production Economics*, *176*, 98–110.

Wang, J. & Wang, S. (2010). *Business Intelligence in Economic Forecasting: Technologies and Techniques*. IGI Global.

Wang, Z., Sundin, L., Murray-Rust, D., & Bach, B. (2020). *Cheat Sheets for Data Visualization Techniques*. Proceedings of the 2020 CHI Conference on Human Factors in Computing Systems, 1–13.

Wedel, M. & Kannan, P. (2016). Marketing analytics for data-rich environments. *Journal of Marketing*, *80*, 97–121.

11

EMERGING TECHNOLOGIES IN THE DIGITAL AGE: BIG DATA, IOT, CLOUD COMPUTING, AND BLOCKCHAIN

11.1 Learning Outcomes

By the end of this chapter, you should be able to:

- Define cloud computing
- Describe the cloud computing categories and deployment models
- Explain the benefits of cloud computing
- Describe big data and its characteristics
- Discuss the various applications and challenges of big data
- Define the Internet of Things (IoT)
- Describe the key components of IoT
- Discuss the benefits and applications of IoT
- Describe blockchain and its key features
- Explain how blockchain works
- Discuss the benefits of blockchain for business, and its applications in various industries

11.2 Introduction

The ongoing development of digital technologies offers businesses many opportunities to adopt innovative solutions. Cloud computing, big data, IoT, and blockchain technologies can be collectively used for a number of business activities including data collection, storage, analytics, automation, and security, in addition to improving business performance and competitive advantage. In this chapter, we will learn about big data, cloud computing, IoT and blockchain technologies. The concepts, components, applications, and challenges associated with each of these four technologies will be addressed in the following sections.

11.3 Cloud Computing

What is Cloud Computing?

Cloud computing can mean different things to different people. In simple terms, it means storing and accessing data and programs on the Internet instead of on a user's computer hard drive (Griffith, 2020). For some, it is synonymous with 'IT outsourcing', while for others, it comprises any computing services provided over the Internet or yet again any bought-in computer service, which is located outside an organization's firewall but used in-house (Woodford, 2020). With cloud computing, users connect to the cloud, which 'appears as a single entity as opposed to the traditional way of connecting to multiple servers located on company premises' (AlSudiari and Vasista, 2012, p. 159).

Cloud computing services can easily expand their offerings globally as a result of the 'online nature of their services and the lack of any requirement for local infrastructure build or supply chain set-up costs' (Abed and Chavan, 2019, p. 177). Consequently, cloud computing services are rapidly growing worldwide, with big names such as Microsoft, Google, IBM, and Amazon 'all expanding their cloud computing offerings to provide faster, cheaper, more convenient and powerful solutions to their global consumers' (Abed and Chavan, 2019, p. 177; Groll, 2016).

In a typical cloud computing architecture, the *client's side* consists of the client's computer or computer network as well as the application(s) required to access the cloud computing system (Strickland, n.d.). It is important to note that some cloud computing systems such as web-based email programs leverage existing web browsers while other cloud computing systems require their own specific applications to provide network access to the clients. These applications are known as 'middleware' as they act as the bridge between the client's system and the cloud systems. On the other hand, the *cloud side* is made up of computers, servers, and data storage systems. It also has a central administration server that monitors traffic and clients' demands using protocols that are strictly adhered to and makes use of middleware.

Some Simple Examples of Cloud Computing

Cloud computing is quickly becoming one of the most popular technologies, and a means whereby businesses can acquire and improve their competitive advantage. Some examples of its use are outlined in Table 11.1.

Table 11.1 Examples of Cloud Computing Applications

Examples of Cloud Computing	Cloud Computing Applications
Google Drive and Microsoft OneDrive	These are forms of cloud computing storage (Griffith, 2020; Nolledo, 2020). They allow users to save files online which can then be accessed from anywhere using a computer or any smart device such as a tablet or smartphone.
Web versions of Microsoft Office	Users do not need to install the programs on their PCs; instead, they access the web-based apps via a web browser (Griffith, 2020).
Web-based email services (e.g. Gmail)	The email program is not being run on the user's computer but on the service's computer cloud (Strickland, n.d.).

Cloud Computing Categories

To cater for the needs of a wide variety of users, three main types of services are offered by the cloud: Infrastructure as a Service (IaaS), Platform as a Service (PaaS), and Software as a Service (SaaS) (Singh, 2014).

Infrastructure as a Service (IaaS) provides the infrastructure and computational resources necessary for the running of applications, and includes the storage, networks, processing units, etc. (Xue & Xin, 2016; Kulkarni et al., 2012). It allows users to deploy and run both operating systems and applications without having to take on the responsibilities of deployment and systems or applications management and maintenance (Xue and Xin, 2016; Aniruddha and Chaudhari, 2013). Singh (2014, p. 55) describes the IaaS service model as one which offers 'Web-based access to storage and computing power. The consumer does not need to manage or control the underlying cloud infrastructure but has control over the operating systems, storage, and deployed applications'.

Platform as a Service (PaaS) acts as a deployment environment for application developers to implement and maintain their applications (Thiyagarajan and Ramachandrarao, 2015). The PaaS service model 'provides the tools to build and host web applications' (Singh, 2014, p. 55). Mell and Grance (2011, p. 3) describe PaaS as a model whereby,'The consumer does not manage or control the underlying cloud infrastructure including network, servers, operating systems, or storage, but has control over the deployed applications and possibly configuration settings for the application-hosting environment'.

With **Software as a Service (SaaS)**, providers install their own applications for users to access and use as service either by paying a fee or using a pay-per-use model, without any concerns of installation and maintenance (Assante et al., 2016; Xue and Xin, 2016). Compared to traditional systems, SaaS does not require the users to own the applications or the hardware resources necessary to run the applications. Users do not even need to know the infrastructure and platform required to run the applications (Kumar, 2014; Al-Roomi et al., 2013). SaaS provides seamless applications access to users, making it scalable and widely accessible, although users do not have control over components, security, and application customization, as pointed out by Goel and Sharma (2014). Mell and Grance (2011, p. 3) describe Software as a Service (SaaS) as a model whereby 'the consumer uses an application, but does not control the operating system, hardware or network infrastructure. The consumer does not manage or control the underlying cloud infrastructure including network, servers, operating systems, storage, or even individual application capabilities, with the possible exception of limited user-specific application configuration setting.'

Cloud Computing Deployment Models

There are four main deployment or delivery models for cloud computing: public cloud, private cloud, community cloud, and hybrid cloud (Dillon et al., 2010). Table 11.2 below lists the main features of each model.

Table 11.2 Cloud Computing Deployment or Delivery Models (adapted from Dillon et al. (2010))

	Access	Privacy and Security Issues	Additional Features	Examples
Public Cloud	Services are offered to everyone over the Internet	Usually of high concern Users assumed to be untrustworthy	Each service provider has their own policy, value, costing, and charging model (Vimal and Prabakaran, 2014)	Email services
Private	Services are offered for private organizational usage	High security, more reliable, trusted users	Costly, as organizations must spend more to have their own private clouds	
Community Cloud	Share use of a cloud usually between organizations with similar missions and requirements (Cheng and Lai, 2012)	High security, trusted users amongst different organizations Data storage is, however, shared	Services may be managed by a third party or by the organizations themselves. As a result of the shared usage, cost is usually reduced, unlike the private cloud	Educational cloud in universities for research purposes
Hybrid Cloud	A composition of two or more clouds, either private, public or community	Private cloud features can be used to protect sensitive data Critical applications can be on the private cloud and others on the public cloud	Usually used for back-up purposes	

Why Cloud Computing?

Cloud computing offers a range of technological and sociological benefits (Yang and Tate, 2009). The main goals of cloud computing are to reduce operating costs and increase throughput, performance, reliability, availability, agility, and scalability (Strickland, n.d.; Erdogmus, 2009). In fact, 'the foundation of cloud computing is the delivery of services, software and processing capacity over the Internet, reducing cost, increasing storage, automating systems, decoupling ... service delivery from underlying technology, and providing flexibility and mobility of information' (Singh, 2014, p. 53).

Benefits of Cloud Computing

The main benefits of cloud computing can be summed up as: efficiency, flexibility, ease of set-up, and reduction of IT costs (AlSudiari and Vasista, 2012) as outlined below.

- **Access anytime, anywhere:** Clients can access their applications anytime and anywhere as long as they have access to the Internet. Access is not confined to accessing one's hard drive on one's computer or internal network (Strickland, n.d.). Cloud computing also allows the simultaneous sharing of documents and files over the Internet (Xue and Xin, 2016).
- **Lower cost:** The cloud side has all the processing and storage power. As such, considerable economies of scale can be achieved with the computing power being generated from a centralized and standardized data centre (Yang and Tate, 2009). The client side just needs to have a computer device with enough processing power to run the middleware necessary to connect to the cloud system, without the need to invest in advanced hardware or a large hard drive for increased memory or fast processing capabilities. This, therefore, drastically reduces the costs incurred by the client (AlSudiari and Vasista, 2012).
- **Flexibility and lower cost to organizations:** Organizations do not have to invest in a large number of applications to be installed and run in-house. They can just connect to cloud computing companies and pay them for access to the programs they need as and when they need them (Strickland, n.d.). Additionally, by shifting their capital expenses regarding software and hardware acquisitions and maintenance to operating expenses, organizations can reduce costs which can then be passed on to clients.
- **Scalability:** With cloud computing, users can adjust their resources based on changes to their business needs (Xue and Xin, 2016). This is because cloud computing has the advantage of being able to make resources available quickly, which removes the need for capacity planning (Armbrust et al., 2010).
- **Space saving:** Servers and digital storage devices take up space. Cloud computing offers the option of storing data on someone else's hardware, removing the need for the client to have the physical space (Strickland, n.d.).

- **Environmental benefits:** Due to the advanced electrical and cooling systems used by centralized data centres, cloud computing promises to reduce environmental costs and ensure high energy efficiency compared to traditional dispersed enterprise data centres (Katz, 2009).

Concerns Regarding Cloud Computing

The main concerns of cloud computing remain security and privacy, with security often cited as the primary challenge (Opara-Martins et al., 2015; Nazir & Jamshed, 2013; Kumar et al., 2018). Kumar et al. (2018, p. 693) clearly pointed out that the three critical properties of data, namely confidentiality, integrity, and availability, are 'tested a lot' in the cloud environment.

- **Data theft:** The clouds are subject to malicious attacks including data theft. Many of the service providers do not own their servers and acquire these services from external providers for cost and flexibility reasons, leading to an increased risk of data being stolen from external servers (Chou, 2013). Similarly, service providers are subject to other cyberattacks, including theft of user account details such as users' personal information, credit card details, and even encrypted passwords (Kaur and Singh, 2015).
- **Authentication attack:** Hackers are always trying to gain access to users' credentials and confidential information, particularly during the authentication process (Xue and Xin, 2016). A successful attack can lead to the accessing of users' and organizations' sensitive data.
- **Privacy:** Insufficient control and lack of regulatory compliance are often the root causes of privacy issues in cloud computing (Xue and Xin, 2016; Kaur and Singh, 2015). Service providers often do not have adequate control of the data and the information stored on servers. As a result of this lack of control, cyberattacks and breaches can occur. Also, in the cloud environment, users might not know the exact location of their data. Therefore, clients' privacy may be comprised as a result of ease of access from anywhere and at any time (Kaur and Singh, 2015).

Definition: Cloud Computing

Your local hard drive is not cloud computing. Any programs or services delivered over the Internet and not from your local network are classified as cloud computing.

'Cloud computing is a model for enabling ubiquitous, convenient, on-demand network access to a shared pool of configurable computing resources (e.g., networks, servers, storage, applications, and services) that can be rapidly provisioned and released with minimal management effort or service provider interaction' (Mell and Grance, 2011, p. 2).

Definition: Cloud Computing

Cloud computing is becoming more and more pervasive due to its ability to be rapidly provisioned. While this is one if its biggest strengths, its ubiquitous nature also limits the user's visibility of how their data is managed. Security and privacy of content thus becomes a major issue.

Stop and Reflect: Privacy

Privacy is often a sensitive issue when it comes to cloud computing. 'Cloud Computing can bring many uncertainties with respect to compliance with privacy regulations' (AlSudiari and Vasista, 2012, p. 167). For example, as pointed out by AlSudiari and Vasista (2012, p. 165), it is common practice for cloud providers to offer their facilities to users without individual contracts, where the users are subject to the providers' published terms and service. If these terms of service give the cloud provider rights over users' information, then the users are likely bound to those terms. In such cases, what do you think the risks are to users' data? What do you think can be done to ensure that users have more control over their data?

Stop and Reflect: Security

Cloud computing offers affordable, accessible, and convenient services, but cloud consumers are subject to various threats from hackers, spammers, terrorists, data breaches, and political challenges (Hu, 2015). Due to these potential threats, corporate executives have been hesitant to hand over their 'all important' data to another company, although the counterargument is that cloud computing services are compelled to ensure that they have reliable security measures in place to protect their clients' data or risk losing their reputation and, worst of all, their clients (Strickland, n.d.). Are large storage capacity and ease of access to data worth the trade-off of data ownership and control? To what extent can the security measures of cloud computing services be trusted, especially if the data location is not local or national?

Stop and Reflect: PaaS vs SaaS

According to Santosh and Goudar (2012, pp. 356–360), 'the difference between PaaS and SaaS is that with PaaS, users can develop the applications on cloud or host the completed applications whereas with SaaS, they can only host the completed applications'. When do you think PaaS will be a better option as opposed to SaaS? Would you argue that SaaS is safer than PaaS?

11.4 Big Data

What is Big Data?

Peter Drucker famously stated that 'You can't manage what you don't measure.' (Carter, 2023)

As a result of the increased adoption of e-commerce worldwide and the technology advancements in data acquisition, processing, and storage, business managers can measure, analyse, and understand more about their business, and translate this knowledge into improved evidence-based decision-making and strategic planning. Big data enables the new culture of decision-making for the data-driven organizations based on 'what do we know?' rather than 'what do we think?' (McAfee et al., 2012). The explosion of digital data availability can be effectively exploited to generate meaningful information that can translate into relevant decisions made by artful, compelling, and visionary leaders who understand the need to align problems with the right data in order to take effective decisions.

The term 'big data' has become ubiquitous among various industries and in academia, with many different definitions of the term offered. Since 2011, the interest in big data has been increasing exponentially and interwoven with various technical and social-technical issues, such as privacy, and an exact and consensual definition has yet to be formulated. While 'big' suggests significance, complexity, and challenges, its quantification for the purpose of definition is difficult (Ward and Barker, 2013). Based on all previous definitions of big data offered by various industries and academics, De Mauro et al. (2015, p. 103) proposed this consensual definition of the term: 'Big Data represents the Information assets characterized by such a High Volume, Velocity and Variety to require specific Technology and Analytical Methods for its transformation in Value'.

Comparably, TechAmerica Foundation's Big Data Commission states: 'Big data is a term that describes large volumes of high velocity, complex and variable data that require advanced techniques and technologies to enable the capture, storage, distribution, management and analysis of the information' (Mills et al., 2012, p. 10).

Characteristics of Big Data

The three main characteristics of big data are volume, velocity, and variety (Laney, 2001). Industry experts from IBM and Oracle suggest two additional characteristics: veracity and value.

Volume

Definition: Volume refers to the mass quantities of the data that organizations can harness to generate insights on business operations in order to improve the quality of decision-making across the enterprise. According to survey results presented in IBM's 2012 Executive Report, over 50% of 1,144 respondents (comprising business and IT professionals from various disciplines across 26 industries in 95 countries) considered a data size of between one terabyte and one petabyte to be big data. Its results also acknowledges that the volume of data is increasing at an exponential rate and whatever is considered 'high volume' today will not be high enough tomorrow (Schroeck et al., 2012).

Purpose: The businesses and organizations have been collecting massive volumes of their transactional data to identify the patterns or historical trends in their business operations in order to address the problems that they would not have been able to tackle before and also to develop evidence-based strategic decision-making.

Example: Spotify is one of the most successful companies which use big data to improve their customer experiences. In 2018, Spotify users generated 600 GB of data daily and it has been using this big data to perfect its algorithms in order to understand its customers' preferences and to develop personalized content.

Velocity

Definition: Velocity is the rate at which data are generated and/or acquired, and the speed with which they are analysed and subsequently acted upon if necessary. The advancement of digital devices such as smartphones and sensors has enabled us to create or capture the data at unprecedented speed (Gandomi and Haider, 2015).

Purpose: There has been a growing demand for these data to be analysed in real time so that evidence-based decisions can be made, and to acquire the most up-to-date business insights.

Example: According to Twitter blog, it processes nearly 4 million events per second which generate petabyte scale data every day in 2021.

Regarding data velocity, Laney (2021) suggested the following architectural solutions:

- periodically extract, transform, integrate, and reorganize the real-time production data into operational data stores for operational reporting and tactical analysis;
- use caches which allow instant access to transactional data by buffering back-end systems and updating according to the business rules;
- use the point-to-point distribution model for data routing among databases and applications;
- consider the data requirements and decision cycles for designing the architecture to balance the data latency.

Variety

Definition: Variety refers to the diverse types of data and data sources. The complexity of various data types, which may be structured and/or semi-structured and/or unstructured, requires careful and efficient management. It is necessary to acquire, integrate and analyse the collection of both traditional and non-traditional data sources from both within and outside of the enterprise.

Purpose: The dramatic increase in the utilization of sensors and smartphones, along with social-networking and social-collaboration techniques, has led to the generation of data in a variety of formats such as text, data from webpages, social media data including tweets, audio, photos, video, social interactions, click streams, log files, etc. (Schroeck et al., 2012).

Example: Big data used in social media platforms such as Facebook, Instagram, and TikTok use a variety of data formats such as text, audio, photo, video and live streaming.

To overcome the challenges posed by the variety of big data, Laney (2001) recommended the use of:

- data profiling to explore the unrevealed relationships and to resolve the data anomalies among a variety of data sources;
- an XML-based data format which is useful as a 'universal translator' to increase data portability;
- data access middleware to enhance the direct connectivity between applications and databases;
- distributed query management software to add a data routing and integration intelligence layer;
- metadata management solutions for contextual consistency with enterprise data;
- advanced indexing techniques to relate or link the data from a variety of incompatible data types.

Veracity

Definition: Veracity refers to the quality and provenance of the big data, according to TechAmerica Foundation's Big Data Commission.

Purpose: In spite of a high level of data integrity being an essential big data requirement, even the most rigorous data cleansing methods cannot eliminate the inherent uncertainty or unreliability of some data, although these data may still contain valuable information (Gandomi and Haider, 2015).

In their IBM Executive Report, Schroeck et al. (2012) suggest that it is necessary to know the context of the data in order to manage the uncertainty by integrating multiple less reliable sources to create a more accurate and meaningful data point. This can be done by applying more advanced mathematical data modelling techniques such as robust optimization and fuzzy logic.

Example: Data uncertainty reflects the inherent unreliability of some sources of data, such as uncertainty in regard to energy production, weather conditions, or the sentiments and truthfulness of humans.

Value

Definition: Oracle (2022) introduced value as an essential characteristic of big data. Even though the data that we collect/acquire, integrate, and process satisfy the other characteristics of big data, they will not be useful if the valuable information cannot be discovered. Only when we can explore and discover the value in our big data in terms of increasing efficiencies, developing new products, better customization to enhance the customers' experiences and satisfaction, and increasing the enterprise's competitive advantages, can we identify big data as capital for the enterprise.

Purpose: Oracle also highlights the need to be aware of 'low value density', which means that the value generated from a large amount of data is relatively low. It is important to ask the right questions, recognize patterns, and have well-defined assumptions and rigorous analysis to predict a particular behaviour so that a high value can be generated from a discovery process conducted on the large volumes of multiple data sources.

Example: Harnessing big data has provided great value to Netflix, not only in understanding its users' preferences and matching them with its contents, but also in personalizing the artwork to be more appealing to its users.

Big Data Applications

Oracle (2022) states that big data can facilitate business activities such as: product development, predictive maintenance, customer experience, fraud and compliance, machine learning, operational efficiency, and innovation.

The top 22 uses of big data by various industries, according to Oracle (2022), are illustrated in Table 11.3.

Table 11.3 Top 22 Uses Of Big Data By Various Industries (prepared by the authors, adopted from Oracle (2022)

Industry	Use Cases	Description
Manufacturing	Predictive Maintenance	Big data helps to predict equipment failure by analysing both structured data of equipment details and multi-structured data on log entries, sensor data, error messages, equipment temperature, and other factors so that equipment uptime can be maximized more cost effectively.
	Operational Efficiency	Big data helps to analyse the production process so that customer feedback can be proactively responded to and future demands can be predicted.
	Production Optimization	Big data helps to examine the flow of items through the production lines and identify areas for improvement or generating benefits.

(Continued)

Table 11.3   (Continued)

Industry	Use Cases	Description
Retail	Product Development	Big data helps to explore the relationships among key attributes of past and current products and the commercial success of the offerings to predict the new products and services that will match with anticipated customer demand.
	Customer Experience	Big data helps to gain insight into the customer experience by analysing the data from social media, web visits, call logs, and interactions with the customers so that businesses can fine-tune their operations to provide personalized offers, increase customer loyalty and handle issues proactively.
	Customer Lifetime Value	Big data helps in understanding consumer behaviour and spending patterns so that businesses can identify the valuable customers and provide the targeted exclusive offers by analysing large amounts of sales transaction data.
	In-store Shopping Experience	Big data helps to examine the data from mobile apps, in-store purchases, and geolocations to improve the in-store shopping experience and to encourage customers to complete purchases.
	Pricing Analytics and Optimization	Big Data helps to investigate end-to-end profit and margin analysis so that businesses can understand market segmentation and future opportunities, and identify any pricing improvements.
Healthcare	Genomic Research	Big data helps in investigating disease genes and biomarkers so that medical professionals can identify the potential health issues that their patients may be facing in future, and take the necessary preventive and proactive steps. Moreover, it also allows them to design personalized and therefore more effective treatments for their patients.
	Patient Experience and Outcomes	Big data enables health professionals to examine a wide range of patients' historical health information and obtain a comprehensive view of patient care so that healthcare organizations can provide better and more cost-effective treatment and improved quality of care.
	Claims Fraud	Big data helps the relevant personnel to review significant numbers of reports regardless of their formats to verify the accuracy of healthcare claims in insurance incentive programs so that healthcare organizations can discover potential claims fraud from unusual behaviours.
	Healthcare Billing Analytics	Big data helps accounting and finance personnel to evaluate the large amount of billing and claims data from various data sources in diverse formats to identify where to improve for ensuring better cash flows and reducing any loss in revenue.

Industry	Use Cases	Description
Oil and Gas	Predictive Equipment Maintenance	Big data helps to improve the tracking of equipment utilization, the equipment's condition, and other issues so that oil and gas companies can maintain the optimal life of their equipment and machinery while improving their safety by forecasting possible faults or errors that could occur in the future.
	Oil Exploration and Discovery	Big data helps to process the extensive amount of data captured during the drilling and production process so that oil and gas companies can select new drilling sites based on evidence-based decisions.
	Oil Production Optimization	Big data helps to analyse the sensor and historical data regardless of their volume, variety, velocity, and veracity, and conducts the complicated mathematical modelling to optimize oil well production.
Telecommunications	Network Capacity Optimization	Big data helps to conduct the complex data analytics on telecommunication network usage data; as a result, we can identify the areas or time intervals with excessive capacity and plan for load balancing by rerouting bandwidth. It also enables the forecasting of telecommunication network demand and any potential usage peaks.
	Telecom Customer Churn	Big data helps to examine the vast amount of customers' network usage data and to identify the usage patterns so that telecommunication organizations can predict the demand and plan for better service provision to increase their customers' satisfaction and their retention rate.
	New Product Offering	Big data helps to gain insights into customer behaviour and enables businesses to customize their services for diverse customer segments with various offerings so that they can increase their customers' satisfaction rather than losing them to their competitors.
Financial Services	Fraud and Compliance	Big data helps to investigate the exponentially growing financial data to identify any unusual patterns indicating fraud and any financial activities which do not comply with financial regulations.
	Drive Innovation	Big data helps financial institutions to acquire a better understanding of customer behaviours and needs, and identify market trends so that they can improve their products and services.
	Anti-money Laundering	Big data helps to investigate the immense amount of financial data derived from various sources to identify any financial activities which can lead to unlawful transactions such as money laundering. It enables financial institutions to discover potential fraud patterns as proof of proper diligence and suspicious activity reports by complying with anti-money laundering laws and regulations.
	Financial Regulatory and Compliance Analytics	Big data helps financial institutions to conduct audits of their massive amounts of financial data to ensure compliance with all regulatory requirements.

Challenges in Big Data Applications

Big data applications face several challenges due to the characteristics of big data, namely its volume, velocity, veracity, and variety. Regarding the volume of big data, it is also important to consider that the relative value of each data point decreases proportionally when the data volume increases, which can result in poor financial justification for exponential increases in data storage demand. Therefore, the various data sources need to be profiled to identify and subsequently eliminate any data redundancies, and to monitor data usage in order to identify the 'cold spots' of unused data which can be reduced or offloaded to offline storages (Laney, 2001). Another challenge that velocity, veracity, and variety of big data is incremental learning for non-stationary data (Najafabadi et al., 2015).

In big data applications where machine learning data analytics are applied to streamed data, several challenges are encountered due to the diverse data formats, velocity of streamed data, validity of data analysis, integration for highly distributed data, noisy and poor data quality, the scalability of data modelling algorithms and data storage, high-dimensional data and the difficulty of handling unsupervised and uncategorized data, and parallel processing (Najafabadi et al., 2015).

In addition to the data integrity challenges, there are statistical challenges that we need to consider in high-dimensional big data. Fan et al. (2014) state that the massive volume and high dimensionality of big data present several challenges that are not encountered in traditional datasets. These challenges are heterogeneity, noise accumulation, spurious correlations, and incidental endogeneity.

Heterogeneity: When aggregating big data, it is important to be aware of and to safeguard the rich diversity of various sub-populations of big datasets. There could be instances when some subpopulations with unique features will be identified as outliers and discarded when there are insufficient observations in these subpopulations.

Noise accumulation: Numerous dimensions (variables) in big datasets can lead to an accumulation of noise and estimation errors because rules applied in predictive modelling depend on these dimensions. When conducting classification analysis, this will result in poor classification when there are multiple weak dimensions which do not contribute to the reduction of classification error.

Spurious correlation: When a great number of dimensions are examined in big data analysis, it is necessary to investigate the correlations between them and be aware of spurious correlation because, among large numbers of dimensions, some may be highly correlated. This spurious correlation can lead to invalid or false findings.

Incidental endogeneity: When a substantial number of dimensions are included in regression modelling, there is some possibility that incidental endogeneity may emerge when some of these dimensions (predictors) correlate with the residual values of that regression model. This can lead to a violation of the endogeneity assumptions required for the validity of the regression.

Definition: Big Data

Big data is a term that describes large volumes of high velocity, complex, and variable data that require advanced techniques and technologies to enable the capture, storage, distribution, management, and analysis of the information (Mills et al., 2012, p. 10).

Definition: Volume

Volume in big data refers to the mass quantities of the data that organizations can harness to generate insights into business operations in order to improve the quality of decision-making across the enterprise.

Definition: Velocity

Velocity in big data is the rate at which data are generated and/or acquired, and the speed with which they are analysed and subsequently acted upon if necessary. The advancement of digital devices such as smartphones and sensors has enabled us to create or capture data at unprecedented speed (Gandomi and Haider, 2015).

Definition: Variety

Variety in big data refers to the diverse types of data and data sources. The complexity of various data types, which may be structured and/or semi-structured and/or unstructured, requires careful and efficient management. It is necessary to acquire, integrate and analyse the collection of both traditional and non-traditional data sources from both within and outside the enterprise (Schroeck et al., 2012).

Definition: Veracity

Veracity in big data refers to its quality and provenance, according to the TechAmerica Foundation's Big Data Commission. Data uncertainty reflects the inherent unreliability of some sources of data, such as uncertainty in regard to energy production, weather conditions or the sentiments and truthfulness of humans. Despite the fact that a high level of data integrity is an essential big data requirement, even the most rigorous data cleansing methods cannot eliminate the inherent uncertainty or unreliability of some data, although these data may still contain valuable information (Gandomi and Haider, 2015).

Definition: Value

Oracle (2022) introduced value as an essential characteristic of big data. Even though the data which we collect/acquire, integrate, and process satisfy the other characteristics of big data, the data will not be useful if the valuable information cannot be discovered. Only when we can explore and discover the value in our big data in terms of increasing efficiencies, developing new products, ensuring better customization to enhance customers' experiences and satisfaction, and increasing the enterprise's competitive advantages, can we identify big data as capital for the enterprise.

Stop and Reflect: Big Data

There are five main characteristics of big data, which are volume, velocity, variety, veracity, and value.

Assume that your organization has enormous amount of sales data which has been generated by your customers' purchases minute by minute.

- Can we classify this sales dataset as big data? Provide your justification based on your assumptions.

Stop and Reflect: Uses of Big Data

Oracle (2022) states that big data can facilitate business activities such as: product development, predictive maintenance, customer experience, fraud and compliance, machine learning, operational efficiency, and innovation. Big data applications have been used in various industries such as manufacturing, retail, healthcare, oil and gas, telecommunications, and financial services for product development, customer experience optimization, compliance analysis, etc.

- How do these big data applications impact on your daily-life activities? Explain with some examples.

Stop and Reflect: Big Data Challenges

Big data applications are facing data integrity challenges as well as statistical challenges derived from high dimensional big data. The massive volume and high dimensionality of big data present many challenges that are not encountered in traditional datasets. These challenges are heterogeneity, noise accumulation, spurious correlations, and incidental endogeneity.

● As a data scientist, what are the measures or approaches that you will take to overcome these challenges?

11.5 Internet of Things

What is the Internet of Things (IoT)?

The Internet of Things (IoT) is a network of physical objects or 'things' that are embedded in electronics. These things include sensors, actuators, software, and the network connectivity used to connect and exchange data with other devices and systems over the network or Internet. Put simply, any device that is able to connect to the Internet and has sensors that transmit data without human interaction or control, can be considered to be an IoT device or object. IoT objects or devices include everything from everyday items such as coffee makers, smart TVs, and vehicles to industrial applications such as traffic congestion monitors, air pollution sensors, asset tracking, smart manufacturing, and smart power grids.

Technologies that Enabled IoT

The advancement in *network, wireless and mobile technologies*, IPv6, broadband Internet, 5G networks, smart devices with Wi-Fi capabilities and embedded *sensor technology* (discussed in Chapters 5 and 6) has contributed to the broader implementation of IoT. Further, the increased availability of *cloud computing platforms* allows both enterprises and consumers to gain access to the infrastructure they require in order to scale up without having to manage it all with XaaS solutions (refer to cloud computing section). Advances in *neural networks (AI)* have enabled natural-language processing (NLP) in IoT devices (such as digital personal assistants Alexa, Cortana, and Siri), making them inexpensive, and feasible for home use. Further, the ready access to large amounts data stored in the cloud and in *machine learning and analytics*, enables businesses to gather insights faster and more easily (IBM, 2022).

Key Components of IoT

The Internet of Things (IoT) is made up of several key components that work together to enable devices to collect, process, and communicate data. Table 11.4 lists the main components (IBM, 2022).

Table 11.4 Key Components of IoT (prepared by the authors, adopted from IBM 2022)

Component	Description	Examples
Smart devices	Objects embedded with sensors and connected to the internet	Smart locks and video doorbells
Connectivity	Use of network and internet protocols to connect devices and exchange information	Cellular networks, WiFi, Bluetooth
Data processing	Processing of data collected by IoT devices on the cloud	Verification of temperature data, computer vision for intruder detection
User interface IoT applications	Applications that allow users to interact with IoT devices and data	Smartphone apps, websites

1   **Smart devices**: These are objects that are embedded with sensors and connected to the Internet, enabling them to collect and transmit data. Examples include smart locks and video doorbells that allow users to control access to their home remotely.

2   **Connectivity:** IoT devices use various network and Internet protocols to connect, collect, and exchange information. Wired and wireless connections such as cellular networks, satellite networks, WiFi, Bluetooth, and wide-area networks are used to connect the sensors and devices to the cloud.

3   **Data processing:** The data collected by IoT devices is processed by software on the cloud. This can be a simple task, such as verifying that temperature data falls within an acceptable range, or a complex task, such as using computer vision to detect intruders on a property.

4   **User interface IoT applications:** IoT applications allow users to interact with the data collected by IoT devices. These applications integrate data from various devices and may use machine learning or artificial intelligence to analyse data and make informed decisions. A graphical user interface, such as a smartphone app or website, may be used to manage IoT devices.

IoT technology has the potential to revolutionize many industries by enabling the development of new applications and services that leverage the data generated by IoT devices. For example, in the healthcare industry, IoT devices can be used to monitor patient health and alert medical professionals to potential health issues. In agriculture, IoT sensors can be used to monitor soil moisture and temperature, enabling farmers to optimize crop yields. However, the security and privacy of IoT data must be carefully managed to ensure that users' personal information is protected.

Benefits and Applications of the Internet of Things (IoT)

IoT benefits for business

The Internet of Things (IoT) may be characterized by three primary features that can bring numerous benefits to different business organizations:

1   **Big data:** The IoT generates large amounts of data through interconnected smart devices, resulting in big data that is high in volume and variety. This data is generated in real-time or near real-time, with greater accuracy than traditional data sources. By collecting and analysing this data, organizations can gain valuable insights into strategic threats and opportunities.

2   **Multiple data sources:** Interconnected IoT devices allow organizations to collect and combine data from multiple sources. This provides greater insights into unexpected activity and enables businesses to efficiently monitor and regulate the performance, quality, and reliability of products and services.

3   **Linking data from multiple sources:** Linking data from various sources can provide organizations with a more holistic view of their customers and lead to new product and service lines, creating new streams of revenue. For example, data on a customer's purchasing behaviour can be collected from multiple sources and integrated to provide the customer with a more personalized shopping experience.

By leveraging IoT technology, businesses can gain a significant competitive advantage, as well as improved profitability. IoT offers numerous benefits to businesses, as highlighted in the following list (Brous et al., 2020).

1   **Real-time and accurate data insights:** IoT technology provides businesses with access to real-time and accurate data insights. This allows for better forecasting and trend analysis, which can help organizations identify strategic threats and opportunities. For example, a smart meter installed in a residential building can provide real-time data on energy usage, allowing energy companies to forecast demand and adjust their operations accordingly.

2   **Potential for new products and services:** IoT technology can provide businesses with vast amounts of data, which can be used to identify new opportunities for products and services. For instance, a car manufacturer can use IoT sensors to gather data on driver behaviour and preferences, enabling them to design new features and services that cater to the needs of their customers.

3   **Improved service delivery to customers:** By leveraging IoT technology, businesses can improve the delivery of their services to customers. For example, a restaurant can use IoT devices to monitor kitchen equipment and inventory levels, ensuring that they always have the necessary ingredients to prepare meals for customers. This can help to reduce waiting times and improve the overall dining experience for customers.

4   **Efficient monitoring and regulation of business activities:** IoT technology enables businesses to efficiently monitor and regulate their business activities, which can improve the quality and reliability of their products and services. For example, a manufacturer can use IoT sensors to monitor the performance of their equipment, allowing them to detect and address potential problems before they lead to production downtime or product defects.

5   **Ability to remotely monitor and regulate business activities:** IoT technology also allows businesses to remotely monitor and regulate their operations. For example, a home security company can use IoT devices to monitor and control security systems in homes and businesses, enabling them to respond quickly to potential security threats and ensure the safety of their customers.

Applications of IoT

IoT is being implemented in many different industries and domains, including healthcare, energy, agriculture, construction, and government. Below are a number of examples of how IoT is being implemented in various business sectors.

Smart homes

IoT technology can provide for the well-being and convenience of residents via smart homes. Through Internet-connected technologies, smart home devices such as smartphones, remote sensors, heating, and lighting systems and other IoT devices can improve the efficiency and safety of the home. For example, smart door locks enable users to lock their homes from anywhere using a smartphone app. Video doorbells allow users to receive video calls via their doorbell when someone is at their front door. These devices also enable users to unlock their homes remotely using smartphone apps, giving access to family and friends if necessary. Likewise, smart meters installed in individual homes and businesses provide information about both real-time use and historical usage patterns that customers and the utilities can analyse to identify ways to improve power-consumption efficiency (Chowdhury et al., 2020; Lanner, 2018).

Wearables

Wearables are devices that are worn under, with, or on top of clothing. Many of us use wearables to monitor various aspects of our lives such as physical activity (exercise), sleep patterns, heart activity, and other health-related functions. They are also being used for law enforcement, emergency management, public safety, and other purposes. The wearing of smart helmets can improve worker safety and operations in hazardous industrial and manufacturing environments. The technology embedded in the helmets can detect hazards such as voltage, and alert the wearer to the approach or movements of a non-visible vehicle.

Industrial IoT

The IoT involves more than just consumer products and how they interact to provide consumers with an interconnected experience. In industrial settings, many companies are utilizing IoT to better understand consumer needs in real time, become more responsive, improve machine and system quality on the fly, streamline operations, and discover new ways to operate. *Industrial IoT (IIoT)* is the application of IoT technology in industrial settings, utilizing smart industrial devices in manufacturing, retail, health, and other enterprises to improve business efficiency. Industrial devices, ranging from sensors to equipment, provide businesses with detailed, real-time data that can be used to improve business operations. They provide insights into supply chain management, logistics, human resources, and production. IIoT also relies on business intelligence software such as predictive and prescriptive analytics solutions and reporting, which give deeper insights and facilitate smarter, faster decision-making that drives operational efficiency on an industrial scale (Sniderman et al., 2016).

Healthcare

The healthcare sector uses IoT for the remote monitoring of patients' health status. Wearables and other IoT-enabled home monitoring equipment can help doctors keep a better track of their patients' health. They can monitor patients' adherence to treatment plans as well as any need for immediate medical attention. IoT helps healthcare providers to be more vigilant and proactive in their interactions with patients. Data received from IoT devices can assist healthcare providers to determine the appropriate treatment for patients and achieve the desired outcomes. IoT devices equipped with sensors are also used in hospitals to track the real-time location of medical equipment such as wheelchairs, defibrillators, nebulizers, oxygen pumps, and other hospital equipment.

Automotive

Sensors are able to detect potential equipment failure in vehicles on the road and can give the driver details about the fault, as well as advice. Sensor-driven analytics and automation improve the efficiency of automobile production and maintenance. For example, industrial sensors are used to create 3D real-time images of interior automotive components. Diagnostics and troubleshooting can be done much faster, and the IoT system can automatically order replacement parts.

Manufacturing

Predictive maintenance and wearable technology are used in production to prevent unwanted downtime and increase worker safety. Machine failure can be predicted with IoT applications, saving production downtime. When IoT devices/sensors identify an approaching malfunction in production-line equipment, preventative maintenance can be carried out. Equipment can be checked immediately for accuracy or removed from the production line until it is fixed. Sensors can also detect when manufacturing output is being harmed, allowing for prompt repairs or replacement of damaged equipment. Workers are warned about possible dangers via wearables such as helmets and wristbands, as well as computer vision cameras (Sniderman et al., 2016).

Retail

The IoT can connect data, analytics, and marketing activities across several locations. IoT applications enable retailers to manage inventory, improve customer experience, optimize supply chains, and cut costs. Retail companies use IoT-connected devices such as RFID inventory tracking chips, cellular and Wi-Fi networks, beacons, and smart shelves to collect IoT data from in-store and digital channels, and use analytics including artificial intelligence to identify customers' behaviour patterns and preferences in real time. For example, smart shelves fitted with weight sensors enable RFID-based data collection, and transfer the data to an IoT application which automatically checks the inventory and issues a warning when stocks are low (Pratt, 2022).

Logistics and transport

Supply chain management, vendor relationships, fleet management, and scheduled maintenance operations benefit from a variety of IoT applications. Shipping companies, using industrial IoT devices can keep track of assets and optimize fuel use on shipping routes. Sensors for track-and-trace and temperature-control monitoring could be imbedded in the inventory itself. For example, IoT monitoring applications can monitor temperature-sensitive items such as food, floral, and pharmaceutical products, and provide alerts when temperatures rise or fall to a level that threatens the product (Taliaferro et al., 2019).

Government/public sector

IoT applications are increasingly being used by governments to address issues in infrastructure, health, and the environment. IoT applications facilitate smart cities solutions that collect and analyse data from IoT devices and sensors installed in physical infrastructure such as streetlights, water meters, and traffic signals. The government then uses this information to improve public utilities and services, for example by detecting urgent infrastructure maintenance needs of streets, bridges, and pipelines, reducing energy consumption with smart lighting systems, and evaluating air quality and radiation levels (Chowdhury et al., 2020; Pratt, 2022).

IoT Concerns and Challenges

The widespread adoption of IoT devices has given rise to a number of concerns and challenges, including security, privacy, connectivity, power dependence, and costs.

Security is a major issue for IoT devices, as they are vulnerable to various forms of attacks, such as physical tampering, internet-based software assaults, network-based attacks, and hardware-based attacks. With the increasing number of IoT devices in use, it becomes more challenging to protect the data that is collected and transmitted by these devices.

Privacy is another critical concern, particularly as IoT devices are utilized in sensitive industries such as healthcare and banking. As data privacy regulations become more stringent globally, businesses are legally obligated to safeguard data. However, integrating encryption and security protocols with IoT devices can be challenging, particularly when dealing with a large number of devices (Borgini, 2022).

Connectivity and power dependence are further challenges for IoT systems. Since they rely on Internet and cloud services, any disruption to the Internet connection can impact their functionality. Businesses need to have a proactive outage plan and understand how outages can affect their devices. Troubleshooting and incident management protocols can help mitigate the effects of outages, as can ensuring that employees know what to do when devices are down (Borgini, 2022).

Finally, in terms of **cost**, the deployment of IoT devices requires a significant investment of time and money (Borgini, 2022). Companies need to carefully plan and budget for integrating IoT devices into their existing network.

Definition: Internet of Things

The Internet of Things (IoT) is a network of physical objects equipped with sensors, software, and connectivity that enables the exchange of data with other devices and systems over the Internet.

Definition: IoT Devices

IoT Devices are physical objects that contain embedded sensors and are connected to the Internet, enabling them to gather, transmit, and receive data.

Definition: IoT Applications

IoT Applications comprise software and services that gather data from multiple IoT devices, which is then analysed using Machine Learning or Artificial Intelligence (AI) to make informed decisions.

Stop and Reflect: Internet of Things

How does the IoT impact your daily life and work through energy management and consumer conveniences? Can you provide examples of IoT devices you use and how they have benefited you?

Stop and Reflect: IoT Challenges

While the IoT has tremendous benefits such as energy management and consumer conveniences, there are also cyber risks that consumers should be aware of.

- What are the possible risks of having so many devices connected to the Internet?
- Do you think the advantages of the IoT outweigh its disadvantages?

Stop and Reflect: Privacy Issues

Privacy paradox: Although we speak about the importance of protecting privacy, our actions and choices relegate privacy to secondary importance.

- To what extent do you believe that privacy is often undervalued or disregarded in practice, despite being widely acknowledged as important? Can you reflect on specific instances where you have made choices that appear to prioritize convenience or other benefits over safeguarding your privacy?

11.6 Blockchain

What is a Blockchain?

A blockchain is a decentralized network of digital ledgers, commonly referred to as data blocks, that store and record transactional information. Each block is secured using a cryptographic hash function and shared among all network participants. Because the

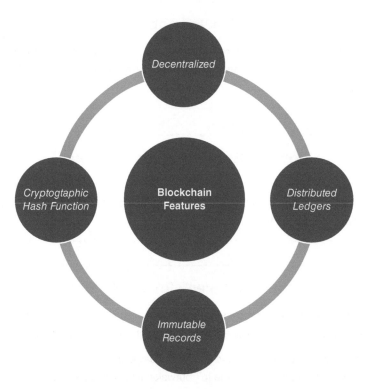

Figure 11.1 Key Features of Blockchain (Adapted from Gupta, 2020)

network is decentralized, there is no central entity controlling the devices, making the digital ledgers accessible to anyone with permission (Gupta, 2020).

How Blockchain Works

Each transaction in the blockchain is recorded as a 'block' of data. The information recorded in the *distributed digital blocks* is *immutable*, which means that once the information has been recorded in the block (digital ledger) and appended to the chain, it cannot be altered or deleted. If there is an error in recording the information, then the corrections need to be updated in another digital block and appended to the previous erroneous block, and both of these blocks will be visible.

These digital blocks are connected and secured using a *cryptographic hash function* that makes them resistant to unwarranted modification of the data in the ledgers. Any attempt to alter or delete an information block will break the cryptographic chain and all nodes in the network will be alerted of that change. Due to this encryption feature, blockchain is immutable and tamper-proof, removing the possibility of tampering by a malicious actor – thus ensuring that information is always *secure* and the *authenticity of a transaction is verified* and confirmed by participants in the network. Further, in the decentralized network, because there is no intermediary to manage the agreement between the business participants, blockchain technology enables the automation of agreements using smart contracts.

A *smart contract* is a computer program that can be built into the blockchain to facilitate, verify, or negotiate a contract agreement (Hayes, 2022). By using smart contracts, businesses can standardize the recording of transactions in the network. Smart contracts implement the rules governing transactions between two or more parties by establishing terms and conditions to which the involved parties agree, such as the price of products/services, shipping methods, transaction completion time, and financing terms (Gupta, 2020; Hayes, 2022).

How is Blockchain Different from Bitcoin?

Bitcoin is a virtual currency, also known as cryptocurrency, that has been the most prominent user of blockchain technology. It was created by Satoshi Nakamoto in 2008 and allows for direct buying, selling, and exchanging without intermediaries such as banks or governments. Blockchain technology is the underlying mechanism that powers Bitcoin cryptocurrency. It transparently records transactions in public distributed digital ledgers, which are verified through cryptography. This makes the transaction information immutable but accessible to everyone (Gupta, 2020; Hayes, 2022).

However, blockchain technology is not solely limited to Bitcoin and cryptocurrencies. It is increasingly being used innovatively in various spheres, such as finance, healthcare, media, government, and more. The following sections discuss the applications of blockchain in these industries.

Blockchain for Business

Blockchain has transformed the way businesses operate and function. The properties of blockchain technology, as we discussed above, enable blockchain networks to provide better transparency, traceability, secure transactions, and cost reduction for business (Figure 11.2) (Geroni, 2021; Gupta, 2020).

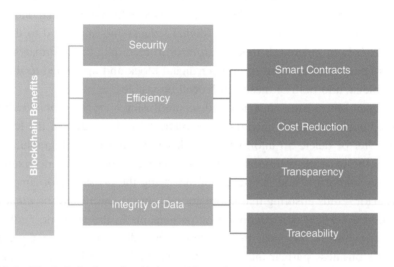

Figure 11.2　Blockchain Benefits (Adapted from Geroni 2021, Gupta 2020 and Hayes, 2022)

With no single centralized authority to control and manage the blockchain network, transactions in the blockchain network are verified, validated, approved, and managed by multiple peer nodes. Once a transaction is validated, each node keeps a copy of the transaction record and is updated when new records (blocks) are approved and added to the chain. Transactional information in each block can include who, what, when, where, how much, and even the condition of goods – such as the temperature of a food shipment (IBM, 2022). These records of transactions enable businesses to trace information to its source and track the movement of its assets – tangible (a product) or intangible (intellectual) – throughout the supply chain network. Editing the blockchain is only possible if there is a consensus between all nodes on the network. This way, the blockchain ensures the *transparency, accuracy*, and *traceability* of information in the network (Hayes, 2022).

Because the same set of data is kept on multiple nodes/computers, businesses do not need to worry about data corruption or downtimes as there are several copies of the data throughout the network, thus providing *data resilience* for organizations and businesses.

Further, as the blockchain is a decentralized network, it does not need a central authority for the verification of transaction information. It eliminates the costs associated with third-party hosting, verification, and maintenance, thereby contributing to cost reductions for businesses, which in turn can be passed on to customers.

The use of cryptography makes it extremely difficult to alter information on the blockchain without notice, ensuring secure transactions in the blockchain network. Better security, the elimination of intermediaries, and decentralised transaction processing all contribute to more secure and efficient transactions on the blockchain network (Geroni, 2021; Gupta, 2020; Hayes, 2022).

Blockchain Applications

The number of businesses embracing blockchain is steadily increasing, with industry leaders swiftly realizing the technology's promise and accessibility. Blockchain is being used in government sectors as well as in a variety of industries including finance, health, and supply chains, among others. The following are some examples of how blockchain is assisting many sectors to transform their operations by means of trusted data, end-to-end visibility, process automation, and the creation of new business values.

Supply chain management

Blockchain enables the tracking of items at every stage of the supply chain, from origin to delivery to destination. Using blockchain, all partners in a supply chain can record and verify the originality and integrity of information such as price, date, location, quality, certification, and other relevant information about their products. Overall, blockchain has considerably improved supply chain management and operations.

Food supply chain

Australian meat processor, Thomas Foods International, and grocery retailer, Drakes Supermarket, have partnered to trace the entire lifecycle of a food product from paddock to plate, tracing the origin of a piece of steak back to one of four individual farms using IBM Food Trust blockchain technology (Jassal, 2019; Nott, 2019). The IBM Food Trust™ is a blockchain-based solution comprising a collaborative network of growers, processors, wholesalers, distributors, manufacturers, retailers, and others, who can track goods as they move through their supply chain while enhancing visibility and accountability across the food supply chain (IBM, 2020a).

Pharmaceutical supply chain

PharmaPortal™ is a blockchain platform established by Sonoco ThermoSafe, a company that supplies temperature-controlled packaging, and enables pharmaceutical manufacturers and carriers to collaborate on the safe delivery and end-to-end traceability of biologics, vaccines, and other temperature-sensitive products (IBM, 2020b).

Supply chain logistics

TradeLens is an IBM blockchain-based platform that digitizes the shipping processes, enabling information sharing, greater transparency, and collaboration across supply chains. The Royal Malaysian Customs Department (RMDC) adopted TradeLens to modernize its shipping processes, which gives the RMDC more time to prepare for the arrival of shipments, enabling it to be more efficient and thorough in terms of fraud and forgery detection, as well as providing a more consistent and transparent revenue-collection process. The Canadian Pacific's (CP) intermodal shippers use the TradeLens platform for the secure and transparent transfer of their container-shipping documents (IBM, 2015).

Banking and Finance

Australia's ANZ bank, in collaboration with the Commonwealth Bank, Westpac, and property company SCENTRE has created a blockchain-based bank guarantee platform. The platform transforms financial guarantees using IBM Blockchain, digitalizing financial guarantees between landlords and tenants in commercial property leasing, which enables a tenant to request a guarantee from an online platform (Dobson, 2019).

Healthcare

The main issue in the healthcare industry is ensuring secure access to patients' data without jeopardizing their privacy. Blockchain is used for health record-keeping, clinical trials, and patient monitoring. It improves safety and displays information while ensuring transparency and privacy. Blockchain enables large volumes of medical records to be stored, edited, or removed securely while giving users and parties access to up-to-date and authentic patient records and evaluations via electronic health records (EHRs) and ensuring patients' medical privacy (Haleem et al., 2021).

Medicalchain (www.medicalchain.com) is a blockchain-based electronic health record platform that consolidates patient records from various sources and provides secure data storage. Doctors, hospitals, and laboratories can access patient information that has a record of origin and protects the patient's identity from outside sources.

Furthermore, health and pharmaceutical industries can use blockchain technology to eliminate counterfeit medications, allowing for the traceability of all these products, and helping to determine the manufacturing source (Haleem et al., 2021).

Blockpharma (www.blockpharma.com) is a blockchain-based application that traces drug sales online. The Blockpharma application interfaces with pharmaceutical companies' information systems to identify counterfeit medicines by scanning the supply chain and verifying all points of shipment, from product manufacture to the point of sale, when the pharmaceutical companies release the products.

Public sector and government

Governments can use blockchain to keep permanent records of asset transactions involving land, property, and automobiles on a public ledger. The public sector can use blockchain-based solutions to secure and protect government and citizens' data, streamline public service processes, while reducing fraud, waste and corruption and increasing the trustworthiness and accountability of government systems. Some applications of blockchain in government and public sectors (Pandey, 2020) include:

- *Land registration and ownership*: Using blockchain, governments can store records of asset transactions, such as land, property, and vehicles, permanently on a public ledger. This ensures transparency, eliminates fraud, and streamlines the transfer of ownership. For example, in Sweden, the country's land registry authority is exploring blockchain technology to reduce the time and costs involved in transferring property titles. The system records every property transaction on a blockchain, making it easier to trace and verify property ownership (https://www.finyear.com/Sweden-launch-leading-blockchain-solution-for-Land-registry_a36479.html).
- *Contracts:–* Blockchain enables the creation of smart, self-executing contracts, eliminating the need for intermediaries. Contracts are executed on the blockchain, making them publicly accessible and secure within the network. For instance, a blockchain-based platform called 'We.Trade' allows small and medium-sized businesses to create, sign and execute trade transactions with each other, eliminating intermediaries and reducing costs (https://techmonitor.ai/technology/emerging-technology/ibm-backed-blockchain-platform-we-trade-shutting-down).
- *Social-benefits management*: Blockchain technology can help ensure that the social benefits provided by government systems are not misused. For instance, blockchain-based systems can track the use of benefits, such as unemployment benefits or food stamps, reducing fraud and improving accountability.
- *Validation of documents*: Cloud-based blockchain solutions can be used to validate citizens' digital documents. For instance, Estonia's digital ID system uses blockchain technology to store citizens' personal data and provide secure access to government services (https://www.pwc.com/gx/en/services/legal/tech/assets/estonia-the-digital-republic-secured-by-blockchain.pdf).
- *Patent protection*: Since blockchain can permanently time-stamp transactions at any time, companies or individuals can file patents without undergoing the cumbersome submission process. Blockchain-based platforms can also prevent unauthorized use or duplication of patented technology.

Media & entertainment

Key issues in the entertainment industries are theft and copyright infringement. By providing transparency, security, and control, blockchain-based solutions can improve the media supply chain and reduce copyright infringements. Greater transparency helps with the identification of intermediaries who are adding significant cost to advertisers' budgets.

Definition: Blockchain

Blockchain is a decentralised distributed digital ledger that stores blocks of transactional information that are linked to each other and secured using a cryptographic hash function that is shared among all the participants in the distributed peer-to-peer computer network.

Definition: Blockchain

Information recorded in the distributed digital ledgers/blocks is *immutable*, which means that once the information has been recorded in the block (digital ledger) and appended to the chain, it cannot be altered or deleted.

Definition: Blockchain

Blockchain is a distributed technology. The digital ledgers/blocks are distributed and shared among all the participants in the decentralized peer-to-peer network. In a *decentralised* (no one entity/central control of the network) *distributed peer-to-peer network*, every node is independent but interconnected to other nodes; thus, distributed digital ledgers/blocks are accessible to anyone who has permission.

Stop and Reflect: Blockchain Applications

As discussed in the 'Blockchain Applications' section, blockchain technology has many potential applications beyond cryptocurrency. Blockchain technology has the potential to offer solutions for environmental dilemmas.

• Think about how blockchain technology can be used to reduce poverty and help clean up our oceans.

Stop and Reflect: Cloud, Big Data, IoT, and Blockchain Technologies

In what ways has the integration of cloud, big data, IoT, and blockchain technologies contributed to achieving the Sustainable Development Goals (SDGs)? How can these technologies be further leveraged to address specific SDG targets, such as reducing food waste, improving resource efficiency, or promoting sustainable consumption and production? What are some potential challenges and risks associated with the adoption of these technologies, and how can they be mitigated to ensure a more equitable and sustainable future?

11.7 Chapter Summary

The fusion of cloud computing, big data, IoT, and blockchain facilitate effective and secure communication, connection, and transference of data between devices. Cloud computing provides a scalable, reliable, and agile platform for big data, IoT, and blockchain capabilities to interoperate and gives secure access to data, insights, and solutions for businesses.

11.8 Further Reading

Ashraf, I. (2014). An overview of service models of cloud computing. *International Journal of Multidisciplinary and Current Research*, 2, 779–783.

Jansen, M. (2011). What does it service management look like in the: An ITIL based approach. *Proceedings of the 2011 International Conference on Applied, Numerical and Computational Mathematics, and Proceedings of the 2011 International Conference on Computers, Digital Communications and Computing*, 87–92. https://dl.acm.org/doi/abs/10.5555/2047950.2047964

Marr, B. (2021). *35* amazing real-world examples of how blockchain is changing our world. https://bernardmarr.com/35-amazing-real-world-examples-of-how-blockchain-is-changing-our-world/

Marr, B. (2022). The 5 biggest blockchain trends in 2022. https://bernardmarr.com/the-5-biggest-blockchain-trends-in-2022/

Omurgonulsen, M., Ibis, M., Kazancoglu, Y., & Singla, P. (2021). Cloud computing: A systematic literature review and future agenda. *Journal of Global Information Management*, 29, 1–25.

Parmentola, A., Petrillo, A., Tutore, I., & De Felice, F. (2022). Is blockchain able to enhance environmental sustainability? A systematic review and research agenda from the perspective of Sustainable Development Goals (SDGs). *Business Strategy and the Environment, 31*(1), 194–217. doi:10.1002/bse.2882

Rountree, D. & Castrillo, I. (2014). *The Basics of Cloud Computing: Understanding the Fundamentals of Cloud Computing in Theory and Practice* (Hai Jiang, Technical Editor). Syngress/Elsevier.

Zhang, Q., Cheng, L., & Boutaba, R. 2010. Cloud computing: State-of-the-art and research challenges. *Journal of Internet Services and Applications*, 1, 7–18.

Discussion Questions

(Suggested answers are provided in the teaching guide.)

1 Give examples of SaaS, PaaS, and IaaS.
2 What can be done to eliminate or mitigate the risks associated with cloud computing?
3 Discuss the factors that have made IoT increasingly popular.
4 Discuss the application of the Internet of Things in various industry/business sectors.

Case Study: Microsoft vs USA District Court – Data Locations and Access

By the authors based on information obtained from Abed and Chavan (2019, pp. 173–176), Groll (2016) and Bort (2015).

Microsoft Office 365 'is everywhere' (Bort, 2015, p. 1). As one of the most popular examples of cloud-based office software and email platforms, Microsoft has positioned itself as a very attractive cloud computing provider.

In 2014, Microsoft was issued with a search warrant from the US District Court for the Southern District of New York, seeking access to the contents of an individual's email account in relation to a narcotics trafficking investigation. Microsoft refused, claiming that the data was not stored in the USA but in Ireland, and therefore was outside of US jurisdiction. Microsoft was then issued a warrant for the second time and ordered to hand over the data in the account. The company complied, but delivered only the contents of the email account stored within the USA. Microsoft also advised the Justice Department that the data they were seeking were most likely in the Ireland-based storage. For the Justice Department to gain access to the data, Microsoft would need to transfer the data to a US-based storage which Microsoft refused to do. As a result, the court ruled that Microsoft Corporate was in civil contempt of the court. Eventually, the United States Court of Appeals quashed the warrant as Microsoft satisfied the warrant by providing all data stored within the USA, and forcing Microsoft to retrieve data from Europe was deemed to be against 'extraterritoriality' and could cause international conflicts.

Due to similar issues, many countries have decided to pass 'data localisation laws' forcing companies to store users' data within their country's borders. Some governments are trying to legislate frameworks to formally mandate how domestic data can be accessed. However, it is also argued that 'although countries and their lawmakers put lots of effort [in]to updat[ing] their legislation in regard to the cloud phenomenon, it has been proven that international law is not agile enough to compete with cloud computing developments' (Abed and Chavan, 2019, p. 178).

In this instance, Microsoft successfully showed that the company takes the privacy of users' data seriously. However, the US Government's persistent efforts to access the data without the clients' consent alerted cloud users to the many security concerns they face. This has resulted in many cloud users in the US signing cloud service contracts with overseas providers. Some users are going further to encrypt their data, using services provided by companies such as Whisper Systems. With data encryption, access to data is more difficult because, even if the data are supplied, the encryption will make it impossible to view the actual content.

Questions

1   What are the concerns and issues that you can identify in this case study with regard to cloud computing?
2   Do you think data localization laws will help to protect the privacy of clients who use cloud services? Why or why not?
3   Do you think that all data should be stored locally to ensure better security and privacy management? What would be the arguments for and against such a proposition?
4   What do you think are the impact that big companies like Microsoft can bring about to address security and privacy concerns within the world of cloud computing?

Case Study: Making Humanitarian Action Easier, Humanitech, Australian Red Cross

By the authors based on information obtained from Young and Jurko (2020), TypeHuman (2021) and The National Blockchain Roadmap (2020).

As part of the Australian Red Cross's (ARC) commitment to create a nation that takes humanitarian action, ARC facilitates the deployment of volunteers in support of community outcomes and is investing in technology that can help to achieve humanitarian outcomes via new initiatives such as Humanitech. Humanitech is an initiative of the Australian Red Cross which seeks to achieve better humanitarian outcomes through the use of new and emerging technology such as blockchain, artificial intelligence and robotics.

Today, volunteers and humanitarian workers for multiple charity organizations asking volunteers to go through a lengthy sign-up process to verify their compliance with requirements such as police checks and Working with Children Checks, and other relevant qualification verifications, with every organization for which they volunteer.

The ARC realized that a standardized accreditation process could enable volunteers to share their credentials with partner organizations. This would expedite the sign-up and deployment processes, benefiting volunteering overall. Thus, in order to overcome the expensive and slow process of conducting background checks of volunteers and humanitarian workers, the Australian Red Cross partnered with TypeHuman to streamline the background checking process, and to increase the sector's capacity to take effective humanitarian action.

In collaboration with the ARC, TypeHuman designed and developed *Ponto*, a digital credential platform which enables organizations to issue and verify decentralized, digital credentials in the form of a badge for activities such as humanitarian response training, first-aid, and working with children. Badges are stored in a digital wallet on a phone or the Web, and leverage blockchain to reduce the cost of integration for humanitarian organizations, and broaden the availability and portability of individuals' credentials.

Using blockchain technology, partners can issue volunteers with unalterable digital representations of documents such as police and Working with Children checks or first aid and training certificates. These encrypted digital credentials are kept in people's digital wallets and can be shared with other organizations in the network upon request. The blockchain credentials offer individuals mobility between organizations, recognizing the background checks already performed along with other experience and qualifications gained along the way.

The decentralized system is based on a user-in-control approach to personal data management, whereby the individual is the focal point of his or her data, and decides what to share and with whom. This approach gives volunteers ownership of their own data and control of the way it is shared. This also eliminates the need for organizations to store data centrally on their systems, thereby strengthening data security.

One of the challenges impeding the growth and utility of the *Ponto* blockchain system is the digital coordination problem, which is the way that other organizations can issue and recognize the digital credentials. To support the emergence of this open credential

(Continued)

ecosystem and to address the digital coordination problem, a group of organizations that trust each other to verify volunteers' credentials have come together to establish the Trust Alliance. Members of the Trust Alliance include the Australian Red Cross, Oxfam Australia, RedR Australia, Telstra Foundation, Swinburne University, RMIT, Bridge of Hope, and EWBA.

Questions

1   What issue was faced by the ARC in regard to accepting and deploying volunteers?
2   What strategy did ARC apply to address the identity verification issue prior to volunteers' deployment? Describe the technology implemented by ARC to address the identify verification issue for humanitarian workers.
3   Describe how the technology implemented by ARC to address the identify verification issue benefits the humanitarian workers and the charity organizations.
4   Based on the information in this case, how do you think blockchain technology can be used for identity management in the context of the Internet of Things (IoT) while preserving privacy in its applications in various industries, for example healthcare scenarios, supply chain and retail? Discuss with examples.

11.9 References

Abed, Y. & Chavan, M. (2019). The challenges of institutional distance: Data privacy issues in cloud computing. *Science, Technology and Society, 24*, 161–181.

Agrawal, D., Bernstein, P., Bertino, E., Davidson, S., Dayal, U., Franklin, M., Gehrke, J., Haas, L., Halevy, A., Han, J., Jagadish, H.V., Labrinidis, A., Madden, S., Papakonstantinou, Y., Patel, J., Ramakrishnan, R., Ross, K., Shahabi, C., Suciu, D., Vaithyanathan, S. and Widom, J. (2011) *Challenges and Opportunities with Big Data 2011-1*. Cyber Center Technical Reports. Paper 1.

Al-Roomi, M., Al-Ebrahim, S., Buqrais, S., & Ahmad, I. (2013). Cloud computing pricing models: A survey. *International Journal of Grid and Distributed Computing, 6*, 93–106.

AlSudiari, M. A. & Vasista, T. (2012). Cloud computing and privacy regulations: An exploratory study on issues and implications. *Advanced Computing, 3*, 159.

Aniruddha, S. & Chaudhari, D. (2013). Cloud computing: Infrastructure as a service. *International Journal of Inventive Engineering and Sciences, 1*, 1–7.

Armbrust, M., Fox, A., Griffith, R., Joseph, A. D., Katz, R., Konwinski, A., Lee, G., Patterson, D., Rabkin, A., & Stoica, I. (2010). A view of cloud computing. *Communications of the ACM, 53*, 50–58.

Assante, D., Castro, M., Hamburg, I., & Martin, S. (2016). The use of cloud computing in SMEs. *Procedia Computer Science, 83*, 1207–1212.

Borgini, J. (2022). Top advantages and disadvantages of IoT in business. https://www.techtarget.com/iotagenda/tip/Top-advantages-and-disadvantages-of-IoT-in-business

Bort, J. (2015). Everyone is talking about how Microsoft Office 365 is suddenly beating Google Apps. https://www.businessinsider.com.au/how-office-365-is-beating-google-apps-2015-3

Brous, P., Janssen, M., & Herder, P. (2020). The dual effects of the Internet of Things (IoT): A systematic review of the benefits and risks of IoT adoption by organizations. *International Journal of Information Management, 51*, 101952.

Carter, A. D. (2023). Diversity intelligent leadership coaching in practice. *Advances in Developing Human Resources*, 15234223231193359

Cheng, F.-C. & Lai, W.-H. (2012). The impact of cloud computing technology on legal infrastructure within internet – focusing on the protection of information privacy. *Procedia Engineering, 29*, 241–251.

Chou, T.-S. (2013). Security threats on cloud computing vulnerabilities. *AIRCC's International Journal of Computer Science and Information Technology, 5*, 79–88.

Chowdhury, M. J. M., Ferdous, M. S., Biswas, K., Chowdhury, N., & Muthukkumarasamy, V. (2020). A survey on blockchain-based platforms for IoT use-cases. *The Knowledge Engineering Review, 35*.

De Mauro, A., Greco, M., & Grimaldi, M., (2015). *What is Big Data? A Consensual Definition and a Review of Key Research Topics*. In AIP Conference Proceedings, *1644* (1), 97–104. American Institute of Physics.

Dillon, T., Chen, W., & Chang, E. (2010). Cloud computing: Issues and challenges. IEEE *International Conference on Advanced Information Networking and Applications, Apr 20–Apr 23 2010 Perth, Western Australia*. IEEE, 27–33.

Dobson, N. (2019). Why ANZ bank is optimistic about blockchain technology. https://www.ibm.com/blog/why-anz-bank-is-optimistic-about-blockchain/?mhsrc=ibmsearch_a&mhq=Why%20ANZ%20bank%20is%20optimistic%20about%20blockchain%20technology%20

Erdogmus, H. (2009). Cloud computing: Does nirvana hide behind the nebula? *IEEE Software, 26*, 4–6.

Fan, J., Han, F., & Liu, H. (2014). Challenges of big data analysis. *National Science Review, 1*(2), 293–314.

Gandomi, A. & Haider, M. (2015). Beyond the hype: Big data concepts, methods, and analytics. *International Journal of Information Management, 35*(2), 137–144.

Geroni, D. (2021). Hybrid blockchain: The best of both worlds. 101 Blockchains.

Goel, N. & Sharma, T. (2014). Cloud computing – SPI framework, deployment models, challenges. *International Journal of Emerging Technology and Advanced Engineering, 4*.

Griffith, E. (2020). What is cloud computing? https://www.pcmag.com/news/what-is-cloud-computing

Groll, E. (2016). Microsoft vs. the Feds, cloud computing edition. https://foreignpolicy.com/2016/01/21/microsoft-vs-the-feds-cloud-computing-edition/

Gupta, M. (2020). *Blockchain for Dummies®* (3rd IBM limited edition edn.). John Wiley & Sons, Inc.

Haleem, A., Javaid, M., Singh, R. P., Suman, R., & Rab, S. (2021). Blockchain technology applications in healthcare: An overview. *International Journal of Intelligent Networks, 2*, 30–139.

Hayes, A. (2022). Blockchain explained. *Investopedia*, 5.

Hu, T.-H. (2015). *A Prehistory of the Cloud*. MIT Press.

IBM. (2015). Maersk and IBM Introduce TradeLens Blockchain Shipping Solution. https://newsroom.ibm.com/2018-08-09-Maersk-and-IBM-Introduce-TradeLens-Blockchain-Shipping-Solution

IBM. (2020a). IBM Food Trust: A new era in the world's food supply. https://www.ibm.com/blockchain/solutions/food-trust

IBM. (2020b). The pharmaceutical industry on blockchain. https://www.ibm.com/blockchain/resources/transparent-supply/pharma

IBM. (2022). What is IoT? https://www.oracle.com/au/internet-of-things/what-is-iot/#technologies-iot

Jassal, S. (2019). Drakes Supermarket and Thomas Foods International collaborate to pilot IBM Food Trust in South Australia [Press release].

Katz, R. H. (2009). Tech titans building boom. *IEEE Spectrum, 46*, 40–54.

Kaur, M. & Singh, H. (2015). A review of cloud computing security issues. *International Journal of Education and Management Engineering, 5*, 32–41.

Kulkarni, G., Sutar, R., & Gambhir, J. (2012). Cloud computing – infrastructure as service – Amazon EC2. *International Journal of Engineering Research and Applications, 2*, 117–125.

Kumar, K. K. M. (2014). Software as a service for efficient cloud computing. *Environment, 7*, 10.

Kumar, S., & Goudar, R. H. (2012). Cloud computing-research issues, challenges, architecture, platforms and applications: a survey. *International Journal of Future Computer and Communication, 1*(4), 356.

Kumar, P. R., Raj, P. H. & Jelciana, P. (2018). Exploring data security issues and solutions in cloud computing. *Procedia Computer Science, 125*, 691–697.

Laney, D. (2001). 3D data management: controlling data volume, velocity and variety. *META Group Research Note, 6*(70), 1.

Lanner. (2018). 5 examples of IoT devices in your next smart home. https://www.lanner-america.com/blog/5-examples-iot-devices-next-smart-home/

McAfee, A., Brynjolfsson, E., Davenport, T. H., Patil, D. J., & Barton, D. (2012). Big data: The management revolution. *Harvard Business Review, 90*(10), 60–68.

Medicalchain (2018). https://medicalchain.com/Medicalchain-Whitepaper-EN.pdf

Mell, P. & Grance, T. (2011). *The NIST Definition of Cloud Computing*. NIST.

Mills, S., Lucas, S., Irakliotis, L., Rappa, M., Carlson, T., & Perlowitz, B. (2012). Demystifying big data: A practical guide to transforming the business of government. TechAmerica Foundation, Washington.

Najafabadi, M. M., Villanustre, F., Khoshgoftaar, T. M., Seliya, N., Wald, R., & Muharemagic, E. (2015). Deep learning applications and challenges in big data analytics. *Journal of Big Data, 2*(1), 1–21.

Nazir, A. & Jamshed, S. (2013). Cloud computing: Challenges and concerns for its adoption in Indian SMEs. *International Journal of Software and Web Sciences, 4*, 120–125.

Nolledo, M. (2020). What is Google Drive? A guide to navigating Google's file storage service and collaboration tools. https://www.businessinsider.com.au/what-is-google-drive-guide-2020-7

Nott, G. (2019). Drakes tracing steaks back to farm of origin with IBM blockchain. *CIO. com*.

Opara-Martins, J., Sahandi, R., & Tian, F. (2015). A business analysis of cloud computing: Data security and contract lock-in issues. *2015 10th International Conference on P2P, Parallel, Grid, Cloud and Internet Computing (3PGCIC), 2015*. IEEE, 665–670.

Oracle. (2022). What is big data? https://www.oracle.com/au/big-data/what-is-big-data/#:~:text=Put%20simply%2C%20big%20data%20is,been%20able%20to%20tackle%20 before

Pandey, A. (2020). How governments can harness the potential of blockchain. https://www.mckinsey.com/business-functions/mckinsey-digital/our-insights/tech-forward/how-governments-can-harness-the-potential-of-blockchain

Pratt, M. K. (2022). Top 8 IoT applications and examples in business. https://www.techtarget.com/iotagenda/tip/Top-8-IoT-applications-and-examples-in-business

Schroeck, M., Shockley, R., Smart, J., Romero-Morales, D., & Tufano, P. (2012). *Analytics: The Real-World use of Big Data: How Innovative Enterprises Extract Value from Uncertain Data, Executive Report*. IBM Institute for Business Value and Said Business School at the University of Oxford.

Singh, J. (2014). Cyber-attacks in cloud computing: A case study. *International Journal of Electronics and Information Engineering*, *1*, 78–87.

Sniderman, B., Mahto, M., & Cotteler, M. J. (2016). Industry 4.0 and manufacturing ecosystems. Retrieved from Deloitte Industry Report: https://www2.deloitte.com/tr/en/pages/manufacturing/articles/industry-4-0-manufacturing-ecosystems-exploring-world-connected-enterprises.html

Strickland, J. (n.d.). How cloud computing works. https://computer.howstuffworks.com/cloud-computing/cloud-computing.htm

Taliaferro, A., Ernst, R., Ahmed, U., Harolikar, A., & Ray, S. (2019). Creating IoT ecosystems in transportation. Retrieved from Deloitte Insights. https://www2.deloitte.com/us/en/insights/focus/internet-of-things/transportation-iot-internet-of-things-ecosystem.html

The National Blockchain Roadmap, Australian Government Department of Industry, Science, Energy and Resources (2020). Promoting and protecting critical technologies. https://www.industry.gov.au/data-and-publications/national-blockchain-roadmap/sectoral-opportunities

Thiyagarajan, D. & Ramachandrarao, G. (2015). Platform-as-a-Service (PaaS): Model and security issues. *TELKOMNIKA Indonesian Journal of Electrical Engineering*, *15*, 151–161.

TypeHuman (2021). Red Cross – digital identity and credential solution. https://www.typehuman.com/project/australian-red-cross

Vimal, D. & Prabakaran, N. (2014). Challenges and issues of deployment on cloud. *International Journal of Innovative Research in Computer and Communication Engineering*, *2*, 3095–3101.

Ward, J. S. and Barker, A. (2013). Undefined by data: A survey of big data definitions. *arXiv preprint arXiv:1309.5821*.

Woodford, C. (2020). Cloud computing. https://www.explainthatstuff.com/cloud-computing-introduction.html

Xue, C. T. S. & Xin, F. T. W. (2016). Benefits and challenges of the adoption of cloud computing in business. *International Journal on Cloud Computing: Services and Architecture, 6*, 1–15.

Yang, H. & Tate, M. (2009). Where are we at with cloud computing? A descriptive literature review.

Young, L and Jurko, I. (2020). *Future of Vulnerability: Humanity in the Digital Age.* Humanitech, Australian Red Cross, Melbourne.

INDEX

Page numbers in *italics* refer to figures; page numbers in **bold** refer to tables.